New Markets,
New Opportunities?

*Economic and Social
Mobility in a
Changing World*

Nancy Birdsall
Carol Graham
Editors

CARNEGIE ENDOWMENT
FOR INTERNATIONAL PEACE

BROOKINGS INSTITUTION PRESS
Washington, D.C.

Copyright © 2000
THE BROOKINGS INSTITUTION
1775 Massachusetts Avenue, N.W., Washington, D.C. 20036
www.brookings.edu

Library of Congress Cataloging-in-Publication data

New markets, new opportunities? : economic and social mobility in a
changing world / Nancy Birdsall and Carol Graham, eds.
    p.   cm.
Includes bibliographical references and index.
    ISBN 0-8157-0917-X
    1. Income distribution—Latin America. 2. Equality—Latin America.
3. Social mobility—Latin America. 4. Income distribution—Europe,
Eastern. 5. Equality—Europe, Eastern. 6. Social mobility—Europe,
Eastern. I. Birdsall, Nancy. II. Graham, Carol, 1962–
    HB523 .N49 1999
    305.5′13—dc21   99-050451
                                                                      CIP

9 8 7 6 5 4 3 2 1

The paper used in this publication meets minimum requirements of the American
National Standard for Information Sciences—Permanence of Paper for Printed
Library Materials: ANSI Z39.48-1984.

Typeset in Adobe Garamond

Composition by Cynthia Stock
Silver Spring, Maryland

Printed by Automated Graphic Systems
White Plains, Maryland

Foreword

The dramatic entry of the emerging market countries into the global economy has raised new questions about inequality and opportunity worldwide. Indeed, as the international financial crisis of 1997–98 suggested, even the most apparently successful fast-growing economies of East Asia are not immune to the increased inequality and insecurity that global financial contagion implies for their citizens. And because many emerging market countries are also in the midst of transitions to more democratic and decentralized political systems, the effects of inequality on public support for market policies are also a concern.

New Markets, New Opportunities? focuses on social mobility and opportunity as an essential part of the debate on income inequality in both developed and developing economies. The essays in this book attempt to provide answers to two critical questions. To what extent is the increase in inequality that has accompanied the turn to the market in the emerging economies remediated by increasing the opportunities for advancement, particularly for those at the bottom of the income ladder? Does the creation of greater opportunities help generate wider political support for a country's move to the market?

Relying on the contributions of scholars with expertise in inequality and mobility issues in the United States and in developing countries, the book provides a summary of the latest research on the economics and politics of social mobility. It elaborates on the conceptual issues involved and the challenges of accurately documenting trends. It concludes with analy-

v

ses of the economics of opportunity-driven mobility in two regions where market reforms have been extensive, Latin America and Eastern Europe, and with analyses of the politics and public perceptions of opportunities in the two regions.

The chapters draw on discussions at a workshop on mobility sponsored by the Brookings Center on Social and Economic Dynamics and the Inter-American Bank, held in Washington, D.C., in June 1998. Valuable contributions and comments came from many participants, including the staff of the Brookings Institution, the Inter-American Development Bank, and the World Bank.

Michael H. Armacost
President
The Brookings Institution

Jessica Mathews
President
Carnegie Endowment for
International Peace

Acknowledgments

The editors of this volume wish to thank George Akerlof, Gary Burtless, Martin Cumpa, William Easterly, Paul Glewwe, Rebecca Harris, Veronika Kabalina, Nora Lustig, Samuel Morley, Sherman Robinson, and John Steinbruner for their valuable contributions to the 1998 conference. They also thank Kristine McDevitt for coordinating the conference and the volume's publication, Stefano Pettinato for research assistance, James Schneider for editing the manuscript, Eloise C. Stinger and Carlotta Ribar for proofreading the pages, and Susan Fels for compiling the index.

The editors acknowledge generous financial support for this project from the John D. and Catherine T. MacArthur Foundation and the Tinker Foundation; and, for their support of the editors' initial organizing efforts, the Inter-American Development Bank and the Council on Foreign Relations.

The views expressed in this book are those of the authors and should not be ascribed to any of the persons whose assistance they acknowledge, or to the trustees, officers, or other staff members of the Brookings Institution or the Carnegie Endowment for International Peace.

Contents

PART I

Issues and
Concepts

NANCY BIRDSALL
CAROL GRAHAM

1

Mobility and Markets: Conceptual Issues and Policy Questions

The closing years of the twentieth century have been marked by the consolidation worldwide of the market economy. With the end of the cold war the new countries of the former Soviet Union and the newly liberated countries of eastern Europe adopted at least the trappings of market-driven systems. In Latin America the dismantling of state-run enterprises and the opening of markets that began in the 1980s as a response to the debt crisis dramatically accelerated in the 1990s. In East Asia, after three decades of fast growth under market approaches that ranged from laissez-faire in Hong Kong to a government-led market in Korea, a financial crisis in the late 1990s produced still another round of market-oriented consolidation. In India and Pakistan, and even in China, economic policy changes have been inevitably directed toward liberalization. In Africa and the Middle East, those countries that more quickly and fully adopted market policies have been widely acknowledged to have the best prospects for escaping economic backwardness. Even among industrialized countries, U.S. prosperity, compared with recession in Japan and slowdown in Europe, seems to vindicate devotion to market principles.

Meanwhile, the apparent triumph of market systems was accompanied by increasing adherence to democratic systems of governance. Open markets and democratic systems seem to go hand in hand.

3

But the prevalence of the market economy has not been without costs. Inequality across and within countries has persisted and possibly worsened.[1] Market competition rewards those countries and people with the wherewithal (property, connections, and, increasingly central in the information age, education and skills) to exploit the new rules.[2] Along with greater inequality has come increased insecurity as even people with good jobs and rising income work in more volatile and flexible labor markets and as the globalization of markets generates constant adjustments in the nature and location of production and thus of jobs.

Despite these problems, voters throughout the democratic world have for the most part endorsed the market reforms, choosing the potential for more dynamic growth in more open societies even with the accompanying risks of inequality and insecurity. In a global system that seems unfair and unstable, democracy and open markets persist and grow stronger, belying concerns about isolationist backlash and resort to authoritarian populism.

Why? And will this trend persist, or are open markets and democratic systems vulnerable? In this book we build on studies of inequality, markets, and democracy to explore how market reforms and other political and policy changes affect changes in individuals' and households' status, both in absolute terms and relative terms, and in their perceptions of their status.[3] In other words, we use conventional measures of status, especially income and education, to measure people's *mobility* in different societies and under different policy regimes.

Why focus on mobility? One explanation for voters' continued endorsement of market reforms is that the reforms create new opportunities in more meritocratic systems, that market signals are perceived to reward hard work, innovation, and talent more fairly than more centralized and statist economic systems do. Perhaps increased inequality has created increased opportunities, or at the least is associated with changes in incentives that generate both new opportunities and new risks for people. Perhaps it is the existence of such opportunities that makes the move to the market politically acceptable in regions of high and increasing inequality such as

---

1. Schultz (1998). This provides the most comprehensive recent survey and deals with both inequality across and within countries.

2. Birdsall (1998); and Birdsall (1999).

3. For example, on Latin America, see the essays by Birdsall, Graham, and Sabot (1998); Lora and Londoño (1998); Graham and Naim (1998); Graham (1998); and Graham and Kane (1998). See also Haggard and Webb (1994).

Latin America and in those of visible and painful downward mobility for many, as in eastern Europe and parts of the former Soviet Union.

But increased inequality and insecurity may simply reflect deep and persistent differences in the capacity of individuals and households to exploit markets or to achieve equal access to education, employment, or property rights. Amartya Sen's well-known definition of poverty, for example, focuses on people's capabilities to participate as productive members of society rather than focusing only on their incomes. Sen notes that the opportunity to convert personal incomes into capabilities depends on a variety of personal circumstances, including age, gender, and health status, and on other circumstances such as the physical environment and the state of available public services.[4] This broader and less static view of poverty underlies our approach to inequality and mobility.

If inequality reflects discrimination against certain groups or results from linguistic, cultural, or historical handicaps that ensure the intergenerational transmission of poverty, then mobility, measured over lifetimes and even generations, will be constrained. Acceptance of continued market reform could be the short-run outcome of the limited political voice of those excluded from new opportunities, and time and greater accountability of public policy to the median voter could generate a political backlash against market policies.[5] The signs of such a backlash are present, if limited, as the twenty-first century approaches.

In short, the central idea behind the essays in this volume is that mobility provides a better measure of changing opportunities than do the traditional measures of inequality, and that understanding mobility is critical to the discussion of inequality and of what to do about it. This is especially the case in the new market economies of eastern Europe and Latin America, which are undergoing major economic and political transformations.

In addition, we recognize that people's perceptions of their own mobility and access to opportunity, perceptions that may or may not square with reality, are critical to their opinions about the market and thus to their voting behavior. These perceptions are often influenced by relative income differences as much if not more than by absolute ones, particularly as absolute income levels increase.[6] Because the sustainability of open markets in democratic societies hinges ultimately on voter support, we also explore

4. Sen (1995).
5. For theoretical discussions of such a possibility, see Benabou and Ok (1998); and Piketty (1995).
6. See Easterlin (1974).

the links among actual and perceived mobility, and between perceptions and political behavior.[7]

Mobility and Markets: Major Themes

The chapters in this book lay some groundwork for new research on the effects of economic change on mobility and on the implications of those changes for democracy and markets. New research needs to cross disciplinary boundaries and go beyond existing concepts and models. Progress is necessary in a number of areas; we have framed this book through themes that we feel are critical.

Unbundling Inequality: Concepts and Measures

Central to our exploration of the effects of economic change on mobility is whether people are willing to accept more inequality (or the persistence of great inequality) if economic change generates more opportunities and thus more mobility, including mobility that is downward.[8] Inequality and mobility and their link to economic change requires consideration of two points: the nature of the inequality measured and the time period over which it is measured.

THE NATURE OF INEQUALITY. The nature of inequality governs the effect of market reforms and economic change on mobility. Some inequality is constructive and rewards innovation and productivity. Some is destructive and blocks the productive potential of the poor.[9] The former communist econo-

7. Of course it is not possible to distinguish completely between the economic or market reform process and the political changes that have preceded, accompanied, and in some cases reinforced open markets: more civil liberties, more active civic participation in nongovernmental groups, more power to local governments, and more accountability of government to citizens in general. Perhaps even in the face of great and growing inequality, the stronger accountability of increasingly democratic societies is improving voters' perceptions of market reforms and their long-run benefits for them and their children—so that, for example, in eastern Europe it is the transition to democracy that has made the tough reality of increased downward as well as upward mobility more palatable. In the fourth section of this book, though, the authors consider how market reforms have affected political perceptions and behavior, not how political changes have affected perceptions of market reforms.

8. We discuss later the various possible definitions of mobility, which include absolute and relative mobility, time dependence, positional movement, share movement, and directional income movement. See chapter 5 by Gary Fields.

mies are examples of systems in which there were insufficient rewards for risk taking, hard work, and productivity; that is, insufficient constructive inequality. But destructive inequality can in addition entail inequality of access to productive assets, such as land, capital, education, and even the "asset" that contacts and personal connections provide, as has occurred historically in Latin America. Destructive inequality creates an unlevel playing field from the start and makes it difficult for even the most innovative and hardworking poor to take advantage of economic opportunity.

The nature of inequality affects the extent to which it impinges on growth and economic efficiency. By definition, destructive inequality inhibits aggregate growth. Constructive inequality may in fact encourage growth. Unfortunately it is not easy to distinguish empirically between these two types of inequality. But a good indirect approach is to analyze access to opportunities by measuring the extent and nature of social mobility.

In the 1990s, economists produced a large body of new work on the links between inequality and growth in developing countries.[10] For much of the postwar period the conventional wisdom was of a trade-off between augmenting growth and reducing inequality. For those following Nicholas Kaldor, a high level of savings was considered a prerequisite to growth in capital-poor societies; concentration of income would generate high savings because the rich have a higher propensity to save than the poor.[11] For those following Simon Kuznets, growth was seen as necessarily increasing income inequality in poor economies because over a long initial period labor would shift from sectors with low productivity to those with high productivity, and income gaps would widen.[12] In a sense the conventional wisdom assumed that most inequality is inevitable and in any event "constructive."

More recent empirical studies suggest that the relationship is less simple, and at least some measured inequality is destructive. Alberto Alesina and Roberto Perotti identify several ways inequality hinders growth. High inequality creates perverse fiscal incentives: the rich have few incentives to

9. This dual concept of inequality was emphasized by Sheahan and Iglesias (1998).

10. We do not attempt here to provide an extensive literature review. We also limit ourselves to the economics literature, realizing that there is a rich discussion of the effects of inequality in a number of other disciplines, including philosophy. See Rawls (1971). We also limit the discussion to inequality rather than the broader concept of equity. For an excellent discussion of the concept of equity and its role in increasing economic efficiency, see Young (1994).

11. Kaldor (1978).

12. Kuznets (1955).

pay taxes and the poor have strong incentives to vote for higher taxation.[13] High inequality may also hinder investments because it increases investors' fears about political instability on the one hand and on the other hand implies a smaller base of people in society with the capacity to save and invest. Nancy Birdsall, David Ross, and Richard Sabot note that higher levels of inequality may reduce the poor's propensity to save and to invest in the education of their children.[14] Karla Hoff explores how, in the presence of market failures, inequality can exacerbate efficiency losses, perpetuate itself, and trap people in poverty. Because of imperfect capital markets, for example, access to credit may be restricted to those who have collateral wealth; a person's initial assets may be an important determinant of his or her ability to finance the high-return investments, including education, that make it possible to escape poverty. This poses a particular problem for investments in human capital because future earnings cannot be used as collateral. The implication is that initial assets determine productive potential.[15]

Economists have also developed models that explain inequality and its persistence even in the absence of market failures. George Akerlof describes a phenomenon he calls the economics of identity, which stems from individuals' ties to particular social groups. Because leaving such groups threatens individuals' identity, they are often reluctant to do so, even if it means giving up opportunities to escape poverty. This is applicable to a variety of social groups, ranging from adolescents in ghetto gangs to ethnic minorities and immigrants.[16] Steven Durlauf analyzes the role of neighborhood effects in determining individuals' economic success and the productivity of investing in children's education. He shows how stratification and neighborhood feedback effects with behavioral norms in poor neighborhoods can discourage economic effort and perpetuate inequality.[17]

13. See Alesina and Perotti (1994).

14. See Birdsall, Ross, and Sabot (1995); and Birdsall, Pinckney, and Sabot (1998). The latter sets out a model in which, given imperfect capital markets, new and equal opportunities for the poor will increase the poor's savings and investments, setting off a dynamic process of equitable growth.

15. Hoff (1996). Chapter 6 by Behrman, Birdsall, and Székely, meanwhile, demonstrates that in Latin America imperfect capital markets are associated with a stronger link between family background variables and children's schooling.

16. Akerlof (1997).

17. Durlauf (forthcoming). Another group of studies attempts to overcome the limitation of static, rational-actor-based models in explaining economic processes and outcomes and relies on agent-based modeling techniques to capture the interactive dynamics between individuals and their environments. Epstein and Axtell (1996) demonstrate how individual traits such as expectations acquired from repeated economic interactions among agents can lead to high and persistent inequality even without market failures.

Empirical evidence suggests that the restraining effects of inequality on growth are essentially a story of destructive inequality: blocked or limited mobility and opportunity for low-income groups. The transition to a market economy, coupled with a transition to democratic government, provides a historic opportunity to break these vicious inequality circles. In regions such as Latin America, the defeat of inflation has improved the situation of the poor. There and in eastern Europe trade liberalization makes it possible to reduce corruption and insider rents that favor a protected corporate elite. Throughout the developing and developed world, privatization has the potential to increase competition and improve access to services. In fact, however, recent studies suggest that the effects of these initial market reforms on inequality in the emerging market economies have been mixed. Studies for several countries in Latin America indicate that trade liberalization, for example, increases inequality of wages in manufacturing as demand for skilled workers increases faster than supply.[18] Recent cross-country analyses suggest that effects at the level of the entire economy may be more benign: trade liberalization affects relative prices as well as relative wages and may favor low-income consumers.[19]

In the medium term the implementation of a second stage of reforms, in sectors such as health and education, finance, social security, and labor markets, could attack the roots of destructive inequality. What distinguishes these reforms from past efforts to deal with inequality is that they address its causes. Rather than merely mitigating the effects of poverty, they increase the productive potential of the poor by emphasizing fiscally sustainable, productivity-enhancing measures and avoiding microeconomic disincentives that create dependence. Instead of relying on redistributive transfers, they increase the capacity of the poor to benefit from opportunities, for example, by providing incentives that encourage them to make investments in education. Depending on their extent and depth, these reforms should be reflected in greater social mobility in the countries where they are most vigorously followed. The dynamics, of course, will differ among countries and regimes, depending on the scale of the economic changes and such initial conditions as inequality itself.[20] In the former communist countries there is little doubt that with dramatic changes in incentives inequality has increased from a low level. Some of that increase was

18. Robbins (1996).
19. Lora and Londoño (1998); and Londoño, Spilimbergo, and Székely (1997).
20. Londoño and Székely (1997); and Berry (1997). See also Morley (1995). For the former communist economies, see Milanovic (forthcoming); and Vecernik (1997).

necessary to spur productivity and innovation and therefore opportunity. In Latin America, in contrast, distribution patterns remain very similar to what they were before the reform period. Latin America began its reforms with the most unequal income distribution of any region in the world, a distribution that seems so far to have blocked the productive capacity of the poor and constrained the region's growth.

THE MEASUREMENT OF MOBILITY: INEQUALITY OVER TIME. The authors in this volume are concerned with two distinct aspects of mobility, neither of which is easily captured in conventional measures of income inequality. The first is lifetime income and mobility. The incomes of doctors in the United States, for example, when measured at any point in time are unequal because in their early years as interns they earn little compared with what they will earn later in their careers. Annual measures of the distribution of bricklayers' incomes will exhibit much less inequality because bricklayers' earnings opportunities do not increase as much with time as do those of doctors (figure 1-1). Obviously, in economies undergoing major structural change the situation is more complicated because many people will change occupations during their lifetime, some occupations will emerge and others disappear, and the lifetime income profiles of different occupations may shift altogether.

In short, typical measures of inequality tell us nothing about doctors' or bricklayers' lifetime income or mobility. Measures of inequality are like snapshots; they reflect differences in income at a specific point in time, but not whether those at the top or bottom of the income ladder are moving up or down or expect to do so. They therefore tell us little about what is happening to people's opportunities and to their well-being over a prolonged period of policy change.

A second measure of inequality is intergenerational within families or "dynasties." Societies differ in the extent of their intergenerational mobility—the extent to which parents' (and grandparents' and so on) place in the income or other ranking of their generation determines the place of their children (and grandchildren and so on). At one time, land ownership or bloodline mattered. With the global turn to the market, it appears that it is education that matters, and thus some combination of parents' investments in children and of public policy determines intergenerational mobility.[21]

---

21. There is a considerable literature on this subject. For detail and references, see chapters 2 and 6.

Figure 1-1. *Earnings Curves of Doctors and Bricklayers*

Earnings

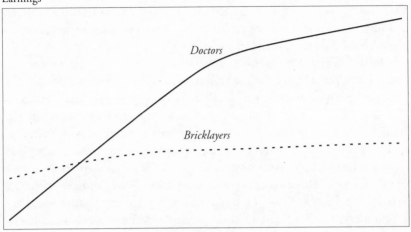

Years of experience

Lifetime income mobility is likely to be influenced by business cycle volatility, and intergenerational mobility by such structural changes in economies as the opening of trade markets and divestiture of state-owned enterprises.[22] In the longer term, patterns of mobility are also influenced by broader trends in the global economy, in particular the transition to growth led by high technology. In the nineteenth century's embrace of industrialization, economic opportunities and rewards were largely determined by a capital-labor divide with by far the largest rewards going to those who owned capital rather than to those who provided manual labor. With the turn to high technology growth, a similar divide exists between educated and uneducated workers, increasing the opportunities and rewards of the educated and decreasing the returns to the labor of the uneducated.

Crossing Regional Boundaries

The issues involving equality, opportunity, and mobility cut across developed and developing countries. Although there are obviously differences, especially that most developed economies have not faced economic

---

22. See chapter 2 for a useful discussion of the problems of measuring lifetime mobility.

crises as severe as the developing countries have nor have had to implement
such extensive policy reforms, many of the core issues remain the same.
Questions about the role of parents' occupation and education in determining the opportunities of children are central in both contexts, as are
those about differential returns to skilled and unskilled labor.

In this book we explore mobility and economic change in various set-
tings. The United States, for example, is often cited as the land of opportunity, where high and increasing levels of inequality are tolerated because of
the abundance of opportunity. In recent work, Isabel Sawhill notes that
high mobility in the United States, defined as the extent to which children
end up economically better off than their parents, has been in large part
associated historically with faster average income growth than in, for example, Europe. Differences between the United States and Europe in the
extent of social mobility—the extent to which children's relative social and
economic status is related to their parents' relative status—are not that
great. She notes that the differences across families in children's future opportunities in the United States are more and more a function of access to
college education, and that with spiraling private costs of higher education, parents' income and education are increasingly important in determining who goes to college.[23]

Latin America, meanwhile, leads the developing world in introducing
extensive market reforms.[24] The region's traditionally high levels of inequality
appear to be destructive, based on the unequal distribution of such crucial
assets as land and education as well as on policy distortions that have favored the rich and discriminated against the poor. Thus the distribution of
opportunity as well as income has been especially unequal. In this book
we explore whether recent reforms are improving opportunities for low-
income groups and how those groups perceive the changes that have
occurred. We analyze the limited empirical data that exist on mobility
trends as well as some new data that document public perceptions about
those trends.

In the former communist economies of eastern Europe and the former
Soviet Union, a very different situation predated reform: one of destructive
equality, in which there were insufficient incentives for productivity and
innovation, and opportunities were rationed according to political and other
noneconomic criteria. Reforms have increased inequality but at the same

---

23. For detail, see chapter 2; and McMurrer and Sawhill (1998).
24. For detail see Birdsall, Graham, and Sabot (1998).

time have generally improved the manner in which opportunities are allocated. In most cases, market principles such as greater returns to higher education coexist with older patterns such as greater opportunities for the nomenklatura and their children. Not surprisingly, changing patterns of income distribution coupled with very visible differences among winners and losers from market policies have had significant effects on the public's perceptions about how markets work in those regions. In this book we explore the empirical data on mobility since reforms began in a number of countries in eastern Europe as well as data that detail people's perceptions about their own mobility patterns vis-à-vis the rest of society.

Eclectic Methods

The economic literature on income distribution and economic growth has expanded substantially in the past decade in both theory and empirical work. Important contributions on developing countries have been made possible by the development of better and more consistent data.[25] Contributions have also come from the increasing use of household panel data by economists concerned with economic policy questions.

Meanwhile, studies of social mobility have been primarily the domain of sociologists. They have focused mainly on developed countries and have not directly addressed relations among economic growth, economic policy, and mobility.[26] With a few exceptions, economists have until recently been less concerned with social mobility and the conceptual and measurement problems surrounding it. Angus Deaton and Christina Paxson have studied questions pertaining to mobility within generations in the United States, largely through the exploration of short panels, focusing on the role of education and other variables in determining income mobility.[27] Sawhill in this volume, among others, has studied intergenerational mobility, com-

25. Deininger and Squire (1996), for example.

26. There are some exceptions for the developing countries. One for Brazil is Pastore and Zylberstajn (1997). We refer here primarily to the economics literature. There is a rich body of sociology literature that addresses issues of social status and social structure as well as of income mobility. It also provides occupational categories as a means to measure social mobility. These issues are, for the most part, beyond the scope of our study. See, for example, the works of Erikson and Goldthorpe (1985); Duncan, Featherman, and Duncan (1972); and Ganzeboom, Treiman, and Ultee (1991).

27. Deaton and Paxson (1994) have looked at trends in Taiwan as well as in the United States. For a comparison of U.S. and European data and approaches to earnings mobility, see Atkinson, Bourguignon, and Morrisson (1992).

paring income and other characteristics of parents and their grown children in the developed economies.[28]

With the nearly universal turn to the market in the former communist countries and in the developing world has come new interest in understanding mobility in rapidly changing environments. Taking advantage of the wave of market reforms, the authors in this volume link mobility to traditional economic concerns about growth and efficiency, combine these new concerns with the literature on the politics of economic reform, exploit a variety of different methodologies, and provide case studies from several regions. Our methods are exploratory: we rely on new conceptual approaches to issues of inequality and opportunity, take novel approaches to exploiting the empirical data that exist, and report in several chapters on new data sets we have developed.

Absolute versus Relative Mobility

Whether one measures a lot or a little mobility depends in part on exactly what is being measured. Confusion about absolute versus relative mobility is at the heart of confusion about whether certain societies really are mobile. Absolute mobility is defined as movement of individuals across a fixed income threshold established in a base year for the population as a whole. By this definition, a large number of people will be considered mobile, regardless of their relative position within a distribution. Factors such as economic growth and the natural tendency of incomes to increase with a person's age tend to ensure high absolute mobility.[29] Relative mobility is defined as individuals' mobility relative to others, normally for a given age, and will reflect the influence of factors such as education, inheritance, and luck. Both absolute and relative mobility will of course look different in different economies and within economies over time as a function of policy changes, societal differences in age distribution, and so forth.

We are interested in both kinds of mobility. For many countries, the extent of absolute mobility is an important issue for the period under study, which covers years of severe economic crisis, extensive macroeconomic adjustments, and the subsequent resumption of economic growth. As a starting point, we establish absolute mobility rates in a number of coun-

---

28. See Behrman (1984); and Solon (1992).

29. These conceptual differences underlie a widespread debate about mobility rates in the United States. See McMurrer and Sawhill (1998); and Krugman (1992).

tries in Latin America and explore how or if they have been affected by market reforms. We are also concerned with relative mobility and thus the differential effects of market reforms on different groups, defined, for example, by education.

Critical Variables

Another departure from standard approaches to the study of mobility is our focus on the effects of structural economic changes on mobility. A major question in Latin America and in the former communist economies, for example, is the extent to which the demand for labor has changed because of market reforms. The relative weights of variables that determined mobility rates in the pre-reform economies, such as education and occupational skills, may have changed, and the change may differ from country to country. Few studies assess the effects of economywide changes across countries and over time on patterns of mobility. In this book we make an initial attempt to do so by presenting the state of the art in mobility studies in each regional context, exploiting a series of cross-sections of countries and bringing new data to bear in a few case studies.

An emphasis on education emerges, not only as a contributor to mobility patterns but as a result of them. Both the sociological and economics studies on mobility have focused on education as a key variable. Yet these studies have for the most part treated education as an exogenous variable. Nancy Birdsall and Juan Luis Londoño suggest why the distribution of education is in fact as likely to be an outcome of past inequality.[30] Thus for some groups in the region, education or lack of education reflects lost opportunities in the past rather than serving as a vehicle for change.[31] We treat education as both a contributor to and an outcome of inequality and mobility patterns.

Political Economy and Public Perceptions

This book also departs from the established literature in incorporating political economy and institutions-based approaches. As mentioned ear-

---

30. Birdsall and Londoño (1997).

31. McMurrer and Sawhill (1998), meanwhile, find that in the United States access to good quality education, which is very important in determining mobility rates, is increasingly correlated with distribution of income patterns, which is becoming more unequal.

lier, public perceptions and expectations about mobility are as important as objective trends in determining voter behavior and therefore the sustainability of market policies.[32] The last section of this volume explores the conceptual and methodological challenges involved in measuring public perceptions about objective mobility trends and presents initial results of surveys taken in Latin America and eastern Europe.

Related to this political economy approach is the role of institutions in creating equal opportunities. Throughout this volume the authors explore the influence of public education, credit markets, and political and other institutions on trends in mobility. It is clear from the results presented here that institutions can be critical in creating equal opportunity or in stacking the deck against the poor, resulting in destructive inequality.

Contents of the Volume

The first section of the book sets out the conceptual issues involved in the study of the economics of opportunity. Isabel Sawhill focuses on mobility as a measure of access to opportunity, explores recent trends in the United States, and lays out the resulting policy choices, with a particular emphasis on the role of education. Joseph Stiglitz examines the trade-offs among social justice, economic efficiency, and individual responsibility, and how different societies' resolutions of these trade-offs affect their equality of opportunity and level of mobility.

The second section explores measurement challenges involved in the study of mobility. Jere Behrman defines the concept of social mobility as movements between periods in socioeconomic status indicators for specific entities. He reviews the state of the art in approaches to the study of income mobility and explores the challenges involved in applying them to the limited data that exist for developing countries, Latin America in particular. Gary Fields unbundles the concept of income mobility into five aspects: time dependence, positional movement, share movement, symmetric income movement, and directional income movement. He explores how reliance on one or another of these leads to different conclusions about mobility. Both authors explore issues of relative versus absolute mobility and how they affect the definition and measurement of mobility.

---

32. For a discussion of how inequality can lead to "populist" voting, see Alesina and Perotti (1994). For a discussion of voting patterns and economic policies in Latin America, see Remmer (1993). For a discussion of social policies, voting, and market reforms, see Graham (1994).

The third section of the book provides some empirical evidence of mobility patterns and their causes in Latin America and eastern Europe. Nancy Birdsall, Jere Behrman, and Miguel Székely construct indexes of intergenerational mobility for countries of Latin America and use the indexes to explore the effects of economic policies, macroeconomic conditions, and education programs on that mobility. They find that the depth of financial markets and the emphasis on basic schooling in public spending increase intergenerational mobility. Although the immediate effects of market reforms and education policy reform on current income distribution have not been evident, longer-run effects on mobility seem likely.

Katherine Terrell examines worker mobility and winners and losers in the postcommunist economies. She defines winners and losers along two dimensions: changes in their relative earnings and in finding jobs and avoiding unemployment. She finds that the winners in the transition so far have been young, educated men whose skills have enabled them to exploit new opportunities in the private sector of the economy. The growth in women's returns to education has lagged behind men's returns, and the skills of older workers are now much less valued in the new market economies.

In a study of mobility trends in Chile, David Hojman focuses on what he calls "market-driven, medium-term mobility," the changes in mobility trends that are driven by policy alteration. Chile's highly unequal income distribution remains very similar to what it was before the reforms, despite major strides in reducing absolute poverty. Though income has increased across the board, by far the largest increases have gone to managerial (skilled) personnel. Hojman develops a model in which increases in absolute income gaps may lead to consumption effects that reduce welfare—even if, as in Chile, income and consumption are increasing rapidly.

The fourth section of the book explores the issues of public perceptions and politics. Carol Graham analyzes how the existing studies on the political economy of reform fail to account for the effects of mobility trends—both upward and downward—on voting patterns. She reports the results of a regionwide survey of public opinion about markets and democracy in Latin America. One result was greater optimism among younger groups, probably reflecting their greater capacity to adapt to market changes and related demands for skilled labor. She also assesses the implications of the results of a pilot study of public perceptions versus objective mobility trends in Peru for the development of new political economy research on mobility, public perceptions, and the political sustainability of reform. She concludes that objective trends are usually poor predictors of subjective assessments, in part because upwardly mobile groups tend to have initially higher expectations than do the very poor.

Richard Webb, who conducted the pilot study of perceptions versus objective trends in Peru, details the findings of the study in his chapter. The most striking is that the responses of the top 30 percent of the sample—people who did best in income terms—were more pessimistic in their individual self-assessments than were those of other groups in the sample. There are various explanations, including higher expectations among more educated urban groups, reluctance to make definitive statements among rural respondents, and difficulties in accurately assessing earnings and income trends among respondents, particularly the self-employed. Beyond informing the research on mobility and perceptions, these findings also introduce methodological questions for all surveys that compare responses of urban and rural residents.[33]

Finally, Petr Matějů compares objective mobility trends (occupational mobility) with perceptions in eastern Europe. Like Webb, he finds that there is often little correlation between objective trends and public perceptions of those trends. He also finds that subjective assessments rather than objective trends have the most influence on how people vote. This points to the importance of better understanding what determines people's perceptions of their past mobility and future opportunities and the links of these perceptions to voting patterns.[34]

This volume must be viewed as an initial exploration into uncharted waters. The links between inequality, opportunity, and political behavior are far from established. There are also substantial problems with finding adequate data, particularly panel data, for the emerging market countries. Important major countries such as Russia, where resolving the problems of inequality and the opening of opportunity may be key to a very fragile political stability, are not covered in this volume, in large part due to data problems.[35] We view ours as an initial effort to frame the issues and lay the foundation for cross-regional collaboration in a new line of research on the economics of opportunity. Thus what is missing may be as important as what we are able to report.

33. See Putnam (1993).

34. These issues and their linkage to the sustainability of market policies are the focus of Carol Graham's ongoing research at the Brookings Institution.

35. Researchers from Russia attended an exploratory workshop sponsored by the Brookings Center on Social and Economic Dynamics in June 1998 that laid the foundations for this book. At that workshop, the basis for the future collection of the relevant data in Russia was established.

References

Akerlof, George. 1997. "Social Distance and Social Decisions." *Econometrica* 65 (5).

Alesina, Alberto, and Roberto Perotti. 1994. "The Political Economy of Growth: A Critical Review of the Literature." *World Bank Economic Review* 8 (3).

Atkinson, A.B., F. Bourguignon, and C. Morrisson. 1992. *Empirical Studies of Earnings Mobility.* Chur, Switzerland: Harwood Academic Publishers.

Behrman, Jere. 1984. "Intergenerational Earnings Mobility in the United States: Some Estimates and a Test of Becker's Intergenerational Endowments Model." *Review of Economics and Statistics* (June).

Behrman, Jere, and Paul Taubman. 1985. "Intergenerational Earnings Mobility in the United States: Some Estimates and a Test of Becker's Intergenerational Endowments Model." *Review of Economics and Statistics* 67 (1):

Benabou, Roland, and Efe A. Ok. 1998. "Social Mobility and the Demand for Redistribution: The POUM Hypothesis." *Economic Research Reports,* RR #98-23, C. V. Starr Center for Applied Economics, New York University.

Berry, Albert. 1997. "The Income Distribution Threat in Latin America." *Latin American Research Review* 32 (2).

Birdsall, Nancy. 1998. "Life Is Unfair: Inequality in the World." *Foreign Policy* (Summer).

———. 1999. "Education: The People's Asset." Brookings Center on Social and Economic Dynamics, Working Paper Series 5 (August).

Birdsall, Nancy, and Juan Luis Londoño. 1997. "Asset Inequality Matters: An Assessment of the World Bank's Approach to Poverty Reduction." *American Economic Review* 87 (May).

Birdsall, Nancy, Carol Graham, and Richard Sabot, eds. 1998. *Beyond Tradeoffs: Market Reforms and Equitable Growth in Latin America.* Brookings and InterAmerican Development Bank.

Birdsall, Nancy, David Ross, and Richard Sabot. 1995. "Inequality and Growth Reconsidered." *World Bank Economic Review* 9 (September): 477–508.

Birdsall, Nancy, Thomas C. Pinckney, and Richard Sabot. 1998. "Why Low Inequality Spurs Growth: Savings and Investment by the Poor." In Andres Solemano, ed., *Social Inequality: Values, Growth and the State.* University of Michigan Press.

Deaton, Angus, and Christina Paxson. 1994. "Intertemporal Choice and Inequality." *Journal of Political Economy* 102 (3): 437–68.

Deininger, Klaus, and Lyn Squire. 1996. "A New Data Set Measuring Income Inequality." *World Bank Economic Review* 10 (3): 565–91.

Duncan, Otis Dudley, David L. Featherman, and Beverly Duncan. 1972. *Socioeconomic Background and Achievement.* Seminar Press.

Durlauf, Stephen. Forthcoming. "Neighborhood Feedbacks, Endogenous Stratification, and Income Inequality." In Barnett, Gandolfo, and Hillinger, eds., *Disequilibrium Dynamics: Theory and Applications.* Cambridge University Press.

Easterlin, Robert. 1974. "Does Economic Growth Improve the Human Lot? Some Empirical Evidence." In Paul A. David, ed., *Nations and Households in Economic Growth.* Academic Press.

Epstein, Joshua, and Robert Axtell. 1996. *Growing Artificial Societies: Social Science from the Bottom Up.* Brookings.

Erikson, Robert, and John H. Goldthorpe. 1985. "Are American Rates of Social Mobility Exceptionally High? New Evidence on an Old Issue." *European Sociological Review* 1 (1).

Ganzeboom, Harry B. G., Donald J. Treiman, and Wout C. Ultee. 1991. "Comparative Intergenerational Stratification Research: Three Generations and Beyond." *Annual Review of Sociology* 17: 277–302.

Graham, Carol. 1998. *Private Markets for Public Goods: Raising the Stakes in Economic Reform*. Brookings.

———. 1994. *Safety Nets, Politics, and the Poor: Transitions to Market Economies*. Brookings.

Graham, Carol, and Cheikh Kane. 1998. "Opportunistic Government or Sustaining Reform: Electoral Trends and Public-Expenditure Patterns in Peru, 1990–1995." *Latin American Research Review* 33 (1).

Graham, Carol, and Moises Naim. 1998. "The Political Economy of Institutional Reform in Latin America." In Birdsall, Graham, and Sabot, eds. *Beyond Tradeoffs: Market Reform and Equitable Growth in Latin America*, Brookings and InterAmerican Development Bank.

Haggard, Stephan, and Steven B. Webb, eds. 1994. *Voting for Reform*. Oxford University Press.

Hoff, Karla. 1996. "Market Failures and the Distribution of Wealth: A Perspective from the Economics of Information." *Politics and Society* 24 (4): 411–432.

Kaldor, Nicholas. 1978. "Capital Accumulation and Economic Growth." In Nicholas Kaldor, ed., *Further Essays on Economic Theory*. New York: Holmes and Meier.

Krugman, Paul. 1992. "The Right, the Rich, and the Facts: Deconstructing the Income Distribution Debate." *American Prospect* (Fall): 19–31.

Kuznets, Simon. 1955. "Economic Growth and Income Inequality." *American Economic Review* 45 (March): 1–28.

Lora, Eduardo, and Juan Luis Londoño. 1998. "Structural Reforms and Equity in Latin America." In Birdsall, Graham, and Sabot, eds., *Beyond Tradeoffs*.

Londoño, Juan-Luis, and Miguel Székely. 1997. *Latin America after a Decade of Reforms*. Washington; InterAmerican Development Bank.

Londoño, Juan-Luis, Antonio Spilimbergo, and Miguel Székely. 1997. "Income Distribution, Factor Endowments, and Trade Openness." InterAmerican Development Bank, Office of the Chief Economist, Working Paper Series (October).

McMurrer, Daniel,and Isabel Sawhill. 1998. *Getting Ahead: Economic and Social Mobility in the United States*. Washington: Urban Institute Press.

Milanovic, Branko. Forthcoming. *Poverty and Inequality during the Transition*. Washington, World Bank.

Morley, Samuel A. 1995. *Poverty and Inequality in Latin America*. Johns Hopkins University Press.

Pastore, Jose, and Helio Zylberstajn. 1997. "Social Mobility: The Role of Education in Determining Status." In Nancy Birdsall and Richard Sabot, eds., *Opportunity Forgone: Education in Brazil*. Washington: InterAmerican Development Bank.

Piketty, Thomas. 1995. "Social Mobility and Redistributive Politics." *Quarterly Journal of Economics* 110 (August).

Putnam, Robert. 1993. *Making Democracy Work: Civic Traditions in Modern Italy*. Princeton University Press.

Rawls, John. 1971. *A Theory of Justice*. Harvard University Press, 1971.

Remmer, Karen. 1993. "The Political Economy of Elections in Latin America." *American Political Science Review* 87 (2): 393–407.

Robbins, Donald. 1996. "HOS Hits Facts: Facts Win. Evidence on Trade and Wage Inequality in the Developing World." Harvard Institute for International Development.
October.

Schultz, T. Paul. 1998. "Inequality in the Distribution of Personal Income in the World:
How It Is Changing and Why." Yale University Economic Growth Center, Discussion
Paper 784 (January).

Sen, Amartya. 1995. "The Political Economy of Targeting." In Dominique Van de Walle
and Kimberly Nead, eds., *Public Spending and the Poor: Theory and Evidence.* Johns Hopkins
University Press and the World Bank. 11–24.

Sheahan, John, and Enrique Iglesias. 1998. "Kinds and Causes of Inequality in Latin
America." In Birdsall, Graham, and Sabot, eds., *Beyond Tradeoffs.*

Solon, Gary. 1992. "Intergenerational Income Mobility in the United States." *American
Economic Review* 82 (3).

Vecernik, Jiri. 1997. *Markets and People.* Aldershot, U.K.: Avebury Press.

Young, Peyton. 1994. *Equity: In Principle and in Practice.* Princeton University Press.

ISABEL V. SAWHILL

2 | *Opportunity in the United States: Myth or Reality?*

In this chapter, I argue that opportunity matters. By this I mean that it is not sufficient to look only at the distribution of income at a point in time; one must also consider the rules of the game that gave rise to the distribution and the amount of social mobility these produce. Imagine a society in which incomes were as unequal as they are in the United States but in which everyone had an equal chance of receiving any particular income and in which there was substantial income mobility. The economic game would then be an unbiased lottery. Those people who were risk-averse might not like the idea of losing and might argue, in the spirit of John Rawls, that society ought to create a more equal distribution of income a priori. Others might welcome the chance to do exceedingly well, or at least the chance for their children to do exceedingly well. But—and this is the important point—no one could argue that the system was unfair.

There are at least three reasons to focus more attention on opportunity and social mobility. The first is that Americans have always cared more about equal opportunity than about equal results. The second is that it is

This chapter is based in part on Daniel P. McMurrer and Isabel V. Sawhill, *Getting Ahead: Economic and Social Mobility in America* (Washington: Urban Institute, 1998). I am particularly indebted to Daniel McMurrer for his work on the earlier book, many of the results of which are reported here.

22

hard to get any consensus on how much inequality is too much. Virtually no one favors a completely equal distribution of income. It is understood that some inequality in rewards is what drives individual effort and, as such, is essential to economic growth. But many would argue that current inequalities far exceed those needed to encourage work, saving, and risk taking, and that we need not worry about the optimal degree of inequality in a society that has clearly gone beyond that point. The argument is, however, hard to prove and will not satisfy those who are persuaded that inequality is the price we pay for a dynamic economy and the right of each person to retain the benefits from his or her own labor. In light of these debates, if any public consensus is to be found, it is more likely to focus on opportunity than on equality.

Still another reason to focus on opportunity is that it gets at the underlying processes that produce inequality. It addresses not just the symptoms but the causes of inequality. And a deeper understanding of these causes can inform not only one's sense of what needs to be done but also, as I have argued, one's sense of whether the existing distribution of income is a "good" or a "bad" one.

Three Societies

Consider three hypothetical societies, all of which have identical distributions of income as conventionally measured. (That is, if one ranked the annual incomes of all families and asked how society's total income was divided among them, the answer would be the same in each case). The first society is a meritocracy. It provides the most income to those who work the hardest and have the greatest talent, regardless of class, gender, race, or other less relevant characteristics. The second society, which I will call a fortune cookie society, is one in which where one ends up is less a matter of talent or energy and more a matter of luck. The third society is class stratified. Family background is all-important and you need to pick your parents well. The children in this society largely end up where they started, so social mobility is low to nonexistent.

The United States and most other advanced countries are mixtures of these three types. Given a choice among the three, most people would probably choose to live in a meritocracy. Not only do the rules determining success in a meritocracy produce greater social efficiency but, in addition, most people consider them inherently more just. Success depends on individual action. In principle, by making the right choices, anyone can succeed, whereas in a class-stratified or fortune cookie society, they are buffeted by forces outside their control. So, *even if the distribution of income in each case were identical,* most of us would judge them quite differently. In fact, we might even prefer to live in a meritocracy with a less equal distribution of income than in a class-stratified or fortune cookie society with a more equal distribution.

How Much Mobility Is There in the United States?

Much confusion has accompanied attempts to discover how much mobility there is in the United States because of a failure to specify exactly what one means by mobility. So I start with a simple example that may clarify matters. In my example, I deal with a society in which there are only three people, Minnie, Mickey, and Mighty.

Minnie, Mickey, and Mighty start with incomes (or other valued goods) of $20,000, $30,000 and $40,000 respectively. Now imagine that Minnie's children do extremely well, moving from an income of $20,000 to one of $80,000. Mighty's children, by contrast, experience a fall in income from $80,000 to $20,000. Mickey's children experience no change. This is the sort of *intergenerational* social mobility we would expect to find in a meritocracy. It is a story of rags to riches (or the reverse) in a generation. *Note that the distribution of income, as conventionally measured, has not changed at all.* As Joseph Schumpeter once described it, the distribution of income is like the rooms in a hotel—always full but not necessarily with the same people.

This same rags-to-riches story can occur over a lifetime as well as between generations. That is, there can be *intragenerational* social mobility. Those at the bottom of the income scale often move up as they accumulate skills and experience, add more earners to the family, or find better jobs. Those at the top may move down as the result of layoffs, divorces, or business failures. Thus, any snapshot of the distribution of incomes in a single year is likely to be a misleading indicator of the distribution of incomes over a longer period such as a lifetime. For example, in a society in which everyone was poor at 25 years old but rich at age 55, the distribution of annual incomes for the population as a whole would be quite unequal; but everyone's lifetime income would be the same.

Thus, it is theoretically possible for the annual distribution of income to become more unequal at the same time that the Minnies of the world are improving their status. Is this what happened over the past few decades in the United States? The answer is yes and no. On the one hand, there is a lot of income mobility within the population. About 25 or 30 percent of all adults move between income quintiles (say, from the lowest fifth to the second lowest fifth) every year, and this rate increases with time, approaching 60 percent over a ten-year period.[1] So there is considerable upward and downward movement. A lot of the Minnies in our society have moved up and a few may have even traded places with the Mickeys of the world. On the other hand, many people remain stuck at the bottom for long periods, and what data we have do not suggest that there is more mobility now than there was twenty or thirty years ago.[2] So one cannot dismiss complaints about growing income inequality with the argument that it has been accompanied by *more* opportunity than in the past for everyone to share in the new wealth.

But what about Minnie and Mighty's children? Suppose one looks at mobility across generations instead of looking at it across only Minnie and Mighty's life cycles? Here, the news is much more positive. Social mobility in America appears to have increased at least since 1960 and probably going back to the middle of the last century. This conclusion is based on studies that show less association now than in the past between some measure of family background and eventual adult career success.[3] This association has declined by as much as 50 percent since the early 1960s, according to Michael Hout. Scholars such as Hout have spent countless hours attempting to piece together a reliable story about social mobility in the United States, using survey data that span many years and several generations. Despite their best efforts to ensure comparability of income or occupational codes across years, problems remain, and it is only in the past few decades that solid data on this topic have been available at all.[4]

1. Burkhauser and others (1996); and Sawhill and Condon (1992). For more detail and a more complete set of citations see McMurrer and Sawhill (1998, chap. 4). Also, see Gottschalk and Danziger (1998).

2. Studies of intragenerational mobility have relied on longitudinal data, typically from the Panel Study of Income Dynamics or from the National Longitudinal Survey. These data have been available only since the late 1960s.

3. Featherman and Hauser (1978); Hout (1988); Grusky (1989); Grusky and Diprete (1990); Biblarz and others (1996); and Hout (1996).

4. Most studies of intergenerational mobility have relied on Occupational Changes in a Generation, first fielded as a supplement to the Current Population Survey by the Census Bureau in 1962 and repeated in 1973. Earlier work had to rely on more localized samples or on much less reliable data. More recent work, such as Hout's, has also used the General Social Survey cross-sectional data

What has produced this increase in social mobility? The major suspects are a massive broadening of educational opportunities, the increased importance of formal education to economic success, and more meritocratic procedures for assigning workers to jobs (basing assignments on "what you know rather than who you know"). In addition, the extension of opportunities to some previously excluded groups—most notably women and blacks—has produced greater diversity in the higher as well as the lower ranks. But paradoxically, this diversity has not necessarily produced more intergenerational mobility because blacks and women now have more "status" and like white men before them are passing this on to their heirs.

What about Economic Mobility?

Now return to our three-person society and consider a second scenario. In this one the economy booms and Minnie, Mickey, and Mighty all double their incomes from $20,000, $30,000, and $40,000 to $40,000, $60,000 and $80,000. Clearly, everyone is better off, although the relative position of each (as well as the distribution of income) is exactly the same as before. It is this sort of economic mobility rather than social mobility per se that has primarily been responsible for America's reputation as the land of opportunity.

Historically, the growth of the economy has been the most important source of upward mobility in the United States and the reason that children tend to be better off than their parents.[5] In a dynamic economy a farmer's son can become a skilled machinist and the machinist's son a computer programmer. Each generation is better off than the last one even if there is no social mobility. (Class-based differentials in fertility aside, social mobility is, by definition, a zero-sum game.)

But as important as it was historically, economic mobility has been declining over the past few decades for the simple reason that the rate of economic growth has slowed. Young men born after about 1960, for example, are earning less (in inflation-adjusted terms) than their fathers' generation did at the same age.[6] It would be nice to assume that a higher rate of growth

---

on about 1,500 adults that have been collected by the National Opinion Research Center (NORC) almost every year since 1972. Models of the process of social mobility have also gone through several evolutions. For a nice review of this literature and some of the methodological developments, see Haveman (1987, chap. 6).

5. This finding comes from the same studies cited in note 3. In the literature, what I call economic mobility is often termed "structural mobility."

6. The data and more detail are provided in McMurrer and Sawhill (1998).

is in the offing. New technologies and new markets abroad make many observers optimistic, but whatever the force of these developments, they have not yet produced a discernible increase in intergenerational mobility.

In sum, both these factors—the increase in social mobility and the decline in economic mobility—have affected prospects for the youngest generation. The good news is that people are increasingly free to move beyond their origins. The bad news is that fewer destinations represent an improvement over where they began. For those concerned about the material well-being of the youngest generation, this is not a welcome message. But for those concerned about the fairness of the process, the news is quite good.

The United States versus Other Countries

The distribution of income in the United States is, according to all the evidence, less equal than in other industrialized countries.[7] Given the level of affluence that most Americans have achieved, it is somewhat surprising that they have not been more generous in sharing their income with the less fortunate. One possible reason for this state of affairs is the peculiarly American belief in meritocracy, the idea that success is the result of a person's own efforts and talents rather than the social class into which that person was born. This belief in meritocracy has been much noted. Alexis de Tocqueville described it as early as the 1830s, and it has, if anything, grown stronger since then.[8] A commonly held view is that such beliefs have undermined public support for a more radical politics and inhibited the growth of the labor movement in the United States.[9] When those who are relatively poor believe that they or their children will rise in status over time, they are less likely to complain about the status quo and more likely to accept the prevailing system.[10] Such beliefs also weaken support for redistributional measures and may help to explain why the United States

7. See, for example, Atkinson (1995).

8. One should distinguish between American ideology and American practice. Some scholars who have studied the actual degree of social mobility around the time of Tocqueville, using the best available data, find little evidence of a rags-to-riches pattern. See Pessen (1974).

9. See, for example, Erikson and Goldthorpe (1985) and a series of articles in the *Woodrow Wilson Quarterly*, winter 1987.

10. In a 1998 paper Benabou and Ok argue that the coalition in favor of laissez-faire policies depends on expectations of future income growth, so that if a sufficiently large proportion of the population expects their future incomes to exceed the mean income for the society as a whole, they will resist redistributional measures. The authors analyze the Panel Study of Income Dynamics and find that over a twenty-year period, a majority of agents expect to have future incomes above the mean.

has done less to redistribute income through progressive taxes and social welfare benefits than most other industrialized countries.

The idea that America is exceptional in the degree of opportunity it provides to its citizens has never been proved. In a classic study done in the 1950s, S. M. Lipset and R. Bendix found little support for the hypothesis that the United States had a higher rate of social mobility than other countries. However, given the difficulties of comparing data from one country with that of another, one can never be sure about such matters. Despite much recoding of the data from various national surveys to make them more comparable, uncertainties remain.[11] However, the preponderance of the evidence suggests that the United States is not a more open society than the older democracies of western Europe.[12] Moreover, efforts to discover political or policy variables that explain these differences among industrialized countries have not proved very successful.[13]

Families Matter

One thing seems certain. No country has succeeded in eliminating the effects of family background on later success. These effects are strong. They work not just directly but more importantly through their influence on the kind of education a child gets. That is, more successful parents are particularly adept at obtaining a good education for their children. Over the years a vast reservoir of research has demonstrated time and again that the kind of family into which a child is born has as much or more influence on that child's adult success than anything else we can measure.[14] The income, education, or occupational status of a parent are strong predictors of how well children do.

11. The CASMIN (Comparative Analysis of Social Mobility in Industrial Nations) project, which has done much of this recoding, covers nine countries: England and Wales, France, Hungary, the Republic of Ireland, Northern Ireland, Poland, Scotland, Sweden, and West Germany.

12. See, for example, Erikson and Goldthorpe (1992).

13. Ishida and others (1995) do not include the United States in their study but add Japan to the CASMIN sample. They conclude, "Similarity among nations is found not only in the pattern of interaction between origin and destination but also in the way in which both origin and destination are related to education in industrial nations" (p. 180).

14. The relative impact of family background versus education depends on how well family background is measured, but when one includes in family background hard-to-measure influences that affect siblings similarly, the role of background looms at least as large as that of education. For further discussion and some evidence see Jencks and others (1979); Haveman (1987); Haveman and Wolfe (1995); and Hauser and Sweeney (1997).

Why are families so important? There are at least three possibilities. The first is that well-placed parents can pass on advantages to their children without even trying: they have good genes. The second is that they have higher incomes, enabling them to provide better material environments for their children. The third is that, on average, they are simply better parents, providing their children an appropriate mix of warmth and discipline, emotional security, intellectual stimulation, and coaching about how to relate to the wider world.

It has proved difficult to disentangle the separate influence of each. However, as Susan Mayer demonstrates in her recent book, *What Money Can't Buy*, the role of material resources has probably been exaggerated.[15] Most studies have failed to adjust for the fact that parents who are successful in the labor market have competencies that make them good parents as well. It is these competencies rather than the income they are able to provide that help their children succeed. I do not want to leave the impression that income does not matter at all. It enables families to move to better neighborhoods, relieves the stresses of daily living that often produce suboptimal parenting, and most obviously enables parents to purchase the necessities. Still, additional income assistance of the sort that our political system is likely to deliver is unlikely to produce major changes in children's life prospects.

Genes clearly matter. We know this from studies of twins or siblings who have been raised apart. However, IQ or other measures of ability are at least somewhat malleable, and, differences in intelligence are only a partial explanation of who ends up where on the ladder of success.[16]

Good parenting and an appropriate home environment are much harder to measure, but studies suggest they may explain a substantial portion of the relationship between family background and later success in school or in the labor market.[17]

The more general conclusion is that, for whatever reason, families matter. So unless we are willing to take children away from their families, the deck is stacked from the very beginning. And even if one could remove children from their homes, the pesky little matter of differences in genetic endowments would remain. Since a meritocracy has no good way

15. Mayer (1997).
16. Dickens and others (forthcoming). Similar results are reported using 1962 data in Jencks and others (1972).
17. Duncan and Brooks-Gunn (1997).

of dealing with these two fundamental sources of inequality, it is a pipe dream to think that it can provide everyone with an equal chance to succeed. But there are means to compensate for at least some of these initial differences.

Education and Opportunity

The education system has always been viewed as the primary means of compensating for initial differences, and the broadening of educational opportunities in the United States is thought by most scholars to be the major reason for the increase in social mobility that has occurred over the last century.[18] The United States spends more per capita on education than most other countries, and a larger fraction of its population has completed high school.

Despite this progress, family background continues to be a strong influence. There are two possible reasons for the failure of the educational system to produce greater opportunity. The first is that the elementary and secondary education system does not do a very good job of compensating for differences in family background. The second is that higher education has become increasingly important in determining success, and not everyone is guaranteed access to this level of education. In fact, it is precisely at this level of the education system that family resources become most important.

Elementary and Secondary Education

Most school funds are raised through property taxes, and as a result, spending per pupil is typically higher in wealthier than in poorer districts.[19] Legal challenges in state courts have had some success in reducing these disparities, but they can do nothing about the two-thirds of the variation in spending per student that is due to funding differences between rather than within states.[20] Attempts by the federal government to compensate for these differences have foundered on the limited federal contribution to

18. Michael Hout (1988), for example, finds that the association between family background and later success is almost completely eliminated among individuals who complete college.

19. U.S. Department of Education (1997). See also Parrish and others (1995).

20. Riddle and White (1996).

total school spending (7 percent of the total) and a strong political bias toward keeping control of education in local hands.

In addition, not all spending on education is equally effective, and it would be a mistake to assume that a simple equalization of spending per child, or even compensatory spending on behalf of the most disadvantaged, would solve all of the problems. However, other things being equal, it would surely help. In the meantime, efforts to improve school performance, whether through market-based reforms such as school vouchers and charter schools or through reductions in class size, better teacher training, or making schools, students, and teachers more accountable for results, could all increase the effectiveness of schools and thus their ability to help less privileged children overcome initial disadvantages. Poorly performing schools disproportionately hurt students from disadvantaged backgrounds. Students from more advantaged backgrounds have alternative sources of support and instruction, such as their family or community. Thus, the stronger the education system and the more it tilts resources toward the least well off, the more likely it is to serve as an engine of social mobility.

Higher Education

The influence of family background is even stronger at the higher education level. It affects the likelihood that a student will enroll in college, the type of institution attended, and the likelihood of completing a degree. Among 16- to 24-year-old high school graduates in the top fifth of the family income distribution in 1995, 83 percent enrolled in college in the fall after high school graduation, compared with 56 percent for those in the broad middle and only 34 percent for students in the bottom fifth.

Comparisons with earlier data reveal that these differences have increased significantly over time, driven primarily by increases in the likelihood of college enrollment among those from higher-income families.[21] High school graduates from families with incomes in the top fifth of the distribution were 30 percent more likely to enroll in college in 1995 than in 1979, while those from families with incomes in the lowest fifth were only 10 percent more likely to do so.

This relationship between college attendance and family background holds true *even when controlling for high school achievement.* More than 95

21. Heckman and Cameron (1997).

percent of the highest achievers from backgrounds of high socioeconomic status went to college within two years of high school graduation versus 77 percent of the highest achievers from low-SES backgrounds. Indeed, these high achievers from low-SES backgrounds were no more likely to make it to college within two years of graduation than the low achievers from high-SES backgrounds.[22]

Given that college tuition increases have far outpaced the rate of inflation in the economy as a whole, the increasing effect of family background on college enrollment is not surprising.[23] The tuition increases have made it ever more difficult for students from less affluent families to afford college tuition, particularly at many of the four-year private institutions, without significant public or private assistance. Recently enacted tax credits designed to offset higher education expenses may help somewhat in this regard, but they may also further inflate the cost of college.

At the same time, partly as a result of these tuition increases, students from wealthier families are enrolling more and more in the most-affordable public universities, increasing the competition for spaces in these institutions.[24] Thus, less affluent students face pressure from two sides: increasing tuition at already hard-to-afford private colleges and universities and increased competition at many public institutions.

Even when the difference in the likelihood of attending college is ignored and attention is restricted to those who actually enroll, family background continues to be important. It affects who graduates: in 1994, among students who had enrolled in college five years earlier seeking a bachelor's degree, 53 percent of those from families in the top quarter of the socioeconomic scale had received a bachelor's degree compared with 39 percent from families in the middle and 22 percent from families in the lowest quarter.[25]

Thus, family background has a significant and increasing effect on who goes to college, where, and for how long. With the rewards for going to college greater than ever and family background now a stronger influence over who reaps those rewards, the United States is at risk of becoming more class stratified in coming decades.

22. Heckman and Cameron (1997).
23. Kane (1997).
24. McPherson and Schapiro (1998).
25. U.S. Department of Education (1996).

Conclusion

The United States may not be the land of opportunity celebrated in our literature and in our public philosophy, but there is considerable mobility. Whether looked at intergenerationally or intragenerationally, individuals frequently move up and down the economic ladder. Moreover, there is at least some evidence that the importance of class or family background has declined over the past century.

The most important reason for any progress appears to be the extension of educational opportunities to a much larger proportion of the population. Further progress would seem to hinge, importantly, on improving the effectiveness of elementary and secondary education and ensuring that children from more disadvantaged families receive a larger share of whatever resources are devoted to this purpose.

References

Atkinson, A. B. 1995. "Income Distribution in Europe and the United States." Working Paper 133. Luxembourg Income Study.

Benabou, Roland, and Efe A. Ok. 1998. "Social Mobility and the Demand for Redistribution: the POUM Hypothesis," Working Paper 98-23. New York: C. V. Starr Center for Applied Economics, New York University.

Timothy Biblarz and others. 1996. "Social Mobility across Three Generations." *Journal of Marriage and the Family* 58 (February): 188–200.

Burkhauser, Richard, and others. 1996. "Labor Earnings Mobility in the United States and Germany during the Growth Years of the 1980s." Syracuse University.

Dickens, William, and others. Forthcoming. *Does the Bell Curve Ring True? A Reconsideration*. Brookings.

Duncan, Greg J., and Jeanne Brooks-Gunn. 1997. "Income Effects across the Life Span: Integration and Interpretation." Greg J. Duncan and Jeanne Brooks-Gunn, eds. *Consequences of Growing Up Poor*. New York: Russell Sage Foundation.

Erikson, Robert, and John H. Goldthorpe. 1985. "Are American Rates of Social Mobility Exceptionally High? New Evidence on an Old Issue." *European Sociological Review* 1 (1): 1–21.

———. 1992. *The Constant Flux: A Study of Class Mobility in Industrial Societies*. Clarendon Press.

Featherman, Daniel L., and Robert M. Hauser. 1978. *Opportunity and Change*. Academic Press.

Gottschalk, Peter, and Sheldon Danziger. 1998. "Family Income Mobility—How Much Is There, and Has It Changed?" In James A. Auerbach and Richard S. Belous, eds. 1998. *The Inequality Paradox: Growth of Income Disparity*. Washington: National Policy Association.

Grusky, David. 1989. "American Social Mobility in the 19th and 20th Centuries." Working Paper 86-28. University of Wisconsin Center for Demography and Ecology.

Grusky, David, and Thomas Diprete. 1990. "Recent Trends in the Process of Stratification." *Demography* 27 (November): 617–37.

Hauser, Robert M., and Megan M. Sweeney. 1997. "Does Poverty in Adolescence Affect the Life Chances of High School Graduates." In Greg J. Duncan and Jeanne Brooks-Gunn, eds., *Consequences of Growing Up Poor.*

Haveman, Robert. 1987. *Poverty Policy and Poverty Research: The Great Society and the Social Sciences.* University of Wisconsin Press

Haveman, Ribert, and Barbara Wolfe. 1995. "The Determinants of Children's Attainments: A Review of Methods and Findings." *Journal of Economic Literature* 33 (December): 1829–78.

Heckman, Stephen V., and James J. Cameron. "The Dynamics of Educational Attainment for Blacks, Hispanics, and Whites." Paper prepared for the conference "Financing College Tuition: Government Policies and Social Priorities." Washington American Enterprise Institute.

Hout, Michael. 1996. "Speed Bumps on the Road to Meritocracy: Occupational Mobility of Women and Men in the United States, 1972–1994." Working Paper. University of California, Berkeley Survey Research Center.

Hout, Michael. 1988. "More Universalism, Less Structural Mobility: The American Occupational Structure in the 1980s." *American Journal of Sociology* 93: 1358–1400.

Ishida, Hiroshi, and others. 1995. "Class Origin, Class Destination, and Education: A Cross-National Study of Ten Industrial Nations." *American Journal of Sociology* 101 (July): 145–93.

Jencks, Christopher, and others. 1979. "Who Gets Ahead? The Determinants of Economic Success in America." Basic Books.

———. 1972. *Inequality: A Reassessment of the Effect of Family and Schooling in America.* Basic Books.

Kane, Thomas. 1997. "Rationing College." Paper prepared for the conference "Financing College Tuition: Government Policies and Social Priorities." Washington: American Enterprise Institute.

Lipset, S. M., and R. Bendix. 1959. *Social Mobility in Industrial Society.* University of California Press.

McMurrer, Daniel, and Isabel Sawhill. 1998. *Getting Ahead: Economic and Social Mobility in America.* Washington: Urban Institute Press

McPherson, Michael, and Morton Schapiro. 1998. *The Student Aid Game: Meeting Need and Rewarding Talent in American Higher Education.* Princeton University Press.

Mayer, Susan E. 1997. *What Money Can't Buy: Family Income and Children's Life Chances.* Harvard University Press.

Parrish, Thomas B., and others. 1995. *Disparities in Public School Spending: 1989–90.* U.S. Government Printing Office.

Pessen, Edward, ed. 1974. *Three Centuries of Social Mobility in America.* D. C. Heath.

Riddle, Wayne, and Liane White. 1996. "Expenditures in Public School Districts: Estimates of Disparities and Analysis of Their Causes." In U.S. Department of Education, *Development in School Finance 1996.*

Sawhill, Isabel, and Mark Condon. 1992. "Is U.S. Income Inequality Really Growing? Sorting Out the Fairness Question." Urban Institute Policy Bites 13.

U.S. Department of Education. 1997. *The Condition of Education 1997.*

U.S. Department of Education. 1996. *Digest of Education 1997.*

JOSEPH E. STIGLITZ

3 | Reflections on Mobility and Social Justice, Economic Efficiency, and Individual Responsibility

Although much of modern positive economics is concerned with dynamic issues, economists have tended to approach distributional issues from a static point of view. Economists study the distribution of income at a single point in time or even how this distribution of wages or income changes over time. But they have paid less attention to the mobility of individuals, their prospects for advancement or the chances of a reversal of fortune. In part, this is due to limitations in comprehensive longitudinal data. The same approach, however, has also characterized most normative analysis. Traditional welfare economics, including utilitarian social welfare functions and the related Rawlsian social welfare functions, look at the economy at a point in time.[1] As a result, they do not reflect well basic ideas of social justice. In particular, I will show that utilitarian social welfare functions can rank as two equivalent economies where intuitively one would seem clearly preferable to another. Not only

I am greatly indebted to Ravi Kanbur and Jason Furman for helpful discussions. Some of the general theoretical ideas in this chapter reflect a joint research project with Kanbur. Jessica Seddon and Maya Tudor provided excellent research assistance. I also thank the participants of the MacArthur Inequality and Economic Performance Research Network in Bellagio, Italy, and the Brookings–Inter-American Development Bank meeting on economic mobility for helpful comments.
1. Even within the traditional framework, however, it is clear that one should look at the distribution of lifetime utilities or consumption.

can it be shown that certain widely accepted norms such as equality of opportunity cannot be derived from utilitarianism, but such norms may be inconsistent with utilitarianism; and utilitarian social welfare functions do not reflect many of the attributes of our social and economic systems that public rhetoric, at least, suggests are of first importance.

In addition to developing a broader framework for evaluating alternative economic systems and assessing alternative views of the role of the state, especially in the areas beyond pure public goods, this chapter also seeks to apply this framework to two specific problems, the provision of social insurance and the rationale for inheritance taxes.

This discussion is a continuation of the inquiry into the economic role of the state and the relationship between the government and markets.[2] In recent years that inquiry has begun by identifying ways markets fail to produce efficient outcomes, the special properties of the state (in contrast with other market and nonmarket institutions), and the powers and limitations that are derived from that. There has been a switch from seeing markets and government as substitutes to seeing them as complements.[3]

But much of the activity of the public sector goes beyond correcting market failures. Governments are concerned with redistribution, promoting social justice, and helping change the nature of society from what it might otherwise be (for example, through discouraging the consumption of drugs and encouraging the consumption of education). Today, much of the expenditure of the public sector is associated with the provision of *publicly provided private goods*, like education and social insurance, in contrast to the pure *public goods* on which Paul Samuelson focused attention. Typically, the marginal cost of providing these services to an additional individual is close to the average cost (while for public goods, the marginal cost is close to zero) and exclusion is easy (while for public goods exclusion is prohibitively expensive). The shape of these public programs, if not their very existence, is motivated by concerns that are not well captured in the "market failure" paradigm. Distributional concerns are paramount.

I have titled this chapter "Reflections . . ." because I am more concerned with presenting a set of issues than with providing definitive answers. Although I do not provide a comprehensive alternative framework

2. See Stiglitz (1989, 1991, 1992, 1994, 1998).

3. Or as "market enhancing." See, for example, Aoki, Murdock, and Okuno-Fujiwara (1997); or Hellman, Murdock, and Stiglitz (1998).

here, these results should at least make us cautious about excessive reliance on the traditional concepts of welfare economics.

Criteria for Assessing Economic Systems: Outcomes versus Mobility

For almost a century the concept of Pareto efficiency has dominated the economic profession's evaluation of economic systems and policies. In this tradition, for a "desirable" economic system Pareto efficiency is a necessary condition and an individualistic, social welfare function can be used for a more complete evaluation of alternative economic systems. Although there is some controversy about the meaning or usefulness of social welfare functions, there are, except at the fringes of the profession, few misgivings about the Pareto principle.[4]

Economists have looked at the implications of fairly weak restrictions on social welfare functions in choosing among Pareto-efficient allocations— for example, what are the implications of some weak ideas of egalitarianism for rankings among income distributions?[5] The basic idea was provided by the concept of utilitarianism—measuring the sum of individual utilities—where the marginal utility is decreasing with income. As a result, a mean-preserving spread of the income distribution, which moves people from the middle to the extremes of the income distribution, would make society worse off (from an egalitarian perspective) because the losses of the people made poorer would be larger than the gains of those made richer. Specifically, *an income distribution with a given mean is considered more egalitarian than another distribution with the same mean if the sum of individual utilities, for any utility function characterized by diminishing marginal utilities (for example, a concave function of income), is greater for the first distribution than for the second.*[6]

---

4. The standard argument in favor of the competitive market system is that it is Pareto efficient; the analysis has been extended, for instance, to thinking about alternative tax structures, in the concept of Pareto-efficient tax structures. See Stiglitz (1987).

5. The classic paper in this area is that of Atkinson (1970) who showed how one could translate the Rothschild-Stiglitz (1971, 1972) orderings of probability distributions into orderings of income distributions. These ideas were subsequently generalized by Dasgupta, Sen, and Starrett (1973) and Rothschild and Stiglitz (1973).

6. In more formal terms, *An income distribution (with given mean) $P_1(Y)$ is preferred to another income distribution $P_2(Y)$ with the same mean (which I write as $P_1 >_E P_2$ and describe as P_1 is more egalitarian than P_2) if and only if $\int U(Y)dP_1(Y) > \int U(Y)dP_2(Y)$ for all concave U.*

Anthony Atkinson, Michael Rothschild and Joseph Stiglitz, and Partha Dasgupta, Amartya Sen, and David Starrett then provided alternative characterizations of such rankings. There has been extensive discussion about the implications of further refinements—for example, utilitarian versus Rawlsian social welfare functions—and further generalizations—for example, separable versus nonseparable social welfare functions.

As applied, these approaches have been fundamentally *individualistic, outcome oriented,* and *static.* It is each person's own assessment of his welfare that counts; there are no "interaction" effects, no envy; and the process by which the outcomes are arrived at is of no relevance. But it is clear that such a social welfare function does not fully capture widespread, broader views of social justice.

Ranking Transition Matrices

The belief that we care only about *outcomes* implies that if we are studying an economy with income mobility, the only property that we care about (at least in a steady state) is the steady-state distribution of income. In more formal terms, if an economy is characterized by a Markov transition matrix, which gives the probability that a person whose parents are in the ith income group will be in the jth income group, the only information relevant for standard social welfare rankings is the eigenvector of the transition matrix.[7]

That this ranking system is at variance with our basic concepts of egalitarianism is illustrated by the following example. Consider two societies; one has no mobility and the other has considerable mobility, but with the same asymptotic distribution. For simplicity, assume that there are only two income states: low income and high income. The first society is characterized by the following transition matrix:

$$\begin{pmatrix} 1 & 0 \\ 0 & 1 \end{pmatrix}$$

7. If λ_A is the eigenvector of matrix A, then $A >_E B$ if $\lambda_A >_R \lambda_B$ where the symbol $>_R$ means "stochastically dominates in the sense of Rothschild-Stiglitz (1971) or Atkinson (1970)." Throughout the chapter I focus on Markovian income processes, but of course, there may be more complicated income dynamics.

In other words, with probability 1 a low-income parent will have a low-income child and a high-income parent will have a high-income child. This transition matrix is consistent with any initial distribution of income, which will also become the steady-state distribution of income.

Compare this to the mobile society whose transition matrix is

$$\begin{pmatrix} .5 & .5 \\ .5 & .5 \end{pmatrix}$$

In this society a person has a fifty-fifty chance of being rich or poor regardless of his or her parents' income. Regardless of the initial distribution of income, the distribution of income will rapidly evolve to (0.5 , 0.5), where half the people have high incomes and half have low incomes. This distribution of income, however, is also a feasible steady-state distribution in the immobile society. Although they are equally desirable according to the egalitarian definition, clearly the more mobile society is preferable to the less mobile one.

The Limits of Utilitarianism

This section is devoted to technical issues of transition matrices and may be omitted on first reading without loss of content.

If we use a utilitarian social welfare function, even with time discounting, then (at least in steady state) all matrices with the same steady-state distribution of income yield the same level of social welfare. The same is true of Rawlsian social welfare functions. Evidently, neither of these social welfare functions fully captures our sense of social justice.[8]

There are two interpretations of these results. One is to reject the assumption of time separability and look for nonseparable social welfare functions.[9] The other is to look for rankings of matrices implied by nonseparable period-by-period social welfare functions.

The axioms underlying time separability have a certain degree of persuasiveness.[10] Should the marginal rate of substitution between incomes of

8. The result is even stronger: *social welfare functions that are of the form* $W = W(V_0(U_0), \ldots V_t(U_t) \ldots)$ *rank matrices with the same eigenvector the same (in steady state), even when the period-by-period social welfare functions are not separable themselves.*

9. As note 8 makes clear, even rejecting the time separability does not fully resolve the paradox.

10. For the axioms see, for example, Harsany (1955).

generation t and $t + 1$ depend on income levels of earlier or succeeding generations rather than just the incomes of those involved directly? Although one may be concerned about an individual's parents, should the grandparents also be relevant? As I argue later, there are other aspects of the income generation process that are relevant for the evaluation of social justice, aspects that will not, in any case, be well reflected in any standard social welfare function, whether time-separable or not. The inability of such a static social welfare function to provide a ranking of matrices with the same steady-state distribution is simply another reason for dissatisfaction with the standard approach.

Alternatively, one can try to see the implications of nonseparable, period-by-period social welfare functions. Constructing simple nonseparable social welfare functions that allow the ranking of matrices is not an easy task. Rather than addressing the task directly, I first approach it indirectly by asking whether there are intuitive conditions that might allow matrices to be ranked.

PARTIAL ORDERINGS OF TRANSITION MATRICES. One such condition is the following. If those currently in low-income categories have a higher probability of doing well (and by implication, those in high-income categories have a higher probability of doing poorly) under transition matrix A than under transition matrix B, then A is more egalitarian. It should be obvious that this is a partial ordering: most matrices will have the property that while some persons with initially low incomes may prefer A to B, others may prefer B to A. For simplicity, I shall refer to this as the *egalitarian mobility ranking*.[11] A formal statement of this ranking, and proofs of some of the propositions in this section, are contained in appendix A.

Our sense of the circumstances in which one transition matrix is more egalitarian than another may be sharpened if we look at two special cases. Assume first there are only two income groups in the economy. Consider two transition matrices A and B. In this case it can be shown that A is more egalitarian than B (in the sense of the egalitarian mobility ranking) if and only if A and B have the same steady-state distribution (that is, the same

11. There is a possible objection to this approach. Although the poor may prefer B over A, they may be so much better off that, behind the veil of ignorance, under, for example, matrix B individuals who put some weight on the welfare of their descendants, they might actually prefer to begin life poor, given that poverty gives their descendants better opportunities later. We may wish to restrict ourselves to matrices such that there is sufficiently limited mobility that, behind the veil of ignorance, all individuals would prefer to be born rich rather than poor.

eigenvector), and $a_{11} < b_{11}$ (fewer of the low-income people get stuck in the low equilibrium).

Most matrices cannot be compared by this criterion (if they have different levels of expected income they cannot even be ranked under the standard Atkinson and Rothschild-Stiglitz criteria). In some cases the comparison is trivial; assuming there is an equality-preferring social welfare function with positive marginal social utility of income, any matrix with both a higher mean income and a lower probability of staying poor would be preferred. In this case there is no trade-off. The more difficult case comes in comparing matrices where there is a trade-off between a better asymptotic distribution but less mobility.

In the 2 × 2 case, the criterion of *egalitarian mobility* provides a complete ranking of matrices that generate the same asymptotic distribution of income. In the *n* x *n* case, for *n* > 2, it does not. To provide a more complete ordering, we might want to impose further conditions, a task to which we shall turn shortly.

ALTERNATIVE APPROACHES. There are, in fact, at least two distinct ideas of what might be meant by an "egalitarian" transition matrix. One is captured by the idea of equality of opportunity, that a person's lifetime chances are independent of his or her parents' income.[12] The other captures the idea of compensation, that those whose parents have a low income have a greater chance of doing well, so that "dynastic utility," some way of weighing the levels of utility of successive generations together, is less unequal.

In the 2 × 2 case, perfect equality (equality of opportunity) in the first sense is attained by the matrix

$$\begin{pmatrix} .5 & .5 \\ .5 & .5 \end{pmatrix}$$

or by the matrix

$$\begin{pmatrix} .2 & .2 \\ .8 & .8 \end{pmatrix}.$$

12. In formal terms, $a_{ij} = a_{kj}$ for all i, k where a_{ij} is the probability of being in income group j, given that one's parent is in income group i. The probability of an individual's being in state j does not depend on his parents' state (socioeconomic condition).

The perfect equality in the second sense is attained by the matrix

$$\begin{pmatrix} 1 & 0 \\ 0 & 1 \end{pmatrix}.$$

The children of the rich are poor, and the children of the poor are rich. In ranking matrices with the same steady-state income distribution, the second criterion prefers matrices with small a_{11} (a_{22}), while the first criterion prefers matrices in which $|a_{11} - a_{21}|$ is smaller. The two give quite different rankings.[13]

Standard individualistic, nonseparable, quasi-concave (equality-preferring) dynastic utility functions possessing the usual properties of anonymity can be used to motivate the second criterion. Dynastic utility will be more equal if there is at least some degree of compensation. (If there are three or more groups, there can be "excessive" compensation; if the poor become overcompensated and the rich overtaxed, dynastic utility inequality can be increased relative to more moderate levels of compensation.)

NONSEPARABLE UTILITY FUNCTIONS. More generally, one can use nonseparable utility functions to provide a complete ranking of matrices. One simple nonseparable utility function ranks $W[U(\sum \delta^t Y_t)]$, that is the utility of lifetime dynastic incomes generated by the stochastic process. (This is the same ranking that would emerge if the mobility matrix described an individual's income process, there were perfect capital markets, and we wished to rank matrices by a standard social welfare function.) Clearly, standard results of Rothschild and Stiglitz, Atkinson, and Dasgupta, Sen, and Starrett imply that matrix A will be preferred to B by all social welfare functions that are equality-preferring and anonymous (symmetric), if the Lorenz curve of the present discounted value of income associated with A lies inside that of B.[14]

This is, however, not the only plausible nonseparable utility function. The marginal rate of substitution between income of generation t and $t + 1$ should not depend on income of generations before $t - 1$ or after $t + 2$,

13. For further discussion of the difference between these two concepts, see Shorrocks (1978), Atkinson (1971), and Kanbur and Stiglitz (1986).

14. Rothschild and Stiglitz (1973); Atkinson (1971); and Dasgupta, Sen, and Starrett (1973). Conlisk (1989) and Kanbur and Stiglitz (1986) provide sufficient conditions for this to occur for *monotone* matrices (see the definition in appendix A): $0 \le D(A) \le D(B)$ or $(I + \delta A + \ldots + \delta^\tau A^\tau)$ $(I + \delta B + \ldots + \delta^\tau B^\tau)^{-1} \ge 0$, where it is assumed that the individual lives for τ periods.

that is, interdependence should be limited to at most four generations (one's great-grandfather matters, but not one's great-great-grandfather.) Then the social welfare function will be of the form[15]

$$W = W [. . . V_t(Y_t, Y_{t+1}) . . .].$$

Consider V taking on two limiting shapes. The first case I will call quasi-Rawlsian. In this case the minimum income attained each period is the same, and so it is natural to assume that society simply wants to minimize the number of people for whom either the parent or the child are in that minimum state. The number of people for whom that is not true is proportional to a_{22}. Thus A will be preferred to B if $a_{22} < b_{22}$. The ranking places all the weight on the likelihood that someone in the best-off state remains there.

The alternative extreme is given by $V = V(Y_t + \delta Y_{t+1})$. In this case, A will be preferred to B if

$$(I + \delta A) (I + \delta B)^{-1} \geq 0.$$

The Importance of Process over Outcomes

I have argued that we care not just about the distribution of income but also about income dynamics. A society in which people inherit their position is, at least in current views, less fair than a society in which they have a more equal chance to attain different positions within the income distribution.

More broadly, we care about the *process* by which inequality is generated, what generates the elements of the transition matrix. There seem to be at least two principles that affect our attitudes about the *process* generating inequality, *fairness* and *individual responsibility.* Neither concept is precisely defined, as some of the following discussion should make clear.

---

15. With full separability, social welfare depends solely on each individual's utility, with no concern for the relationship between the income of a parent and a child. The equation below is the simplest symmetric social welfare function that embodies direct interdependence between a parent and child. But one of the implications of this interdependence is that to evaluate the marginal rate of substitution of income between these two generations we need to have data concerning income (consumption) levels of *four* generations.

The idea of fairness is reflected in the value placed on equality of opportunity. One would prefer life choices not to be determined by the roll of dice, but if that is to be the case, one would prefer that the dice not be loaded. One implication of this is that inequality that arises out of luck seems more acceptable than inequality that arises out of inheritance (either of physical or human capital), so long as the chances are the same for everyone. I shall return later to this idea of equality of opportunity.

But not all inheritances are equivalent. For instance, it makes a difference whether the inheritance is an inheritance of ability rather than of physical capital. Why? Presumably because ability is an intrinsic property of the individual; it reflects the individual's own "worth" even if he received that "gift" through no action of his own, just as in the case of inherited physical capital.

Similarly, inequality that is a result of differences in people's willingness to work hard seems more acceptable than inequality that arises from either luck or inheritance. Again, this is because it is an intrinsic attribute of the individual. It reflects a sense of individual responsibility, a consequence of a person's own actions rather than gifts, either gifts of nature or gifts from parents. People who receive higher incomes from working harder "deserve" higher income.

But the line between inherited differences in incomes and inequalities arising from individuals' actions is more blurred. We pay some attention to the fact that willingness to work hard may be an inherited attribute (either genetically or through parental influence). We are more sympathetic, for instance, to those who succeed against odds.

The principle of individual responsibility—by which inequalities that arise from people's own actions are more acceptable than inequalities that arise from other sources—extends beyond simply the decision about how hard or long to work. There are other choices too that give rise to inequality: individuals decide on a level of risk taking. Those who are willing to take more risk have a better chance of a high income but also a better chance of a low income.

The idea of fairness that underlies this discussion of the inequality-generating process is markedly different from Rawls's idea, which focuses only on *outcomes*. In Rawls's view, a just society should be judged simply on how it treats its worst-off person. I would argue that our views of what is a just society are also affected by our perceptions of the rules of the game. It makes a difference whether the rules give each of us an equal chance of being the worst-off person.[16] We care that the rules are fair. But because we often cannot tell whether they are or are not fair, we also care about how they are determined.

Some might argue that I am confusing attitudes toward inequality with the trade-offs associated with more or less inequality. To be sure, one of the reasons we care about individual responsibility is that if people are not rewarded for working hard or for taking risks, there will be no incentives to work hard or take risks. If, for instance, government always offsets the gains and losses associated with risk taking, individuals would have no basis to make rational decisions concerning trade-offs between risks and rewards (total returns.) Our views about the degree of acceptable inequality are affected by these trade-offs. Optimal tax theory is based on using a social welfare function to balance carefully these trade-offs.[17] I am, however, trying to make a somewhat different argument: that our feelings about inequality itself, like our feelings about individual responsibility, are not just instrumental; that is, our willingness to accept inequality is not just that, for example, it results in more resources for society, which (were I a Rawlsian) might enable an improvement of the welfare of the worst-off individual. Rather, it is that our attitudes toward inequality are mixed with other, primitive concepts concerning a desirable society, that our sense of fairness and individual responsibility goes beyond simply the more traditional "functional" view that has been emphasized in the economics literature. *Unequal outcomes that serve a social function, are arrived at fairly, or are a consequence of individual exercise of responsibility are more acceptable than those that are not.*

---

16. Rawls motivated his argument that the just society worried about the worst-off individual by thinking about infinitely risk-averse people focusing on *outcomes* behind a veil of ignorance. The question is, "In thinking about justice, do individuals think about outcomes or processes?" Would they prefer a system in which individuals have a fair chance of attaining different outcomes, but where there is, for instance, some scope for them to exercise individual responsibility to avoid the worst outcome, or a system in which the outcome of the worst-off individual is guaranteed to be slightly better, even though all other outcomes are worse? Rawls has been extensively criticized for implicitly assuming all individuals, behind the veil of ignorance, assume that they are infinitely risk averse, even though no person may actually exhibit that degree of risk aversion. The focus on *process* implies that we do not even have to make judgments about what our utility function will be—behind the veil of ignorance.

17. For an exploration of this idea in a setting that shows that individuals may never extract from their experience what that trade-off is, see Piketty (1995).

Ex Post versus Ex Ante Expected Utility

The views presented here are not universally accepted. For instance Ravi Kanbur has argued that society cares about ex post inequality even when it is a result of risk that is voluntarily engaged in.[18] Part of the reason for his argument is that he is concerned that individuals may make *irrational* decisions based on misperceptions of probabilities. Clearly the work of Daniel Kahneman and Amos Tversky showing that there are systematic deviations between individual risk perceptions and objective probabilities provides support for those concerns.[19] But to the extent that this provides a reason for redistribution (for a concern about the resulting inequality), it suggests a form of paternalism: we are concerned about inequality just as we are concerned about people taking drugs because they are taking actions that are not in accord with their own best interest.

How to deal with irrational risk perceptions is, in a sense, no different from how to deal with other kinds of misperceptions. People underestimate the return to investing in school or the consequences of taking some drug (for example, the dangers of addiction). A society that is based on the principle of individual responsibility says that individuals must bear the consequences of those decisions. A society based on paternalism says that people should not have the right to exercise their individual responsibility when someone else (the government) believes that they will not exercise it well in some important arena. The difficulty with the paternalistic doctrine is that it is often hard to draw the line: whose judgment and what criteria? There are innumerable instances of governments taking what in retrospect we view as overreaching actions—from prohibitions on alcohol to attempts to prohibit certain consensual relationships among adults. Should taking undue risk be added to those instances in which the government should exercise paternalistic powers? And if so, where are the bounds?

For analytic purposes we need to distinguish instances of such irrationality from those in which people have rational perceptions but perhaps differ in their attitudes toward risk (some people may be risk lovers) or in their human and physical capital. Then, if we believe in the Pareto principle, a society that allows individuals to engage in bets that may increase ex post inequality but increase everyone's ex ante expected utility must be

---

18. Kanbur (1987).
19. Kahneman and Tversky (1972, 1973).

preferable to one that restricts such trades. All people in one society are better off (or at least as well off) than in the other unless a compelling case can be made that there are significant externalities associated with the ex post inequality. Yet at the same time, just as we were concerned before about individual responsibility and how inequality was generated *because of the implications for the fundamental nature of society*, so too here. Ex post inequality—no matter how generated, even if a part of a Pareto-efficient resource allocation—may be of concern because of the consequences it has for the nature of society.[20]

Although I thus believe that we should focus more on the distribution of ex ante utilities than ex post outcomes, there is a category of risks that requires special attention: those that are involuntarily undertaken. The argument before was that if people voluntarily engage in risk-taking activities, it increases their ex ante expected utility, and the Pareto principle, combined with a skepticism about paternalism, suggests that we should focus on their ex ante expected utility. But this argument does not apply to risks thrust upon a person. A society in which companies release high levels of pollutants, so that there is a higher risk of cancer, imposes an additional risk (additional dispersion in ex post outcomes) without an offsetting increase in ex ante expected utility. The additional risk is not a result of individuals' exercise of individual responsibility.

I have tried to give some sense of ranking of different sources of inequality. It would be nice if one could give more precision to these ideas and be able to derive them from some higher-order principles. Such an approach might attempt, for instance, to provide some axiomatic basis to the concepts of fairness and individual responsibility and then formulate a social welfare function that places weight on the outcomes, the transitions, *and* the fairness of the process by which those transitions occurred.

Equality of Opportunity

The idea that we care not so much about outcomes but about opportunities has received increasing attention, especially in political dialogue. We at least pay lip service to the view that children from disadvantaged homes should have the same life chances that are afforded children of the more advantaged. One of the reasons for the increased emphasis on educa-

---

20. The distribution of political power may depend on ex post inequality (not on ex ante expected utility).

tion is that it promotes equality of opportunity, and the fact that children from lower-income households are much less likely to attend college is cited as evidence of a lack of equality of opportunity.[21]

Equality of opportunity may require compensatory actions. That is, if we define an individual's "opportunity set" by his wage, then for individuals of equal ability,

$$w = w(E, H).$$

The wage is a function of education and home "investment," which is controlled by parents, not the individual. Equalizing w requires undertaking higher levels of E to offset lower levels of H.[22]

Equality of opportunity is perfectly consistent with inequality of outcome. People could have the same opportunity set, but some seize the opportunities while others do not. Some work hard and others do not.

There is a growing consensus that society has no responsibility to undo the inequality arising from individual decisions, given that they have comparable opportunities. The principle of individual responsibility with equality of opportunity suggests that once we have truly equalized opportunities, any inequalities arising from the extent to which individuals take advantage of those opportunities are socially acceptable. A decade ago there was less agreement on this premise: those from disadvantaged homes might be more inclined not to seize the opportunities that were afforded them, and public actions might be required to offset these differences in proclivities. Underlying these differences in views are fundamental differences in beliefs about the nature of individuals, including their freedom to "choose" who they are and the extent to which their preferences are socially determined. Traditional economics has taken the individual as the basic unit of analysis, with his characteristics exogenously determined. We all recognize that the nature of the individual is influenced both by genetics and the social milieu in which he exists. But what are the differences for which society should take offsetting actions?[23]

21. But there is some evidence that even if they were given the same or better opportunities (for instance, free education) they might not avail themselves of those opportunities to the same extent. Preferences are molded by family background, raising the troublesome question of the extent to which one thinks of preferences in a way similar to other inheritances.

22. For more extensive discussion of these issues, see Arrow (1973) and Stiglitz (1973).

23. Roemer (1998) examines the boundaries of social intervention to create equality of opportunity.

Appendix B shows that *if we care only about outcomes, and not processes, we cannot derive the principle of equality of opportunity from generally accepted social welfare functions.*

The argument is even stronger when it comes to *equal access to goods* (including education as a good). In general, *inequality of opportunity may be welfare increasing, given an individualistic social welfare function that values only outcomes.* The point is illustrated forcefully in figure 3-1, where *BB* is the initial budget constraint for all individuals. *E* is the initial endowment point, which lies strictly in the interior. The figure shows the consequences of increasing *P* for some individuals and decreasing it for others. Note that all individuals, whether they are net buyers or sellers of the good, are better off. Thus *the inequality of opportunity has made all individuals better off and has increased social welfare.*[24]

Thus, if we subscribe to the principle of equality of opportunity, we must take it as a principle in its own right, an essential part of our idea of social justice, not simply as a corollary of more general principles derived from egalitarian social welfare functions.

The Nature of Society

One of the reasons that we care about inequality and the processes by which it is generated is that we believe it has a fundamental impact on society. A society in which people perceive themselves as facing a fair game in which there is equality of opportunity is fundamentally different from a society in which some people, simply by right of birth, have attained a position of privilege. The views of individuals—of themselves, of their responsibilities to themselves as well as to others—may be markedly different in the two situations, and these perceptions may well affect behavior, including social interactions.

There are some concerns that go beyond those raised so far, where I have taken "utility functions" (behavior) as given, not shaped by the environment in which people live. But we know that this assumption is not valid, and although we have great difficulties in formulating generally accepted approaches to welfare analysis with endogenous individuals, still our concept of a just society may well take into account how the *rules* of society themselves shape the people in it.

---

24. The point about inequality and utilitarianism is made more generally in Stiglitz (1982).

Figure 3-1. *Welfare Consequences of Unequal Opportunity*[a]

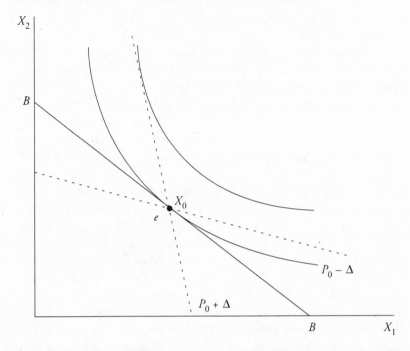

a. Increasing inequality of opportunity may increase social welfare. If utility is a convex function of p, then inequality in prices may be welfare enhancing.

So far, my focus has been on showing that in ranking societies we look not only at *outcomes*, the distributions of income, but at the *dynamics* that determine those outcomes (the transition matrices) and the underlying forces, the *processes*, that determine the dynamics. Matters are more complicated than the above discussion suggests. The mobility in the society as described by the transition matrix may itself be a function of the distribution of income. This may be because the transitional matrix is an expression of institutional arrangements, which are themselves endogenous. A plausible example of this comes from agriculture in developing countries. In circumstances of great inequality the institution of sharecropping will emerge, solidifying the unequal distribution. But when land is distributed in a more egalitarian manner, farms will be owner managed, resolving the agency costs and making it easier for small farmers to maintain or even extend their property. In this case there may be multiple equilibria land distributions: a highly unequal distribution would tend to perpetuate itself as would a highly equal distribution.[25]

Algebraically, we could define the transition matrix as a function of the income distribution $A(Y)$ and then a steady-state income distribution would be Y^*, satisfying $A(Y^*) Y^* = Y^*$. In these circumstances there may exist multiple equilibrium distributions. Even if economies were valued simply by their transition matrices, those matrices are now *functions* and the task is to rank not a matrix of numbers but a matrix of functions. The difficulties are highlighted by the fact that some of the equilibrium distributions associated with $A(Y)$ may be preferable to some of the equilibrium distributions associated with $B(Y)$, but other of the equilibrium distributions may be strictly less preferred, while still others may not be rankable.

The dependence of the stochastic process on the wealth distribution raises another set of issues: while traditionally economists have focused on trade-offs (for example, between inequality and average income), in the presence of agency costs more egalitarian distributions may actually lead to higher average incomes.[26] There may even be Pareto-efficient redistributions. Clearly, from the perspective of evaluating outcomes, such redistributions (as those associated with land reforms) should increase welfare; but once the *process* of redistribution is taken into account, critics might claim that such redistributions are not desirable. By contrast, advocates of such redistributions might argue that even if they lead to lower incomes, they may be desirable, especially if they undo inequalities that were created through unjust processes.

The Measurement of Inequality: A Digression

Conventional measures of inequality may both overstate and understate the true extent of inequality, and changes in the discrepancy between measured and actual inequality may obscure real changes in the extent of inequality in society.

Traditional measures have focused on inequality in the consumption of private goods among households. My concern here is inequality in *total* consumption (welfare, however measured) among individuals. There may be marked discrepancies not only in the levels, but changes in the level,

---

25. For an early discussion of this, see Braverman and Stiglitz (1989). For an excellent example of such dynamics, see Banerjee and Newman (1993).

26. See, for instance, Hoff (1994, 1996) and Stiglitz (1993b) and the references cited there.

between the two. For instance, there may be inequality in the distribution of consumption within the family. Women may work harder and receive less consumption.[27] Offsetting this effect (which implies that traditional statistics understate true inequality[28]) are three effects that may work in the opposite direction.

—Public goods (typically not included in "measured" income) may be taking on an increasingly important role, especially as a country's GDP increases.[29]

—What matters is not current inequality but lifetime inequality. Changes in the transition matrix between income at time t and income at time $t + 1$ may result in lower lifetime inequality associated with the same (or even higher) levels of current inequality.[30] For instance, for the United States, changes in lifetime inequality seem markedly less than changes in current inequality.[31] Moreover, improvements in capital markets may result in less lifetime inequality of welfare associated with even a given (year-to-year) transition matrix. Similarly, lower rates of interest may result in less inequality of lifetime inequality associated with a given transition matrix.

—Families may choose to share among themselves (either at a single moment of time or intertemporally), so that actual inequality may be less than measured inequality.

Application 1: A Comprehensive Lifetime Insurance Plan

In the past hundred years, advanced industrialized economies have developed comprehensive social insurance plans that set out to reduce inequality arising from certain risks. Such social insurance has been characterized by several problems.

---

27. The discrepancies between consumption and other social indicators for male and female children provide dramatic evidence of such differentiation. See for instance, Sen (1989); Klasen (1996); and Svedborg (1990). Government policies may have exacerbated these differences. Apps and Stiglitz (1981) point out, for example, that the corporate income tax encourages consumption inside the firm, particularly of executives, who are predominantly male.

28. These observations are especially important in analyzing trends in inequality. If, for instance, intrafamilial discrimination has diminished as more women have entered the corporate world, then increased interhousehold inequality could be consistent with decreased individual inequality.

29. That is if public goods have an income elasticity greater than unity.

30. Earlier, the discussion of transition matrices focused on intergenerational transitions.

31. Sawhill (1994).

—It has confused risks with redistribution. Growing old is not really a risk. It is totally predictable. How long one lives is a risk. An annuity is designed to mitigate the risk to annual consumption arising from excessive longevity. Annuity markets have not, at least in the past, functioned well, partly because of high transactions costs, possibly partly because of severe problems in asymmetries of information.[32]

—Programs have been compartmentalized so that there are separate social insurance programs for each such risk. Most of these separate programs face severe moral hazard problems. Unemployment insurance, for instance, may induce individuals not to search for a job as actively as they might otherwise.

Although discussions of these programs may often have been confusing in articulating the precise role for government, especially about whether the role was due to market failures or distributional concerns, there is now a general recognition of the rationale for government action. There *are* market failures, particularly associated with adverse selection problems in insurance markets; and at the time these programs were initiated, markets did not do a very good job at providing the desired insurance. But there are more fundamental problems: in a compassionate society in which governments provide support for those who fail to provide for themselves, there is a moral hazard (free-rider) problem, which can be addressed by mandating coverage of these risks or providing social insurance directly.[33]

In this case our standard welfare theory provides a good framework both for analyzing the rationale for government actions and for thinking through ways in which the system might be improved. For instance, elsewhere I have proposed a comprehensive social insurance program that would insure lifetime risks rather than individual risks. It would recognize that people could self-insure against many small risks (and even a six-month spell of unemployment is small relative to an individual's lifetime income). Capital markets are imperfect, and government may (does) have a role in offsetting the consequences of the capital market imperfections.

People face many separate risks that are imperfectly correlated: disability, health, unemployment, and longevity risks. By providing insurance against cumulative lifetime risks rather than each separate risk, one can provide greater effective insurance at a given level of moral hazard. In par-

32. Those who know that they are likely to live a long time are especially eager to purchase such insurance.

33. See, for example, Stiglitz (1993a).

ticular, generally accepted principles of insurance argue that people should self-insure against most small risks such as temporary unemployment (since the transaction costs associated with insurance more than offset the benefits of risk reduction associated with such insurance). There are capital market imperfections that make relying on such self-insurance difficult, especially as individuals have come to rely more on social insurance for their retirement. They cannot borrow against their retirement income to sustain consumption during a short bout of unemployment. The restrictions on borrowing can be understood: without some restrictions, they might borrow so extensively that the social justification for mandatory pensions—that without such requirements, people might become dependent on the state for support in their old age—might be undermined. But we may have pursued this argument too far: unemployment (defined by, for example, existing criteria) is a risk that currently is (to a large extent) socially borne. Agglomerating this risk with longevity risk (associated with pensions), providing insurance against large lifetime risks, would enable most individuals to bear fully the risk of short bouts of unemployment. Doing so would serve to mitigate the strong moral hazard effects currently observed with unemployment insurance.

Similar arguments hold for agglomerating health and disability risks with longevity and unemployment risks. The provident funds (of Malaysia and Singapore) may provide a model for such agglomeration. The provident funds are designed to enable individuals to draw on their individual accounts for a variety of needs. As currently designed they provide no lifetime risk insurance. If risks were fully independent and variances of individual risks were small enough, individual risk pooling through individual accounts would provide a good approximation of lifetime insurance. (In such circumstances, perfect capital markets too would enable individuals to provide effective self-insurance for themselves. The moral hazard associated with society's unwillingness to let individuals bear the full consequences of profligacy would still lead to the government's wishing to impose mandates on contributions to the provident funds and limits on withdrawals associated with particular circumstances.)

Although standard theory provides a good framework for thinking about how the current system of social insurance might be improved, implicitly it has taken a stand on individual responsibility. It says that certain outcomes (poverty-level incomes for the aged) are unacceptable, even if they are the result of a person's failing to take appropriate actions, such as saving for retirement. And because these outcomes are unacceptable, it deprives the individual of his right to exercise individual responsibility. In effect, it puts our concerns about outcomes over our concerns about individuals' rights to exercise individual responsibility.

These conflicts between outcome-oriented concerns about equality and process-oriented concerns about individual responsibility arise in the design of social insurance programs. For instance, proposals affording people the right to invest all or a fraction of their individual accounts in qualified private funds illustrate these conflicting views. One might argue that such proposals (with explicit incorporation of any implicit taxes and subsidies embedded in current structures) would not only increase transparency and give people greater opportunity to exercise individual responsibility but also would improve welfare. After all, individuals would only avail themselves of this opportunity if they believed it increased their expected utility; and so long as they were rational, and so long as the implicit taxes in the current system are reflected under the system with choice, no one should be adversely affected. But what happens if people invest poorly and as a result inequality actually increases? Can we say that they have exercised their individual responsibility and leave it at that? (Presumably the system will be designed to ensure a socially acceptable minimum, for example, through a part of the system in which people are not allowed to invest in private accounts.) Some have suggested in effect that the government provide partial insurance for such investments.[34] Such partial insurance can be thought of as an attempt to reconcile our concerns about outcomes (we do not want too much inequality) and our concerns about providing individuals the right to exercise individual responsibility.

Over the past couple of decades there has been a shift in thinking about the importance of social insurance in improving economic justice. The shift has been concomitant with an increase in concerns about individual responsibility. I sense that there is no general perception of a *right* or *societal obligation* to maintain an individual in retirement at a certain fraction of before-retirement income. Although views on specific forms of egalitarianism might explain why society provides certain levels of health insurance for all people, there is no similar argument for retirement insurance defined relative to income while working. Rather the concern is about an individual's absolute level of income during retirement; and that concern is compatible with the consolidated approach to social insurance discussed in this section. People should have the right to decrease their retirement income if they *choose* to have an extended period of unemployment.

34. Feldstein (1998).

To be sure, in a world with no asymmetries of information, society might well provide social insurance against a wide variety of social risks, from the risk of cancer to the risk of one's human capital becoming technologically obsolete. A just society might provide complete insurance or even compensatory payments. But information is imperfect, and social insurance is provided against observable risks, which are affected both by exogenous events and by actions. For such risks one cannot put aside the behavioral consequences of the provision of social insurance. But if my discussion in the previous sections is correct, then in thinking about the role of social insurance for various risks individuals face, one needs to go beyond the traditional focus on outcomes and behavioral responses and pay attention to the *processes* by which unequal outcomes are generated.[35]

Application II: Inheritance Taxes

Inheritance taxes provide an interesting context within which to explore views about inequality. Most advanced industrial countries have adopted inheritance taxes. Such taxes reflect broadly held views of ethical principles. I want to consider how such taxes can be interpreted through various models of equality.

Some years ago, I showed in a series of papers that inheritance taxes may (and indeed were likely to) increase inequality—that is, differences in individual consumption levels.[36] The reasoning was simple. Inheritances should be viewed as intergenerational consumption smoothing. In standard models in which there is regression toward the mean (in the vernacular, "from rags to riches and back to rags in three generations"), parents who inherit above average amounts of physical capital or abilities share their good fortune with their descendants. The result is that, in general, those with above average ability consume less than their wage income, and those with below average ability consume more. Taxing inheritances discourages this consumption smoothing and thus increases the inequality of consumption (though it may at the same time decrease inequality in income).[37] Those concerned with *outcomes* alone would, on these grounds, argue against taxing inheritances.

---

35. We do this, for instance, in our tax code. Gambling losses are treated differently from losses on more "legitimate" investments.

36. See Bevan and Stiglitz (1979); and Stiglitz (1976a, 1976b, 1978).

37. Under some circumstances it may actually increase the range of consumption, even though on average it reduces its dispersion.

Utilitarianism provides an even stronger case against inheritance taxes. Again, the reasoning is simple: inheritances are, from the perspective of a utilitarian, doubly blessed, for they give utility to both the giver and the receiver; the giver, however, does not take into account the second effect (only the effect of his gift on his own utility, which does put weight on that of his descendants). Presumably, therefore, bequests should be encouraged. Appendix C presents a more formal exposition of the argument that, from a utilitarian perspective, inheritance should be subsidized.

But neither formulation fully captures our sensibilities about inheritance. Inheritances do result in inequality of opportunity: those who inherit more have opportunities opened up for them that are not available to others.[38] We worry too that a society in which people attain positions of status (high income) as a result of inheritance is, in some fundamental way, different from societies in which position is attained on the basis of each individual's own work.

Indeed, even when inheritances are Pareto improvements, society may wish to discourage them. Allowing an individual to give money to his children increases his welfare and that of his children. In the absence of envy it has no direct adverse effects on anyone else. Yet such a transfer does result in inequalities of opportunity.

These conflicts between equality of opportunity, individual rights, and the Pareto principle in the context of inheritances of wealth are troublesome enough. But consider the problem of human capital. Some parents may "invest" more than others in their children. Such investments may lead to inequalities of opportunity. Should such investments be restricted simply because some parent decides he does not want to make these investments? To improve equality of opportunity, should society provide compensation to those who are unlucky enough to be born into families where parents are not willing to make such investments? Should the parents be taxed to finance these investments so that parents who choose not to invest will not be better off than those who do?[39] But does that imply that the

---

38. In the previous models, assume some parents care about their children and some do not. Then inheritances smooth consumption within one set but leave consumption in the other set unaffected. Thus inheritances still unambiguously reduce inequality of outcomes, even though they increase inequality of opportunities.

39. Or should we assume that the parents who choose to invest more must be getting sufficient pleasure out of doing so that in fact we do not need to tax the parents who do not—we should not just focus on direct consumption.

parents who want to invest more in their children effectively force others either to do so or to pay the price?

What is clear is that we do not view the accident of birth just like any other random event, part of the roll of the dice. When we say the system is unfair, we do not say, "Well, he had a chance of being born to a rich person." But in thinking about inheritances—including inheritances of human and physical capital as well as individual traits—we are forced to reflect upon what we consider to be attributes, actions, and outcomes for which individuals should take *individual responsibility*, the random occurrences somehow determined by a more or less fair process, and the circumstances in which a just society takes action.

Concluding Remarks

The two applications, social insurance and inheritance, provide a good testing ground for our views about social justice and the role of government. In the first case, standard welfare theory provides a framework within which we can understand the role of government, though even here there is a conflict between outcome-oriented concerns over inequality and process-oriented concerns over the exercise of individual responsibility. In the second case the conflict between standard welfare approaches and generally held views concerning such taxes is more apparent: utilitarianism suggests that we should subsidize bequests, while broader concepts of social justice are far less supportive of inheritances.

More generally, I have argued that our views of social justice are not well reflected in the standard approach, which focuses on outcomes that can be evaluated using a social welfare function. Widely held views concerning the desirability of social mobility and equality of opportunity cannot be derived from, and are sometimes inconsistent with, standard specifications of social welfare functions. Although I have attempted to articulate the ways in which the standard formulations are deficient, I have not succeeded here in formulating a general alternative. That must await another occasion.

Appendix A: Ordering Transition Matrices

The egalitarian mobility ranking can be formally defined as follows. Let a and b be two vectors. We write:

$$a >_{sI} b.$$

If a stochastically dominates b, in the sense that every risk-averse individual prefers a to b (a and b need not have the same mean). Let

$$A >_e B$$

if, regardless of the income of an individual, he prefers to be confronted with matrix A rather than B.

It should be obvious that this is a partial ordering: most matrices will have the property that while some individuals with initially low incomes may prefer A to B, others may prefer B over A.

The analysis is complicated by the possibility that even if a lower-income individual has a higher probability at a higher income next period (or generation), the *future* prospects of a high income could be worse than, say, those of a middle-income individual. A sufficient condition to restrict ourselves to matrices such that there is sufficiently limited mobility that, behind the veil of ignorance, all individuals would prefer to be born rich rather than poor, is that the cumulative distribution for those of higher income stochastically dominates the cumulative distribution for those of lower income. That is,

$$\text{if } D_{ij} \equiv \sum_{l=1}^{i} a_{il},$$

then $D_{ij} \leq D_{i^*j}$ for $i^* \leq i$. For the case of two groups, the condition is $a_{11} \geq 1 - a_{22}$ (see figure 3-1).

Matrices with this property are called monotone matrices.[40]

In the case of two income groups the equilibrium fraction of the population in the lower income group 1 is given by the solution to the equation

$$a_{11} \lambda^* + (1 - a_{22}) (1 - \lambda^*) = \lambda^*.$$

This defines the relationship that must exist between a_{11} and a_{22} for matrices to generate the same distribution of income. Intuitively, I suggested that $A >_E B$ if A and B have the same equilibrium income distribution, and $a_{11} < b_{11}$. (Fewer of the low-income people get stuck in the low equilibrium.) This in turn implies that a_{22} is also smaller. Figure 3-A1 shows the set of parameters for which the matrices can be ranked, along the straight line satisfying

$$a_{11} = [a_{22} (1 - \lambda^*)/\lambda^*] + 1 - [(1 - \lambda^*)/\lambda^*].$$

40. Keilson and Kester (1977).

Figure 3-A1. *Ranking Transition Matrices*

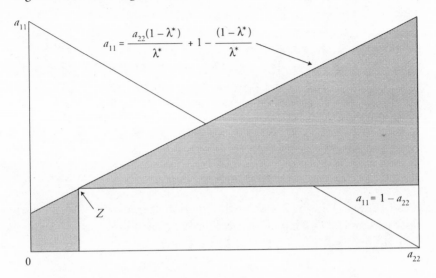

$$a_{11} = \frac{a_{22}(1 - \lambda^*)}{\lambda^*} + 1 - \frac{(1 - \lambda^*)}{\lambda^*}$$

$$a_{11} = 1 - a_{22}$$

Smaller values of a_{11} represent more equality.

Matrices below the line generate lower values of λ^* and thus higher levels of expected income. If there is an equality-preferring social welfare function with positive marginal social utility of income, then decreasing λ^* both increases mean income and decreases the number of poor and would be preferred. Those below the upward-sloping line and to the left of any point Z on the line are strictly preferred to the point Z. Points below the line and to the right and above Z represent a trade-off: while the asymptotic distribution is preferred, there is less egalitarian social mobility.

Things become considerably more complicated when one moves to three-income groups. Then, matrices that generate the same final distribution of income satisfy the equations

$$a_{11}\lambda_1 + a_{21}\lambda_2 + a_{31}(1 - \lambda_1 - \lambda_2) = \lambda_1$$

and

$$a_{12}\lambda_1 + a_{22}\lambda_2 + a_{32}(1 - \lambda_1 - \lambda_2) = \lambda_2.$$

Thus there are six independent parameters constrained by two linear equations, leaving four degrees of freedom. Under the previously defined criteria, $A >_E B$ if, among matrices with the same λ and λ_2, there is a smaller probability of being stuck in either a low-income state or a high-income state:

$$a_{11} < b_{11},$$
$$a_{11} + a_{12} < b_{11} + b_{12},$$
$$a_{33} = 1 - a_{31} - a_{32} < b_{33} = 1 - b_{31} - b_{32}, \text{ and}$$
$$a_{33} + a_{32} = 1 - a_{32} < 1 - b_{32},$$

which implies that

$$a_{32} > b_{32}$$

and

$$a_{32} + a_{31} > b_{31} + b_{32}.$$

Clearly, although in the 2×2 case the criterion of *egalitarian mobility* provided a complete ranking of matrices that generated the same asymptotic distribution of income, in the 3×3 case it does not.

Appendix B: The Impossibility of Deriving Equality of Opportunity from Outcome-Oriented Social Welfare Functions

In this appendix I show that equality of opportunity (in the sense defined in the text) *cannot* be derived from utilitarian principles. That is, the *indirect* social welfare function

$$W = \Sigma V(w, I)$$

may be either convex or concave in w, where w is now taken as exogenous and I is lump-sum income. With $I = 0$, w determines the individual's opportunity set. To see that V may be convex in w, I differentiate twice, using Roy's identity:

$$V_w = LV_I,$$

where L is labor supplied.

$$
\begin{aligned}
V_{ww} &= L_w V_I + LV_{Iw} \\
&= L_w V_I + L(V_I L_I + LV_{II}) \\
&= V_I(L_w + LL_I) + L^2 V_{II} \\
&= V_I[(L_w)_U + 2LL_I + L^2 V_{II}] \\
&> \text{or} < 0 \text{ as} \\
&\quad (L_w)_U > \text{or} < -(2LL_I + L^2 V_{II})
\end{aligned}
$$

where I have used the fact that

$$V_{Iw} = V_{wI} = L_I V_I + L V_{II}$$

and

$$L_w = (L_w)_U + L L_I.$$

It is thus clear that the social welfare function may be concave or convex in w. *If we care only about outcomes, and not processes, then we cannot derive the principle of equality of opportunity from generally accepted social welfare functions.*

Appendix C: Utilitarian Perspectives on Inheritance Subsidies

Assume that each individual includes in his utility the discounted utility of his descendant:

$$U_t = u(c_t) + d U_{t+1}[B_t] = \sum u(c_T)\delta^{T-t}.$$

He chooses c_t to maximize U_t, where, for instance,

$$c_t + B_t = Y_t + B_{t-1}$$

and where, for simplicity, we take Y_t as given. By contrast, social welfare is

$$W = \sum U_t = \sum u(c_t) + \sum [(1 - \delta^{n+1})/1 - \delta]u(c_t).$$

It is clear that the social welfare function puts greater weight on future generations' consumption than does the individual in his own decision. For instance, in a two-generation model (in which only the first generation has the option of leaving a bequest), the private solution maximizes

$$u(c_1) + \delta u(c_2),$$

where $c_2 = Y_2 + B = Y_2 + Y_1 - c_1$, while social welfare maximization entails maximizing

$$u(c_1) + (1 + \delta)u(c_2),$$

subject to the same constraint. *Inheritances should be subsidized.*

References

Aoki, Masahiko, Kevin Murdock, and Masahiro Okuno-Fujiwara. 1997. "Beyond the East Asian Miracle: Introducing the Market-Enhancing View," in M. Aoki, H. Kim, and M. Okuno-Fujiwara, eds., *The Role of Government in East Asian Development.* Oxford University Press.

Apps, Patricia. 1981. *A Theory of Inequality and Taxation.* Cambridge University Press.

Apps, Patricia, and Joseph Stiglitz. 1979. "Individualism, Inequality, and Taxation."

Arrow, Kenneth. 1973. "Higher Education as a Filter." *Journal of Public Economics* 2 (July): 193–216.

Atkinson, Anthony B. 1970. "On the Measurement of Inequality." *Journal of Economic Theory* 2 (3): 244–63.

———. 1971. "The Distribution of Wealth and the Individual Life-Cycle." *Oxford Economic Papers* 23 (2): 239–54.

Banerjee, Abhijit V., and Anthony F. Newman. 1993. "Occupational Choice and the Process of Development." *Journal of Political Economy* 101 (April): 274–98.

Bevan, David, and Joseph Stiglitz. 1979. "Intergenerational Transfers and Inequality." *Greek Economic Review* 1 (1): 8–26.

Conlisk, John. 1989. "Ranking Mobility Matrices." *Economics Letters* 29: 231–35.

Dasgupta, Partha, Amartya Sen, and David Starrett. 1973. "Notes on the Measurement of Inequality." *Journal of Economic Theory* 6 (2): 180–87.

Feldstein, Martin. 1998. "Savings Grace." *New Republic,* April 6: 19.

Harsanyi, John C. 1955. "Cardinal Welfare, Individualistic Ethics, and Interpersonal Comparisons of Utility." *Journal of Political Economy* 63 (June): 309–71.

Hellman, Thomas, Kevin Murdock, and Joseph Stiglitz. 1998. "Financial Restraint and the Market Enhancing View."

Hoff, Karla. 1994. "The Second Theorem of the Second Best." *Journal of Public Economics* 54 (June): 223–42.

———. 1996. "Market Failures and the Distribution of Wealth: A Perspective from the Economics of Information." *Politics and Society* 24 (December): 411–32.

Kahneman, Daniel, and Amos Tversky. 1972. "Subjective Probability: A Judgment of Representativeness." *Cognitive Psychology* 3: 430–54.

———. 1973. "On the Psychology of Prediction." *Psychological Review* 80: 237–51.

Kanbur, Ravi. 1987. "The Standard of Living: Uncertainty, Inequality and Opportunity," in Geoffrey Hawthorn, ed., *The Standard of Living: The Tanner Lectures,* pp. 59–69. Cambridge University Press.

Kanbur, Ravi, and Joseph Stiglitz. 1982. "Mobility and Inequality: A Utilitarian Analysis." Economic Theory Discussion Paper 57, University of Cambridge.

———. 1986. "Intergenerational Mobility and Dynastic Inequality." Princeton University Economic Research Program Research Memorandum 324.

Keilson, J., and A. Kester. 1977. "Monotone Matrices and Monotone Markov Chains." *Stochastic Processes and Their Applications* 5: 231–41.

Klasen, Stephan. 1996. "Nutrition, Health, and Mortality in Sub-Saharan Africa: Is There a Gender Bias?" *Journal of Development Studies* 32 (6): 913–32, 944–48.

Piketty, Thomas. 1995. "Social Mobility and Redistributive Politics." *Quarterly Journal of Economics* 110 (August): 551–84.

Roemer, John. 1998. *Equality of Opportunity*. Harvard University Press.

Rothschild, Michael, and Joseph Stiglitz. 1971. "Increasing Risk I: Its Economic Consequences." *Journal of Economic Theory* 3 (March): 66–84.

———. 1972. "Addendum to Increasing Risk I: A Definition." *Journal of Economic Theory* 5 (April): 306.

———. 1973. "Some Further Results on the Measurement of Inequality." *Journal of Economic Theory* 6 (April): 188–204.

Sawhill, Isabel. 1994. "Income Inequality and the Underclass," in Dimitri B. Papadimitriou, ed., *Aspects of Distribution of Wealth and Income*, pp. 194–98. Jerome Levy Economics Institute Series. St. Martin's Press.

Sen, Amartya. 1989. "Women's Survival as a Development Problem." *Bulletin of the American Academy of Arts and Sciences* 43.

Shorrocks, Anthony F. 1978. "The Measurement of Mobility." *Econometrica* 46 (September): 1013–24.

Stiglitz, Joseph E. 1973. "Education and Inequality." *Annals of the American Academy of Political and Social Sciences* 409 (September): 135–45.

———. 1976a. "Estate Taxes, Growth and Redistribution." In Ronald E. Grieson, ed., *Public and Urban Economics: Essays in Honor of W. Vickrey*, pp. 225–32. Lexington, Mass.: Lexington Publishing.

———. 1976b. "Notes on Estate Taxes, Redistribution and the Concept of Balanced Growth Path Incidence," pt. 2. *Journal of Political Economy* 86 (2): 137–50.

———. 1978. "Equity, Taxation and Inheritance." In W. Krelle and Andrew F. Shorrocks, eds., *Personal Income Distribution*. Proceedings of IEA Conference, Noordwijk aan Zee, Netherlands, April 1977, pp. 271–303. North-Holland.

———. 1982. "Utilitarianism and Horizontal Equity: The Case for Random Taxation." *Journal of Public Economics* 18 (June): 1–33.

———. 1987. "Pareto Efficient and Optimal Taxation and the New Welfare Economics." In A. Auerbach and M. Feldstein, eds., *Handbook on Public Economics*, pp. 991–1042. North Holland: Elsevier Science Publishers. (Also NBER Working Paper 2189.)

———. 1989. *The Economic Role of the State*. Basil Blackwell and Bank Insinger de Beaufort NV.

———. 1991. "The Economic Role of the State: Efficiency and Effectiveness." In T. P. Hardiman and Michael Mulreany, eds., *Efficiency and Effectiveness in the Public Domain*, pp. 37–59. Dublin: Institute of Public Administration.

———. 1992. "Rethinking the Economic Role of the State: Publicly Provided Private Goods." Lecture delivered at Universitat Pompeu Fabra, Barcelona (November 15).

———. 1993a. "Perspectives on the Role of Government Risk-Bearing within the Financial Sector." In Mark S. Sniderman, ed., *Government Risk-Bearing*, pp. 109–30. Norwell, Mass.: Kluwer Academic Publishers.

———. 1993b. "Remarks on Inequality, Agency Costs, and Economic Efficiency." Paper prepared for a workshop, "Economic Theories of Inequality," Stanford Institute for Theoretical Economics, Stanford University.

———. 1994. *Whither Socialism?* MIT Press.

———. 1998. "Redefining the Role of the State: What Should It Do? How Should It Do It? And How Should These Decisions Be Made?" Lecture given at MITI, Tokyo, Japan.

Svedborg, Peter. 1990. "Undernutrition in Sub-Saharan Africa: Is There a Gender Bias?" *Journal of Development Studies* 32 (4): 933–43.

PART II

Defining and Measuring Mobility

JERE R. BEHRMAN

4

Social Mobility: Concepts and Measurement

The effect of market reforms on poverty and inequality in Latin America and the Caribbean is a topic of considerable recent discussion. Agreement is growing that these reforms have helped reverse increases in poverty caused by the economic crises in most countries in the region in the 1980s. But the poor fared worse in the counties that delayed reform the longest. Agreement is less uniform regarding the effects of reform on income distribution. Some recent studies suggest that reforms have halted and perhaps reversed trends toward increasing inequality, while others are less optimistic.[1] In any case Latin America and the Caribbean continue to have relatively great income inequalities in comparison with other regions (tables 4-1 and 4-2), and it is unlikely that there will be radical changes in these inequalities in the near future. Some commentators suggest that such inequalities may make the sustainability of reforms in the region very difficult, particularly in light of heightened pub-

Jere Behrman wrote this chapter as a consultant to the Inter-American Development Bank. Useful comments were received from participants in the Brookings Institution Center on Social and Economic Dynamics/Inter-American Development Bank Workshop on Social Mobility at the Brookings Institution in 1998. The author is solely responsible for the content of this chapter.

1. Recent studies include Berry (1997); Londoño and Székely (1997); Lustig and Székely (1997); Morley (1994); and Psacharopoulos and others (1992). Appendix table 4-A1 summarizes world data on the relation between income growth on one hand and inequality and income of the poor on the other.

Table 4-1. *Decade Averages of Inequality Indices, by Region, 1960s–1990s*[a]

Region	Overall averages	Gini coefficients			
		1960s	*1970s*	*1980s*	*1990s*
Latin America and Caribbean	49.78	53.24	49.06	49.75	49.31
Sub-Saharan Africa	46.05	49.90	48.19	43.46	46.95
Middle East and North Africa	40.49	41.39	41.93	40.45	38.03
East Asia and the Pacific	38.75	37.43	39.88	38.70	38.09
South Asia	35.08	36.23	33.95	35.01	31.88
Industrial countries and high-income developing countries	34.31	35.03	34.76	33.23	33.75
Eastern Europe	26.57	25.09	24.63	25.01	28.94

Source: Deininger and Squire's (1996, table 3) calculations based on various sources as described in their text. Appendix table 4-A2 gives summaries over the entire time period for individual countries in the Latin American and Caribbean region. Table 4-A3 gives the number of observations for each decade on which this table is based.

a. Figures reported are unweighted averages of Gini coefficients of economies in each region. The sample includes 108 economies. Changes within regions may be caused by the fact that not all economies have observations for all decades.

lic expectations of benefits from postreform growth within the more democratic political contexts of most countries in the region.[2]

But income inequality measurements in cross-sectional data are snapshots of a moment in time. In practice, income distributions change under the effect of various transition mechanisms. These may affect social welfare by changing the shape of the spot income distributions captured in the usual snapshots. Two societies with the same snapshots of income distribution may have different levels of social welfare because they have different degrees of social mobility. For example, Milton Friedman asserted decades ago that a given extent of income inequality in a rigid system in which each family stays in the same position in each period may be more a cause for concern than the same degree of income inequality due to great mobility and dynamic change associated with equality of opportunity.[3] Similarly, others have argued that to assess the impact of market reforms in the region and the probable sustainability of these reforms, including political support for them, it is essential to characterize the extent of social mobility both across generations and within generations and whether the mobility has been affected by the recent reforms.[4]

2. Berry (1997); and Schemo (1998).
3. Friedman (1962).
4. Birdsall and Graham (1998).

Table 4-2. *Income Shares of Various Quintiles, by Decade and Region,*
1960s–1990s
Percent

Quintile and region	Overall average	1960s	1970s	1980s	1990s
Lowest quintile					
Latin America and Caribbean	3.86	3.42	3.69	3.67	4.52
Sub-Saharan Africa	5.26	2.76	5.10	5.70	5.15
East Asia and the Pacific	6.34	6.44	6.00	6.27	6.84
South Asia	7.74	7.39	7.84	7.91	8.76
Eastern Europe	9.34	9.67	9.76	9.81	8.83
Middle East and North Africa	6.66	5.70	n.a.	6.64	6.90
Industrial countries and high-income developing countries	6.42	6.42	6.31	6.68	6.26
Middle class (third and fourth quintiles)					
Latin America and Caribbean	33.21	28.13	34.59	33.58	33.84
Sub-Saharan Africa	34.06	32.72	32.15	35.40	33.54
East Asia and the Pacific	37.02	36.29	36.88	37.18	37.53
South Asia	37.25	37.05	37.89	37.17	38.42
Eastern Europe	40.65	39.69	41.59	41.25	40.01
Middle East and North Africa	36.28	35.30	n.a.	35.88	36.84
Industrial countries and high-income developing countries	40.99	39.89	40.61	41.21	41.80
Top quintile					
Latin America and Caribbean	55.12	61.62	54.18	54.86	52.94
Sub-Saharan Africa	51.79	61.97	55.82	48.86	52.37
East Asia and the Pacific	45.73	45.90	46.50	45.51	44.33
South Asia	43.01	44.05	42.19	42.57	39.91
Eastern Europe	36.11	36.30	34.51	34.64	37.80
Middle East and North Africa	46.32	49.00	n.a.	46.72	45.35
Industrial countries and high-income developing countries	40.42	41.22	41.11	39.89	39.79

Source: Deininger and Squire's (1996, table 4) calculations based on various sources as described in
their text.
n.a. Not available.

To date, however, little attention has been paid to measuring actual or
perceived social mobility and changes in it in the region.[5] This chapter
attempts to contribute to the studies on social mobility in Latin America
and the Caribbean by summarizing some conceptual problems regarding

5. There have been a few very recent empirical studies of selected aspects of the relations between
macroeconomic conditions and social mobility in the region (see chapter 6).

measuring social mobility and then briefly discussing implications for exploring social mobility there.

What Is Meant by Social Mobility?

Social mobility is used by social scientists to refer to movements by specific entities between periods in socioeconomic status indicators. Four of the terms used in this general statement, however, merit elaboration because they are used differently by different authors, which at times leads to confusion.

First, *movements* is used to mean both *total* and *relative* movements (with the latter often referred to as *exchange*). There is *total mobility*, for example, if in a three-person society between two periods, everyone's income doubles from (1, 2, 3) to (2, 4, 6).[6] But there may (depending on the exact definition used) be no relative mobility. Mobility (at least the nonrelative component) in this example is just total income change, and it is not clear what insight is gained by calling such total income change mobility. Also, although total social mobility has a clear meaning for quantitative indicators such as income, the meaning beyond the relative aspect is not clear for inherently relative indicators such as relative social status within a society. Nevertheless a lot of studies (for example, those on intergenerational occupational mobility) focus on total social mobility, albeit usually with awareness of the relative dimension.

There is *relative (exchange) mobility* if in the same three-person society there is a transfer between two periods from the third to the first person so that the incomes change from (1, 2, 3) to (3, 2, 1). Here there is mobility even though total income and income distribution both are the same across the two periods. Thus relative mobility has meaning distinct from income growth and income distribution. The distinction between relative mobility and income distribution hinges on persons being anonymous for the latter but not the former. Therefore the change implies relative social mobility because there has been a marginal change between persons one and three but no change in income distribution because persons one and three have simply exchanged positions in the income distribution.

---

6. For specificity, here and later I use income as an example of the relevant socioeconomic indicator for which social mobility is a matter of concern (except in cases in which some other specific indicator better illustrates a point).

As is illustrated in the examples in the preceding paragraphs, there may be change in total income without relative mobility and with no change in income distribution and there may be relative mobility with no total income change and with no change in income distribution. There also may be changes in income distribution with no change in total income—from (1, 2, 3) to (2, 2, 2), but this inherently involves relative mobility.

Thus total mobility can be decomposed conceptually between the total income change and the change in relative mobility. The change in relative mobility further can be decomposed into mobility without a change in income distribution and mobility with a change. Consider the following three transitions:

(1) (1, 2, 3) to (2, 4, 6),
(2) (2, 4, 6) to (6, 4, 2), and
(3) (6, 4, 2) to (4, 4, 4).

The overall movement from (1, 2, 3) to (4, 4, 4) can be decomposed into the total income change (transition 1), a change in relative mobility without a change in either total income or the income distribution (transition 2), and a change in relative mobility without a change in total income but with a change in income distribution (transition 3).

A second term, *periods*, may be short relative to individuals' lives or adulthoods (months, years, quinquenniums) or intergenerational (parents' versus children's education, adult earnings, incomes, or occupations). The duration that periods have in efforts to characterize social mobility obviously depends on what aspect of social mobility is of interest. For questions relating, for instance, to fluctuations in a person's position in the distribution of earnings or income over the person's life cycle, annual data may be very informative. But for questions relating to intergenerational mobility some means of characterizing socioeconomic status over the adulthoods of the relevant generations may be necessary.

Third, *socioeconomic status indicators* that are most commonly used in empirical studies of social mobility include income, earnings, occupation, education, nature of marital matches, political participation, social participation, and social status measures. Some of these indicators (income, earnings, years of schooling, number of representatives in parliament) inherently are continuous variables and others are categorical (occupation, school attended). At times the categorical variables are represented as continuous by, for example, representing occupation by mean or median earnings and education of those in a particular occupation.

Some of the continuous empirical measures used are cardinal (income, earnings, years of schooling, number of representatives in parliament) and others are ordinal (relative social status, relative income or earnings). Whether the indicators used in a particular case are continuous or categorical and, if continuous, are cardinal or ordinal has implications for the type of mobility that can measured (relative only versus total) and the type of empirical analysis that is undertaken.

Fourth, the *specific entities* of interest generally are individuals or families, but in some cases are groups of individuals or families identified by such demographic or cultural characteristics as gender, birth cohort, race, ethnicity, language, religion, and location or such previous behavioral decisions as education, marital status, migration status, number of children, and labor force participation. Which entity is of interest often ties in closely with the relevant time period. For individuals, for example, the concern generally is with intragenerational mobility and the time periods most common are one year or a few years. For families the concern generally is intergenerational, so the time period of interest, though not always the empirical representation, is longer (completed education, lifetime income or earnings, primary occupation).

Why Care about Social Mobility?

Although it seems clear why society might care about the total income available and about the distribution of that income among its members under the plausible assumption that more income increases welfare, it may not be so clear why society should care in addition about relative social mobility. Holding total income and income distribution constant, after all, relative social mobility is greater if wealthier people more frequently change places with poorer people than if such exchanges occur less frequently. But the number of poorer people is the same whether there are more or fewer of such exchanges; they just are different people in different periods.

The possible bases for arguing that, in addition to total income and income distribution, relative social mobility is important include the following (some of which also relate to overall social mobility).

First, if there are means of transferring resources across periods, longer-run income rather than one-period income is likely to be of interest because that is the true intertemporal constraint on consumption. Longer-run income is likely to be distributed more equally than one-period income, and probably with fewer people below some poverty cutoff than in one-period income if there is greater relative social mobility.[7] This point holds whether periods refer to years within the life cycle of an individual or to different generations.

Within a generation, for example, there may be different life-cycle earnings paths because some people are initially investing relatively heavily in human capital, such as education, and thus have steeper long-term earnings paths than others. Heavy investors in the early stages of their lives may appear to be relatively poorer than they are on the average over their full lives. Within a cross-sectional sample, moreover, some may be in their peak earnings year and others may be before or after their peak earnings. There may also be stochastic income shocks that persist for relatively short parts of the life cycle. All three possibilities point to one-year characterizations of the income distribution as overstating longer-run inequality and possibly poverty as compared with longer-run income measures.[8]

If there are intergenerational transfers of physical or financial assets (bequests, gifts) or human resource investments (parental investments in child health, nutrition, and schooling), there may be similar effects across generations. If, for example, there are independent shocks such as luck in the stock market across generations in the same family line, from the point of view of considering family dynasties even lifetime income measures may overstate inequalities among family dynasties and intergenerational poverty.

Note that this first point is not an argument that social mobility per se is desirable but that the extent of social mobility provides information about income distribution over a longer period than can be observed in the data.

A second argument for the importance of relative mobility is that if there are stochastic elements in innate abilities or preferences that affect

7. Whether poverty is understated or overstated by short-term measures rather than longer-term measures because of transitory shocks depends on whether the long-term measure is above or below the poverty line. If an individual is above (below) the poverty line in terms of long-run income, negative (positive) transitory shocks of sufficient magnitude mean that a short-term measure may indicate that the individual for the short term is below (above) the poverty line for some periods though above (below) the line in most periods. If, as in most societies, most people are above the poverty line according to longer-run measures, poverty rates are likely to be estimated to be lower for longer-run than for shorter-run indicators.

8. Perhaps ironically, for these same reasons annual income measures are likely to result in overestimates of intergenerational mobility in comparison with longer-run income measures. For the United States, for example, recent studies find that parent-child income correlations are about twice as high (about 0.4 rather than 0.2) if there is control for transitory fluctuations in annual income (Behrman and Taubman, 1990; Solon, 1992; and Zimmerman, 1992) than if there is no such control.

marginal prices ("weights," "values") that determine relative social standing, social mobility by many indicators is likely to be greater, all other
things being equal. This does not mean that social mobility is good or bad
in itself, but only that measured mobility will be greater if there are larger
stochastic elements in abilities and preferences and if these stochastic elements have larger effects on the marginal prices of characteristics that affect social standing. Although these factors might cause measured social
mobility to be greater, there is not something obviously good or bad about
social mobility being greater for such reasons. If the stochastic abilities or
preferences are basically innate or fixed characteristics of individuals, this
consideration is likely to be more important for considering intergenerational
mobility than for considering intragenerational mobility.

Third, if there are greater changes in the values to society of different
abilities or preferences because of technological change, new discoveries,
disasters, or resource depletion, social mobility by many indicators is likely
to be greater. Again, this does not mean that social mobility is good or bad
in itself, but only that measured mobility will be greater if such changes are
greater and if prices of abilities and preferences are more responsive to
them. Perceptions seem to be widespread that there are likely to be large
costs for economic adjustments if social institutions are so rigid that prices
of abilities and preferences do not change even in the presence of large
changes. Thus, for this reason, some social mobility is likely to reflect better adjustment capacity than no social mobility. But more developed economies may be able to cope better than less developed economies in facing
the same shocks. To illustrate, weather shocks are likely to be less deleteri-
ous for agriculture if there are more sophisticated water control systems,
technologies that are less dependent on local microeconomic conditions,
and better transportation and communication systems, all of which tend
to be truer in more developed economies. If more developed economies
can cope better with shocks for such reasons, more development, other
things being equal, may be associated with less social mobility.

Fourth, social mobility is important because the greater average social
distance among members of more rigid rather than more flexible societies
is likely to have negative externalities regarding economic and other transactions.[9] If so, greater social mobility is likely to imply greater efficiency
and productivity through more efficient transactions. This possibility seems
to relate primarily to relative social mobility. If a society is very rigid and

9. See, for example, Akerlof (1997).

everyone's incomes double with no change in relative social mobility, for example, the social distances would seem not to be changed.

Fifth, people may perceive that society is fairer if there is greater relative social mobility either because of transitory shocks or because of changing rewards for different skills. If so, greater relative social mobility may be related to greater social and political cohesion, or at least greater political support for the system from those in the lower part of the distribution. For those in the upper part there are incentives for political support because they have done well, but also incentives to change the system so that there is less relative social mobility and they can preserve their relatively good situation.

Sixth, greater relative social mobility may, for instance, hinder getting information on the credit risks of a potential borrower or the work intensity of a potential worker in a task in which monitoring is difficult. If so, greater relative social mobility may imply less effective functioning of markets because transaction partners are more anonymous and there is more uncertainty regarding their difficult-to-observe characteristics. In such a situation the incentives increase for statistical discrimination on the bases of such easily observed characteristics as gender, race, caste, ethnicity, region of origin, language, and age and for signaling productive capabilities through schooling, training, exam performance, accreditation, licensing, and other forms of credentialing.

Seventh, there may be costs of adjusting to changes because of habit, in which case greater relative or overall social mobility may reflect greater costs. This would seem to be a more serious problem for shorter-run mobility—intragenerational rather than intergenerational.

Eighth, in the transition from a very rigid society to a more flexible one, there may be an imbalance between changes in social mobility and changes in expectations, which may lead to frustrated expectations. These may have direct welfare costs and reduce social and political cohesiveness. Again, this would seem to be a greater problem for intragenerational than for intergenerational mobility.

Thus underlying greater social mobility may be a number of benefits and costs possible for both relative and total mobility. And some of the possibilities have direct effects on welfare themselves while others, especially the first one in this discussion—where longer-run income rather than one-period income is likely to be of interest—reflect more measurement problems with regard to income and income distribution based on available, usually short-run, data than that relative social mobility per se is directly good or bad.

How Is Social Mobility Statistically Modeled and Measured?

How social mobility has been modeled and measured has, not surprisingly, varied depending on aspects of it that I have discussed earlier as well as the available data.[10] I review some of the more prominent approaches to modeling social mobility statistically in this section.[11] Some of this material is fairly technical. I attempt to present brief summaries of the more technical material and refer interested readers to sources with more extensive discussions should they be interested in pursuing the topics. Nevertheless use of some of the technical terminology is almost unavoidable to keep the summaries to a reasonable length.

Before turning to these statistical models it is important to note that there is an enormous literature on behavioral models of intergenerational relations, human resource investments, and marriage that relates to social mobility. The studies of intergenerational relations and human resource investments, for example, address how family background affects the socioeconomic success of children through channels such as genetic endowment and investment in children's education. Studies of marriage address how marriage matches are made. These matches often reflect positive assortative mating on some attributes such as schooling. Assortative mating on schooling, in turn, may occur in part because of information obtained through schooling or activities correlated with schooling about the pool of alternatives. There also may be negative assortative mating on endowments rewarded in the labor market because of specialization within families on market versus home production. There is an extensive literature on the nature of these marriage choices and on how marriages may affect or reflect social mobility. It is beyond the scope of this chapter to summarize these large literatures. But it should be kept in mind that the studies of such behaviors underlie many of the concerns and interpretations of statistical measures of social mobility and their implications.[12]

---

10. This section builds in part on Atkinson, Bourguignon, and Morrisson (1992), to which the interested reader is referred for more extensive discussion of a number of the topics.

11. Some of the statistical models that I discuss, such as permanent income and earnings relations, also are consistent with models of optimizing behavior.

12. Some examples of these literatures on behaviors related to social mobility (with other references in these) are Becker (1975, 1991); Behrman (1997); Behrman and Knowles (1999); Behrman, Pollak, and Taubman (1982, 1995); Behrman, Rosenzweig, and Taubman (1994, 1996); Burdett and Coles (1997); Cole, Mailath, and Postlewaite (1992, 1995); Mulligan (1997); and Neumark and Postlewaite (1996).

Permanent Income Model

In addition to short-run total income and income distribution, the first reason as to why social mobility may be of interest relates to the so-called permanent income model of Milton Friedman and Simon Kuznets because of the role of transitory fluctuations or shocks.[13] In its simplest form, current income for individual (household, family) i in period t (Y_{it}^c) has a permanent component (Y_i^p) that depends on i's basic characteristics such as education and other assets and a transitory component (u_{it}) that represents chance events that are independent of the permanent component:

$$(1) \qquad\qquad Y_{it}^c = Y_i^p + u_{it}.$$

One measure of mobility here is the proportion of the variance in Y_{it}^c (σ_{Yc}^2) that is accounted for by the variance in u_{it} (σ_u^2) as opposed to the variance in Y_i^p (σ_{Yp}^2). If the stochastic term u_{it} is distributed independently and identically across periods and individuals, this mobility measure equals σ_u^2/σ_{Yc}^2 or $\sigma_u^2/(\sigma_{Yp}^2 + \sigma_u^2)$. Thus mobility increases and long-run inequality decreases the greater the size of the variance of the transitory term relative to the variance in income—or, almost equivalently, the less the correlation in current income across periods, which is $\sigma_{Yp}^2/(\sigma_{Yp}^2 + \sigma_u^2)$.[14] Although I have presented this discussion in terms of income, the basic point carries over to any continuous cardinal socioeconomic indicator of mobility. Also, while permanent income considerations usually are emphasized with regard to intragenerational mobility, parallel considerations may hold for intergenerational mobility.

Lifetime Earnings Profiles and Earnings Functions

The first reason discussed earlier as to why social mobility may be of interest in addition to short-run total income and income distribution also

---

13. Friedman and Kuznets (1954).

14. For example, Atkinson, Bourguignon, and Morrisson (1992, p. 6) show that if the income inequality measure used is the coefficient of variation (the standard deviation relative to the mean) and if mean income is constant across periods, long-run inequality is $[(1 + r)/2]^{\frac{1}{2}}$ times one-period inequality, where r is the income correlation across periods. For $r = 0.5$, this implies that the long-run coefficient of variation is 13 percent less than the one-period coefficient of variation.

Figure 4-1. *Life-Cycle Earnings Paths*

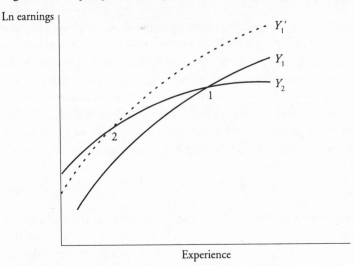

relates to lifetime earnings profiles (which may carry over to lifetime income profiles) that have been emphasized by various authors.[15]

First, if life-cycle earnings profiles are upward sloping as are those illustrated in figure 4-1, a snapshot at any time for an individual worker is likely to misrepresent his or her lifetime earnings, that is, understate them if the snapshot is in the initial years of work experience and overstate them if it is during peak earnings years. Therefore the inequality indicated by a snapshot is likely to be greater than the inequality in lifetime earnings simply because different workers have different work experience. In addition, comparisons of measured total earnings mobility resulting from differences in total earnings for all workers depend on the composition of work experience for the comparison groups. A comparison among cross-sectional earnings for Thailand in 1960, 1980, and 2000, for example, all else equal, would underestimate the extent of total lifetime earnings mobility between 1960 and 1980 and overestimate it between 1980 and 2000: a much larger share of the work force in 1980 comprised young workers with little work experience than it did in 1960 or 2000 because of the fertility boom in the 1970s.

15. See, for example, Mincer (1974).

Further, because of differences in on-the-job training or learning, lifetime earnings profiles may take different shapes for different individual-job matches. In some jobs new workers take relatively long to acquire the skills and to establish their reputation regarding productivity (the latter in jobs in which monitoring of work effort is very costly). In such jobs the initial compensation is relatively low, but earnings rise relatively rapidly with experience, as for curve Y_1 in figure 4-1, in comparison with the earnings profiles in other jobs for initially identical workers (Y_2). For initially identical workers to take both types of jobs (abstracting from other factors such as uncertainty), the present discounted values of wages for these workers from the two types of jobs must be equal, so the earnings profiles must cross. Point 1 in figure 4-1 is the crossover or overtaking experience.

This simple figure illustrates why, if there are different lifetime earnings profiles, the use of annual earnings or income data without controlling for earnings and income mobility is likely to result in overestimates of lifetime income inequality even among people with the same work experience who were identical at the start of their work lives. By assumption, the two life-cycle earnings profiles represented by the solid lines Y_1 and Y_2 imply the same lifetime earnings. But if one looks at a snapshot at any level of work experience other than at the overtaking point, there appears to be inequality.

If workers initially are not identical, such snapshots at certain stages of the work experience may not even reveal the correct ordering of individuals in the lifetime earnings and income distribution. For example, in figure 4-1 the dashed curve Y_1' has been added for a worker in the first job with greater ability than the workers represented by Y_1 and Y_2 (for simplicity it is assumed that the worker with greater ability would not earn more than the worker represented by Y_2 in job 2). Because of this worker's greater ability, it is assumed that in job 1 earnings are higher at every level of experience than are those for the worker type portrayed by Y_1, so the present discounted value of earnings for Y_1' is greater than for Y_1 or for Y_2. Nevertheless, if a snapshot of the earnings distribution is taken for experience less than point 2 (the crossover point for the worker with more ability), it will indicate that in the short-run earnings distribution the worker with less ability and less lifetime earnings has greater annual earnings.

The usual approach for estimating the impact of on-the-job training and other human capital investments on earnings is to estimate earnings functions that can be interpreted to be derived from wage production functions in which the inputs include human capital investments such as schooling and training, innate characteristics such as abilities and motivation, and labor market conditions. A standard simplified form of such functions that has been widely used in empirical research is the semilog form:

$$(2) \qquad Y_{it} = a_{i0} + a_{i1}S_{it} + a_{i3}E_{it} + a_{i4}E_{it}^{2} + v_{it},$$

where Y_{it} is ln earnings of individual i in time period t, S_{it} is years of schooling of individual i before time t, E_{it} is work experience of individual i before time t (sometimes represented by potential experience defined as age at time t minus years of schooling minus age at starting school), and v_{it} is a stochastic earnings shock that is assumed to be distributed independently across individuals and over time.[16] Experience is included in quadratic or sometimes higher-order polynomial form to allow for the diminishing marginal impact of experience on earnings that underlies the concave shape of the earnings profiles in figure 4-1. Conditional on the assumptions necessary to yield this relation, good estimates of it permit the distinction between the distributions of short-run (annual) and lifetime earnings so that the importance of earnings mobility over the life cycle is illuminated. Such estimates can also identify the contribution of transitory shocks to earnings mobility, parallel to the role of transitory shocks in relation 1.

Good estimates of relation 2 are difficult to obtain under plausible assumptions regarding factors that are unobserved by analysts and uncontrolled in most estimates. As written, to be more explicit, the parameters in relation 2 are specific to an individual because of differences in abilities, motivations, school quality, labor market conditions due to cohort effects, and so forth across individuals. The individual-specific parameters under certain assumptions control for the unobserved factors and permit consistent estimation of the parameters of the observed variables, including those pertaining to lifetime earnings profiles for different jobs. For example, if individual ability and motivation enter into relation 2 additively and also affect past investments in schooling and job experience, the estimated effects of schooling and experience will be biased (probably upward) unless there is control for ability and motivation; the individual-specific constant provides such control.

But most studies assume that all the parameters are the same across sample people. This assumption means, first of all, under plausible assump-

---

16. The use of "potential experience" so defined to represent work experience is common in empirical studies because of the lack of data on actual work experience in many surveys.

tions about human capital determinants and labor market conditions (supported in most of the few studies that attempt to explore them), the estimated schooling and experience effects probably are biased.[17] The assumption also means that most estimates do not provide any information about the possible importance of the job crossover effects due to the differential on-the-job training illustrated in figure 4-1, although some studies that do address this possibility report estimates that are consistent with it.[18] Finally, it points to the importance of being very clear about what untested assumptions empirical estimates are conditional upon so that people can use appropriate caution.[19]

There are three other possibly important aspects of mobility that are not addressed in most empirical earnings studies that focus on relation 2 but that may be important regarding what can be learned in empirical studies of earnings mobility.

First, there is the question of matching people with jobs. Employers may have imperfect information about the qualities of potential employees and workers may have imperfect information about the qualities of potential employers, so that on both sides information problems can be lessened only with work experience. If so, there may be a process of sorting in which better worker-job matches are made as workers acquire more experience, job mobility is likely to decrease with experience, and greater job mobility may be important for making better worker-job matches.

Second, there may be information problems in monitoring employee efforts that may result in end-loaded compensation to increase the cost of an employee's job loss and elicit more effort. This implies that earnings profiles are likely to be steeper for more stable employment and in jobs for which monitoring problems are greater.

Third, demand-side factors are likely to affect earnings mobility. Greater general aggregate demand will probably increase mobility in terms of total

17. Much of the scholarly emphasis has been on biases in estimates of the rate of return to schooling resulting from the usual failure to control for ability. Recent samples of identical twins (which permit control for all unobserved genetic endowments) with control for measurement errors (the downward bias of which is exacerbated in between-sibling estimates), for example, find upward biases of 10 to 100 percent in estimated schooling effects if there is no control for genetic endowments (Behrman and Rosenzweig, 1999). Similar biases may exist for estimates of experience effects.

18. See, for example, Mincer (1974); and Hause (1977, 1980).

19. For example, most earnings function estimates assume implicitly that unobserved ability, motivation, school quality, and cohort effects do not affect earnings or, if they do affect earnings, they do not affect prior investments in years of schooling and work experience. Because such assumptions are not explicit, readers may not be sensitive to their possible importance in interpreting the estimates.

earnings, though lessened aggregate demand may increase measured mobility through job losses and acceptance of lower-paying positions. Shifts in labor demand related to changes in production sectors may change the composition of jobs with respect to the extent of information problems and on-the-job learning, with implications for the extent of earnings mobility.

Thus the nature of earnings profiles and related concerns may be important aspects of social mobility. I discuss in this section earnings profiles, but the effects carry over to other socioeconomic indicators that depend on earnings, such as income and socioeconomic status. These considerations generally are conceptualized and presented with an intragenerational focus. But, as noted earlier, they may have important implications for measuring intergenerational mobility and, for that matter, for comparing aspects of income distribution and mobility across societies.

Markov Statistical Models of Social Mobility for Continuous Socioeconomic Indicators

A common statistical characterization of mobility dating back at least to Francis Galton's 1889 model of regression toward the mean is the first-order Markov model in which the relevant socioeconomic indicator for entity i in period $t(Y_{it})$ depends on the value of that indicator in the previous period (Y_{it-1}) and a stochastic term (w_{it}) that is independent of the previous period indicator and that is independently distributed across individuals and across periods:[20]

$$(3) \qquad\qquad Y_{it} = bY_{it-1} + w_{it}.$$

Thus the previous period indicator carries all relevant past information about individual i, including the past experience regarding transitory shocks (which means that the variance of Y increases with t). The parameter b is positive and is greater than one if there is real growth in Y (if Y is income and there is growth in income). If Y_{it} is defined relative to the mean of its distribution, then the parameter b affects the relative position in the distribution and $b < 1$ implies regression toward the mean (that is more rapid the smaller is b). The parameter b is a measure of immobility. Another

---

20. With data on three (or more) periods the first-order Markov assumption can be tested by its implication that the correlation in Y between periods t and $t + 2$ equals the product of the correlations between t and $t + 1$ and between $t + 1$ and $t + 2$.

frequently used measure of mobility is r, the interperiod correlation in Y. As t goes to the limit, b and r coincide, but along the path b consistently exceeds r.[21]

Estimates of relation 3 or of extensions of this relation (for example, with population groups having different mobilities) may be used to characterize both intragenerational and intergenerational social mobility with continuous socioeconomic indicators such as income and earnings measured, as noted, in either absolute or relative terms.

Markov Transition Matrix–Based Measures of Social Mobility

For some relevant socioeconomic indicators, such as occupation, class, and production sector of employment, data generally are available only in categorical form. For others, even though data are available in continuous form, for some questions categorizing the variables may be of interest (for example, whether income is below the poverty level). A convenient and standard way to characterize social mobility with categorical variables is to use transition probability matrices for movements among segments of the distribution, the relevant categories, terciles, and deciles, between periods. These generally are used in first-order Markov processes with the assumption, as in relation 3, that the previous period indicator carries all relevant past information about an individual. In certain respects transition matrices allow greater flexibility in characterizing mobility than do the approaches based on continuous variables that are discussed in the previous sections (at least as they usually are used) because they allow asymmetries and other nonlinearities. For example, transition matrices easily may capture a situation in which the probabilities of moving in a large jump from the bottom of the income distribution to the top may be larger than the probability of moving from the top to the bottom, with the difference balanced out by differences in the probabilities of moving to the middle.

A transition probability matrix ($\mathbf{P}$) is an $\mathbf{n} \times \mathbf{n}$ matrix, where $\mathbf{n}$ refers to the number of categories. The element in the jth row and kth column of a transition probability matrix ($\mathbf{p}_{jk}$) gives the probability that an entity moves from the jth category to the kth category between periods. The sum across elements in each row must be one because every entity that initially is in the jth category must end up in one of the categories ($\mathbf{\Sigma}_k \mathbf{p}_{jk} = 1$ for each $\mathbf{j}$). In general the sum of elements in each column need not be 1. If the

---

21. Atkinson, Bourguignon, and Morrisson (1992, p. 9).

categories have equal numbers in them and there is what is referred to earlier as relative or exchange mobility so that distribution does not change between periods, the sum of the elements in each column is 1.[22] Following are examples of such matrices for population terciles (so there are three segments) for two special cases of interest: no social mobility (P_N) and "complete" or "perfect" social mobility (P_C):

$$
(4) \quad P_N = \begin{matrix} 1.00 & 0.00 & 0.00 \\ 0.00 & 1.00 & 0.00 \\ 0.00 & 0.00 & 1.00 \end{matrix} ; \quad P_C = \begin{matrix} 0.33 & 0.33 & 0.33 \\ 0.33 & 0.33 & 0.33 \\ 0.33 & 0.33 & 0.33 \end{matrix}
$$

For P_N, there is no relative social mobility, so there are no nonzero off-diagonal elements. If each period is a generation, for example, children end up in exactly the same part of the distribution as their parents: the completely rigid social system noted in the introduction to which Friedman refers. For P_C there is complete social mobility in the sense that the probabilities are equal of ending up in any of the three terciles after the transition, independent of the initial starting point.

One important emphasis in the literature is how to infer the extent of social mobility from transition probability matrices of the types discussed here. In essence the problem is how to reduce such a probability matrix to a scalar that characterizes the extent of social mobility or immobility. A number of possibilities have been proposed and are summarized by Valentino Dardanoni, to which the interested reader is referred for further discussion and references.[23]

—Trace [trace $(P) - 1)/(n - 1)$]. The intuition behind this measure is that the greater the concentration on the diagonal the less the mobility. The obvious limitation is that the trace only distinguishes between being on and off the diagonal, not whether off-diagonal elements are close or far from the diagonal.

—Determinant [$|P|^{1/(n - 1)}$]. The determinant incorporates information about off-diagonal elements as well as diagonal elements. But the determinant is zero (implying complete mobility) if any two rows or any two

---

22. As noted earlier, the term *exchange mobility* is frequently used by sociologists concerned with social mobility in contrast to *structural mobility* if the distribution is changed. If the sum of the elements in each of the rows and of the elements in each of the columns is one, the matrix is said to be *bistochastic*.

23. Dardanoni (1993).

columns are identical, no matter what the distribution of elements else-where in the matrix, which is a definite limitation as a mobility indicator.

—Mean first passage time. If two individuals are drawn from the popu-lation at random and there is a steady-state Markov chain of transitions, the mean first passage time is the expected number of periods that must pass before the first individual achieves the state of the second individual.[24]

—Bartholomew's measure $[\Sigma_j \Sigma_k \pi_{jk}|k-j|]$.[25] The expected number of category boundaries crossed from one period to the next when the chain is in steady state.

—Second largest eigenvalue. This index has been proposed to repre-sent the speed of escape from the initial conditions and of regression to the mean.

Unfortunately, as Dardanoni emphasizes, these mobility indicators do not consistently rank different transition matrices. He illustrates with the following three transition matrices:

$$(5) \quad P_1 = \begin{matrix} 0.60 & 0.35 & 0.05 \\ 0.35 & 0.40 & 0.25 \\ 0.05 & 0.25 & 0.70 \end{matrix} \; ; \quad P_2 = \begin{matrix} 0.60 & 0.30 & 0.10 \\ 0.30 & 0.50 & 0.20 \\ 0.10 & 0.20 & 0.70 \end{matrix} \; ; \quad P_3 = \begin{matrix} 0.60 & 0.40 & 0.00 \\ 0.30 & 0.40 & 0.30 \\ 0.10 & 0.20 & 0.70 \end{matrix} \; ;$$

He shows that any of these matrices may be considered to represent the greatest mobility, depending on which mobility index is used.

Trace	Determinant	Mean first passage time	Bartholomew's measure	Eigenvalue
P_1, P_3	P_1	P_3	P_1, P_2, P_3	P_2

Dardanoni therefore derives a partial social welfare function (SWF) order-ing with an additive SWF placing greater weights on people who start in lower positions in society. Conditional on this SWF, he derives a condition for the partial ordering of alternative transition matrices.[26] He also shows that most of the mobility indices I have described (with the exception of

24. Conlisk (1990).

25. Bartholomew (1982): π is the equilibrium probability vector, which exists and is the unique solution to $\pi' = \pi'P$ if P is regular (that is, for some large enough integer m, P^m is strictly positive).

26. He shows that welfare is greater for transition matrix P than for Q (if both are monotone regular transition matrices for SWF weights and instantaneous utilities that are nondecreasing in income) if $T'\Pi[P(\rho) - Q(\rho)]T \leq 0$ where T is an $n \times n$ summation matrix with zeros below the main diagonal and ones elsewhere and $0 \leq \rho < 1$ is the discount factor.

Bartholomew's measure and a modified eigenvalue measure) do not necessarily imply greater mobility for transition matrices that give individuals
starting with lower initial income better income lotteries.

Such considerations point to the fact that currently there is no one
correct way to measure relative mobility with transition matrices. Different
approaches may yield different rankings for the same matrices, and to make
much progress in such cases may require explicit assumptions about the
SWF. But even with such assumptions, complete orderings of transition
matrices may not be possible.

Axiomatic Approach to Measuring Income Mobility

Gary Fields and Efe Ok contribute an axiomatic approach to characterizing income mobility from longitudinal data.[27] Using seven axioms,
they derive a measure of total income mobility that is additively decomposable into mobility from the transfer of income among individuals with
total income held constant (relative or exchange social mobility) and a change
in the total income available.[28] In particular, they define the relative mobility due to income transfers (M_R) in a growing economy to be twice the
amount lost by losers (twice because every dollar lost by a loser is gained by
a winner):

$$(6a) \qquad\qquad M_R = 2 \ [3(y_{jt} - y_{it + 1})],$$

where j is summed over all losers. Relative mobility due to income transfers in a shrinking economy is defined to be twice the amount gained by
winners:

---

27. Fields and Ok (1996).

28. The axioms are (1) linear homogeneity (an equiproportional change in all income levels both in
the initial and the final distributions results in exactly the same percentage change in the mobility
measure), (2) translation invariance (if the same amount is added to everybody's income in the initial
and final distributions, the new situation has the same mobility as the initial one), (3) normalization
(a one-dollar income gain and a one-dollar income loss both produce one unit of mobility for that
individual), (4) strong decomposability (the level of total income mobility experienced by a population is a function of the levels of mobility experienced by two disjoint and exhaustive subpopula-
tions—the authors also consider weak decomposability), (5) population consistency (in the contexts
of populations of different sizes, if equals are added to equals the results are equal), (6) growth sensitivity (if unequals are added to equals the results are unequal), and (7) individualistic contribution (the
contribution of one individual=s income change to total mobility depends only on the amount of his
or her income change).

(6b) $M_R = 2 \, [3(y_{jt+1} - y_{it})]$,

where j is summed over all winners. Mobility due to income growth (M_Y) in a growing economy is defined to be

(6c) $M_Y = \Sigma y_{jt+1} - \Sigma y_{it}$,

where j is summed over all members of the population. Mobility due to income contraction in a shrinking economy is defined to be

(6d) $M_Y = \Sigma y_{jt} - \Sigma y_{jt+1}$,

where j is summed over all members of the population. Total mobility (M) is defined to be

(6f) $M = \Sigma |y_{jt+1} - y_{it}|$,

where j is summed over all members of the population. They show that with these definitions of mobility

(6g) $M = M_R + M_Y$.

This approach has several advantages over those proposed in previous studies. First, total mobility is decomposed into relative (exchange) mobility and income change mobility as in relation 6g, which is the first exact decomposition of income mobility in the literature. Second, this approach can be applied in per capita terms to allow for comparisons across periods (or surveys) with different numbers of people, which also permits comparisons with base income so that statements can be made such as "average mobility is 10 percent of initial income." Third, the approach does not depend on the Markovian assumptions that have been rejected by empirical studies of Britain, France, and the United States.[29] Fourth, it also does not depend on normative assumptions regarding social welfare functions as in Dardanoni's article.

29. Atkinson, Bourguignon, and Morrisson (1992); and Shorrocks (1976).

Possibilities for Measuring Social Mobility in Latin America and the Caribbean

Given the considerations in the previous discussion, to think about possible measurements of social mobility in a particular context such as Latin America and the Caribbean means that the nature of available data is critical. The obvious data requirement is some way of representing changes in the indicators of social mobility of interest—intragenerationally or intergenerationally or both—for individuals, families, or whatever entities are of interest. It is beyond the scope of this chapter to survey available data in the region that might be used to characterize the extent of social mobility. But it is useful to make a few general comments about possibilities.

Cross-Sectional Household Data

Most of the available household data sets are cross-sectional. With one cross-sectional data set the primary possibilities are two.

First, estimation of cross-sectional relations that pertain to some aspects of social mobility. Some examples follow.

—Permanent income relations of the form of relation 1 can be estimated with assets (human, physical, financial) on the right-hand side, which permits characterization of the importance of transitory fluctuations in intragenerational mobility. Similar relations can be estimated for any other continuous mobility indicator for which data are available both for current values and for the determinants of the longer-run values such as earnings, "full" income, and "full" earnings in which leisure is valued at market wage rates.

—Lifetime earnings (income) relations of the form of relation 2 can be estimated both to identify the transitory component and to estimate the importance of lifetime earnings paths due to learning and experience that permit characterizing intragenerational earnings mobility. Estimation of such earnings functions also can be informative regarding the importance of different earnings paths for different jobs and the importance of specific job tenure.

—Household human resource (schooling, training, health, nutrition) demand relations can be estimated to characterize the relation between the investments and observed dimensions of family background such as parental income, schooling, health, and occupation. These relations can also be estimated to characterize observed time series of policy variables or macroeconomic conditions that are conjectured to be particularly pertinent at certain ages of individuals in the sample such as ages at which decisions are made whether to continue to the next schooling level.

—Marriage market relations can be estimated to ascertain the extent of assortative mating on earnings, income, education, parental education, and so forth.

A cautionary note must be sounded, however. The usual interpretation of cross-sectional estimates of such relations as reflecting causality rather than association is conditional on some very strong assumptions about the nature of the underlying behaviors—that there are no unobserved variables that are correlated with the right-side observed variables, the right-side variables are not behavioral choice variables, and the right-side variables are not contaminated by measurement errors. Most cross-sectional data sets do not permit much, if any, exploration of these assumptions.

A second primary possibility is estimation of relations from cross-sectional current and recall data. If the cross-sectional data have good recall data on indicators of social mobility, they can be used to estimate the Markov models of social mobility for the appropriate continuous variables in relations 3 and 6a–6g and for the appropriate categorical variables. The most common variables for which such data are likely to be available are intergenerational data on occupations and years of schooling, though some data sets may have current and recall data on earnings or wage rates. A basic problem in using recall data, however, is that they are usually noisy, which is likely to mean that measured social mobility will exceed actual social mobility.

Time Series of Cross-Sectional Household Data Sets

For most countries in the region there are several fairly comparable cross-sections of household data sets at different points of time. These permit the following.

First, they allow undertaking all the estimates possible with one cross-sectional household data set, but comparing how these estimates change over time. Such comparisons would be illuminating for understanding how various dimensions of social mobility that can be measured from a single cross-section of data have changed in the time between surveys. This would seem to address fairly directly some of the concerns summarized in my introduction. Under assumptions less strong than to attribute causality in a single cross-section—that the estimation biases are the same across cross-sections—the changes in the estimates in such comparisons may be interpreted to be the change in the true causal effects.

Second, they would allow using successive cross-sectional household surveys to follow specific cohorts over time. Cohorts defined by age and sex (and possibly other characteristics such as years of schooling) can be followed across cross-sectional surveys to identify better than from single cross-sections lifetime paths in earnings, income, inequality, and some dimensions of intragenerational mobility. An illustration is provided by Angus Deaton and Christina Paxson, who estimate the extent to which income inequality increases with age because of the persistent effects of shocks in a permanent income model with a first-order Markov process.[30] Such possibilities are limited for the Latin American and Caribbean region, however, because of the relatively short time spans covered by comparable household cross-sectional surveys and the relatively limited number of such comparable surveys in most countries.[31]

Longitudinal (Panel) Household Data

Longitudinal household data follow households and the individuals in them over time. Such data are what are really wanted to address the questions of interest on social mobility. With such data over periods of sufficient duration, all of the approaches concerning social mobility in the statistical models discussed earlier can be explored (as well as most of the questions concerning intergenerational behavioral relations) with control for most of the estimation problems that plague analyses based on cross-sectional data. The reality, however, is that the region is relatively poor in longitudinal data in comparison with Asia, Europe, and North America. A number of Latin American and Caribbean countries have revolving panels of households in their basic labor force surveys. But in most cases these data are not available in a form that permits use of longitudinal analysis. In addition, at best these data sets could yield very short panels, generally not lasting more than a year or two. There are a very few exceptions in which longer panels exist—for example, the subset of panel data from the living standards measurement surveys in Peru for 1985–97.[32] But even these ex-

---

30. Deaton and Paxson (1994).
31. For example, Deaton and Case use eleven to twenty-two household surveys for each of the three countries that they consider.
32. See Birdsall and Graham (1998).

ceptions are for periods that will permit investigation primarily of intragenerational mobility, not intergenerational mobility (beyond the possibilities that are summarized above for cross-sectional data). Therefore, although one can hope that more longitudinal data will become available because of the importance of the information for addressing as satisfactorily as possible issues related to mobility (as well as many other issues), currently the options for using longitudinal data are limited.

Appendix Tables

Table 4-A1. *World Growth, Inequality, and Poverty* [a]

	Periods of growth (88)		Periods of decline (7)	
Indicator	Improved	Worsened	Improved	Worsened
Inequality	45	43	2	5
Income of the poor[b]	77	11	2	3

Source: Deininger and Squire's (1996, table 5) calculations based on various sources as described in their text.

a. "Improved" in the income distribution implies a decrease of the Gini coefficient; "worsened" implies an increase. The sample includes ninety-five economies.

b. The income of the lowest quintile.

Table 4-A2. *Descriptive Statistics and Coverage of the Deininger and Squire (1996) Data Set on Income Inequality, Selected Economies*

Region and country	Number of obser- vations	Average Gini	Minimum Gini	Maximum Gini	Standard deviation	First year	Last year	Ratio of top quintile income share to bottom quintile share[a]
Latin America and Caribbean	100	50.15	37.92	61.88	6.05	1950	1994	16.02
Barbados	2	47.18	45.49	48.86	2.38	1951	1979	17.56
Bolivia	1	42.04	42.04	42.04	n.a.	1990	1990	8.58
Brazil	15	57.32	53.00	61.76	2.72	1960	1989	23.07
Chile	5	51.84	45.64	57.88	5.76	1969	1994	14.48
Colombia	7	51.51	46.00	54.50	2.68	1970	1991	13.94
Costa Rica	9	46.00	42.00	50.00	2.97	1961	1989	13.13
Dominican Republic	4	46.94	43.29	50.46	3.35	1976	1992	11.06
Ecuador	1	43.00	43.00	43.00	n.a.	1992	1992	9.82
El Salvador	1	48.40	48.40	48.40	n.a.	1977	1977	10.64
Guatemala	3	55.68	49.72	59.06	5.18	1979	1989	20.82

Guyana	2	48.19	40.22	56.16	11.27	1990	1990	9.15
Honduras	7	54.49	50.00	61.88	3.63	1968	1993	27.74
Jamaica	9	42.90	37.92	54.31	4.81	1958	1993	8.75
Mexico	9	53.85	50.00	57.90	3.09	1950	1992	17.12
Nicaragua	1	50.32	50.32	50.32	n.a.	1990	1990	13.12
Panama	4	52.43	47.47	57.00	5.01	1970	1989	22.64
Peru	4	47.99	42.76	55.00	5.42	1971	1994	9.21
Puerto Rico	3	51.11	50.15	52.32	1.11	1969	1989	22.20
Trinidad	4	46.21	41.72	51.00	3.79	1958	1981	18.31
Venezuela	9	44.42	39.42	53.84	4.27	1971	1990	10.93
Sub-Saharan Africa	40	44.71	28.90	63.18	9.18	1968	1993	11.61
East Asia and the Pacific	123	36.18	25.70	53.00	6.55	1953	1993	7.15
South Asia	60	34.06	28.27	47.80	4.54	1951	1992	5.50
Eastern Europe	101	26.01	17.83	39.39	4.71	1958	1995	4.05
Middle East and North Africa	20	40.77	32.00	45.45	3.07	1959	1991	7.14
Industrial countries and high-income developing countries	238	33.19	22.90	56.00	5.76	1947	1993	6.63

Source: Deininger and Squire's (1996, table 1) calculations based on various sources as described in their text.

n.a. Not available.

a. This ratio is the average for all observations included in the data set.

Table 4-A3. *Number of Economies and Observations Included in the Deininger and Squire (1996) Data Set, by Region, 1960s–1990s*

Region	Total		1960s		1970s		1980s		1990s	
	Economies	Observations	Economies	Observations	Economies	Observations	Economies	Observations	Economies	Observations
Latin America and Caribbean	20	100	9	12	15	34	14	35	12	19
Sub-Saharan Africa	24	40	2	2	5	6	11	16	14	16
East Asia and the Pacific	13	123	6	24	10	37	10	46	9	16
South Asia	5	60	4	24	4	13	5	17	4	6
Eastern Europe	19	101	4	9	5	21	8	39	18	32
Middle East and North Africa	6	20	3	4	3	5	5	7	4	4
Industrial countries and high-income developing countries	21	238	11	50	20	68	21	99	14	21
Total	108	682	39	125	62	184	74	259	75	114

Source: Deininger and Squire's (1996, table 2) calculations based on various sources as described in their text.

References

Akerlof, George A. 1997. "Social Distance and Social Decisions." *Econometrica* 65 (September): 1005–28.

Armitage, Jane, and Richard Sabot. 1990. "Education Policy and Intergenerational Mobility." In J. B. Knight and Richard Sabot, eds., *Education, Productivity and Inequality: The East African Natural Experiment*. Oxford University Press.

Atkinson, Anthony B., François Bourguignon, and Christian Morrisson. 1992. *Empirical Studies of Earnings Mobility*. Chur, Switzerland: Harwood Academic Publishers.

Bartholomew, D. J. 1982. *Stochastic Models for Social Processes*, 3d ed. Wiley.

Becker, Gary S. 1975. *Human Capital*, 2d ed. New York: National Bureau of Economic Research.

———. 1991. *A Treatise on the Family*, 2d ed. Harvard University Press.

Behrman, Jere R. 1997. "Women's Schooling and Child Education: A Survey." University of Pennsylvania.

Behrman, Jere R., and James C. Knowles. 1999. "Household Income and Child Schooling in Vietnam?" *World Bank Economic Review* (May).

Behrman, Jere R., and Mark R. Rosenzweig. 1999. "'Ability' Biases in Schooling Returns and Twins: A Test and New Estimates." *Economics of Education Review*. 18 (April): 159–67.

Behrman, Jere R., and Paul Taubman. 1985. "Intergenerational Earnings Mobility in the United States: Some Estimates and a Test of Becker's Intergenerational Endowments Model." *Review of Economics and Statistics* 67 (February): 141–45; reprinted in Behrman, Robert A. Pollak, and Paul Taubman, *From Parent to Child: Intrahousehold Allocations and Intergenerational Relations in the United States*. University of Chicago Press, 1995.

Behrman, Jere R., and Paul Taubman. 1990. "The Intergenerational Correlation between Children's Adult Earnings and Their Parents' Income: Results from the Michigan Panel Survey of Income Dynamics." *Review of Income and Wealth* 36 (June): 115–27.

Behrman, Jere R., Robert A. Pollak, and Paul Taubman. 1982. "Parental Preferences and Provision for Progeny." *Journal of Political Economy* 90 (February): 52–73.

———. 1995. *From Parent to Child: Intrahousehold Allocations and Intergenerational Relations in the United States*. University of Chicago Press.

Behrman, Jere R., Mark R. Rosenzweig, and Paul Taubman. 1994. "Endowments and the Allocation of Schooling in the Family and in the Marriage Market: The Twins Experiment." *Journal of Political Economy* 102 (December): 1131–74.

Behrman, Jere R., Mark R. Rosenzweig, and Paul Taubman. 1996. "College Choice and Wages: Estimates Using Data on Female Twins." *Review of Economics and Statistics* 73:4 (November), 672-685.

Bénabou, Roland. 1996. "Heterogeneity, Stratification, and Growth: Macroeconomic Implications of Community Structure and School Finance." *American Economic Review* 86 (June): 584–609.

Berry, Albert. 1997. "The Income Distribution Threat in Latin America." *Latin American Research Review* 32 (2): 3–40.

Birdsall, Nancy, and Carol Graham. 1998a. "New Ways of Looking at Old Inequities: Market Reforms, Social Mobility and Sustainable Growth (Latin America in Comparative Context)." Brookings and Inter-American Development Bank.

Birdsall, Nancy, Carol Graham, and Richard Sabot, eds. 1998b. *Beyond Tradeoffs: Market Reforms and Equitable Growth in Latin America*. Brookings and Inter-American Development Bank.

Burdett, Ken, and Melvyn G. Coles, 1997. "Marriage and Class." *Quarterly Journal of Economics* CXII:1 (February), 141-168.

Cole, Harold L., George J. Mailath, and Andrew Postlewaite. 1992. "Social Norms, Savings Behavior, and Growth." *Journal of Political Economy* 100 (December): 1092–1125.

———. 1995. "Incorporating Concern for Relative Wealth into Economic Models." Minneapolis: Federal Reserve Bank of Minneapolis.

Conlisk, J. 1989. "Ranking Mobility Matrices." *Economic Letters* 29: 231–35.

———. 1990. "Monotone Mobility Matrices." *Journal of Mathematical Sociology* 15: 173–91.

Dardanoni, Valentino. 1993. "Measuring Social Mobility." *Journal of Economic Theory* 61: 372–94.

Deaton, Angus, and Christina Paxson. 1994. "Intertemporal Choice and Inequality." *Journal of Political Economy* 102 (June): 437–67.

Deininger, Klaus, and Lyn Squire. 1996. "A New Data Set Measuring Income Inequality." *World Bank Economic Review* 10 (September): 565–91.

Deolalikar, Anil B., and Raghav Gaiha. 1993. "Persistent, Expected and Innate Poverty: Estimates for Semi-Arid Rural South India, 1975–84." *Cambridge Journal of Economics* 17 (December): 409–21.

Featherman, David L., F. Lancaster Jones, and Robert M. Hauser. 1975. "Assumptions of Social Mobility Research in the U.S.: The Case of Occupational Status." *Social Science Research* 4 (December): 329–60.

Fields, Gary S., and Efe A. Ok. 1996. "The Meaning and Measurement of Income Mobility." *Journal of Economic Theory* 71: 349–77.

Friedman, Milton. 1962. *Capitalism and Freedom*. Princeton University Press.

Friedman, Milton, and Simon Kuznets. 1954. *Income from Independent Professional Practice*. New York: National Bureau of Economic Research.

Friesen, P. H., and D. Miller. 1983. "Annual Inequality and Lifetime Inequality." *Quarterly Journal of Economics* 98: 139–55.

Galton, F. 1889. *Natural Inheritance*. London: Macmillan.

Geweke, J., R. C. Marshall, and G. A. Zarkin. 1986. "Mobility Indices in Continuous Time Markov Chains." *Econometrica* 54: 1407–23.

Grusky, David B., and Robert M. Hauser. 1984. "Comparative Social Mobility Revisited: Models of Convergence and Divergence in 16 Countries." *American Sociological Review* 49 (February): 19-38.

Hause, J. C. 1977. "The Covariance Structure of Earnings and the On-the-Job Training Hypothesis." *Annals of Economic and Social Measurement* 6: 335–65.

———. 1980. "The Fine Structure of Earnings and the On-the-Job Training Hypothesis." *Econometrica* 48 (4): 1013–29.

Hauser, Robert M. 1986. "Reinventing the Oxcart: Jones' Obsolete Proposal for Mobility Analysis." *Social Forces* 64 (June): 1057–65.

Hauser, Robert M,. and David B. Grusky. 1988. "Cross-National Variation in Occupational Distributions, Relative Mobility Chances, and Intergenerational Shifts in Occupational Distributions." *American Sociological Review* 53 (October): 723–41.

Hauser, Robert M., and John Allen Logan. 1992. "How Not to Measure Intergenerational Occupational Persistence." *American Journal of Sociology* 97 (May): 1689–1711.

Hill, M. Anne. 1990. "Intercohort Differences in Women's Labor Market Transitions." *AEA Papers and Proceedings* 80 (May): 289–92.

Hout, Michael, and Robert M. Hauser. 1992. "Symmetry and Hierarchy in Social Mobility: A Methodological Analysis of the CASMIN Model of Class Mobility." *European Sociological Review* 8 (December): 239–66.

Kanbur, S. M. R., and Joseph E. Stiglitz. 1986. "Intergenerational Mobility and Dynastic Inequality." Woodrow Wilson Discussion Paper 111. Princeton University.

Klerman, Jacob Alex, and Arleen Leibowitz. 1990. "Child Care and Women's Return to Work after Childbirth." *AEA Papers and Proceedings* 80 (May): 284–88.

Lam, David. 1986. "The Dynamics of Population Growth, Differential Fertility, and Inequality." *American Economic Review* 76 (December): 1103–16.

———. 1996. "Demographic Variables and Income Inequality." In Mark R. Rosenzweig and Oded Stark, eds., *Handbook of Population and Family Economics.* Amsterdam: North-Holland.

Lam, David, and Deborah Levison. 1991. "Declining Inequality in Schooling in Brazil and Its Effect on Inequality in Earnings." *Journal of Development Economics* 37 (November): 199–226.

———. 1992. "Age, Experience and Schooling: Decomposing Earnings Inequality in the United States and Brazil." *Sociological Inquiry* 62 (2): 218–45.

Lam, David, and Robert F. Schoeni. 1993. "Effects of Family Background on Earnings and Returns to Schooling: Evidence from Brazil." *Journal of Political Economy* 101 (August): 710–40.

———. 1994. "Family Ties and Labor Markets in the United States and Brazil." *Journal of Human Resources* 29 (Fall): 1235–58.

Light, Audrey, and Manuelita Ureta. 1990. "Gender Differences in Wages and Job Turnovers among Continuously Employed Workers." *AEA Papers and Proceedings* 80 (May): 293–97.

Lillard, Lee, and Robert Willis. 1994. "Intergenerational Education Mobility: Effects of Family and State in Malaysia." *Journal of Human Resources* 29 (Fall): 1126–66.

Londoño, Juan Luis, and Miguel Székely. 1997. "Distributional Surprises after a Decade of Reforms: Latin America in the Nineties." Washington: Inter-American Development Bank.

Lustig, Nora, and Miguel Székely. 1997. "'Hidden' Trends in Poverty and Inequality in Mexico." Washington: Inter-American Development Bank.

Mare, Robert D. 1996. "Demography and the Evolution of Educational Inequality." In James N. Baron, David B. Grusky, and Donald J. Treiman, eds., *Social Differentiation and Social Inequality: Essays in Honor of John Pock*, pp. 117–51. Boulder, Colo.: Westview Press.

Markandya, A. 1984. "The Welfare Measurement of Changes in Economic Mobility." *Economica* 51: 457–71.

McMurrer, Daniel P., and Isabel V. Sawhill. 1997. "Getting Ahead: Economic and Social Mobility in America." Washington: Urban Institute.

Miller, Paul W., and Paul A. Volker. 1985. "On the Determination of Occupational Attainment and Mobility." *Journal of Human Resources* 20 (Spring): 197–213.

Mincer, Jacob B. 1974. *Schooling, Experience, and Earnings.* New York: National Bureau of Economic Research.

Morley, Samuel. 1994. *Poverty and Inequality in Latin America.* Johns Hopkins University Press.

Mulligan, Casey B. 1997. *Parental Priorities and Economic Inequality.* University of Chicago Press.

Narayan, Deepa, and Lant Pritchett. 1997. "Cents and Sociability: Household Income and Social Capital in Rural Tanzania." Washington: World Bank.

Neumark, David, and Andrew Postlewaite. 1996. "Relative Income Concerns and the Rise in Married Women's Employment." Michigan State University.

Piketty, Thomas. 1995. "Social Mobility and Redistributive Politics." *Quarterly Journal of Economics* 110 (August): 551–84.

Prais, S. J. 1955. "Measuring Social Mobility." *Journal of the Royal Statistical Society,* Series A 118: 56–66.

Psacharopoulos, George, and others. 1992. *Poverty and Income Distribution in Latin America: The Story of the 1980s.* Washington: World Bank.

Schemo, Diana Jean. 1998. "Brazil's Reformist Chief Rides a Bucking Bronco." *New York Times,* February 8, 1998, p. 12.

Shorrocks, Anthony F. 1976. "Income Mobility and the Markov Assumption." *Economic Journal* 86: 556–78.

———. 1978. "The Measurement of Mobility." *Econometrica* 46: 1013–24.

Slesnick, Daniel T. 1986. "Welfare Distributional Change and the Measurement of Social Mobility." *Review of Economics and Statistics* 47 (November): 586–93.

Solon, Gary R. 1989. "Biases in the Estimation of Intergenerational Earnings Correlations." *Review of Economics and Statistics* 21 (2): 172–74.

———. 1992. "Intergenerational Income Mobility in the United States." *American Economic Review* 82 (June): 393–408.

Sommers, P. M., and J. Conlisk. 1978. "Eigenvalue Immobility Measures for Markov Chains." *Journal of Mathematical Sociology* 6: 253–76.

Warren, John Robert, and Robert M. Hauser. 1997. "Social Stratification across Three Generations: New Evidence from the Wisconsin Longitudinal Study." *American Sociological Review* 62 (August): 561–72.

Zimmerman, David J. 1992. "Regression toward Mediocrity in Economic Stature." *American Economic Review* 82 (June): 409–29.

GARY S. FIELDS

5 | *Income Mobility: Concepts and Measures*

People's economic positions may change for a variety of reasons. The economy in which they participate may improve or deteriorate because of macroeconomic growth or contraction, employer-specific events and circumstances, business expansions and contractions, and ups and downs in local communities. Individuals may experience major life events with important economic consequences, among them completion of schooling, promotions and other movements up the career ladder, marriage and divorce, poor health, and retirement. Economic mobility studies are concerned with quantifying the movement of given recipient units through the distribution of economic well-being over time, establishing how dependent one's current economic position is on one's past position, and relating people's mobility experiences to the various influences that have been mentioned.[1]

Four methodological aspects of these studies are worth highlighting. First, mobility analysis follows given economic units through time. Consequently, longitudinal (or panel) data are required for research, which makes mobility analysis different from the measurement of poverty, inequality, or

1. Most of what follows is phrased in terms of "income mobility," but it should not be understood as being limited to the study of incomes per se. The concepts and methods presented here apply equally well to "economic mobility" as gauged by income, earnings, or expenditures, as well as to "socioeconomic mobility" as gauged by an occupational or educational index.

economic well-being.[2] Second, mobility analysis can be applied to a variety of recipient units. Those most commonly used are individuals and households. Third, any aspect of economic well-being can be used. Among those that are studied are the income, earnings, expenditures, or occupational attainment of the individual or household. When income and expenditures are used, the data are often per capita. Any measure in dollars should be in real dollars, adjusted for inflation. Finally, I shall limit my attention to the recipient's economic well-being in a base year versus a final year. Other mobility studies assess mobility by looking at economic position in each of T years, but I shall not deal with those studies or measures.[3]

Notwithstanding these points of agreement about the concept of economic mobility, there are also some fundamental disagreements. This is because the term *income mobility* conjures up very different ideas in people's minds. In much the same way that I find it helpful to reserve the term *income distribution* for a generic concept and to use *inequality, poverty, mobility,* and *economic well-being* to distinguish among different specific aspects of the income distribution, so too is it helpful to reserve the term *income mobility* for the generic concept and to use other specific terms for particular aspects of income mobility. These five ideas—time dependence, positional movement, share movement, symmetric income movement, and directional income movement are described in the next section. The following section contrasts these approaches and shows how the choice among them makes a difference in certain illustrative examples. In the next section I look at various mobility measures and their axiomatic foundations.[4]

Five Mobility Concepts

It is said that Joseph Schumpeter likened an income distribution to a hotel.[5] The rooms at the top are luxurious, those on the middle levels are ordinary, and those in the basement are downright shabby. At any given

2. All of these are done using data from comparable cross-sections.

3. Given this range of choices, it would be tedious to talk all the time about changes in income, expenditure, or per capita incomes among individuals, households, parents, and children over a period of years or across the generations. So from now on, for brevity, I will talk in terms of the income mobility of persons through time, with the understanding that the measure of economic well-being may be something other than income, the recipient unit may be something other than persons, and time may be across generations rather than across years.

4. For a more detailed review of the literature on income mobility measurement see Fields and Ok (forthcoming).

5. This is reported in Sawhill and Condon (1992); and Danziger and Gottschalk (1995). The analogy is also used by Jarvis and Jenkins (1996).

time the occupants of the hotel experience very unequal accommodations. At a later time, if one reexamines who is living where, one finds that some have moved to higher floors, some to lower floors, and some have stayed where they were.

The difference in the quality of hotel rooms at each point in time is called inequality. The movement of hotel guests among rooms of different quality is mobility. One way in which these are linked is that the more movement of guests there is among rooms, the greater the long-term equality of accommodations.

But is the movement of guests among rooms all there is to mobility? What if the existing furnishings are redistributed from some rooms to others? Isn't there mobility then? What if the hotel is refurbished so that some of the rooms are made nicer? Don't the lucky residents of the now nicer rooms enjoy upward mobility? What about those whose rooms are not upgraded? Do they suffer downward mobility?

The hotel analogy raises some fundamental questions about what economic mobility is and by extension how it should be measured. The mobility literature is plagued by people talking past one another because one person's idea of mobility is not another's. Five concepts shall be distinguished in this chapter.

Time dependence measures the extent to which economic well-being in the past determines individuals' economic well-being at present. *Positional movement* takes place when there is a change in individuals' economic positions (ranks, centiles, deciles, or quintiles). *Share movement* occurs when individuals' shares of total income change. *Symmetric income movement* arises when individuals' incomes change and the analyst is concerned about the magnitude of these fluctuations but not their direction. Finally, in *directional income movement* income gains and income losses are treated separately. Let us now look at each of these in greater detail.

Time Dependence

Time dependence is a particular form of immobility. It arises when one's current economic position is determined by one's position in the past. Studies of time dependence arise in two contexts. In the *intergenerational* context, the question is to what extent the incomes of sons can be predicted by the incomes of their fathers.[6] In the *intragenerational* context, the

---

6. Yes, the sexist terminology is used nearly always in these studies.

problem is to what extent individuals' incomes at a later date can be predicted by their incomes at an earlier date. To be able to speak about both contexts, one can use the terminology *base income* and *final income*. Again, the reader is reminded that "income" is a shorthand for whichever economic or socioeconomic variable one is interested in measuring.

Data for gauging time dependence may come either in aggregated or in disaggregated form. I take up in turn how to work with each of these two types of data.

TIME DEPENDENCE IN AGGREGATED DATA. An analytical tool that facilitates measurement of time dependence is an intertemporal transition matrix. The rows of the matrix are the income classes of income recipients in the base year, and the columns are the corresponding income classes in the final year. These classes may either be income categories ($0–$10,000, $10,000–$20,000, and so forth) or quantiles (for example, deciles or quintiles). The entries in the transition matrix indicate what fraction of people with a given base year income end up with a given final year income, and thus each row sums to 100 percent. Quantile transition matrices are the type most commonly used, and so those are the ones I begin with here.

Let the population be divided into five income quintiles. One way there might be perfect time dependence is for each recipient's final year income quintile to be identical to his or her base year quintile. If this were the case, all entries in the transition matrix would lie along the principal diagonal running from upper left to lower right, each element on the principal diagonal would equal 100 percent, and thus the transition matrix would be an identity matrix.

$$(5\text{-}1) \qquad P_1 = \begin{bmatrix} 1 & 0 & 0 & 0 & 0 \\ 0 & 1 & 0 & 0 & 0 \\ 0 & 0 & 1 & 0 & 0 \\ 0 & 0 & 0 & 1 & 0 \\ 0 & 0 & 0 & 0 & 1 \end{bmatrix}$$

The identity matrix indicates what I shall call "perfect positive time dependence." The closer the actual transition matrix in a country to the identity matrix, the more immobility in the sense of time dependence there is said to be.

There is, however, a very different way in which there might be perfect time dependence. Suppose that there is a complete reversal of income positions so that all those who start out rich end up poor and all those who start out poor end up rich. Though this is only a theoretical possibility that never arises in practice, what it would produce if it did happen is a transition matrix with all ones along the diagonal running from upper right to lower left.

(5-2)
$$P_2 = \begin{bmatrix} 0 & 0 & 0 & 0 & 1 \\ 0 & 0 & 0 & 1 & 0 \\ 0 & 0 & 1 & 0 & 0 \\ 0 & 1 & 0 & 0 & 0 \\ 1 & 0 & 0 & 0 & 0 \end{bmatrix}$$

The reverse identity matrix arises in the case of so-called perfect negative time dependence. The closer the actual transition matrix in a country to the reverse-identity matrix, the more immobility in the sense of time dependence there is said to be.

Though these two criteria may appear to be contradictory, I assure you that they are not. This is because lying in between perfect positive time dependence and perfect negative time dependence is time independence. Time independence arises when a person's final year income is independent of his or her base year income. This would produce a transition matrix in which each row is the same as every other. In the special case of a quintile mobility matrix, this would mean that every entry would be equal to 0.2.

(5-3)
$$P_3 = \begin{bmatrix} 0.2 & 0.2 & 0.2 & 0.2 & 0.2 \\ 0.2 & 0.2 & 0.2 & 0.2 & 0.2 \\ 0.2 & 0.2 & 0.2 & 0.2 & 0.2 \\ 0.2 & 0.2 & 0.2 & 0.2 & 0.2 \\ 0.2 & 0.2 & 0.2 & 0.2 & 0.2 \end{bmatrix}$$

To be able to implement the ideas of positive time dependence, negative time dependence, and time independence, one needs a way of measuring how close an actual transition matrix is to these various theoretical possibilities. Continuing with the illustration of what might be done if there is a quintile mobility matrix, take as the basis for comparison the number of people that would be observed in cell i,j under the null hypothesis of time independence; this would be the matrix given in 5-3 multiplied by an appropriate scaling factor such that the sum of the expected frequencies is the total sample size N.

$$(5\text{-}4) \quad P_4 = \begin{bmatrix} .04N & .04N & .04N & .04N & .04N \\ .04N & .04N & .04N & .04N & .04N \\ .04N & .04N & .04N & .04N & .04N \\ .04N & .04N & .04N & .04N & .04N \\ .04N & .04N & .04N & .04N & .04N \end{bmatrix}$$

Denoting these expected frequencies by EXP_{ij}, one can then compare them with the observed frequencies OBS_{ij} by making a standard (Pearson) chi-squared calculation

$$\chi^2 = \sum_i \sum_j \frac{(OBS_{ij} - EXP_{ij})^2}{EXP_{ij}}.$$

The calculated chi-squared value would tell how distant an actual transition matrix is from the one that would be observed in the case of perfect time independence. And then, in comparing the chi-squared values obtained in two different mobility situations, one would be able to say that the matrix with the larger chi-squared value is more time dependent and therefore less mobile in this sense of time dependence than the other.[7]

Table 5-1 shows quintile mobility matrices for the United States for 1967–79 and 1979–91, from which chi-squared values may be calculated.

---

7. For tests of statistical significance using an $M \times M$ transition matrix, compare the calculated chi-squared value with the tabulated value with $M(M - 1)$ degrees of freedom.

Table 5-1. *Quintile Mobility Rates for Equivalent Family Income*
Percent

| | 1967–79 transition matrix | | | | |
| | Quintile in 1979 | | | | |
Quintile in 1967	Bottom quintile	Second quintile	Third quintile	Fourth quintile	Top quintile
Bottom quintile	51.3	25.0	15.3	5.9	2.4
Second quintile	21.8	27.0	24.3	19.1	7.8
Third quintile	12.3	21.3	22.7	24.5	19.3
Fourth quintile	8.1	15.0	19.7	26.5	30.7
Top quintile	6.4	11.7	17.8	24.1	40.0

N = 3,277

| | 1979–91 transition matrix | | | | |
| | Quintile in 1991 | | | | |
Quintile in 1979	Bottom quintile	Second quintile	Third quintile	Fourth quintile	Top quintile
Bottom quintile	47.8	25.6	13.1	10.4	3.2
Second quintile	22.1	26.7	24.8	18.3	8.1
Third quintile	12.2	18.9	25.6	21.6	21.8
Fourth quintile	12.3	19.5	18.2	23.1	26.9
Top quintile	5.7	9.0	17.7	27.6	40.0

N = 3,322

Source: Gittleman and Joyce (1998).

The calculated values are 1.153 for 1967–79 and 1.025 for 1979–91. This indicates that the United States had less mobility in the sense of time dependence in 1967–79 than in 1979–91.

Consider now how you would treat aggregated data in which you are given a transition matrix among income classes that contain unequal numbers of people. In similar fashion, you would need to calculate the distance between the observed frequency distribution and the theoretically expected one, but now the calculation would need to be made in a slightly different way. Under time independence, all rows would have identical conditional probabilities, but because the marginal frequencies are different across income classes in this case (whereas they are identical in the case of quintiles or deciles), the expected frequencies would differ proportionately. Again, in comparing two mobility situations, the one with the larger calculated chi-squared statistic could be said to exhibit more mobility in the sense of time dependence than the other.

Finally, it bears mention that the chi-squared statistic is not the only one that might be calculated as a measure of time dependence. Standard statistical packages contain a contingency table procedure that produces a number of such statistics. For instance, the Stata statistical package will tell you, in addition to the standard (Pearson) chi-squared, the likelihood-ratio chi-squared, Cramer's V, gamma, and Kendall's tau-b—all of which are measures of time dependence in the sense of gauging deviations from randomness. Using the data shown in table 5-1, all of these statistics show higher values for the United States in 1967–79 than in 1979—91, and therefore less mobility in the sense of time dependence in the 1970s than in the 1980s. But Thomas Hungerford calculated the lambda asymmetric statistic, Cramer's V, and the contingency coefficient using a different extract from the U.S. Panel Study of Income Dynamics (PSID) and found that each of these produced essentially identical values in the United States in 1969–76 and 1979–86.[8] From this he concluded that income mobility was unchanged between these two seven-year periods.

The preceding methods give practical ways of measuring time dependence in aggregated data. We turn now to the case of disaggregated data.

TIME DEPENDENCE IN DISAGGREGATED DATA. Increasingly researchers are working with microeconomic data rather than published data. Such data sets may contain observations on many thousands or even tens of thousands of income recipients. If you have such disaggregated data on the base year and final year incomes for each income recipient, you could create your own intertemporal transition matrix. However, you would lose a great deal of information by doing this, so you might prefer another option: calculating a measure of time dependence using the disaggregated data directly.

A commonly used measure of income mobility is the ordinary (Pearson) coefficient of correlation between base year income and final year income.[9]

---

8. Hungerford (1993).

9. Friedman and Kuznets (1954) were early users of this statistic. It has been used by many others; see Atkinson, Bourguignon, and Morrisson (1992, table VI) for a partial summary and Organization for Economic Cooperation and Development (1996, table 3.5) for more recent data.

Figure 5-1. *Time Dependence as a Function of the Ordinary and Rank Correlation Coefficients*

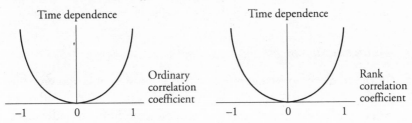

The correlation coefficient can be used to gauge income mobility precisely in the sense of time dependence:[10]

—The closer the value of the correlation coefficient to +1, the more positive time dependence there is.

—The closer the value of the correlation coefficient to −1, the more negative time dependence there is.

—The closer the value of the correlation coefficient to 0, the more time independence there is.

Figure 5-1 shows the relationship between time dependence and the ordinary correlation coefficient.[11]

A related measure of income mobility is the rank correlation coefficient. Denote the poorest individual by 1 and the richest by N in both the base year and final year distributions and calculate the correlation among income ranks. Exactly the same three points as in the previous paragraph apply to the rank correlation coefficient, and thus the graph between time dependence and the rank correlation coefficient has the same U shape as above (figure 5-1).

When these measures have been used to make mobility comparisons, several patterns emerge. First, the correlation coefficient is always positive, so in practice the distinction between measures of time dependence and income movement is more theoretical than practical. Second, as would be expected, the longer the time elapsed between base year and final year, the

---

10. It can also be used to gauge share movement, of which more later.

11. What matters in the present context is that time dependence needs to increase monotonically as one moves away from zero to the right or left. Whether the curve is U-shaped or V-shaped is unimportant for present purposes.

lower the correlation between incomes in the two years.[12] And third, the variations across countries are fairly large.[13]

Let us turn now to measures that are explicitly movement measures.

Positional Movement

In the study of positional movement, the measure of economic well-being is the individual's position in the income distribution.[14] Although the most commonly used measures of economic position are individuals' quintiles or deciles in the income distribution, there is no reason that one could not work with ventiles, centiles, or even ranks.

The main reason that positional analysis is so popular in income mobility studies is that movement among positions is the way most analysts have become accustomed to thinking about mobility.[15] History plays an important role in this. When income mobility studies were first done, it would have been difficult with the available technology to measure and evaluate income changes person by person. The masses of individual information had to be summarized somehow. Analyzing decile or quintile mobility matrices was a convenient and comprehensible way of doing this. Researchers therefore became accustomed to working with such matrices and simply have continued to do so for reasons of hysteresis.

Some observers give a more substantive justification. To them, small income movements are negligible; income changes become important only when the change is large enough that the income recipient crosses a decile or quintile boundary. Figure 5-2 depicts the movement function implied by such measures. (In this figure, Y^* is the income level where the next higher quantile begins and Y_* is the corresponding amount for the next lower quantile.) If such a discontinuous movement function seems odd, positional mobility may not be the right mobility concept for you.

---

12. For example, Moffitt and Gottschalk (1995) estimate one-year correlation coefficients of 0.7 – 0.8 and five-year correlation coefficients of 0.5 – 0.6 for the United States.

13. In the OECD data reported later, the correlation coefficient between 1986 earnings and 1991 earnings ranges from 0.65 for Denmark to 0.79 for Germany.

14. There are parallel literatures examining movement among occupations, industries, and social classes. For a recent analysis, see McMurrer and Sawhill (1998). On measurement issues, see Bartholomew (1982).

15. Most studies use positional measures. See Atkinson, Bourguignon, and Morrisson (1992) for a review of the international literature.

Figure 5-2. *Quantiles Changed as a Function of Income Change*

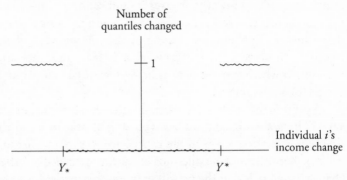

Number of
quantiles changed

But supposing that positional mobility *is* what you want to look at. How might it be measured? A natural benchmark is perfect positional immobility. In this case everybody keeps his or her previous position. (Of course, you will need to have decided whether you are measuring positions in terms of deciles, quintiles, or whatever. The results will be sensitive to that choice.) Perfect positional immobility means that the quantile transition matrix is an identity matrix, as in 5-1.

To gauge how far an actual quantile mobility matrix is from perfect positional immobility, some sort of metric is needed. The most frequently used is the "trace," more commonly called the "immobility ratio." This is the fraction of income recipients who remain in the same quantile as before.[16]

The immobility ratio varies with a number of factors. First, the longer the time period, the smaller the immobility ratio: for example, Richard Burkhauser and colleagues found immobility ratios of 67.6 percent and 69.3 percent comparing quintiles in a given year with those one year later for the United States and Germany, respectively, but when the base year and final year were five years apart, the corresponding immobility ratios were 50.4 percent and 53.4 percent.[17] Second, immobility ratios vary across countries. International comparisons across OECD countries show five-year immobility ratios that range from 0.43 in France to 0.53 in Denmark.[18] Finally, and obviously, the immobility ratio varies inversely with the number of quantiles.

---

16. I have classified the immobility ratio under positional movement because that is how it is ordinarily used. It might alternatively be thought of as a measure of positive time dependence.

17. Burkhauser, Holtz-Eakin, and Rhody (1997).

18. Organization for Economic Cooperation and Development (1996).

The immobility ratio indicates the fraction of people who remain in or change quantiles. However, it gives no indication of how many quantiles the movers move. It seems reasonable to have a measure that is sensitive to that. One such is the mean number of quantiles moved, where zero is assigned to those who do not move at all. (Here too, the results may be sensitive to whether movement is being measured across quintiles, across deciles, or across ranks.)

A great many studies have been done using positional movement measures.[19] In evaluating the studies, you should bear in mind that they are thoroughly relative: a person can experience relative income mobility even if his or her own income does not change, provided that others' incomes change by enough that the person in question experiences a change in position.[20] In positional movement analysis, what matters is one's income *position* vis-à-vis others. But relative considerations might enter in a different kind of way, and that is by looking at one's income *share* vis-à-vis others. I turn now to the concept and measurement of share movement.

Share Movement

Some people, even those who are thoroughgoing relativists, may not care which quintile, decile, or centile of the income distribution they are in—in fact, they may not even know. To the extent that people are relativists in their thinking, what they are much more likely to care about is their income as it compares with that of others. If your income rises by 50 percent but everyone else's rises by 100 percent, you may feel that you have lost ground. Share-movement measures would say that you have experienced downward income mobility, precisely because your share of the total has fallen.

Now that technology allows virtually instantaneous calculations of changes in income shares for samples of thousands or tens of thousands of income recipients, the practical advantage of using quantile mobility matrices rather than share-movement measures is gone. So the choice between these two types of relative mobility approaches is better made on conceptual grounds. Here is a simple self-test.

---

19. See Atkinson, Bourguignon, and Morrisson (1992). A very useful comparative analysis of developed countries is Organization for Economic Cooperation and Development (1996, 1997).

20. Positional movement is also relative in a different sense, which is that the usual measures of positional movement satisfy certain relative mobility axioms. More on this later.

Suppose you start out in a given quantile of the income distribution. Let's say that your income remains stationary while incomes around you are rising, but the fall in position is sufficiently small that you remain in the same quantile that you were in. What is your mobility experience?

If you are a positional movement adherent, you find no income mobility: you were in the xth quantile before and you are in the xth quantile afterwards. "Stop," you say. "That's not me. I *do* experience mobility. I have moved down." If this is your answer, then there surely is a relativist element to your concept of mobility, and it reflects your changing income *share*, not your unchanged *quantile*.

If you think in this way, what should you do to measure mobility? Your own mobility is readily gauged by the change in your income share. The population analogue is an aggregation of the changes in income shares experienced by all the people in the population.

What is it about these changes that you might want to measure? Of course, you would not want to measure the mean change in income shares, because this is identically zero: all the gains in share enjoyed by some must be counterbalanced by losses of share suffered by others. Instead you might look at the standard deviation of changes in income shares, larger values signifying greater share movement. Or you might take the absolute value of the change in each person's income share and average these; here too, a larger value signifies greater share movement.

Thus far, in my review of the literature, I have not seen anyone who has actually measured the change in income shares. However, as noted earlier, the correlation between base income and final income is commonly used as a measure of immobility, and it can easily be shown that the correlation between incomes is the same as the correlation between income shares. So perhaps inadvertently, share movement has been measured.

Note that what share movement measures is *flux*, how much variation there is from base year to final year. Here, the aspect of flux that is being measured is income shares, whereas in the previous section, it was positions in the income distribution. If you are interested in flux but are more concerned about incomes than income shares or income positions, you might find the class of measures presented next more interesting.

Symmetric Income Movement

Imagine that you and I constitute a two-person society and that both of us experience a change in income. You experience a $1,000 income gain and I experience a $1,000 income loss. How much income movement has taken place?

If your answer is $2,000 total or $1,000 per capita, you have revealed much about the concept of mobility that you have in mind. For one, your concept of mobility is symmetric in the sense that gains and losses are both being treated nondirectionally. For another, your concept of mobility is dollar based in that you regard your gain and my loss as being $1,000 regardless of our respective base incomes.

Looking at mobility in this way has been justified formally by Gary Fields and Efe Ok.[21] Denoting base income and final income by x_i and y_i, respectively, their measure of total dollar movement in a population of size n is the sum of the absolute values of income changes ($2,000 in the above example):

$$(5\text{-}5a) \qquad d^{(1)}{}_n(x, y) = \sum_{j=1}^{n} |x_i - y_i|.$$

Corresponding to this is a measure of per capita dollar movement in a population of size n ($1,000 in the above example):

$$(5\text{-}5b) \qquad m^{(1)}{}_n(x, y) = \frac{1}{n} \sum_{j=1}^{n} |x_i - y_i|.$$

Finally, to gauge whether $1,000 per capita is a large or small amount of income change, $m^{(1)}{}_n$ can be expressed as a percentage of the mean base year income:

$$(5\text{-}5c) \qquad p^{(1)}{}_n(x, y) = \sum_{j=1}^{n} |x_i - y_i| \Big/ \sum_{i=1}^{n} x_i.$$

These are measures of total symmetric dollar income movement ($d^{(1)}{}_n$), per capita symmetric dollar income movement ($m^{(1)}{}_n$), and percentage symmetric dollar income movement ($p^{(1)}{}_n$), respectively. Together, these shall be denoted the F-O 1 set of measures.

---

21. Fields and Ok (1996).

To give some idea of the magnitudes involved, Gary Fields and colleagues calculated these measures using data from the U.S. Panel Study of Income Dynamics (PSID).[22] They found that in the United States between 1979 and 1986, $m^{(1)}_n$ = \$16,506 (in real 1982–84 dollars) and the mean in that year was \$33,943 (in the same real dollars). Thus the average income change was 49 percent of the mean base year income. While this is a matter of interpretation, to me, a $p^{(1)}_n$ value of 49 percent is a sign of considerable income flux.

Now, you may object to the perspective taken here by saying, "You haven't taken adequate account of base year income. A \$1,000 income change for me is very important if my base year income is \$1,000. It is much less important if my base year income is \$1,000,000. What matters is by what percentage my income has changed." Gary Fields and Efe Ok have dealt with this concern by formulating measures of income movement that are sensitive to base year incomes.[23] This is achieved by working with the logs of base year and final year income rather than the incomes themselves.[24] The resultant measure of per capita relative income movement is

$$(5\text{-}6) \qquad m^{(2)}_n(x, y) = \frac{1}{n} \sum_{j=1}^{n} |\log x_i - \log y_i| \, .$$

The total measures $d^{(2)}_n$ and percentage measures $p^{(2)}_n$ are defined analogously. Together, these are called the F-O 2 set.

When this was applied empirically to the same PSID data as reported for 1979–86, Fields and colleagues found that $m^{(2)}_n$ = .528. That is, the mean percentage income changes between these two years in the United States was approximately 52.8 percent. Again, it is a matter of perception, but I would say that this is indicative of a high degree of income flux.

One feature of F-O 1 and F-O 2 is that they are exactly decomposable into two parts, one that reflects income changes due to economic growth and the other that reflects income changes due to movements up and down, holding the mean constant.[25] In a growing economy, the breakdown of

---

22. Fields, Leary, and Ok (1998).

23. Fields and Ok (forthcoming).

24. For small income changes, the change in log incomes is very close to the percentage income change. The approximation gets worse and worse as the income change gets larger.

25. No other income mobility measure has been shown to be decomposable in this way. See, for instance, Markandya (1984).

$$d^{(1)}{}_n(x, y) = \sum_{j=1}^{n} |x_i - y_i|$$

into a growth component and a transfer component is given by

$$(5\text{-}7\text{a}) \qquad d^{(1)}{}_n(x, y) = \sum_{j=1}^{n} |x_i - y_i| = G^{(1)}{}_n(x, y) + T^{(1)}{}_n(x, y) \ ,$$

where

$$(5\text{-}7\text{b}) \qquad\qquad G^{(1)}{}_n(x, y) = \sum_{i=1}^{n} y_i - \sum_{i=1}^{n} x_i$$

and

$$(5\text{-}7\text{c}) \qquad\qquad T^{(1)}{}_n(x, y) = 2 \left(\sum_{i \in L_n(x, y)} (x_i - y_i) \right),$$

in which $L_n(x, y)$ denotes the set of people who lost income over time.[26]

Among the panel individuals in the PSID sample, the mean growth of family income was \$1,121 (3.3 percent of average base year income) between 1979 and 1986. But the average income change ($m^{(1)}{}_n$) was \$16,506 (in absolute value) between 1979 and 1986. From these figures, it would be expected that only a small fraction of total income mobility was due to income growth in the economy, and indeed that is what the decomposition in equation 5-7 shows: only 6.8 percent of symmetric income movement as gauged by $m^{(1)}{}_n$ was due to growth in the 1980s. This is because an overwhelming portion of U.S. income mobility (in the sense of symmetric income movement) is accounted for by people moving up or down within the income distribution.

These decompositions tell us, in an accounting sense, why incomes change: but to what extent is it because the economy grew and individuals'

---

26. An analogous decomposition is available in the case of falling total income. There are also analogous decompositions of the F-O 2 measures, obtained by substituting log x in place of x and log y in place of y everywhere in (5-7). See Fields and Ok (1996, forthcoming) for details.

incomes grew along with it and to what extent is it because people moved up or down within a given structure? What has been measured and decomposed is income flux.

Now, it may be that you are not as interested in income flux as you are in the direction of change, in particular how many people are experiencing income gains and losses of what magnitude and which people in the population are the gainers and the losers. Once the distinction between income gains and income losses becomes important to you, you would do better to consider directional income movements.

Directional Income Movement

The three previous subsections were concerned with different aspects of income flux: positional movement, share movement, and nondirectional income movement, respectively. If directional income movements are of concern, you may find the measures discussed in this subsection to be of interest.

Several ad hoc directional indexes are in use, such as the fraction of upward or downward movers and the average amount gained by the winners or lost by the losers. Accompanying the use of these measures is a strong normative judgment, rarely stated explicitly: one income mobility situation is *better* than another when there is a larger fraction of upward movers, when the upward movers gain more on average, and when the downward movers lose less on average.

Whenever an index is used, one has (or should have) a nagging doubt about the robustness of the finding. Just as different poverty and inequality measures can give opposing ordinal judgments, the conclusion that one situation has better mobility than another may hinge on the choice of a particular mobility measure. In what follows, I will work solely with directional income movement. But even given that restriction, if I switch from one measure of directional income movement to another, there are conditions under which different measures will give very different conclusions. However, in other circumstances, one can determine that the same qualitative conclusion holds for a broad class of specific directional movement measures.

The technique I shall use is the familiar criterion of stochastic dominance, applied to directional income movements.[27] Suppose for now that

27. On stochastic dominance, see Hadar and Russell (1969).

Figure 5-3. *Directional Income Movement in Two Chinese Provinces,*
1978–89

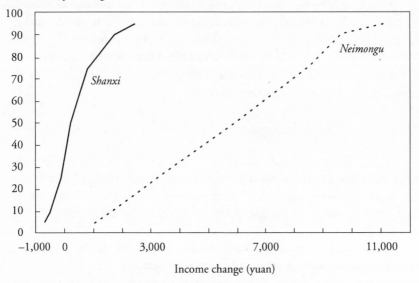

Cumulative percentage

Income change (yuan)

Source: Survey conducted by Chinese Academy of Preventive Medicine.

the measure of income movement is the individual's income change (measured, as always, in terms of real dollars). The population is then arrayed
from most negative income change to most positive. What is needed for
stochastic dominance analysis of income changes is the fraction of people
experiencing income changes less than each possible amount. One distribution of income changes is said to stochastically dominate another if the
percentage of people below any given income change amount is smaller in
the first situation than in the second, or equivalently, if the income change
cutoff for each given percentage grouping is higher in one distribution
than another. Graphically, this means that a better distribution (better in
the sense of stochastic dominance) is one that lies everywhere below or to
the right of another. (One can look at it either way.)

Figure 5-3 shows the distribution of income changes in two provinces
of China over an eleven-year period.[28] Neimongu registered rapid economic

28. The data for these results come from a survey conducted by the Chinese Academy of Preventive
Medicine, and were provided to the author by Professor Victor Nee.

Figure 5-4. *Distribution of Directional Income Movement in the United States, 1970s and 1980s*

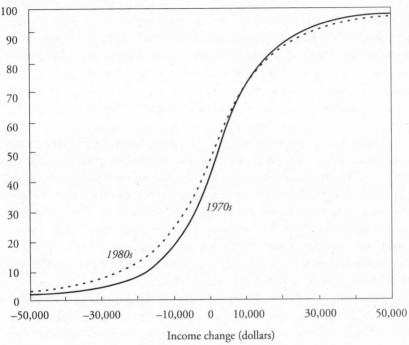

Cumulative percentage

Income change (dollars)

Source: Author's calculations based on data from U.S. Panel Study of Income Dynamics.

growth, while Shanxi suffered an economic decline. The distribution of income changes in Neimongu stochastically dominates the income changes in Shanxi. In this sense economic growth may be said to have brought about a distribution of income changes that was better in Neimongu than in Shanxi.

When two directional income movement distributions are plotted, it is possible that neither dominates the other. This possibility is shown to be a reality in the crossing curves in figure 5-4. These data pertain to directional movement distributions for the United States in the 1970s and the 1980s using the same PSID data described earlier. The 1970s distribution dominates at the lower end of the change distribution, while the 1980s distribution dominates at the upper end. This means that in the 1980s more people lost more dollars than in the 1970s, but those who gained the most in fact gained more dollars in the 1980s than in the 1970s.

Included in the preceding calculation is the judgment that income changes are most appropriately gauged in dollars of income movement. You may not like this practice of measuring income changes independently of base income amounts. For example, suppose that you gain $1,000 of income and I lose $1,000, but your income was twice as high as mine to start with. Your $1,000 income gain is only half as large in percentage terms as my $1,000 income loss. To assign a smaller absolute value change to your income gain as compared with my income loss, we might do as above and measure not changes in income but rather changes in log income for each person in the sample and then test for stochastic dominance between the log-income differences.

This is done in figure 5-5 for the PSID data. When log dollars are used rather than dollars, it is still the case that the distribution of income changes for the 1970s dominates the 1980s distribution for the smallest 90 percent of income changes. However, for the largest 10 percent of income changes, the two curves come together and effectively coincide the rest of the way. No crossing arises, and there is therefore a dominance result. Thus, when directional income movements are measured in log-dollar changes rather than dollar changes, the 1980s distribution of income movements is found to be dominated by the 1970s distribution.

This completes the presentation of the five different classes of mobility measures. We turn now to a comparison of them. First, we shall see how they differ in certain prototypic situations. Then, with that as the base we shall explore the axiomatic foundations of the different approaches.

Different Mobility Concepts in Certain Stylized Examples

Let x_i represent the base-year income of the ith individual, and let x be the vector of x_i's arrayed in some order, which without loss of generality, we will take to be in increasing order. Let y_i be the final-year income of the ith individual and y the vector of y_i's with individuals arrayed in the same order as they were in the x distribution. Then let $x \to y$ denote individual 1's income going from x_1 to y_1, individual 2's income going from x_2 to y_2, and so on.

Let us now examine how mobility changes in some stylized situations.

Example One: Constant Incomes
Suppose that over time, income remains constant for every single person in society. All of the mobility concepts considered above agree on one thing: when $x \to x$, there is no mobility.

Figure 5-5. *Distribution of Directional Income Movement in the United States in Log Dollars*

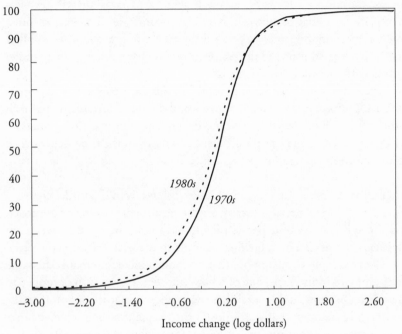

Cumulative percentage

1980s

1970s

Income change (log dollars)

Source: Author's calculations based on data from U.S. Panel Study of Income Dynamics.

Actually, this is the *only* case in which all of the different approaches agree. The differences between them in other cases can be elucidated by means of some other equally simple examples.

Example Two: A Rank-Preserving Equalization

Starting with a given income distribution *x*, let all incomes but two remain the same between base year and final year. For the two that change, let one person transfer a given sum of money to the other, such that their positions remain the same. (Whichever aspect of position is of interest—rank, decile, or quintile—hold that constant when the transfer is made.) What can be said about mobility?

—By the positional movement approach, there is no mobility, because nobody's position has changed.

—By the share movement approach, there is mobility, because the donor's income share shrank and the recipient's income share expanded.

—For the time-dependence approach, it matters what you measure. If you use the correlation coefficient on disaggregated data, you will get a less than perfect correlation between base year income and final year income, and therefore mobility takes place. However, using a quantile mobility matrix, both the donor and the recipient experience no change in quantile, and therefore no mobility takes place.

These differing judgments rendered in this example show two things. One, the positional movement approach and the share movement approach differ from each other. Two, the time-dependence approach implemented on aggregated data may give a different answer from the time-dependence approach implemented on disaggregated data.

Example Three: A Change in Ranks within Given Quantiles

In both of the previous examples the positional movement approach and the aggregate time-dependence approach gave the same answer. Can these ever disagree? The following example shows that the answer is yes.

As in example two, suppose that everyone's income remains the same except for two individuals, one of whom transfers a given sum of money to the other. But now, unlike example two, suppose that the amount transferred is large enough that the donor or the recipient or both change ranks in the income distribution (and of course, those whom they overtake change ranks as well). However, let these changes be small enough so that both donor and recipient remain in the same quantile (decile, quintile, and so on) of the income distribution.

Because the ranks have changed, there is positive positional movement. Yet because everyone remains in the same quantile as before, the quantile mobility matrix is an identity matrix, and therefore mobility is zero.

In this example the discrepancy arises for practical reasons as opposed to conceptual ones. If we had constructed an $N \times N$ transition matrix rather than a 10×10 or a 5×5 matrix, we would have seen positive mobility. It is because we do not do this in practice that no mobility is observed.

Example Four: Proportionate Income Change

Consider two different situations. In situation one, everyone's income is unchanged, so $x \rightarrow x$. In situation two, everyone's income becomes the same nonzero multiple of base year income λ, $\lambda > 0$, which is written as

$x \rightarrow \lambda x$. How do the mobilities in $x \rightarrow x$ and $x \rightarrow \lambda x$, $\lambda \neq 1$ compare with each other?

It turns out to make a stunning difference which approach is adopted.

—By the time-dependence approach, $x \rightarrow x$ and $x \rightarrow \lambda x$ have the same mobility as each other—none.

—By the positional movement approach, $x \rightarrow x$ and $x \rightarrow \lambda x$ have the same mobility—none.

—By the share movement approach, $x \rightarrow x$ and $x \rightarrow \lambda x$ have the same mobility as each other—none.

—By the symmetric income movement approach, $x \rightarrow x$ and $x \rightarrow \lambda x$ have different mobilities. The first, $x \rightarrow x$, has no mobility. The second, $x \rightarrow \lambda x$, has positive mobility. Furthermore, the more different λ is from 1, the more mobility there is.

—By the directional income movement approach, $x \rightarrow x$ and $x \rightarrow \lambda x$ have different mobilities. The first, $x \rightarrow x$, has no mobility. The second, $x \rightarrow \lambda x$, has nonzero mobility. The mobility that there is is positive if $\lambda > 1$ and negative if $\lambda < 1$. Furthermore, the further λ is from 1, the more mobility there is.

These examples show clearly that the income movement approaches are fundamentally different from the others. This is because the income movement approaches say that income mobility takes place whenever someone's real income changes. Furthermore, the larger these income changes in absolute value, the more income movement there has been. The other approaches characterize movement differently.

Example Five: All Incomes Change by a Constant Dollar Amount

Suppose that everyone experiences an income change of $\$\alpha$, $\alpha \neq 0$, which is written as $x \rightarrow x + \alpha$. As was the case in example four, the different mobility approaches give very different answers.

—By the time-dependence approach, $x \rightarrow x + \alpha$ may or may not exhibit mobility: it depends on how time dependence is measured.

—Because no one's position in the income distribution changes, by the positional movement approach, $x \rightarrow x + \alpha$ has no mobility.

—Because the income shares of those below the mean expand and those above the mean contract, by the share movement approach, $x \rightarrow x + \alpha$ has positive mobility.

—Income movement approaches, whether directional or nondirectional, will say that $x \rightarrow x + \alpha$ exhibits positive mobility. Furthermore, the larger α is, the more mobility there is.

Example Six : Manna from Heaven

According to the biblical story, when the Israelites were starving in the desert, a food called manna dropped from the sky. When manna drops from heaven on some people's houses but not on others', those who get the manna enjoy a gain in income, a gain in income share, and possibly a gain in position. Those who do not get the manna have no change in income, a loss in income share, and possibly a loss in position. What do you want to say about the mobility experiences of nonrecipients in such a case? If your view is that they experienced downward mobility, you are a thoroughgoing relativist. At minimum you are a share-movement adherent, and you may be a positional movement adherent as well. But if, in your judgment, those who received no manna had no mobility, the share-movement and positional movement approaches are not for you, and the income movement approach may be more suitable.

Mobility Measures and Axioms

The previous section showed that it makes a difference in theory which approach is used to gauge mobility because the different approaches make fundamentally different judgments about certain key aspects of mobility. This implies that when you choose a mobility concept and a measure of it to take to data, you will want to be sure that it captures what for you is the right approach. We now study the crucial distinctions among the various measures.

Some Mobility Measures

Formally, an income mobility measure is a function $m(x, y)$ defined on the domain of vectors $x = (x_1\, x_2 \ldots x_n)$ and final year incomes $y = (y_1\, y_2 \ldots y_n)$ such that the ith income recipient occupies the same position in the two distributions.[29] There are a great many mobility measures. Among them are the following.

—The correlation coefficient between x and y.

—The rank correlation coefficient, that is, the correlation between income recipients' ranks in distribution x and distribution y.

29. Other mobility measures are defined for the case when there are T years of data to be used.

—The quantile immobility ratio, defined as the fraction of income recipients who remain in the same quintile, decile, or ventile of the income distribution (also called the trace).

—Shorrocks's rigidity index, defined in the two-period case as

$$R \equiv \frac{I(x+y)}{[\mu_x I(x) + \mu_y I(y)] / (\mu_x + \mu_y)} \text{,}$$

where $I(\,.\,)$ is a particular scale-invariant inequality index.

—Fields and Ok's log-dollar per capita measure,

(5-6a) $$m^{(2)}_n(x, y) = \frac{1}{n} \sum_{j=1}^{n} \left| \log x_i - \log y_i \right| .$$

—Fields and Ok's dollar per capita measure,

(5-6b) $$m^{(1)}_n(x, y) = \frac{1}{n} \sum_{j=1}^{n} \left| x_i - y_i \right| .$$

Table 5-2 summarizes the performance of these six measures in the examples. Some noteworthy differences appear. First, when a rank-preserving equalization of income takes place, the rank correlation coefficient is unchanged. Thus, the rank correlation is a measure of positional movement. Second, when people change ranks within given quantiles, the quantile immobility ratio is unchanged. This too is a measure of positional movement, but the positions here are broad groups rather than individual ranks. Third, when all incomes change proportionately, only the Fields-Ok measures declare that mobility has taken place. In this sense the Fields-Ok indices measure income movement in ways that the other indices do not. Fourth, when all incomes change by a constant dollar amount, the Fields-Ok indices capture that movement. Shorrocks's rigidity index changes too, because relative inequality is changed by a uniform increase or decrease in everybody's income. Finally, when manna drops from heaven, the various measures behave very differently. Because incomes change, the two Fields-Ok measures indicate that there was mobility. The rank correlation and quantile immobility ratio register mobility if and only if people change ranks or

Table 5-2. *Mobility in Some Prototypic Situations*[a]

	Mobility if all incomes are unchanged	Mobility if a rank-preserving equalization takes place	Mobility if some people change ranks within given quantiles	Mobility if all incomes change proportionately	Mobility if all incomes change by a constant dollar amount	Mobility if some people gain income, others do not
Correlation coefficient between income in year t and $t + 1$	No	Yes	Yes	No	No	Yes
Rank correlation coefficient between income ranks in year t and $t + 1$	No	No	Yes	No	No	Yes, if and only if someone changes rank
Quantile immobility ratio (quintile, decile, or ventile)	No	Yes, if and only if someone changes quantile	No	No	No	Yes, if and only if someone changes quantile
Shorrocks's rigidity index, two-period case	No	Yes	Yes	No	Yes	Yes
Fields and Ok's log-dollar measure	No	Yes	Yes	Yes	Yes	Yes
Fields and Ok's dollar measure	No	Yes	Yes	Yes	Yes	Yes

a. All measures are defined in the text.

quantiles. The correlation coefficient and Shorrocks's rigidity index will signal mobility because of the nonuniformity of the income changes.

These differences in behavior among the measures highlight their fundamental differences. The two Fields-Ok measures are income-movement measures. The rank correlation coefficient and quantile immobility ratio are measures of positional movement. Shorrocks's R is a measure of share movement. Finally, the correlation coefficient is a measure both of share movement and origin independence. These distinctions will be useful to keep in mind when you decide how best to measure mobility given your conception of what income mobility is.

Axiomatic Foundations

The axiomatic approach to mobility measurement has been developed by a number of authors.[30] The axiomatic foundations of the different measures may be compared and contrasted.

The earlier discussion exhibited one element of commonality: when everyone's income is unchanged, there is no mobility. Anthony Shorrocks (1993) suggested a normalization axiom whereby mobility is at a minimum when all incomes are unchanged, and earlier suggested that a mobility measure should range from zero to one. Combined, these imply that when all incomes are unchanged, mobility is zero, which can be written as the *normalization axiom*: $m(x, x) = 0$. This axiom is hardly controversial: all the mobility measures presented in this chapter satisfy it, as do all others that I know about.

It is also essential to specify how mobility changes when people's incomes change. I consider four concepts.

The first concept is level sensitivity. By the normalization axiom, when everyone's income remains the same, there is no mobility. Such a situation can be thought of as fulfilling two conditions: income shares are maintained and the income level is maintained. Now keep just one of these: keep everyone's income share the same but change the income level. In some mobility conceptions, there is no mobility in such a case. Such a conception can be defined formally as the

normalized level-insensitivity axiom: $m(x, \lambda x) = m(x, x) = 0$ for all $\lambda > 0$.

---

30. It was pioneered by Shorrocks (1978) and continued by King (1983); Cowell (1985); Chakravarty, Dutta, and Weymark (1985); Shorrocks (1993); Fields and Ok (1996, forthcoming); and Mitra and Ok (1998).

Note carefully what this implies: not only is there no mobility in $(1, 2, 3) \rightarrow (1, 2, 3)$ but there is no mobility either in $(1, 2, 3) \rightarrow (2, 4, 6)$. Let us call the measures that fulfill this axiom the (normalized) level-insensitive measures.

A second concept is relativity. A mobility concept is defined to be relative if multiplying everyone's base year and final year income by the same positive scalar leaves mobility unchanged:

relativity axiom: $m(\lambda x, \lambda y) = m(x, y)$ for all $\lambda > 0$.

If you accept the relativity axiom, you are obligated to say that there is the same degree of mobility in the situation $(1, 2, 3) \rightarrow (2, 4, 6)$ as there is in the situation $(2, 4, 6) \rightarrow (4, 8, 12)$, and likewise the situation $(1, 2, 3) \rightarrow (6, 4, 2)$ has the same mobility as the situation $(2, 4, 6) \rightarrow (12, 8, 4)$.

The third concept is what has been called intertemporal scale invariance, although I prefer to call it strong relativity. If you think of mobility as a function of income shares, you can convert the vectors x and y to their corresponding share equivalents by multiplying x by $1/\mu_x$ and y by $1/\mu_y$, obtaining $s_x = x/\mu_x$ and $s_y = y/\mu_y$. You can then define your mobility measure as a function of these shares: $m(s_x, s_y)$. Now, if two different x, y pairs x^1, y^1 and x^2, y^2 have the same s_x, s_y vectors, then $m(x^1, y^1) = m(x^2, y^2)$. More generally, if you choose any multiple $\gamma > 0$ of base year income and any other multiple $\lambda > 0$ of final year income and judge that mobility is necessarily the same in going from γx to λy as in going from x to y, you have a strongly relative mobility notion, $m(\gamma x, \lambda y) = m(x, y)$ for all $\gamma, \lambda > 0$. Combining strong relativity with the normalization axiom produces:

normalized strong relativity: $m(\gamma x, \lambda y) = m(x, y) = 0$ for all $\gamma, \lambda > 0$.

Measures possessing the normalized strong relativity property work in a particular way. To illustrate, take the following mobility situations: $(1, 2, 3) \rightarrow (2, 4, 6)$ and $(1, 2, 3) \rightarrow (3, 6, 9)$. Strongly relative measures would say that these have the same mobility as each other; normalized strongly relative measures would say that the common amount of mobility they both have is zero.

The final concept is translation invariance. If a given amount α is added to or subtracted from everybody's base year and final year income, a translation-invariant mobility measure would declare the new situation to be as mobile as the original one:

translation-invariance axiom: $m(x + \alpha, y + \alpha) = m(x, y)$ for all $\alpha > 0$.

So for example, the situation $(1, 2, 3) \to (2, 4, 6)$ would have the same mobility as the situation $(2, 3, 4) \to (3, 5, 7)$, and so too would $(0, 1, 2) \to (1, 3, 5)$.

These examples bear careful examination. They will help you decide whether you want to use a measure that is level insensitive, relative, strongly relative, or translation invariant. The choice depends, of course, on what you yourself understand the very concept of mobility to be.

Which Mobility Measures Satisfy Which Axioms?

Before choosing a mobility measure to take to data, you will want to know which measures satisfy which properties. Table 5-3 shows this. You are free to choose measures satisfying all four of the preceding normalized axioms, just three, just two, or just one.

Table 5-3 also deals with a technical point. It is obvious that (normalized) level insensitivity, $m(\lambda x, x) = m(x, x) = 0$ for all $\lambda > 0$, is a special case of (normalized) strong relativity, $m(\gamma x, \lambda y) = m(x, y) = 0$ for all $\gamma, \lambda > 0$. For this axiom to be interesting, there must exist a reasonable mobility measure that is level insensitive but is not strongly relative. As shown in table 5-3, Shorrocks's R is precisely such a measure. This means that one is free to make independent choices among these different concepts and measures.

Finally, note that several mobility measures are both relative (in the sense of both relativity and strong relativity) and absolute (in the sense of translation invariance). This contrasts with the case of inequality measures, which may be relative or absolute but not both.[31]

Conclusions

This chapter began by emphasizing that income mobility is a generic concept connoting a wide range of ideas. Five such concepts were time dependence, positional movement, share movement, nondirectional income movement, and directional income movement.

I then went on to consider what these different mobility concepts would produce in certain simple examples. Only when everyone's income stays

31. Eichhorn and Gehrig (1982).

Table 5-3. *Properties of Some Two-Period Mobility Measures*[a]

Properties	Normalization $m(x, x) = 0$	Level insensitivity $m(x, \lambda x) = m(x, x)$	Relativity $m(\lambda x, \lambda y) = m(x, y)$	Strong relativity $m(\gamma x, \lambda y) = m(x, y)$	Translation invariance $m(x + \alpha, y + \alpha) = m(x, y)$
Correlation coefficient between income in year t and $t + 1$	Yes	Yes	Yes	Yes	Yes
Rank correlation coefficient between income ranks in year t and $t + 1$	Yes	Yes	Yes	Yes	Yes
Quantile immobility ratio (quintile, decile, or ventile)	Yes	Yes	Yes	Yes	Yes
Shorrocks's rigidity index, two-period case	Yes	Yes	Yes	No	No
Fields and Ok's log-dollar measure	Yes	No	Yes	No	No
Fields and Ok's dollar measure	Yes	No	No	No	Yes

a. All measures are defined in the text.

the same do they all give the same answer. In other cases they give different answers because they are measuring in light of fundamentally different concepts.

The next section compared measures and axioms. The correlation coefficient, it showed, is a measure of both share movement and time independence, Shorrocks's R is a measure of share movement, the rank correlation coefficient and quantile immobility ratio are measures of positional movement, and the Fields-Ok indices are measures of income movement. I also considered several possible axioms for income mobility, including axioms for normalization, level insensitivity, relativity, strong relativity, and translation invariance and showed that different mobility measures satisfy these different axioms.

The results of this chapter show that how mobility is conceived and how it is measured make an important difference.

References

Atkinson, Anthony B., François Bourguignon, and Christian Morrisson. 1992. *Empirical Studies of Earnings Mobility*. Chur, Switzerland: Harwood Academic.

Bartholomew, David J. 1982. *Stochastic Models for Social Processes*. Wiley.

Burkhauser, Richard V., Douglas Holtz-Eakin, and Stephen E. Rhody. 1997. "Labor Earnings Mobility and Inequality in the United States and Germany during the Growth Years of the 1980s." *International Economic Review* 38 (4): 775–94.

Chakravarty, John Satya, Bhaskar Dutta, and John A. Weymark. 1985. "Ethical Indices of Income Mobility." *Social Choice and Welfare* 2 (1): 1–21.

Cowell, Frank A. 1985. "Measures of Distributional Change: An Axiomatic Approach." *Review of Economic Studies* 52 (1): 135–51.

Danziger, Sheldon, and Peter Gottschalk. 1995. *America Unequal*. Russell Sage Foundation.

Eichhorn, W., and W. Gehrig. 1982. "Measurement of Inequality in Economics." In Bernhard H. Korte, ed., *Modern Applied Mathematics: Optimization and Operations Research*, pp. 658–93. Amsterdam: North Holland.

Fields, Gary S., and Efe A. Ok. 1996. "The Meaning and Measurement of Income Mobility." *Journal of Economic Theory* 71 (2): 349–77.

Fields, Gary S., and Efe A. Ok. Forthcoming. "Measuring Movement of Incomes." *Economica*.

Fields, Gary S., Jesse B. Leary, and Efe A. Ok. 1998. "Income Movement in the United States in the Seventies and Eighties." Working Paper. Cornell University and New York University.

Friedman, Milton, and Simon Kuznets. 1954. *Income for Independent Professional Practice*. New York: National Bureau of Economic Research.

Gottschalk, Peter, and Robert Moffitt. 1994. "The Growth of Earnings Instability in the U.S. Labor Market." *Brookings Papers on Economic Activity* 2: 217–72.

Hadar, Josef, and William R. Russell. 1969. "Rules for Ordering Uncertain Prospects." *American Economic Review* 59 (March): 25–34.

Hungerford, Thomas L. 1993. "U.S. Income Mobility in the Seventies and Eighties." *Review of Income and Wealth* 39 (4): 403–17.

Jarvis, Sarah, and Stephen P. Jenkins. 1996. "Changing Places: Income Mobility and Poverty Dynamics in Britain." Working Paper 96-19. Colchester: ESCR Research Centre on Micro-Social Change, University of Essex.

———.1998. "How Much Income Mobility Is There in Britain?" *Economic Journal* 108 (447): 428–43.

King, Mervyn A. 1983. "An Index of Inequality: With Applications to Horizontal Equity and Social Mobility." *Econometrica* 51 (1): 99–115.

McMurrer, Daniel P., and Isabel V. Sawhill. 1998. *Getting Ahead: Economic and Social Mobility in America*. Washington: Urban Institute Press.

Markandya, Anil. 1984. "The Welfare Measurement of Changes in Economic Mobility." *Economica* 51 (204): 457–71.

Mitra, Tapan, and Efe A. Ok. 1998. "The Measurement of Income Mobility: A Partial Ordering Approach." *Economic Theory* 12 (1): 77–102.

Moffitt, Robert A., and Peter Gottschalk. 1995. "Trends in the Autocovariance Structure of Earnings in the U.S.: 1969–1987." Johns Hopkins University and Boston University.

Organization for Economic Cooperation and Development. 1996. "Earnings Inequality, Low-Paid Employment and Earnings Mobility." *Employment Outlook* (July): 59–108.

———. 1997. "Earnings Mobility: Taking a Longer Run View." *Employment Outlook* (July): 27–62.

Sawhill, Isabel V., and Mark Condon. 1992. "Is U.S. Income Inequality Really Growing?" *Policy Bites 13*. Urban Institute.

Shorrocks, Anthony F. 1978. "The Measurement of Mobility." *Econometrica* 46 (5): 1013–24.

———. 1993. "On the Hart Measure of Income Mobility." In M. Casson and J. Creedy, eds., *Industrial Concentration and Economic Inequality*, pp. 3–21. Brookfield, Vt.: Edward Elgar.

PART III

Economics and Opportunity

JERE R. BEHRMAN
NANCY BIRDSALL
MIGUEL SZÉKELY

6

Intergenerational Mobility in Latin America: Deeper Markets and Better Schools Make a Difference

The effects of market and policy reforms on poverty and income inequality in Latin America and the Caribbean have been a topic of considerable recent discussion. Agreement is increasing that these reforms have had some effects in reversing poverty increases due to economic crises in most countries in the region in the 1980s. At a minimum it is clear that the poor fared worse in the countries that delayed reform the longest. Agreement is less uniform regarding the effects of reform on income distribution. Some recent studies suggest that reforms have halted and perhaps reversed trends toward increasing inequality, while others are less optimistic.[1] In any case the region continues to have relatively great income inequalities in comparison with other major regions, and it is unlikely that there will be radical changes in these inequali-

Nancy Birdsall worked on this paper primarily when she was the executive vice president of the Inter-American Development Bank but also in her current position as senior associate, Carnegie Endowment for International Peace. Jere Behrman collaborated in this paper as a consultant to the Inter-American Development Bank. The authors thank Paul Glewwe, Ricardo Hausmann, Gary Burtless, and other participants in the Brookings Institution Center on Social and Economic Dynamics/Inter-American Development Bank Workshop on Social Mobility for useful comments on the first draft of this chapter. Only the authors are responsible for the content of the chapter.
    1. Recent studies include Berry (1997); Londoño and Székely (1997a, 1979b); Lustig and Székely (1997); Morley (1994); and Psacharopoulos and others (1992).

135

ties very soon.[2] Some commentators suggest that the inequalities may make the sustainability of reforms very difficult, particularly in light of heightened public expectations of benefits from postreform growth within the more democratic political contexts of most Latin American countries.[3]

But income inequality measurements in cross-sectional data are snapshots at a point of time. In practice, income distributions change over time under the effect of various transition mechanisms. The mechanisms may affect social welfare by changing the shape of the spot income distributions captured in the usual snapshots. Two societies with the same snapshots of income distribution at a given time may have different levels of social welfare because they have different degrees of social mobility. For example, Milton Friedman argued that a given extent of income inequality in a rigid system in which each family stays in the same position in each period may be more a cause for concern than if the same degree of income inequality caused great mobility and dynamic change associated with equality of opportunity.[4] Similarly, Nancy Birdsall and Carol Graham have contended that to assess the impact of market reforms in the region and their probable sustainability, including political support for them, it is essential to characterize the extent of social mobility both across and within generations and whether such mobility has been affected by the recent reforms.[5] However, little attention has been paid to measuring social mobility and changes in such mobility in Latin America and how such changes may be related to economic and social conditions and policies.

Schooling is thought to be a major mechanism through which intergenerational social mobility is affected.[6] If schooling has great impact on income and is strongly affected by family background, intergenerational correlations in incomes across families will be high and social mobility as measured by intergenerational relative income changes will be low. If family background is only a minor factor in determining schooling, however, intergenerational social mobility as indicated by relative intergenerational income movements may be high.

2. For example, Deininger and Squire (1996).
3. For example, Berry (1997); and Schemo (1998).
4. Friedman (1962).
5. Birdsall and Graham (1998). See also chapter 1 in this volume.
6. See for example chapter 2. See chapter 4 for a review of concepts and measurements of social mobility. Birdsall and Londoño (1997) emphasize the relevance of the distribution of adults' schooling as an asset that affects not only the distribution of household income but, by influencing household demand for schooling, affects the next generation's schooling.

In this chapter we explore the strength of the association of family background with child schooling and whether this strength is related to some economic and education indicators. Of course, there are many previous studies of associations between family background and schooling of children.[7] These studies almost always find significant associations of child schooling with mothers' and fathers' schooling, with the former about 10 percent more important than the latter at the median of estimates that include both. In about three-fifths of the cases the studies find significant associations with household income or some major component of household income.

But most of the studies are for one sample in a particular country at a particular time. And no previous studies to our knowledge explore how the association of family background with child schooling varies across countries and over time as a function of overall economic conditions and past and current policies. This is what we attempt.

In the next section we summarize some standard arguments about why family background is likely to be associated with schooling and how that association can depend on market reforms and other aspects of policy such as public resources devoted to schooling. In the section on family background we describe child schooling differentials overall and across parental schooling quintiles and child age groups. We also characterize the empirical association of family background, as represented by household income, father's schooling, and mother's schooling, with schooling for children aged 10–21 in Latin America. The description is based on microeconomic data in twenty-eight household surveys from twenty-eight countries for 1980–96. Estimates are made of the associations between the schooling gap—measured as expected schooling (the number of years of school an individual would have if he or she entered school at age 6 and advanced one grade every year) minus the number of years of school that the individual actually has—and family background for each parental schooling quintile for each of four age groups for each of these 28 surveys ($5 \times 4 \times 28 = 560$ sets of estimates).[8] In the subsequent section the extent of intergenerational schooling mobility then is characterized by two indexes: (1) one minus the

7. Behrman (1997) surveys studies that estimate the association of a mother's schooling with child schooling, most of which also include the father's schooling. Behrman and Knowles (1999) review studies of the association of household income (or major components thereof) and child schooling.

8. Because of the small sample size for the subsample for children aged 13–15 in the fifth quintile for the Argentinean 1996 survey, we have 559 sets of estimates.

share of the total variance in the schooling gap for each of these surveys/ quintiles/age groups that is explained by the three variables that we use to represent family background ("proportional intergenerational schooling mobility index") and (2) the product of the first index and the average size of the schooling gap relative to expected schooling in each subsample ("gap-adjusted intergenerational schooling mobility index").[9] We then explore to what extent these intergenerational mobility indexes are associated with basic economic and education indicators for the relevant countries in the relevant time periods. Finally, we draw some conclusions.

Framework for Analysis of the Association between Schooling and Family Background

Gary Becker's 1967 Woytinsky lecture on the determinants of human capital investments is a useful starting point.[10] Within this framework schooling (and other human capital) investments are made until the private marginal benefit of the investment equals the private marginal cost of the investment. Figure 6-1 provides an illustration for one person. The marginal private benefit curve depends on the expected private gains (for example, in wages and salaries in labor markets) due to human capital investment. The curve slopes downward because of diminishing returns to human capital investments.[11] The marginal private cost increases with human resource investments because of the increasing opportunity costs of more time devoted to such investments and because of the increasing marginal private costs of borrowing on financial markets. (If such markets do not easily permit borrowing for such purposes, at some point the marginal private cost curve may become very steep or even vertical.) For a human

9. Both of these indexes are normalized so that their ranges are from 0 to 100 and so that increasing values imply greater intergenerational schooling mobility.

10. Becker (1967). There are numerous other models of how human resource investments in children are made within families (for example Becker 1975, 1991; Behrman, Pollak, and Taubman 1982, 1995; and Mulligan 1997), but a modified version of Becker's Woytinsky lecture serves to communicate the basic points in a simple manner.

11. Diminishing marginal returns might be expected (at least at sufficiently high investment levels) because of fixed genetic endowments (innate ability, for example) for a given person and because human capital investments such as schooling take time, so that greater investments imply greater lags before beginning to obtain the postinvestment returns and a shorter postinvestment period in which to reap the returns.

Figure 6-1. *Private Marginal Benefits and Private Marginal Costs of Human Resource Investments*

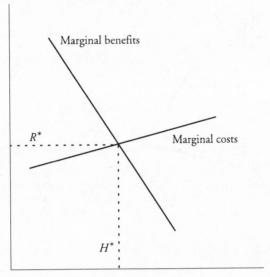

Marginal benefits, marginal costs

Marginal benefits

R^*

Marginal costs

H^*

Human resource investments

capital investment such as schooling, the private returns net of costs are maximized at level H˙.

If all markets function perfectly and schooling is an investment only (with neither consumption gains nor consumption losses), everyone invests in schooling until the expected rate of return equals the expected rate of return on alternative investments (at the level H* in figure 6-1) no matter what their family background. In this case the channels of any association between family background and schooling are virtually nonexistent.

Given real-world market imperfections, however, there are many reasons why there may be associations between family background and schooling, even if schooling is purely an investment. To illustrate, consider what happens if the marginal private benefits or the marginal private costs or both are associated with family background in the presence of market imperfections. (Because we use income and parental schooling to represent family background in our empirical estimates in the section on family background, we use these indicators of family background as concrete examples in our discussion here.)

Figure 6-2. *Private Marginal Benefits and Private Marginal Costs of Human Resource Investments, with Marginal Benefits Dependent on Income*

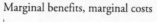

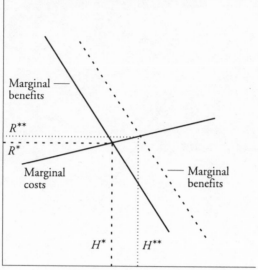

Human resource investments

Figure 6-2 illustrates the implications of the marginal private benefits for human capital being associated with family background, with two alternative curves indicated, each depending on a different family background. The dashed curve is drawn everywhere above the solid curve. For the two (otherwise identical) individuals, the private incentives are to invest at level H* or level H**, depending on family background. Figure 6-3 illustrates the implications of two different marginal cost curves, depending on family background, with the dashed line lower than the solid line. With the solid line the private incentives are to invest at level H*, which is less than the privately optimal level of human capital investment at level H*** if the dashed line is relevant.

We first consider why, given market imperfections, we could expect higher marginal private benefits and lower marginal private costs for higher-income households with better-educated parents. We then do the same for lower-income households with less educated parents. The first case would

Figure 6-3. *Private Marginal Benefits and Private Marginal Costs of Human Resource Investments, with Marginal Costs Dependent on Income*

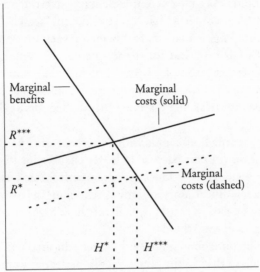

Human resource investments

yield the generally seen positive association between parents' and children's schooling; the second case could offset that association partly or entirely.

For the higher-income households, on the benefits side the considerations are the following.

1. Households may invest directly in children's education at home and through tutoring, or indirectly by improving their health and nutrition. If markets for these investments (or for financing these investments) are imperfect, and given that the costs of such investments—of helping with homework, for example—are likely to be lower for higher-income households with more educated parents, the marginal private benefits of schooling are likely to be greater for such households.

2. Children's genetic endowments may interact with schooling investments in producing education. If children's endowments are correlated with parental endowments that in turn are correlated with household income and with parental schooling because of direct effects of such endowments

on income and through parents' human capital stocks, including their education, the marginal private benefits of investing in schooling will be higher for higher-income and better-educated parents.[12]

3. Households may make complementary investments in searching for a job and have contacts that affect children's search for jobs after completing schooling. If markets for financing such investments are imperfect and the costs are less for higher-income households with more educated parents (for example, because of more attractive possibilities for working in family enterprises and better connections for other employment opportunities), the marginal private benefits again are greater for such households.

4. Higher-income households with better-educated parents may have better information (in part because of better chances for joining a family enterprise and better connections). Given imperfect markets for information, they face less uncertainty regarding schooling investment decisions and, holding risk aversion constant, therefore have higher marginal private benefits than poorer households.

5. Higher-income households with better-educated parents may have less risk aversion, so that, in the presence of imperfect insurance markets or simply insurance that has positive private costs, their private incentives are to invest more in schooling than otherwise identical lower-income households with less-educated parents.

6. Higher-income households with better-educated parents may have better means of dealing with stochastic events—for example, through their connections they may be more able than poorer households to offset a bad performance on admissions examinations by their children—and therefore have private incentives to invest more in schooling than otherwise identical lower-income households with less educated parents.

7. Higher-income households with better-educated parents may have lower discount rates and thus invest more generally, including in schooling, than lower-income households with less-educated parents.

8. Public policies may favor higher-income, better-educated households, providing more or better-quality schooling to such households in

12. Behrman, Rosenzweig, and Taubman (1994, 1996), using special twins data, present evidence that schooling investments respond positively to child genetic endowments. Behrman and Taubman (1989) present estimates that variations in such endowments are consistent with most of the variance in child schooling. The enormous literature on the associations between schooling of adults and their household earnings and income is surveyed in Psacharopoulos (1994) and Rosenzweig (1995).

response to their greater economic and political power.[13] François Bourguignon argues that as long as the rich invest more in education than the poor (see case 1), any improvement in the education system—particularly in the part of the system used primarily by those who are better off, such as higher education in most countries—will benefit the rich more than the poor.[14]

9. For higher-income households, on the cost side, there is the following consideration. Weak and imperfect capital markets mean that even creditworthy parents who are poor may have difficulty borrowing and will face higher costs of borrowing. This implies that the marginal private costs for such investments are higher for poorer parents and of course lower for higher-income parents. For poorer households without collateral, it may be impossible to borrow at all because current or future human capital is generally not recognized as collateral. Additionally, given their greater access to capital markets, higher-income parents may be more able to smooth out income shocks by borrowing, and their children will have greater chances of going through the education system without interruptions. Children of poorer parents may have to drop out of school when faced with a shock, which increases the cost of acquiring the same years of education without interruption.

However, it is also possible, though less intuitively obvious, for marginal private benefits to be higher for poorer, less educated parents, and marginal private costs to be lower.

For lower-income households, on the benefits side are the following:

1. Public policies may favor the poor. Many governments, even in the face of greater economic and political power of better-off households, favor poorer households as part of programs to reduce poverty and inequality by targeting school spending to poor households or by allocating additional education spending to basic education, which is more likely to favor the poor.

---

13. This case relates to endogenous policy choices (Rosenzweig and Wolpin, 1986) that, depending on the mechanism, can also favor lower-income households (as noted later). In the first through seventh cases and in the ninth case, higher-income, better-educated parents have private incentives to invest more in the schooling than do the parents of otherwise equal children from lower-income households because the higher-income households cope better with other market imperfections or because they have unobserved characteristics that increase investments and are associated with household income and parental schooling.

14. Bourguignon (1998).

For lower-income households on the cost side are the following:

2. Some governments or private providers of schooling exempt poorer households from paying school fees for children, lowering marginal costs for them.

3. The opportunity costs of attending school instead of participating in the labor market are likely to be lower for poorer households if, for example, children from better-off families have more or better alternatives because their families have more land for farming or own their own enterprises where children can work or the families are better connected with other employers.

Thus, within this simple framework, there are reasons originating in both market failures and policy choices for why family background in general and household income and parental schooling in particular may be related to the marginal private benefits and the marginal private costs of schooling investments, and thus to schooling investments themselves.[15]

Three points merit emphasis. First, because associations may have different signs, positive or negative, the total association may be positive or negative, and in any particular context there may be both positive and negative effects in part offsetting each other.

Second, the associations do not necessarily imply causality. For genetic endowments, preferences, and connections, for example, the associations with household income and parental schooling do not reflect causal effects but simply that these observed family background indicators are proxies for unobserved factors. For characterizing many aspects of intergenerational mobility, however, the basic question is one of association, so the limited degree to which inferences of causality might be made is not troublesome.

Third, these considerations also point to a link between the extent of association of family background and schooling on the one hand and the economic environment and education and other policies on the other hand. We return to this link and its implications later.

Family Background and Schooling Gaps in Latin America

We characterize the schooling gap for a child as the expected years of schooling, that is, the number of years the child would have completed had he or she entered at age 6 and advanced one grade each year, minus the

---

15. If schooling has consumption effects, moreover, they also may result in family background–schooling associations (with the sign depending on the nature of the consumption effects) in addition to any that exist because of the investment dimension of schooling.

number of years of schooling the child actually had completed at the time of the survey. We use twenty-eight household surveys from twenty-eight Latin American countries taken between 1980 and 1996. These include all the surveys that we have in usable form and that have the necessary variables for our analysis.[16] We consider schooling gaps separately for four age groups: 10–12, 13–15, 16–18, and 19–21 years old. We consider these age groups separately because family background is likely to matter more for older children.[17]

The decision to stay in or to leave school is likely also to depend on the position of a child's family within the economy. Therefore for each survey we also consider (for each age group) five quintiles of households categorized by parental schooling. Parental schooling represents an important component of permanent household income and may also represent such nonincome characteristics as genetic endowments and preferences regarding schooling. (Remember that we are interested in characterizing associations of child schooling with family background, not in identifying causal effects.)

Both child ages and parental schooling have the advantage of being characteristics that are not likely to be affected by recent macroeconomic conditions nor by the policy variables that we use for additional analysis in the next section.

Schooling Gaps

Table 6-1 gives the country and years for the household surveys that we use and, for each survey, the mean overall schooling gap, the average schooling gap as a percentage of the schooling expected with initiation of schooling at age 6 and promotion of one grade each year, and the mean schooling gap for each parental schooling quintile. The results, in summary, follow.[18]

---

16. See Duryea and Székely (1998) for a more detailed description of the data.

17. Another advantage of considering the age groups separately is that this lessens the risk of biases due to school continuation selectivity on unobserved ability. Cameron and Heckman (1998), for example, note that most of the studies on the effects of parental background on children's educational attainment conclude that the effect of family background declines after secondary schooling but claim that these estimates suffer from omitted ability bias because more able children normally progress farther in the education system, which affects the estimates of family background effects. We avoid this problem by subdividing the surveys by age groups in this section and by controlling for age groups in the estimates in the next section.

18. See Behrman, Birdsall, and Székely (1998) for a more complete description of these results.

Table 6-1. *Schooling Gaps as Percentage of Expected Schooling Conditional on Age for Ages 10–21 Overall and Schooling Gaps in Years Overall and by Parental Schooling Quintiles, by Country, Selected Years, 1980–96* [a]

		Average schooling gap		Schooling gaps in years, by parental schooling quintiles				
Country	Year	Years	Percent of expected schooling for age	1	2	3	4	5
Argentina (Greater	1980	2.0	19.2	3.4	2.2	2.1	1.5	0.6
Buenos Aires)	1996	2.5	27.2	3.1	2.2	1.9	1.2	1.4
Bolivia (urban)	1986	1.6	16.3	2.4	1.4	1.5	1.5	1.2
	1995	1.4	15.8	2.2	1.7	1.3	1.0	1.0
Brazil	1981	5.5	57.5	7.7	6.3	5.6	4.6	3.2
	1995	4.6	48.0	6.9	5.6	4.4	3.7	2.6
Chile	1987	1.7	17.4	2.9	2.0	1.4	1.3	0.9
	1994	1.5	14.7	2.3	1.9	1.3	1.1	0.8
Colombia	1995	3.3	36.8	4.7	3.5	2.9	2.6	2.7
Costa Rica	1981	3.2	30.2	4.6	3.7	3.0	2.6	1.9
	1995	3.1	30.6	4.6	3.6	3.2	2.6	1.7
Ecuador	1995	2.7	26.5	4.3	3.5	2.4	2.0	1.2
El Salvador	1995	4.1	43.1	6.0	5.4	4.1	3.1	1.7
Honduras	1989	5.2	50.9	6.8	5.8	4.9	4.6	3.6
	1996	4.7	45.2	6.3	5.4	4.7	3.9	3.0
Mexico	1984	3.4	37.5	4.7	3.7	3.3	3.1	2.3
	1989	3.1	33.7	4.8	3.3	2.7	2.4	2.2
	1992	2.9	32.7	4.6	3.5	2.5	2.3	1.6
	1994	2.9	32.9	4.6	3.5	2.7	2.0	1.9
Nicaragua	1993	4.6	44.9	5.7	5.2	4.6	4.2	3.5
Panama	1995	2.1	20.5	3.7	2.4	1.7	1.4	1.0
Paraguay	1995	3.5	36.3	5.0	4.2	3.3	2.7	2.2
Peru	1985	2.7	28.1	4.7	3.1	2.1	1.9	1.5
	1996	2.6	31.8	4.0	3.0	2.6	1.8	1.3
Uruguay (urban)	1981	2.3	23.4	3.6	2.9	2.3	1.7	1.2
	1995	2.0	18.9	3.2	2.5	2.0	1.5	1.0
Venezuela	1981	3.6	35.5	5.1	4.1	3.4	3.0	2.4
	1995	2.7	26.9	4.0	2.6	2.6	2.5	2.0
Average[b]	. . .	3.0	31.5	4.5	3.5	2.9	2.4	1.8

Source: Authors' calculations from household survey data. Household surveys for Bolivia and Uruguay are urban only and for Argentina are for Greater Buenos Aires only.

a. Schooling gap defined to be schooling that would have been attained at age when surveyed if child had begun schooling at age 6 and progressed one grade every subsequent year minus actual number of completed grades ("expected schooling").

b. Equally weighted country averages (not population weighted).

—The size of the schooling gap for the region as a whole is large. The average schooling gap across all surveys is 3.0 grades or 31.5 percent of the expected schooling, meaning that on the average a 16-year-old who would have completed 10 grades of schooling if he or she had started at age 6 and advanced one grade each subsequent year in fact had completed fewer than 7 grades.

—The gap ranges widely across countries. For recent years the largest gaps—of more than four years—are for Brazil, Honduras, and Nicaragua, which is consistent with data based on school enrollments collected by UNESCO. The smallest gap is for Chile (excluding Bolivia, where only urban households were covered).

—For most countries for which there is more than one survey, gaps narrowed between surveys during the intervening periods of up to 14 years. There are a few exceptions: in Mexico between 1992 and 1994 and in Argentina between 1980 and 1996 the gap widened.

—Within countries gaps tend to be larger the lower the income quintile. The average gaps across all twenty-eight surveys narrow in higher parental schooling quintiles, suggesting that family background is influential in determining the schooling gaps. The average gap across surveys for the first quintile is 4.5 grades, more than twice as large as the average across surveys for the fifth quintile, which is 1.8 grades.

—There is some tendency for countries with large average schooling gaps to have relatively larger gaps between the means for the first and the fifth parental schooling quintiles.

—For most countries for which there is more than one survey, the differences in the mean schooling gaps between the first and fifth parental schooling quintiles narrowed between surveys. So over time there has been a tendency toward equalization of children's schooling relative to parents' schooling.

Table 6-2 gives the mean schooling gaps for the four age groups. The gaps are larger for older age groups, consistent with human capital models that emphasize the advantage of obtaining a given level of education when as young as possible in order to have as long as possible a period after schooling in which to reap the returns. The differences in gaps by age vary across surveys, in general being larger than the average gap shown in table 6-1. All these findings are consistent with our expectations and with data from other sources. For most countries for which there is more than one survey, the difference in gaps between the oldest and the youngest groups decreased over time.

Table 6-2. *Schooling Gaps in Years for Age Groups 10–12, 13–15, 16–18, and 19–21, by Country, Selected Years, 1980–96* [a]

| Country | Year | Schooling gaps by age group | | | |
		10–12	13–15	16–18	19–21
Argentina (Greater	1980	0.7	1.2	2.3	3.9
Buenos Aires)	1996	1.4	2.8	2.0	3.9
Bolivia (urban)	1986	0.7	1.1	1.7	3.1
	1995	0.8	1.1	1.6	2.8
Brazil	1981	3.1	4.5	6.0	8.0
	1995	2.5	3.6	5.1	7.1
Chile	1987	0.5	1.1	2.1	3.8
	1994	0.5	0.9	1.7	3.2
Colombia	1995	2.2	2.7	3.5	5.3
Costa Rica	1981	1.1	1.8	3.7	6.0
	1995	1.3	1.9	3.4	5.7
Ecuador	1995	1.1	1.8	3.1	4.8
El Salvador	1995	2.3	3.2	4.6	6.3
Honduras	1989	2.5	3.6	5.7	8.0
	1996	2.0	3.2	5.2	7.6
Mexico	1984	1.8	2.6	3.9	6.5
	1989	1.7	2.3	3.5	5.5
	1992	1.6	2.3	3.4	5.4
	1994	1.6	2.2	3.5	5.6
Nicaragua	1993	2.0	3.2	5.1	7.4
Panama	1995	0.8	1.3	2.3	4.0
Paraguay	1995	1.7	2.5	3.9	6.1
Peru	1985	1.3	2.0	3.0	4.7
	1996	2.2	2.3	2.8	4.2
Uruguay (urban)	1981	0.9	1.6	2.6	4.4
	1995	0.7	1.2	2.2	3.8
Venezuela	1981	1.6	2.4	3.9	6.3
	1995	1.1	1.8	3.0	5.1
Average [b]	. . .	1.5	2.2	3.4	5.3

Source: Authors' calculations from household survey data. Household surveys for Bolivia and Uruguay are urban only and for Argentina are for Greater Buenos Aires only.

a. Schooling gap defined to be schooling that would have been attained at age when surveyed if child had begun schooling at age 6 and progressed one grade every subsequent year minus actual number of completed grades.

b. Equally weighted country averages (not population weighted).

Estimates of Association between Family Background and Schooling Gaps

How strongly are these schooling gaps associated with family background? To explore this question, we regress the schooling gap (*SGAP*) on three indicators of family background: father's schooling (S_f), mother's schooling (S_m), and household income (Y_h).[19] There are also two controls (*CON*, whether a household is rural or urban, and limited demographic characteristics of the household, for example, whether it is headed by a woman), and a stochastic disturbance term (*e*):

(1) $$SGAP = a_0 + a_1 S_f + a_2 S_m + a_3 Y_h + a_4 CON + e.$$

We estimate relation (1) for each of the 559 (28 × 5 × 4 – 1) survey-quintile age group subsamples.[20] We subdivide the surveys by quintiles and by age groups because: (a) we are particularly interested in the poorest households in the bottom quintile; (b) we anticipate that there may be nonlinearities in the associations between our indicators of family background and schooling gaps for each age group; (c) we anticipate that there are differences across age groups; and (d) this increases our sample size for the estimates of the relation between family background and survey-specific economic and social indicators to which we turn in the next section.

The first three columns of table 6-3 summarize the average values of the coefficient estimates for the three indicators of family background for each survey (averaged across quintiles and age groups), for each quintile (averaged across surveys and age groups), and for each age group (averaged across surveys and quintiles). To make the income units comparable across surveys, we transformed the survey incomes into 1985 U.S. dollars adjusted for purchasing power parity.[21]

The results of our estimations for the 559 subsamples are consistent with our expectations and with results of numerous studies in which a single sample is analyzed.[22] The coefficients of income are negative—increased income reduces the schooling gap—and are more negative the poorer

---

19. When the child for which the gap is measured earns an income, we subtract such income from the total household per capita income.

20. See note 8.

21. Adjustment factors were obtained from World Penn Tables, 1995, and from World Bank World Development Indicators, 1998.

22. The results are discussed in detail in Behrman, Birdsall, and Székely (1998).

Table 6-3. *Average Coefficient Estimates for Father's Schooling, Mother's Schooling, and Household Head's Income in Estimates for Schooling Gaps for Ages 10–21, by Surveys, Parental Schooling Quintiles, and Age Groups*[a]

		Average coefficient estimates		
Country	Year	Father's schooling	Mother's schooling	Household current income[b]
Argentina (Greater	1980	–0.084	–0.145	–6.51E–05
Buenos Aires)	1996	0.0459	0.386	–1.28E–04
Bolivia (urban)	1986	–0.100	–0.144	–1.27E–06
	1995	–0.090	–0.094	–1.13E–04
Brazil	1981	–0.171	–0.222	–2.35E–04
	1995	–0.214	–0.220	–2.01E–04
Chile	1987	–0.055	–0.082	–6.42E–05
	1994	–0.040	–0.071	–2.64E–05
Colombia	1995	–0.116	–0.203	–3.35E–05
Costa Rica	1981	–0.086	–0.152	–1.71E–04
	1995	–0.265	–0.261	–1.26E–04
Ecuador	1995	–0.110	–0.182	–5.02E–05
El Salvador	1995	–0.161	–0.192	–2.94E–04
Honduras	1989	–0.077	–0.179	–2.98E–04
	1996	–0.139	–0.299	–3.70E–04
Mexico	1984	–0.202	–0.212	–5.47E–05
	1989	–0.169	–0.195	–8.13E–05
	1992	–0.122	–0.210	–9.53E–05
	1994	–0.120	–0.144	–8.52E–05
Nicaragua	1993	–0.124	–0.184	–2.90E–04
Panama	1995	–0.070	–0.134	–1.18E–04
Paraguay	1995	–0.169	–0.221	–1.84E–04

the quintile and the older the child. The same pattern holds for mother's and father's education; the coefficient of the mother's education is on average more than three times larger for the richest compared with the poorest quintile.[23] The effects of differences in parents' education and income ex-

23. The absolute value of mothers' education tends to be higher in the subsamples than the value for fathers' education; this may simply reflect the fact that fathers' more than mothers' education is reflected in household income.

Table 6-3 *(continued)*

| Country | Year | Average coefficient estimates | | |
		Father's schooling	Mother's schooling	Household current income[b]
Peru	1985	–0.124	–0.094	–1.09E–04
	1996	–0.063	–0.106	–1.29E–04
Uruguay (urban)	1981	–0.028	–0.115	–1.08E–04
	1995	–0.083	–0.113	–1.00E–04
Venezuela	1981	–0.153	–0.204	–7.80E–05
	1995	–0.085	–0.143	–5.87E–05
Quintile				
1	. . .	–0.170	–0.214	–3.03E–04
2	. . .	–0.081	–0.149	–1.76E–04
3	. . .	–0.137	–0.197	–1.23E–04
4	. . .	–0.073	–0.115	–6.96E–05
5	. . .	–0.036	–0.062	–2.63E–05
Age group				
10–12	. . .	–0.065	–0.098	–8.98E–05
13–15	. . .	–0.105	–0.160	–1.35E–04
16–18	. . .	–0.115	–0.176	–2.12E–04
19–21	. . .	–0.210	–0.303	–2.61E–04
Overall average	. . .	–0.098	–0.148	–1.30E–04

Source: Author's estimations from household survey data.

a. Survey averages are averages across quintiles. Quintile and overall averages are averages across countries, with countries equally weighted.

b. Household incomes were transformed into PPP adjusted 1985 U.S. dollars to make the coefficients comparable across surveys.

plain considerable gaps within some countries. For example, for the lowest quintile and oldest age group in Brazil, at average education and household income for that group, the predicted total schooling gap is 6.8 years. This is sizable given that in the past three decades the average education of the labor force in the region increased by only 1.5 years.[24]

24. Inter-American Development Bank (1998).

Is Intergenerational Mobility Associated with Macroeconomic Conditions and Education Policy?

We turn now to the question of whether and how the association between family background and children's schooling, a measure of (im)mobility, is itself associated with the economic and social environment. Our first step is to construct indexes that capture the extent of the association. We then estimate an equation in which the indexes are associated with indicators of macroeconomic and education conditions.

Indexes of Mobility

We use the results of estimating equation 1 to construct for each of the 559 subsamples two basic intergenerational schooling mobility indexes: the proportional intergenerational schooling mobility index (the share of the total variance associated with the weighted average of the three family background variables, where the weights are the coefficient estimates) and the gap-adjusted intergenerational schooling mobility index, defined as the proportional index multiplied by the average gap relative to the expected schooling for that subsample.[25] We normalize each of these indexes so that they fall between 0 and 100 inclusively and so that increases within this range indicate greater intergenerational schooling mobility (and lesser influence of family background). The two indexes are positively correlated (with a correlation coefficient of 0.79) but represent somewhat different aspects of intergenerational mobility related to schooling. Our proportional intergenerational schooling mobility index is constructed to be invariant to the absolute magnitude of the average schooling gap. Urban Bolivia in 1986 and Honduras in 1989 have the same proportional intergenerational

---

25. We thus use the first three family background measures to represent variations in family background across households in each subsample. An alternative interpretation is that this relation represents an intergenerational adjustment toward equilibrium. If the schooling gap is expected schooling (S_e) minus schooling actually attained (S) and in equilibrium schooling is the same for the father, mother and child, relation 1 can be solved to obtain $S = (a_o - S_e + a_3 Y_b + a_4 CON + e)/(-1 - a_1 - a_2)$. The equilibrium value changes over time, of course, because the numerator is not constant. From this perspective the impact of family background on the equilibrium schooling can be viewed as $a_3 Y_b/(-1 - a_1 - a_2)$, which is an alternative way of characterizing the impact of family background on schooling. We do not explore this alternative in this chapter because in our judgment it would place undue emphasis on the role of current household income (the only common Y_b variable across the surveys that we use).

schooling mobility index (42.0). But the average schooling gaps from these two surveys differ substantially—1.6 grades and 5.2 grades, respectively. There is a sense, therefore, in which it can be argued that family background had a more important absolute effect on the schooling gap in Honduras in 1989 than in urban Bolivia in 1986 because the gap is so much larger in the former. Our gap-adjusted intergenerational schooling mobility index captures the fact that the absolute magnitude in terms of grades of schooling of the family background association with the gap is much larger for Honduras in 1989 than for urban Bolivia in 1986—at the averages for these two surveys, 53.7 versus 85.0—even though the proportional intergenerational schooling mobility index is identical for these two surveys.

We believe that the three family background variables reflected in our two indexes are likely to provide, if anything, an underestimate of the total effects of family background because they are correlated less than perfectly with some aspects of family background that may be relevant, such as long-run income or wealth, influence, and connections.[26]

The three variables turn out to be consistent with about a sixth of the sample variations across children in schooling gaps, across all age groups and all surveys (table 6-4, column 1).[27] They tend to be consistent with more of the variation for older age groups, when, as we have noted, family background is likely to be more important to the marginal decision to stay in or leave school.[28] They are consistent with less variation in the

---

26. Behrman and Knowles (1997) report, for example, that for a Vietnamese household survey the estimated impact of indicators of household income increases in magnitude an average of 50–60 percent if a permanent income measure is used instead of current income. Likewise, studies of intergenerational earnings and income correlations for the United States find correlations that are about twice as high if more permanent income measures are used rather than annual measures (Behrman and Taubman, 1990; Solon, 1992; and Zimmerman, 1992). We were not able to explore what would happen with a permanent income measure in the present study, however, because the information to construct such a measure is not available in most of the household surveys that we used. With regard to parental schooling, we are limited to years of completed schooling. But school quality also may have an effect on income, and school quality, while correlated with years of schooling, is far from perfectly correlated with it (see Behrman and Birdsall, 1983, for a study for Brazil). This again suggests that our representation of family background is partial. There are a number of studies, finally, that control for unobserved family endowments by using family or longitudinal data or both and find that there are effects of unobserved family background factors beyond the effects of observed family background such as parental schooling, income, and occupation (Behrman and others, 1980; Behrman and Wolfe, 1984; Pitt, Rosenzweig, and Hassan, 1990; Rosenzweig and Schultz, 1987; and Rosenzweig and Wolpin, 1995).

27. See Behrman, Birdsall, and Székely (1998) for a more complete description of the age-specific results.

28. The proportion of variance explained across age groups for each survey is shown in Behrman, Birdsall, and Székely (1998, p. 35).

Table 6-4. *Average Proportion of Variance Explained by Family Background Variables for Each Survey and Resulting Intergenerational Mobility Indices, by Surveys, Parental Schooling Quintiles, and Age Groups*[a]

| | | *Average proportion of variance explained by family background* | *Intergenerational mobility indexes*[b] | |
| | | | *Proportional mobility index* | *Gap-adjusted mobility index* |
Country	*Year*			
Argentina (Greater	1980	0.1653	8.6	73.1
Buenos Aires)	1996	0.1093	12.4	59.0
Bolivia (urban)	1986	0.0874	42	85.0
	1995	0.0967	80.2	95.0
Brazil	1981	0.2668	0.00	0.00
	1995	0.2773	27.2	34.5
Chile	1987	0.1087	85.2	96.0
	1994	0.0942	100	100
Colombia	1995	0.1580	95.1	92.7
Costa Rica	1981	0.1729	9.9	51.3
	1995	0.1875	69.1	79.6
Ecuador	1995	0.1883	75.3	89.3
El Salvador	1995	0.2141	54.3	61.0
Honduras	1989	0.2286	42	53.7
	1996	0.2068	50.6	57.6
Mexico	1984	0.1301	61.7	73.7
	1989	0.1764	46.9	66.9
	1992	0.1600	44.4	63.8
	1994	0.1550	48.1	71.5
Nicaragua	1993	0.1652	50.6	55.4
Panama	1995	0.1648	63	85.7

two urban Bolivia samples (which yielded surprisingly low average schooling gaps, given Bolivia's per capita income, and even given that the sample is urban only).

Columns 2 and 3 in table 6-4 give the average values of the two intergenerational schooling mobility indexes for the twenty-eight surveys, the five quintiles, and the four age groups. The range of values across surveys is from 100 (Chile, 1994) to 0 (Brazil, 1981) by construction (the end

Table 6-4 (continued)

| Country | Year | Average proportion of variance explained by family background | Intergenerational mobility indexes[b] | |
			Proportional mobility index	Gap-adjusted mobility index
Paraguay	1995	0.2075	53.1	63.0
Peru	1985	0.2453	46.9	68.3
	1996	0.2014	58	75.8
Uruguay (urban)	1981	0.1426	70.4	86.9
	1995	0.1177	70.4	86.9
Venezuela	1981	0.1669	66.7	75.4
	1995	0.1603	77.8	84.0
Quintile				
1	...	...	53.1	55.4
2	...	...	55.6	63.2
3	...	...	63	76.4
4	...	...	58	79.6
5	...	...	38.3	80.2
Age group				
10–12	...	...	66.7	78.0
13–15	...	...	50.6	72.7
16–18	...	...	28.4	61.2
19–21	...	...	2.5	36.8
Overall average	...	...	54.3	71.1

Source: Author's estimations from household survey data.

a. Survey averages are averages across quintiles. Quintile, age group, and overall averages are averages across countries with countries equally weighted.

b. See text for definition of intergenerational mobility indexes.

points happen to be the same for the two indexes). The range in averages across quintiles is smaller than across surveys. The proportional index does not have a strong association with the parental schooling quintiles. The gap-adjusted index does, with the means increasing monotonically from 55.4 for the first quintile to 80.2 for the fifth. For both mobility indexes, means for the age groups also have, as would be expected, monotonically decreasing values.

Estimates of the Mobility-Macroeconomic Association

As noted earlier, in the discussion of the framework for analyzing the association between family background and schooling, a variety of economic and other factors are likely to affect the direction and magnitude of the association. One example is public spending on education. Public spending is likely to directly affect incentives for private schooling investments, although the sign of such effects would depend on how such spending is distributed among children with different family backgrounds and among school levels.

The economic environment also may affect the association between family background and schooling by changing the extent of market imperfections facing different households, thus changing the returns to schooling or the price of schooling differentially across families. Market imperfections arguably are related to the extent of overall economic development; where average education is lower, for example, failures in the markets for capital and information are likely to be exaggerated. In addition, economic policies (for example, barriers to international trade) may alter the extent of market imperfections, and macroeconomic instabilities may tend to increase problems with market imperfections through, for example, increasing problems of evaluation of investments (including those in human capital) due to increased uncertainty regarding future price movements. Studies using aggregate data indicate, for example, that countries in the region that have been subject to greater volatility in macroeconomic variables have had lower secondary school enrollment rates.[29] More open economies may improve access to the labor market for previously excluded groups and may increase returns to labor differentially depending on skills. Inflation could change the relative price of schooling, especially private schooling, if school fees rise faster or slower than wages. A deeper financial market is likely to loosen the effect of family income on schooling by improving families' ability to borrow.

Thus macroeconomic measures of market development, of the level of development, and of instability, and aggregate measures of education policies may affect how great intergenerational schooling mobility is by affecting the extent of market imperfections and the extent to which policies related to schooling offset or increase such imperfections. In this section we explore whether there is empirical evidence from recent Latin American

29. Inter-American Development Bank (1996).

experience consistent with such possibilities. We undertake this exploration by regressing our two intergenerational mobility indexes for our 559 subsamples on a parsimonious set of four macroeconomic and three aggregate education policy variables.[30]

Macroeconomic variables: GDP per capita (purchasing power parity adjusted), trade openness (exports plus imports divided by GDP), financial depth (M2 divided by GDP), and the inflation rate.[31]

Education policy variables: government expenditures on all levels of education over GDP, government expenditures on primary schooling per person of primary school age adjusted for purchasing power parity, and average school quality, as represented by average schooling of teachers.

These variables were selected on the basis of their availability and their probable centrality for the question being investigated.[32] To capture the macroeconomic effects over the time that children in the samples were making schooling decisions at the margin, we use different reference periods for each age group. For children in the 10-12 age group we use averages over two years (the year of the surveys and the previous year); for those aged 13-15, 16-18, and 19-21 we use three-, four-, and five-year averages, respectively.

Table 6-5 presents the correlations among the two intergenerational mobility indexes and these four macroeconomic and three aggregate variables. The two indexes are fairly highly correlated. Each is positively correlated with the trade openness, financial depth, and school quality variables, and negatively correlated with overall educational expenditures and infla-

---

30. We also included a dummy variable equal to 1 for the subsamples from urban surveys only (Bolivia, Argentina, and Uruguay). The coefficients on and significance of all variables do not change.

31. Sources for the macroeconomic variables are, respectively, the World Penn Tables, 1995, and World Bank, *World Development Indicators, 1998;* World Penn Tables, 1995, and International Monetary Fund, *International Financial Statistics,* various issues; constructed from data in International Monetary Fund, *International Financial Statistics,* various issues; and constructed from data in Inter-American Development Bank (1997). Sources for the education policy variables are, respectively, *UNESCO Statistical Yearbook,* 1982–97; and constructed with data from *UNESCO Statistical Yearbook,* 1982–97. To adjust for purchasing power parity, we use the World Penn Tables, 1995, and the World Bank, *World Development Indicators, 1998.* To obtain the number of persons in primary school, we use the United Nations Population Statistics, 1996 revision; calculated from the twenty-eight household surveys used for the econometric estimation of the family background index.

32. We also have explored the inclusion of some other aggregate variables (for example, Gini coefficients to represent distribution), but they do not have statistically significant coefficient estimates nor do they affect the other estimates significantly. So in the interests of simplicity and clarity we do not include these variables in the estimates.

Table 6-5. *Bivariate Correlations among Variables Used in Analysis of Associations between Intergenerational Schooling Mobility and Macroeconomic Variables and Aggregate Education Policy Indicators, and Means and Standard Deviations (Based on 559 Observations)*

	Correlations among variables								
	1	*2*	*3*	*4*	*5*	*6*	*7*	*8*	*9*
Intergenerational mobility indices									
Proportional intergenerational mobility index	1.00	...	...	...	...	...	...	...	...
Gap-adjusted intergenerational mobility index	0.79	1.00	...	...	...	...	...	...	...
Basic macroeconomic variables with quintile interactions									
GDP per capita	0.07	–0.01	1.00	...	...	...	...	...	...
Trade openness	0.10	0.11	–0.20	1.00	...	...	...	...	...
Financial depth	0.25	0.15	0.09	0.53	1.00	...	...	...	...
Inflation rate	–0.15	–0.15	–0.13	–0.31	–0.51	1.00	...	...	...
Aggregate education policy indicators									
Government expenditures on education/GDP	–0.04	–0.05	–0.03	0.51	0.32	–0.10	1.00	...	...
Government expenditures on primary education/population 6–12 years old	0.06	–0.06	0.67	–0.14	0.18	–0.05	0.23	1.00	...
Educational quality indicator	0.25	0.23	0.06	0.19	0.40	0.48	–0.22	–0.16	1.00

tion rates.[33] Though the absolute magnitudes of these correlations are not very large (all are smaller than 0.25), their signs generally are consistent with improved macroeconomic performance and education policies increasing intergenerational mobility, with the notable possible exception of overall education expenditures.

Table 6-6 presents two sets of random effects multivariate estimates for the two mobility indexes.[34] For the first estimate for each dependent variable, the right column variables are the seven macroeconomic and education variables and additive dummy variables for the parental schooling quintiles and child age groups. For the second estimate for each dependent variable, in addition are included multiplicative quintile dummy variables to allow the coefficients for the first and fifth quintiles to differ from those for the other three quintiles. We focus on the possibilities that the coefficients may differ for the bottom and top quintiles because we are interested in these quintiles (particularly the bottom one) from a distributional perspective and because our expectation, reinforced by the patterns in the dependent variables noted earlier, is that any nonlinearities are likely to be manifested most clearly in the tails of the distribution.

We note four important characteristics of these estimates.

First, the specifications are significant and consistent with a fair amount of the variance in the intergenerational schooling mobility indexes. Chi-square tests indicate that each of these four estimates is significant at the 0.0000 level. The R^2s indicate that these associations are consistent with from 18.6 to 28.9 percent of the variance in the intergenerational schooling mobility indexes, with greater consistency with the gap-adjusted index. Particularly given the limited representation of the macroeconomic environment and education policies by just seven fairly crude aggregate variables, this consistency supports our basic conjecture that macroeconomic and education factors importantly shape the associations between family background and schooling investment gaps and therefore intergenerational mobility. Moreover, on a general level the four specifications suggest the same sign patterns for most of the coefficient estimates of the four macro-

33. But the first is positively and the second negatively correlated with GDP per capita and expenditures on primary schooling.

34. We use random effects because of the possibility of correlated disturbances caused by the use of twenty age-quintile subsamples from each survey. For each estimate a Hausman specification test accepts the null hypothesis that the differences between fixed effects and random effects coefficients are not systematic (chi-square tests and probability levels are given in the table).

Table 6-6. *Estimates of Associations between Intergenerational Mobility Indices and Macroeconomic Variables and Policy Indicators*

Items	Proportional intergenerational mobility index		Gap-adjusted intergenerational mobility index	
Basic macroeconomic variables with quintile interactions				
GDP per capita	−3.78E−06 (1.21)	−4.51E−06 (1.39)	−2.14E−06 (1.58)	−2.14E−06 (1.56)
Quintile 1		5.97E−07 (0.19)		−3.18E−07 (0.29)
Quintile 5		2.55E−06 (0.81)		9.37E−08 (0.08)
Trade openness	0.0004 (0.03)	0.00261 (0.16)	0.0041 (0.55)	0.00484 (0.63)
Quintile 1		−0.0218 (1.19)		−0.00813 (1.26)
Quintile 5		0.00113 (0.62)		0.00522 (0.81)
Financial depth	0.0778 (2.73)	0.0865 (2.69)	0.049 (4.45)	0.0498 (4.12)
Quintile 1		0.0262 (0.52)		0.0206 (1.16)
Quintile 5		−0.0669 (1.31)		−0.0273 (1.52)
Inflation rate	0.0029 (0.30)	0.00590 (0.53)	0.0104 (2.95)	0.0128 (3.21)
Quintile 1		−0.0322 (1.76)		−0.0155 (2.40)
Quintile 5		0.0163 (0.88)		0.00277 (0.42)
Aggregate education policy indicators				
Government expenditures on education/GDP	−0.0047 (1.19)	−0.004783 (1.13)	−0.0022 (1.35)	−0.00238 (1.42)
Quintile 1		−0.00875 (1.68)		0.00370 (2.01)
Quintile 5		−0.00886 (1.70)		−0.00268 (1.45)
Government expenditures on primary education/population 6–12 years old	0.0000336 (1.21)	0.0000229 (0.78)	0.000023 (2.04)	0.0000192 (1.63)
Quintile 1		0.0000128 (0.38)		5.02E−06 (0.43)
Quintile 5		0.0000476 (1.38)		0.000017 (1.40)
Educational quality indicator	0.0040 (2.24)	0.00313 (1.60)	0.0016 (2.14)	0.00157 (1.99)
Quintile 1		−0.00136 (0.53)		−0.000891 (0.98)
Quintile 5		0.00597 (2.31)		0.00101 (1.10)

Additive quantile dummy variables (with quintile 1 as reference category)				
Quintile 2	0.0024 (0.48)	0.00996 (0.23)	0.0040 (2.31)	0.00323 (0.21)
Quintile 3	0.0080 (1.64)	0.01556 (0.36)	0.0106 (6.15)	0.00985 (0.64)
Quintile 4	0.0045 (0.91)	0.0121 (0.28)	0.0123 (7.12)	0.0115 (0.75)
Quintile 5	-0.0122 (2.49)	-0.0684 (1.28)	0.0126 (7.27)	0.00706 (0.38)
Additive age group variables (with ages 10–12 as reference category)				
Ages 13–15	-0.00928 (2.11)	-0.00922 (2.14)	-0.00145 (0.94)	-0.00142 (0.93)
Ages 16–18	-0.0241 (5.48)	-0.0241 (5.59)	-0.00636 (4.10)	-0.00636 (4.18)
Ages 19–21	-0.0407 (9.24)	-0.0407 (9.42)	-0.0162 (10.39)	-0.0162 (10.60)
Other estimates and summary statistics				
Constant	-0.0916 (2.97)	-0.0848 (1.87)	-0.0510 (3.97)	-0.049 (2.85)
Overall R^2	0.186	0.227	0.259	0.289
Chi^2 (probability > chi^2)	140.75 (0.0000)	182.84 (0.0000)	260.29 (0.0000)	307.93 (0.0000)
Hausman specification test chi^2 (probability > chi^2)	9.64 (0.7882)	9.87 (0.9994)	4.62 (0.9904)	4.66 (0.0000)
Joint chi^2 tests of significance of groups of parameters (probability)				
Quintile effects				
Additive	19.68 (0.0006)	4.87 (0.3010)	84.53 (0.0000)	27.25 (0.0000)
Multiplicative		36.12 (0.0010)		36.61 (0.0008)
Quintile 1 only		11.68 (0.1117)		20.83 (0.0040)
Quintile 5 only		19.63 (0.0064)		9.30 (0.2315)
Age group effects: additive	97.90 (0.0000)	101.97 (0.0000)	132.53 (0.0000)	138.21 (0.0000)

a. Random effects estimator. Absolute values of z-statistics given in parentheses to right of point estimates ($z \geq 1.96 \Rightarrow$ significant at 5 percent level; $z \geq 1.67 \Rightarrow$ significant at 10 percent level).

economic and three education variables and quintile and age-group controls. Our basic results are generally robust to different specifications.

Second, there is evidence that the effects differ by parental schooling quintiles, though the strength and nature of the results are sensitive to the particular specification used.[35] The single strongest result, in terms of statistical significance, is for the additive quintile effects on the gap-adjusted index. The point estimates for the additive quintile effects suggest a definite monotonic increase in social mobility with higher parental-schooling quintiles. (The estimates are much less precise, and have one deviation from a monotonically increasing pattern, if there also are interactive quintile effects.)

Third, there is strong evidence that the estimates differ by age groups. All of these effects are additive.[36] Joint tests indicate that the additive age group dummy variables are significant at the 0.0000 level in each of the four estimates. The individual parameter estimates indicate, as would be expected, decreasing social mobility with increased age for each of the four estimates.

---

35. For example, joint tests indicate that additive quintile effects are significantly nonzero for three of the four estimates. However, results vary depending on the index. For the proportional intergenerational school mobility index, the point estimates for the additive quintile effects weakly suggest that the fifth quintile has less intergenerational social mobility than the first (and the second, third, and fourth quintiles possibly more), whereas for the gap-adjusted intergenerational mobility index the fifth quintile has more mobility than the first. Similarly, joint tests for the multiplicative quintile effects indicate significance at a high level (0.0010 and 0.0008, respectively) for both intergenerational schooling mobility indexes. But joint tests also suggest that which quintile differs significantly from the other four differs for the two dependent variables: for the proportional intergenerational schooling mobility index, only the interactions involving the fifth quintile differ significantly from the others, while for the gap-adjusted intergenerational schooling mobility index, only the interactions involving the first quintile differ significantly from the others. The individual coefficient estimates indicate that for the proportional intergenerational schooling mobility index, social mobility increased significantly more for the fifth than for the other quintiles with higher-quality schooling. For the gap-adjusted intergenerational schooling mobility index, social mobility increased significantly more for the first than the other quintiles with greater overall educational expenditures but less than for the other quintiles with higher inflation.

36. The substantial age differentials shown, for example, in table 6-2 result only in additive shifts, not differential coefficients for the macroeconomic and aggregate schooling policy variables. Adding interactions with age-group dummy variables does not result in any significant differences. For example, if age-group interactions are added to the second specification for each of the two dependent variables to allow for the possibility that the coefficient estimates of the macroeconomic and aggregate schooling variables differ for the youngest and for the oldest age groups (compared with the middle two age groups), chi-square tests for joint parameter significant reject the significance of these interaction terms: $chi^2 = 10.75$ (probability = 0.7059) and $chi^2 = 12.20$ (0.5902), respectively.

Finally, and most important, a number of the macroeconomic and education variables have significant coefficient estimates with plausible a priori interpretations.

Two of the macroeconomic variables have significant coefficient estimates. The first is for financial depth, which is probably our best single indicator of the extent of general internal market development. Financial depth has significant positive effects that are robust across the four specifications. Within the framework discussed earlier, these provide strong support for the importance of internal market development in increasing social mobility.[37]

The second macroeconomic variable with significant coefficient estimates is inflation, for which there is relatively great a priori ambiguity regarding the expected sign. If inflation effectively increases imperfections in markets by reducing the quality of information because of rapidly changing absolute and relative prices, negative coefficient estimates would be expected. But inflation may work in the opposite direction by increasing the sensitivity to market changes given the high cost of lags in market behavior or may weaken the capacity for families to cope with rapid changes, both of which may lead to positive associations of the intergenerational indexes with inflation. The weakened capacity to cope with change seems to dominate for both intergenerational mobility indexes, with significant coefficient estimates for the gap-adjusted index.

Two of the three education policy variables have significant coefficient estimates. School quality has significant positive effects for all four specifications (based on joint tests with quintile interactions for the second specification). Adjusted for purchasing power parity, government expenditures on primary schools relative to the pool of primary-age students has positive coefficient estimates in all four specifications that are significantly nonzero in the specifications for the gap-adjusted mobility index (based on joint tests with quintile interactions for the second of these specifications). Total government expenditure on education, in contrast, has negative (though not significant even at the 10 percent level) coefficient estimates in all four specifications. These negative estimates weakly suggest that, once there is control for resources devoted to primary schooling and to improving school quality at the basic levels, the total educational expenditures are reflecting

---

37. Financial depth may be representing in part the effects of trade openness on improving the functioning of internal markets because the correlation between these two variables is fairly high at 0.53 (table 6-5).

largely expenditures that, if anything, reinforce family background and reduce intergenerational social mobility, such as public subsidies for tertiary
schooling for children of upper-middle and upper-class families.

Thus there seems to be strong support for our basic conjecture that
market reforms, through affecting the extent of market imperfections and
the nature of aggregate public educational expenditures, can have important effects on the importance of family background in determining schooling and, through this channel, on intergenerational social mobility.
Therefore, although the recent macroeconomic changes and education
policy changes in Latin America have not had as strong an effect on the
current income distribution as some may have hoped, they may have had
important and largely positive effects on increasing intergenerational social
mobility. Such effects may make recent policies more politically acceptable
and therefore sustainable and may have longer-run equalizing and growth-
inducing effects on the economies in the region.

Conclusions

Our empirical results confirm for a large number of countries over
many years that family background has a significant association with the
length of children's schooling. As expected, children of higher-income and
better-educated parents everywhere and at all times are likely to do better.
More to the point of our study, the results also suggest that the implied link
is itself subject to substantial variation across countries and periods, depending on macroeconomic conditions and public policy in education.

Macroeconomic conditions, in particular those related to the extent of
internal market development, shape intergenerational mobility by loosen-
ing the strong link between parents' background and children's education.
Education policies can also loosen the link. Increasing public resources
available for basic schooling in general and for improving school quality in
particular have important beneficial effects on intergenerational mobility.
Increasing other educational expenditures, however, such as those on tertiary education, may reinforce the impact of family background and reduce intergenerational mobility.

Even though the immediate effects of macroeconomic market reforms
and schooling policy reforms on current income distribution may not be
strong, there may be important longer-run effects through increasing
intergenerational social mobility.

References

Becker, Gary S. 1967. "Human Capital and the Personal Distribution of Income: An Analytical Approach." University of Michigan, Woytinsky Lecture. Republished in Gary S. Becker, *Human Capital*, 2d ed., pp. 94–117. New York: National Bureau of Economic Research.

———. 1975. *Human Capital*, 2d ed. New York: National Bureau of Economic Research.

———. 1991. *A Treatise on the Family*, 2d ed. Harvard University Press.

Behrman, Jere R. 1997. "Women's Schooling and Child Education: A Survey." University of Pennsylvania.

Behrman, Jere R., and Nancy Birdsall. 1983. "The Quality of Schooling: Quantity Alone Is Misleading." *American Economic Review* 73 (October): 928–44.

Behrman, Jere R., and James C. Knowles. 1999. "Household Income and Child Schooling in Vietnam." *World Bank Economic Review* 13 (May): 211–56.

Behrman, Jere R., and Paul Taubman. 1989. "Is Schooling 'Mostly in the Genes'? Nature-Nurture Decomposition with Data on Relatives." *Journal of Political Economy* 97 (December): 1425–46.

———. 1990. "The Intergenerational Correlation between Children's Adult Earnings and Their Parents' Income: Results from the Michigan Panel Survey of Income Dynamics." *Review of Income and Wealth* 36 (June): 115–27.

Behrman, Jere R., and Barbara L. Wolfe. 1984. "The Socioeconomic Impact of Schooling in a Developing Country." *Review of Economics and Statistics* 66 (May):296–03.

Behrman, Jere R., Nancy Birdsall, and Miguel Székely. 1998. "Intergenerational Schooling, Mobility, and New Conditions and Schooling Policies in Latin America." Working Paper 386. Inter-American Development Bank, Office of the Chief Economist.

Behrman, Jere R., Robert A. Pollak, and Paul Taubman. 1982. "Parental Preferences and Provision for Progeny." *Journal of Political Economy* 90 (February): 52–73.

———. 1995. *From Parent to Child: Intrahousehold Allocations and Intergenerational Relations in the United States.* University of Chicago Press.

Behrman, Jere R., Mark R. Rosenzweig, and Paul Taubman. 1994. "Endowments and the Allocation of Schooling in the Family and in the Marriage Market: The Twins Experiment." *Journal of Political Economy* 102 (December): 1131–74.

———. 1996. "College Choice and Wages: Estimates Using Data on Female Twins." *Review of Economics and Statistics* 73 (November): 672–85.

Behrman, Jere R., and others. 1980. *Socioeconomic Success: A Study of the Effects of Genetic Endowments, Family Environment and Schooling*. Amsterdam: North-Holland.

Berry, Albert.1997."The Income Distribution Threat in Latin America." *Latin American Research Review* 32 (2) 3–40.

Birdsall, Nancy, and Carol Graham. 1998. "New Ways of Looking at Old Inequities: Market Reforms, Social Mobility and Sustainable Growth (Latin America in Comparative Context)." Brookings and the Inter-American Development Bank.

Birdsall, Nancy, and Juan Luis Londoño. 1997. "Asset Inequality Matters: An Assessment of the World Bank's Approach to Poverty Reduction." *American Economic Review* 87 (May): 32–37.

Bourguignon, François. 1998. "Distributional Incidence of Education Expenditures: Intergenerational and Capital Market Effects." Washington: World Bank; and Paris: Delta.

Cameron, Stephen V., and James J. Heckman. 1998. "Life Cycle Schooling and Dynamic Selection Bias: Models and Evidence for Five Cohorts of American Males." *Journal of Political Economy* 106 (2): 262–333.

Deininger, Klaus, and Lyn Squire. 1996. "A New Data Set Measuring Income Inequality." *World Bank Economic Review* 10 (September): 565–91.

Duryea, Suzanne, and Miguel Székely. 1998. "Labor Markets in Latin America: A Supply-Side Story," Working Paper 374. Washington: Inter-American Development Bank, Office of the Chief Economist.

Friedman, Milton. 1962. *Capitalism and Freedom*. Princeton University.

Inter-American Development Bank. 1996. *Making Social Services Work*. Economic and Social Progress in Latin America, 1996 Report. Washington: Inter-American Development Bank.

———. 1998. *Facing Up to Inequality:* Economic and Social Progress in Latin America, 1998–1999 Report. Johns Hopkins University Press for the Inter-American Development Bank.

Londoño, Juan Luis, and Miguel Székely. 1997a. "Persistent Poverty and Excess Inequality: Latin America 1970–1995," Working Paper 357. Washington: Inter-American Development Bank, Office of the Chief Economist.

———. 1997b. "Distributional Surprises after a Decade of Reforms: Latin America in the Nineties," Working Paper 352. Washington: Inter-American Development Bank, Office of the Chief Economist.

Lustig, Nora, and Miguel Székely. 1997. "'Hidden' Trends in Poverty and Inequality in Mexico." Washington: Inter-American Development Bank.

Morley, Samuel. 1994. *Poverty and Inequality in Latin America*. Johns Hopkins University Press.

Mulligan, Casey B. 1997. *Parental Priorities and Economic Inequality*. University of Chicago Press.

Pitt, Mark M., Mark R. Rosenzweig, and M. N. Hassan. 1990. "Productivity, Health and Inequality in the Intrahousehold Distribution of Food in Low-Income Countries." *American Economic Review* 80 (December): 1139–56.

Psacharopoulos, George. 1994. "Returns to Investment in Education: A Global Update." *World Development* 22 (September): 1325–44.

Psacharopoulos, George, and others. 1992. *Poverty and Income Distribution in Latin America: The Story of the 1980s*. Washington: World Bank.

Rosenzweig, Mark R. 1995. "Why Are There Returns in Schooling?" *American Economic Review* 85 (May): 153–58.

Rosenzweig, Mark R., and T. Paul Schultz. 1987. "Fertility and Investments in Human Capital: Estimates of the Consequences of Imperfect Fertility Control in Malaysia." *Journal of Econometrics* 36 (September-October): 163–84.

Rosenzweig, Mark R., and Kenneth J. Wolpin. 1986. "Evaluating the Effects of Optimally Distributed Public Programs." *American Economic Review* 76 (June): 470–87.

Rosenzweig, Mark R., and Kenneth I. Wolpin. 1995. "Sisters, Siblings and Mothers: The Effects of Teen-Age Childbearing on Birth Outcomes." *Econometrica* 63 (March): 303–26.

Schemo, Diana Jean. 1998. "Brazil's Reformist Chief Rides a Bucking Bronco." *New York Times* (February 8, 1998): 12.

Solon, Gary R. 1992. "Intergenerational Income Mobility in the United States." *American Economic Review* 82 (June): 393–408.

Zimmerman, David J. 1992. "Regression toward Mediocrity in Economic Stature." *American Economic Review* 82 (June): 409–29.

KATHERINE TERRELL

7 | *Worker Mobility and Transition to a Market Economy: Winners and Losers*

The collapse of communism has provided the world with a social experiment of historic dimensions. For a decade now, the economies of the former Soviet bloc countries have been undertaking an enormous number of changes in their laws, institutions, and economic policies as they make the transition to a market system. With incredible speed, borders were opened to global trade and migration, state-owned enterprises were privatized, and the state dismantled the centralized systems of prices, wages, employment, and production. Workers have been facing a new environment in which employment is no longer assured and the structure of jobs is changing dramatically. For some, unemployment has become a harsh reality. For others, the new environment has created opportunities to earn more than they had ever thought possible.

This chapter uses findings from recent studies on the transition economies in central and eastern Europe (CEE) and the newly independent states (NIS) of the former Soviet Union to address the following questions: How much mobility has there been in the emerging labor markets of these countries? Who has been gaining and who has been losing from the transition? In addressing these questions, I focus on two dimensions of the labor market: mobility across labor market states, primarily in and out of employment and unemployment, and movements in workers' relative earnings position. Although the period that is being analyzed (1989–96) is relatively short, it exhibits fundamental systemic changes, many of which will have long-term effects on the lives of the current and future generations of people in the transition economies.

Overview of the Transition Process

The basic characteristics of the centrally planned economies are well known. The state owned nearly all of the productive assets and determined the levels of production and allocation of resources. Foreign trade was also centralized through state trading firms. All able-bodied, working-age people were expected to work and were given virtual job security. Wages were centrally administered by a national wage grid that established differentials for individuals' experience and industrial sector of job. However, communist ideology dictated that wages be relatively uniform. In addition to regulating wages, the central planners regulated employment and admissions to higher education (using political loyalty as a criterion).

Although the basic features of the system were the same in all communist countries, there were of course variations. State ownership was more complete in Czechoslovakia and Russia than in Hungary and Poland (table 7-1). Poland, for instance, maintained private agriculture as well as some small private industries and services. And the dispersion of income varied. In Russia the distribution of income was among the most unequal in the Soviet bloc: the per capita Gini coefficient was 0.26 in 1985. Czechoslovakia was among the most equal, with a per capita Gini coefficient of 0.20 in 1985.[1]

In 1989 when the Berlin wall fell and revolutions broke out, the centrally planned system had already been rapidly disintegrating in Poland and Hungary, but it remained intact in East Germany and Czechoslovakia. In 1990–91, most CEE economies started the transition to a market economy. The Russian reform program began in 1992 with price liberalization in January and mass privatization starting in the autumn. Most countries undergoing transition focused first on establishing macroeconomic stability while they were liberalizing prices and dismantling the centrally planned system. Price liberalization resulted in an outburst of inflation, while the restructuring required by the shift from central planning to the

---

1. Atkinson and Micklewright (1992).

Table 7-1. *Private Sector Output in Eastern Europe as a Percent of GDP,*
by Country, 1990, 1995, 1996

Country	1990	1995	1996
Bulgaria	10	45	45
Czech Republic	5	70	75
Hungary	20	60	70
Poland	25	60	60
Romania	15	40	60
Russia	5	55	60
Ukraine	10	35	40

Sources: Data for 1990 and 1995 are from World Bank (1996, p. 15). Data for 1996 are from European Bank for Reconstruction and Development (1998, pp. 148–203).

market mechanism resulted in large decreases in production and employment. The average real wage also fell dramatically as the countries devalued their currencies, freed most prices, and imposed wage controls. All the CEE and NIS economies except for those of the Czech Republic and Ukraine experienced rapidly rising and persistently high unemployment rates. See table 7-2 for these macroeconomic statistics.

Questions naturally arise as to who gained and who lost from these large structural and systemic changes. There were both price and quantity adjustments in the labor market. Overall real wage levels fell, but enormous dispersion was created with both upward and downward relative mobility of different groups.

Labor Turnover

In this section I examine labor turnover at two levels.[2] I begin at the macroeconomic level by comparing the extent of labor mobility in the economies of the CEE and NIS and between them and the more developed market economy of the United States. I then survey studies analyzing the determinants of people's mobility to derive the characteristics of those who are becoming unemployed or finding employment.

---

2. Labor turnover usually refers to movements into and out of a job (defined as employment with a specific employer), but I use it here to mean labor mobility into and out of employment, unemployment, and out of the labor force.

Extent of Labor Mobility: Cross-Country Comparison

With the abolition of job security, privatization of state-owned enterprises, and shifts in demand for products, observers wondered whether the newly created labor market would be dynamic, with labor moving rapidly from low- to high-productivity jobs. Would employers and workers adjust quickly to the demands of the new market? The ideal model showed workers moving directly from a job in the state sector to a job in the emerging private sector (de novo private firms or privatized state enterprises) without passing through a period of unemployment. The second-best scenario was to experience the new mobility with only short bouts of unemployment.

From the very start, observers have been concerned about potential barriers to labor mobility. First, microeconomists worried that wage controls would prevent relative wages from changing enough to elicit desirable mobility. Second, workers might be prevented from changing jobs if inefficient housing markets and other barriers impeded geographical mobility. Third, jobs in the private sector might not be created rapidly enough to absorb those being laid off in state-owned enterprises. Finally, there was concern that if the social safety nets were too generous, they might themselves become a barrier to mobility, giving workers incentives to stay unemployed or out of the labor force longer.

Most studies approached these concerns by examining the mobility of people across the labor market states of employment (e), unemployment (u), and out of the labor force (o). Several studies have calculated the probabilities (P_{ij}) that an average working-age person remains in his or her original state ($i = j$) or moves from state i to state j over the course of the year, where $i, j = e, u, o$.[3] I have assembled in table 7-3 the probabilities from these new studies to compare the amounts of mobility in these transition economies.

In the early to mid-1990s, labor turnover was relatively high among the employed in the transition economies when compared with the United

---

3. The studies assume that the movements of individuals across states are governed by a Markov process. Thus the probability of transition between labor market states depends only on the state currently occupied. The gross probability of transition from state i to state j is given by

$$P_{ij} = \frac{F_{ij}}{S_i} = i, j, = e, u, o \ ,$$

where F_{ij} is the number of individuals in state i at time t that flowed to state j at time $t + 1$ and S_i is the stock at origin.

Table 7-2. *Macroeconomic Statistics for East European, U.S., and EU Economies, 1990–96*

Category	1990	1991	1992	1993	1994	1995	1996	1997	1998[a]	Average
GDP Growth										
Bulgaria	-4.3	0.5	-7.3	-1.5	1.8	2.1	-10.9	-6.9	1.0	-2.8
Czech Republic	-1.6	-11.5	-3.3	0.5	3.4	6.4	3.9	1.0	-1.0	-0.2
Hungary	-3.5	-11.9	-3.1	-0.6	2.9	1.5	1.3	4.4	5.0	-0.4
Poland	-11.6	-7.0	2.6	3.8	5.2	7.0	6.1	6.9	5.3	2.0
Romania	-5.6	-12.9	-8.8	1.5	3.9	7.1	4.1	-6.6	0.0	-1.9
Russia	-2.0	-5.0	-14.5	-8.7	-12.7	-4.1	-4.9	0.4	0.5	-5.7
Ukraine	-2.6	-11.6	-13.7	-14.2	-23.0	-11.8	-10.0	-3.2	0.5	-10.0
United States	1.3	-0.9	2.7	2.3	3.5	2.0	2.8	3.8	3.3	2.3
European Union 15	2.5	8.5	1.0	-0.6	2.9	2.4	1.7	2.5	2.5	2.6
CPI inflation										
Bulgaria	23.8	333.5	82.0	73.0	96.3	62.0	123.0	1,082.0	45.0	213.4
Czech Republic	9.7	56.6	11.1	20.8	10.0	9.1	8.8	8.5	10.4	16.1
Hungary	28.9	35.0	23.0	22.5	18.8	28.2	23.6	18.3	14.2	23.6
Poland	585.8	70.3	43.0	35.3	32.2	27.8	19.9	14.9	11.9	93.5
Romania	5.1	161.1	210.4	256.1	136.7	32.3	38.8	154.8	56.0	116.8
Russia	5.3	92.7	1,526.0	875.0	311.4	197.7	47.8	14.7	5.6	341.8
Ukraine	4.8	91.0	1,210.0	4,735.0	891.0	376.0	80.0	16.0	n.a.	925.5
United States	5.4	4.3	3.0	3.0	2.6	2.8	2.9	2.3	1.7	3.3
European Union 15	5.5	5.2	4.4	3.6	3.0	3.2	2.5	2.0	n.a.	3.7

Change in average wage

Bulgaria	47.9	-87.4	44.5	33.2	-21.8	23.7	-33.3	0.1	n.a.	*0.9*
Czech Republic	-13.1	-29.7	27.8	21.4	20.1	28.5	15.8	-2.7	n.a.	*8.5*
Hungary	18.9	12.7	17.7	4.6	7.3	-2.3	-0.8	2.9	n.a.	*7.6*
Poland	-24.2	53.1	28.1	1.2	7.4	23.4	13.6	8.3	n.a.	*13.9*
Romania	-32.6	-12.6	-31.8	24.8	6.5	26.0	0.0	-18.3	n.a.	*-4.8*
Russia	26.2	-36.3	-92.8	161.0	72.7	7.7	33.6	5.2	n.a.	*22.2*
Ukraine	23.5	-36.2	-87.2	1.8	36.2	13.2	37.7	12.9	n.a.	*0.2*
United States	2.8	3.1	3.3	3.5	4.2	1.4	3.3	4.2	n.a.	*3.2*

Unemployment rate

Bulgaria	1.5	11.1	15.3	16.4	12.8	11.1	12.5	13.7	14.6	*12.1*
Czech Republic	1.0	4.1	2.6	3.5	3.2	2.9	3.5	5.2	7.0	*3.7*
Hungary	1.9	7.4	12.3	12.1	10.4	10.4	10.5	10.4	9.3	*9.4*
Poland	6.3	11.8	13.6	16.4	16.0	14.9	13.2	10.5	10.0	*12.5*
Romania	0.4	3.0	8.2	10.4	10.9	9.5	6.6	8.8	12.0	*7.8*
Russia	n.a.	2.0	4.8	5.3	7.1	8.3	9.2	10.9	9.3	*7.1*
Ukraine	n.a.	0.0	0.3	0.4	0.4	0.5	1.1	2.3	4.5	*1.2*
United States	5.6	6.8	7.5	6.9	6.1	5.6	5.4	4.9	4.5	*5.9*
European Union 15	8.1	8.5	9.9	11.1	11.6	11.2	11.3	11.0	10.3	*10.3*

Sources: *GDP growth*: Data Stream International. *CPI inflation*: for eastern European countries: EBRD, *Transition Report, 1998*; for United States and European Union 15: Data Stream International, average annual CPI percent change. *Change in average wage*: for eastern European countries: Vienna Institute for Comparative Economic Studies, *Handbook of Statistics: Countries in Transition, 1998*; for United States and European Union 15: Data Stream International. *Unemployment rate*: for European Union countries: EBRD, *Transition Report, 1998* until 1997, 1998 estimated from Business Central Europe; United States and European Union 15: International Monetary Fund, *World Economic Outlook, 1998*. (Before 1993, registered unemployed; after 1993, International Labor Organization definition, using national Labor Force Survey data.)

n.a. Not available.

a. Estimate.

Table 7-3. *Probabilities of Labor Mobility for Six East European Transition Economies and the United States, 1990s*[a]

Country	Reference year	P_{ee}	P_{eu}	P_{eo}	P_{uu}	P_{uc}	P_{uo}	P_{oo}	P_{oe}	P_{ou}
Bulgaria	6/1994–3/1995	0.849	0.059	0.092	0.433	0.323	0.244	0.864	0.092	0.044
Czech Republic	1Q1994–4Q1994	0.947	0.021	0.032	0.319	0.506	0.174	0.936	0.046	0.018
Czech Republic	1Q1996–4Q1996	0.955	0.013	0.032	0.418	0.426	0.147	0.944	0.046	0.010
East Germany	11/1990–11/1991	0.836	0.093	0.071	0.373	0.350	0.277	0.799	0.160	0.041
Poland	1992–93	0.884	0.040	0.076	0.481	0.361	0.158	0.860	0.095	0.045
Poland	1993–94	0.897	0.040	0.063	0.487	0.354	0.159	0.883	0.074	0.043
Slovakia	1Q1994–4Q1994	0.932	0.023	0.045	0.685	0.237	0.078	0.965	0.018	0.017
Russia	1992–93	0.910	0.032	0.058	0.323	0.520	0.157	0.899	0.087	0.014
Russia	1995–96	0.881	0.056	0.062	0.459	0.395	0.145	0.891	0.076	0.034
United States	1992–93	0.919	0.028	0.053	0.053	0.659	0.288	0.796	0.043	0.161

Sources: Bulgaria, Slovakia, United States (Boeri, 1998); Czech Republic (Sorm and Terrell, 1999); East Germany (Bellmann and others, 1995); Poland (Gora and Lehmann, 1995); and Russia (Foley, 1997).

a. Column headings are explained in the text and note 3.

States, a benchmark for a stable, developed market economy (table 7-3).[4] Given the declines and structural changes in production during this period, the probability that a person stayed employed throughout the year (P_{ee}) was relatively small in all these countries as compared with the probability in the United States.[5] There is some variation among these economies, but it is largely explained by the time period in which the probabilities were estimated. The 1994 and 1996 P_{ee}'s in the Czech Republic and Slovakia are relatively high because much of the adjustment (mass layoffs) had taken place in 1991; by 1994–96 the companies were operating on their demand curves, adjusting labor with changes in wages and output.[6] Moreover, as table 7-2 showed, production was growing in 1994–96. The explanation for the high P_{ee}'s in Russia in 1992–93 lies largely in that this was the first year of the market-oriented reforms, when not much adjustment had taken place. Unemployment in Russia was about 5 percent in those years, but by 1995–96, when the Russian P_{ee}'s are in line with the other countries, unemployment had risen to 8 and 9 percent.

Another feature of the adjustment in the transition economies, also shown in table 7-3, is that the probability that someone left a job to "drop out of the labor force" (P_{eo}) was higher than the probability that he or she became unemployed (P_{eu}). Former East Germany is the exception. In most cases this meant early retirement, resulting in many new pensioners being created during the transition.

For many transition economies, the high and persistent unemployment rates are the result of low outflows from unemployment to a job (low P_{ue}). As table 7-3 shows, this is the case in Bulgaria, East Germany, Poland, and Slovakia, where approximately one-third (or less) of those who were unemployed at the beginning of the year found employment by the end of the year. In Russia and the Czech Republic, where the unemployment rates were low in the earlier years, the probability of leaving unemployment for a job was much higher: about one-half of those unemployed found jobs. In both countries the high outflows were explained in part by the rapidly growing gray or informal economy.[7] Nevertheless, in none of these coun-

---

4. In the United States the transition probabilities are relatively stable over time.

5. Staying employed means keeping a job (defined by the employer), but not necessarily the same job or employer.

6. Basu, Estrin, and Svejnar (1999).

7. However the nature of the gray or informal economy varies. In Russia it is largely based on barter and is permeating the entire economy, whereas in the Czech Republic it is better characterized as a growing small-scale service and manufacturing sector. In both, government taxation (and thus enumeration) is avoided.

tries did the movement from unemployment to job approach the rates in the United States, where two-thirds of the unemployed found a job within a year.

Obviously the most efficient mobility is frictionless job-to-job moves in which people change employers without passing through a spell of nonwork. This type of mobility is analyzed by Vit Sorm and Katherine Terrell for the Czech Republic.[8] They show that job-to-job mobility was weak but grew from 1994 to 1996 as the economy pulled out of the 1990–93 recession and labor markets began to function more as real markets. The probability of moving from job to job during a year grew from 2.5 percent in 1994, to 6.0 percent in 1995, and 5.8 percent in 1996. However, the rate of frictionless mobility declined when economic activity declined in 1997 and 1998.

Those who are out of the labor force (primarily pensioners) in the CEE and NIS economies are more likely than their counterparts in the United States to remain out. In the United States 20 percent of those out of the labor force at the beginning of the year find a job (P_{oe}) or are actively seeking a job (P_{ou}) by the end of the year. The probability that someone returns to the labor force $(P_{oe} + P_{ou})$ in the transition countries ranges from 4 percent to 14 percent. This in part reflects government policies in many transition countries that provided disincentives through, for example, pension reductions or higher tax on pensions for retired people who return to the labor market.

Who Is Gaining and Who Is Losing from Labor Turnover?

Several researchers have analyzed the types of people who are most likely to become unemployed and who are most likely to move quickly out of unemployment into a job. The studies use a common methodology to estimate the determinants of the transition probabilities out of employment and unemployment. They estimate multinomial logit functions with data on individuals from quarterly *Labor Force Surveys*. Some use annual panel data for individuals while others examine quarterly transition probabilities.[9] All studies include the principal human capital and demographic

8. Sorm and Terrell (1999).

9. For examples of annual panel data, see Bellmann and others (1995); and Sorm and Terrell (1999). For analyses of quarterly transition probabilities, see King and Adamchik (1999); and Stefanova

characteristics of people in their analysis of the determinants of the transition. However, there is much variation in the number and type of other determinants—job characteristics (industry of job and whether a job was in the private or public sector) or regional characteristics (dummies for regions and local demand conditions).

The findings of studies for several CEE countries and Russia with respect to the principal human capital and demographic determinants are shown in table 7-4. A review of this evidence shows a clear pattern as to who are the winners and losers from the transition. With a few exceptions, people who are younger, less educated, single, or women are more likely than those who are older, more educated, married, or men to lose or quit their job and become unemployed (that is, they have higher P_{eu}'s). And except for age, people with these characteristics (less educated, single, women) are also less likely to leave unemployment for a job (they have lower P_{ue}'s). Thus although the young become unemployed at a higher rate, they also generally leave at a higher rate and thus have shorter periods of unemployment than older persons. Less educated, unmarried women are both more likely to become unemployed and remain unemployed longer. The exception is that in Russia women are less likely than men to become unemployed and more likely to find a job.

Although the findings suggest that the transition is demanding people with higher skills, in some studies this finding is simply differentiating between two groups: those with basic (compulsory junior high school) education and those with more education. Thus those with a basic level of education are clearly the vulnerable group in all countries.

The explanations for the finding that, compared with married women, married men are less likely to be laid off or quit and more likely to be hired out of unemployment lie in decisions on both sides of the labor market. It can be argued that societal roles for men and women, supported by government policy, may be putting married women at a disadvantage in the labor market. These are traditional societies where men are typically assumed (even in surveys) to be the head of the household and women are assumed to be

---

and Terrell (1998). The probability of an individual moving from origin to destination state during the sampling interval is given by

$$\Pr[Y_i = j] = \frac{\exp(B_j'Z_i)}{\sum_k \exp(B_k'Z_i)}, \ j, k, = u, o, e \ ,$$

where Z is a vector of personal and origin state characteristics.

Table 7-4. Demographic Characteristics of Mobility into and out of Unemployment, Selected Countries, 1990s[a]

	Bulgaria		Czech Republic (1)		Czech Republic (2)	East Germany		Poland	Russia (1)	Russia (2)
Characteristic	Men	Women	Men	Women	All	Men	Women	All	All	All
Probability of leaving a job for unemployment (P_{eu}) is higher for the:										
Younger	n.a.	n.a.	yes	yes	yes	yes[g]	yes	yes	yes	yes
Less educated	n.a.	n.a.	yes	yes	yes	no[h]	no[h]	yes	yes[j]	yes[j]
Women	n.a.	n.a.	yes		yes[e]	yes[i]		yes	no	no
Single	n.a.	n.a.	yes	yes	yes[e]	yes	n.s.	yes	yes[k]	n.s.
Unemployment for a job (P_{ue}) is higher for the:										
Older	n.s.	n.s.	no[c]	no[c]	no	no	n.s.	yes	no	n.s.
More educated	yes[b]	yes[b]	yes[d]	yes[d]	yes	n.s.	yes	yes	n.s.	yes
Men	n.s.	n.s.	yes		yes[f]	yes[i]		yes	no	no
Married	n.s.	n.s.	yes	no	n.s.	yes	n.s.	n.s.	yes[l]	yes[l]

Sources: Bulgaria: Jones and Kato (1997); refers to 1994–95. Poland: King and Adamchik (1999); refers to 1995–96, nonagricultural workers, education dummies. Czech Republic (1): Stefanova and Terrell (1998); refers to 1994–96, education dummies. Russia (1): Foley (1997); refers to 1992–93 RSLMS data; age in years. Czech Republic (2): Sorm and Terrell (1999); refers to 1994–96, education in years. Russia (2): Foley (1997); refers to 1995–96 RSLMS data; age in years; 5 education dummies. East Germany: Bellmann and others (1995); refers to 1990–91.

a. n.s. means not significant; n.a. means not available. Findings are based on logit analysis and, except where noted, data are from national Labor Force Survey.

b. Anyone with more than a basic compulsory education.

c. People ages 15–25 were more likely to find a job than those more than 25 years old.

d. Anyone with more than the basic (compulsory) education.

e. The probabilities for married women and married men are significantly different; single women and single men are not significantly different. Married men have lower P_{eu} than married women; both of their P_{eu}'s are lower than for single men whose P_{ue} is not significantly different from single women.

f. The probabilities for married women and married men are significantly different, the P_{ue} of men is much higher than that of women.

g. People less than 25 years of age are as likely to leave as the middle aged group (25–40); both groups are more likely to leave than the older group.

h. More educated are more likely to leave.

i. The base probability of one is higher than the base for the other.

j. Less educated include primary school, apprenticeship and vocational school (coefficient not significantly different from each other), the technical and university levels were significantly different from elementary and from each other.

k. Not in general. However, the interaction term for married women shows they tend to exit from e to u at a higher rate than single men in 1992–93. The coefficient on this interaction term was not significant in 1995–96.

l. Married men are more likely to leave than single men and married women are less likely to leave than single men.

responsible for raising the children. Employers might therefore be biased by these traditional views to favor men in hiring and women in firing. And because these traditional family values are supported in government policies that oblige employers to provide women with generous maternity leave (full pay for six months, for example, or a job held available for them for three years) and child care leave, the new private sector employers, as well as state-operated entities under hard budget constraints, may actually hire fewer women, finding them to be more costly than men on the margin. Finally, a reduction in government provision of free child care in many countries has also contributed to a reduction of the labor supply of married women.

Changes in Welfare as Measured by Earnings and Income

In this section I survey the findings on income and earnings mobility in the transitional economies at the macro- and microeconomic levels. I begin by assessing the extent to which the dispersion of income and earnings has grown in the CEE and NIS. I then examine which groups' earnings are rising more rapidly relative to others to define the winners and losers in the transition process.

Dispersion of Earnings and Income: Comparisons among Countries

The removal of the planned economy wage grid alone would result in an increase in wage dispersion as the compressed wage structure changed to reflect the needs of the market. Further widening of the wage dispersion would be expected as a result of the changing labor market opportunities for different population groups. Finally, with the onset of unemployment and the changing ability of the state to provide a social safety net, further changes in total income of various groups in the populations within and across the transitional economies should be expected.

As table 7-5 shows, there were general and marked increases in the inequality of the distribution of earnings and per capita household disposable income from the late 1980s to the early 1990s. Several conclusions may be drawn from these statistics. First, during the socialist period of the late 1980s the dispersion was more similar in these countries than in the 1990s. However, even during the 1980s, income was distributed more equally in the CEE countries than in the Soviet republics. Within the CEE countries, Hungary had relatively higher dispersion of income than the others.

Table 7-5. *Levels of Inequality in East European Transition Economies and the United States, Selected Periods, 1987–94* [a]

Country	Gini – earnings		Gini – income		P90/P10 – earnings		P90/P10 – income	
	1987–89	1993–94	1987–89	1993–94	1987–89	1993–94	1987–89	1993–94
Bulgaria	0.21	0.28	0.33	0.34	2.56	—	—	4.33
Czech Republic	0.20	0.26	0.20	0.23	2.43	3.15	2.44	4.11
Hungary	0.27	0.34	0.23	0.23	3.14	3.72	2.81	2.66
Poland	0.21	0.28	0.28	0.32	2.43	3.38	3.07	3.92
Romania	0.19	0.28	0.24	0.26	1.94	3.49	—	3.18
Russia	0.27	0.45	0.27	0.41	3.45	14.86	3.16	15.10
Ukraine	0.24	0.36	0.23	0.26	3.04	8.04	2.76	5.07
United States			0.35	0.36	5.85		5.85	6.22

Sources: Columns 1, 3, 5, and 7: Atkinson and Micklewright (1992). Columns 2, 4, and 6: Cornia (1996) and Milanovic (1998). For the United States; Gottschalk and Smeeding (1997).

a. Earnings denotes gross monthly earnings. Income denotes disposable per capita household income (net of taxes and including transfers). P90/P10 denotes the ratio of earnings to income at the top (90th) decile to income at the bottom (10th) decile.

Table 7-6. *Share of Total Income, Top and Bottom Deciles, Four Countries, Selected Years, 1988–96*

Country	Reference years	Bottom decile[a]		Top decile[a]	
		Earlier	Later	Earlier	Later
Czech Republic[b]	1989, 1993	0.057	0.059	0.164	0.174
Czech Republic[c]	1988, 1992	0.053	0.050	0.170	0.205
Hungary[d]	1992, 1996	0.012	0.013	0.147	0.158
Slovakia[b]	1989, 1993	0.058	0.059	0.164	0.169
Russia[c]	1992, 1996	0.019	0.011	0.333	0.339

Sources: b. Garner and Terrell (1997). Income refers to total per capita disposable (net) income including transfers (individual distribution). *Family Budge Survey* data. c. Vecernik (1995). Income refers to net monthly earnings. *Microcensus* data. d. Galasi (1998). Income refers to net household per capita income, individual distribution. *Hungarian Household Panel Survey*. e. Commander, Tolstopiatenko, and Yemsov (1999). Income refers to total per capita income. *Russian Longitudinal Monitoring Survey (RLMS)*.

a. Except for Hungary, where figures refer to bottom and top 5 percent.

Second, an interesting pattern of inequality has emerged with the transition: there was a marked and dramatic increase in inequality of both earnings and income in the NIS economies, whereas the increase was moderate in the CEE countries. The most unequal distributions of income in the 1990s were in Russia and Ukraine (see table 7-5), but Armenia, Kyrgyz Republic, and Estonia (not shown in the table) also showed great inequality. The degree of dispersion in these countries is similar to that found in the high-inequality countries of Latin America and thus the world. Still, Bulgaria, the Czech Republic, Hungary, Poland, and Romania have experienced moderate increases in inequality and at present are at the same levels as the middle-inequality nations of the Organization for Economic Cooperation and Development but lower than in the United States.

Third, the widening of the income distribution seems to have been driven by increasing shares of income in the top decile in all countries (table 7-6). However, what was occurring to the share of income of the lowest decile differs across the NIS-CEE divide. In Hungary, the Czech Republic, and Slovakia the bottom decile of the population maintained its share of income, while in Russia the bottom decile lost its share.

Fourth, in all countries the increase in inequality, as measured by the Gini coefficient, has been higher for the distribution of earnings than for the distribution of income (see table 7-5).

As shown in detailed studies by Thesia Garner and Katherine Terrell for the Czech Republic and Slovakia, Simon Commander and Une Lee for Russia, and more generally in the 1998 UN Development Programme report, this difference in the patterns of change in inequality in the NIS relative to CEE economies has been brought about by the way governments managed (or failed to manage) the transition to market economies.[10] For example, the CEE governments were able to liberalize prices with better control of inflation than those of the NIS (see table 7-2). The CEE countries handled this in part by wage controls but largely by more restrictive monetary and fiscal policies. However, an important factor explaining the difference in Russia's and central Europe's growth in inequality and relative share of income at the bottom was the differences in their tax and transfer policies.

In Russia, overall tax revenue has been steadily declining since the early 1990s. Tax compliance for entrepreneurial and self-employment income has been negligible. Employers avoid the high payroll taxes (40 percent) with under-the-counter cash payments as well as in-kind payments. Because this has left the government reliant on the VAT, the tax incidence falls disproportionately on the middle and lower end of the income distribution.[11] The untaxed informal economy has not grown as large in central Europe as in Russia, and these countries have been undertaking tax reforms that have made their tax structures more progressive. Using a Gini decomposition analysis, Thesia Garner and Katherine Terrell have shown that, all else equal, changes in tax payments have reduced inequality in the Czech and Slovak Republics.[12] Using the same methodology, Simon Commander and Une Lee concluded that changes in tax payments from 1992 to 1996 have contributed to the increase in inequality in Russia.

Governments in formerly communist countries had to reengineer the social safety nets to reduce the level of security for all and provide targeted security to the needy. In addition, new systems needed to be built to handle unemployment. The CEE countries were generally very effective in restructuring their transfers (social welfare) to better target the lower end of the income distribution. For example, Garner and Terrell have shown that in the Czech Republic, after much restructuring of the safety net, the share of

10. Garner and Terrell (1998); Commander and Lee (1998); and UN Development Programme (1998).

11. Commander and Lee (1998).

12. Garner and Terrell (1998).

total income in the bottom decile that comprised government transfers (including social assistance, family benefits, health benefits, and unemployment benefits) rose from 8.2 percent in 1989 to 16.8 percent in 1993, whereas the share for the top decile remained about the same, at 3.1 percent in 1989 and 3.2 percent in 1993.[13] Studies have shown that, after an initial adjustment period, most of the CEE economies have provided unemployment assistance that is adequate and yet does not unduly prolong periods of unemployment.[14] But because of low government revenues, most observers have considered social assistance and unemployment benefits in Russia inadequate. Commander and Lee showed that changes in transfers have contributed to the increase in inequality in Russia, while Garner and Terrell found the opposite result for the Czech and Slovak Republics.[15] The difference in growth of inequality in Russia (and the NIS in general) and the CEE had largely to do with the relative maintenance of the real values of pension incomes as inflation took its toll.[16] The ratio of the average pension to the average wage was nearly 20 percent higher in the CEE countries than in the NIS. And because real wages fell less in the CEE countries, the real value of pensions was higher than in the NIS.

Who Is Gaining and Who Is Losing in Terms of Earnings?

Because the former centrally planned economies inherited a system of low wage differentials between groups with different skills, one could expect the rate of return on education to increase as these countries moved toward a market economy.[17] But the human capital and experience gained under communism may not be very useful in a market economy. Proponents of this hypothesis argue that the inherited education system did not promote fungible skills. If correct, this hypothesis would predict that the rate of return to education and experience would fall during the transition period. Various researchers have estimated Mincer-type earnings functions

13. Garner and Terrell (1997). Similarly, in Slovakia the share of transfers in total income in the bottom decile rose from 10.7 percent in 1989 to 17.1 percent in 1993, and the share in the top decile rose slightly from 3.1 percent in 1989 to 3.7 in 1993 (Garner and Terrell, 1997).

14. Ham, Svejnar, and Terrell (1998 and 1999); Puhani (1999); Terrell and Sorm (1999); and Wolff (1997).

15. Garner and Terrell (1998).

16. Pension income comprises between one-third to one-half of total income in the bottom three deciles of the Czech and Slovak distributions of household income in 1989 and 1993 (Garner and Terrell, 1997).

17. This section draws partially from Svejnar (1999).

Table 7-7. *Returns to a Year of Education, by Country, 1990s*[a]

Country	Reference years	Communism		Transition		Percent change	
		Men	Women	Men	Women	Men	Women
CEE							
Czech Republic[b]	1984, 1993	0.024	0.042	0.052	0.058	116.7	38.1
Czech Republic[c]	1989, 1996	0.027	0.038	0.058	0.070	114.8	84.2
East Germany[d]	1989, 1991	0.044		0.041		-6.8	
East Germany[e]	1988, 1991	0.077		0.062		-19.5	
Poland[f]	1987, 1992	0.05	0.071	0.07	0.085	40.0	
Slovakia[b]	1984, 1993	0.028	0.044	0.049	0.054	75.0	22.7
NIS							
Russia[g]	1991, 1994	0.031	0.054	0.067 0.093	0.096	116.1	77.8
United States[e]	1989	...	...	0.085	0.103	...	...
Latin America							
Argentina[h]	1989	...	...	0.103		...	...
Chile[h]	1989	...	...	0.120		...	...
Mexico[h]	1984	...	...	0.141		...	...
Venezuela[h]	1989	...	...	0.084		...	...
Europe							
Germany[h]	1987	...	...	0.049		...	...
Great Britain[h]	1984	...	...	0.068		...	...
Switzerland[h]	1987	...	...	0.079		...	...

Sources: b. Chase (1998); c. Munich and others (1998); d. Bird, Schwarze, and Wagner (1994); e. Krueger and Pischke (1995); f. Rutkowski (1996); g. Brainerd (1998); h. Psacharopoulos (1994).

a. Figures are reported coefficients from human capital (Mincer, 1974) earnings functions. The exception is the study by Chase (1998), which corrects the women's earnings functions for selectivity bias.

in the CEE countries, and some very interesting generalizations have emerged.[18]

Estimates of earnings functions using microeconomic data from the Czech Republic, Poland, Russia, and Slovakia indicate that returns to a year of education increased dramatically from communism to the early transition period (table 7-7).[19] A year of education raised earnings by only 2 to 5 percent during communism, but by the mid-1990s the rate of return was between 5 and 9 percent, similar to the estimates for the United States and other more developed market economies in Europe.[20]

The one exception to this pattern of increased returns is that in the former East Germany the rate of return to a year of education fell in the early part of the transition.[21] No clear explanation has been offered for this exception. The authors suggest that the type of education gained under communism was not useful, but there is no reason to believe that the education received in communist East Germany differed from that in the former Czechoslovakia. I hypothesize that the type of transition that occurred in East Germany was unique. Because of its special relationship with the former West Germany, East Germany was pulled immediately into a powerful market system, complete with competition from the skilled workers in the west. It did not go through the slower transition found in the other CEE and the NIS economies, whose labor markets were more insulated.

These studies also suggest that women enjoyed a higher rate of return to education than men under communism and that although they still have a higher return than men, the gap narrowed as the transition started.[22] The last two columns of table 7-7 show that in the Czech Republic and Russia the returns for men more than doubled, and in Slovakia they rose by

18. Mincer (1974).

19. Data on the Czech Republic are drawn from Chase (1998); and Munich, Svejnar, and Terrell (1998). Data on Poland are taken from Rutkowski (1996). Russian data are reported by Brainerd (1998). Chase (1998) also reports on data from Slovakia.

20. However, these rates are not nearly as high as the rates in Latin America, largely because the average number of years of schooling is much greater in the former communist countries than in Latin America; the law of diminishing returns applies to education as well.

21. Psacharopoulos's (1994) review of the literature for more than sixty countries indicates that there has been a pattern of declining returns to education, which may be explained largely by increased levels of education in most countries. For more on returns to education in the former East Germany, see Bird, Schwarze, and Wagner (1994); and Krueger and Pischke (1995).

22. Psacharopoulos (1994) shows that around the world the returns to a year of education are higher for women than for men, even after correction for selectivity bias. However, the findings with respect to level of education show a more mixed pattern.

75 percent, while the returns for women rose by far less during the same period.

Not shown in table 7-7 are the results of studies that have estimated the returns to education using the highest education level attained rather than years of education. These studies yield similar patterns in terms of the growth of returns and differences by gender. However, the rate of increase in returns varies by level of education. Peter Orazem and Milan Vodopivec have shown that in Slovenia the rate of return to all five levels of education rose for men from pretransition (1987) to transition (1991); this was also the case for women in all but the lowest two levels of education, where the return did not change.[23] The gain for men was relatively higher than that for women in all levels of education except academic high school. Daniel Munich and colleagues have found the same pattern in the Czech Republic for men and women: people at all levels of education experienced an increase in the rate of return to their education from 1989 to 1996. The rate of increase in the return was highest for vocational school graduates and lowest for those with an apprenticeship education.[24] The gains over time for each level, except academic high school, were greater for men than for women. In Hungary, Lazlo Halpern and Gabor Korosi also found that the rate of return to twelve years of education (all high schools) rose faster than the rate of return to university education.[25]

There is, then, a pattern in some of the CEE transitional economies that those who have completed high school (especially vocational high school and especially men) are gaining more than others in the transition. Why the returns to vocational education are rising faster than the returns to a university (and higher) level of education is a puzzle. I would speculate that this pattern reflects the types of skills demanded by the transition and the new private firms. The university-educated are still largely employed in the public sector (administration, education, and research institutes). This pattern may also reflect the fact that those who were selected for political reasons for a university education may not have been best suited for that education.

23. Orazem and Vodopivec. The five levels are elementary, vocational high school, academic high school, two years of university, and four or more years of university.

24. This finding that the returns to vocational education are rising and relatively high in the NIS and CEE countries is consistent with Psacharopoulos's (1994) finding that vocational-technical education has a higher return after a worker has eight years of education. This is the case in these former communist countries.

25. Halpern and Körösi.

What about the return to "general human capital" as captured by potential experience in the labor market since leaving school?[26] Here the evidence from several countries indicates that, unlike schooling, the return to experience obtained under communism at best remained the same but more often fell during the transition. This is the case for the Czech Republic, East Germany, Hungary, and Poland.[27] The exception is Slovenia, where Peter Orazem and MilanVodopivec found that the returns to experience rose from 1987 to 1991. The explanation for the Slovene exception seems to lie in the sharp increase in relative wages of retirement-age workers, which may have been brought about by large outflows of these workers from the Slovene labor force in the early years of the transition. For the majority of the transition economies, however, there is strong evidence that older workers are losing ground to younger workers because older workers' experience is not being valued in the labor market.

Conclusions

This chapter has surveyed studies of the changing welfare of various groups in the transitional economies of central and eastern Europe and the newly independent states of the former Soviet Union. The dissolution of communist-era job security, combined with the changing demands of the market, has created an unstable environment for workers and employers, forcing them to be more proactive in the labor market. The questions asked are how much mobility has been brought about by this systemic shift, and who is gaining and who is losing?

From comparisons among countries it is evident that the transition to a market economy has created substantial labor turnover and changes in the earnings structure. Although the recent scholarly studies do not have data that would allow one to compare countries in terms of the most efficient type of labor turnover, namely job-to-job mobility, sufficient data exist to show that workers in some countries have had shorter durations of

26. The variable for potential experience that is used in most Mincerian earnings functions is simply age minus years of schooling minus 6, where 6 is the age at which most people start school. Thus the return to experience can be viewed as a return to aging.

27. For the Czech Republic, see Chase (1998); and Munich, Svejnar, and Terrell (1998). For East Germany, see Bird, Schwarze, and Wagner (1994); and Krueger and Pischke (1995). For Hungary, see Halpern and Körösi (1997). For Poland, see Rutkowski (1996).

unemployment than their counterparts in the other transition economies. In all countries, large numbers of workers became unemployed or left the labor force in the early years of the transition. In all but the Czech Republic and Russia one observes a serious problem of long-term unemployment in these early years, resulting from the fact that the pool of unemployed has remained fairly stagnant, with only about one-third of the unemployed leaving in a given year. Until 1996 between 40 and 50 percent of the unemployed in the Czech Republic and Russia had been leaving unemployment for a job within a given year.[28] Higher demand was one factor driving the higher outflows (and thus shorter duration of unemployment) in the Czech Republic until 1996. Moreover, in both countries—perhaps to a greater extent in Russia—there is a growing gray economy that is providing employment.

Cross-country evidence from household surveys taken before and during the transition indicates that overall wage and income inequality has risen substantially in all transition economies, but the increase was greater in Russia and the NIS than in the CEE countries. Although in all transition countries most of the increase has been driven by upward mobility at the top of the income distribution, there is also evidence that those at the very bottom fared worse in Russia and the other NIS, where the tax and transfer system has been weaker than in the CEE countries.[29]

Within each transition country the evidence points to a very clear pattern of winners and losers. People with more education have gained because they are less likely to become unemployed and more likely to find a job if unemployed than their less educated counterparts. Moreover, the returns to education have been rising in all the transition economies, except former East Germany, which had a very different transition experience. There is some evidence that the fastest growth in earnings may have been among the vocational high school graduates. What role education has played in determining this outcome has not been explored here but would be an interesting analysis for another study. However, a leading conjecture is that education gives people the ability to adapt to change and the changing environment.

28. Although relatively high for the region, the transition probabilities out of unemployment to a job in these two countries were still lower than those in the United States in 1992–93.

29. The Russian government's social expenditures (on education, welfare benefits, unemployment benefits, and so forth) are relatively low, largely due to its inability to obtain tax revenues.

Younger workers have also had an advantage. Although they are more likely to quit or lose their jobs, they leave unemployment at a more rapid rate and therefore have shorter periods out of work. Meanwhile, earnings function analyses have shown that returns to experience (age) have declined. Younger workers are gaining relative to older workers in the earnings structure. And many older workers were pushed into early retirement in the early part of the transition, so that older people in general may be considered to be the losers (especially in the NIS economies, where the pensions have not kept up with inflation).

Finally, the other winners in the transition are men. Married women may be considered the biggest losers because they are more likely to become unemployed and less likely to leave unemployment compared to the other marital status and gender groups. And although earnings function analyses have shown that under communism women had a higher return to education than men, the gap has been closing during the transition.

In sum, the winners in the transition process have so far been young educated men whose skills have enabled them to exploit new opportunities in the private sector of the economy. The losers are women and older workers, whose human capital has been relatively devalued. Older workers also have few incentives to acquire the new skills that are relevant to the emerging market economy. These outcomes are the result, in part, of how governments have managed the transition and reflected societal attitudes in that process. For example, those countries that have successfully strengthened and targeted their social safety nets have managed to protect such vulnerable groups as the unemployed and pensioners and have moderated increases in inequality from below by allowing those in the bottom income deciles to maintain their share of income. However, protective labor legislation and reduction in government-provided child care has contributed to making married women in childbearing years losers in the labor market. Governments therefore have some scope for changing the winners and losers in the next phase of the transition, if they so choose.

References

Atkinson, Anthony B., and John Micklewright. 1992. *Economic Transformation in Eastern Europe and the Distribution of Income.* Cambridge University Press.

Basu, Swati, Saul Estrin, and Jan Svejnar. 1999. "Employment and Wage Behavior of Enterprises under Communism and in Transition: Evidence from Central Europe and Russia." William Davidson Institute Working Paper 114, University of Michigan.

Bellmann, Lutz, and others. 1995. "The Eastern German Labor Market in Transition: Gross Flow Estimates from Panel Data." *Journal of Comparative Economics* 20 (2): 139–70.

Bird, Edward, Johannes Schwarze, and Gert Wagner. 1994. "Wage Effects of the Move toward Free Markets in East Germany." *Industrial and Labor Relations Review* 47 (3): 390–400.

Boeri, Tito. 1998. "Labor Market Flows in the Midst of Structural Change." In S. Commander, ed., *Enterprise Restructuring and Unemployment in Models of Transition*. Washington: EDI Development Studies, World Bank.

Brainerd, Elizabeth. 1998. "Winners and Losers in Russia's Economic Transition." *American Economic Review* 88 (5): 1094–1116.

Chase, Robert S. 1998. "Markets for Communist Human Capital: Returns to Education and Experience in Post-Communist Czech Republic and Slovakia." *Industrial and Labor Relations Review* 51 (3): 401–23.

Commander, Simon, and Une Lee. 1998. "How Does Public Policy Affect the Income Distribution? Evidence from Russia, 1992–1996." Washington: World Bank

Commander, Simon, Andrei Tolstopiatenko, and Ruslan Yemestov. 1999. "Channels of Redistribution: Inequality and Poverty in Transition." *Economics of Transition* 7(2): 411–48.

Cornia, Giovanni Andrea. 1996. "Public Policy and Welfare Conditions during the Transition: An Overview." *MOCT-MOST* 6 (1): 1–17.

European Bank for Reconstruction and Development. 1998. *Transition Report 1998: Financial Sector in Transition*.

Foley, Mark C. 1997. "Labor Market Dynamics in Russia." Economic Growth Center Discussion Paper 780, Yale University.

Galasi, Peter. 1998. "Income Inequality and Mobility in Hungary, 1992–1996." UNICEF Innocenti Occasional Papers, Economic and Social Policy Series 64.

Garner, Thesia, and Katherine Terrell. 1998. "A Gini Decomposition Analysis of Inequality in the Czech and Slovak Republics during the Transition." *Economics of Transition*, 6(1): 23–46.

———. 1997. "Changes in Distribution and Welfare in Transition Economies: Market vs. Policy in the Czech Republic and Slovakia." William Davidson Institute Working Paper 77, University of Michigan.

Gora, Marek, and Hartmut Lehmann. 1995. "How Divergent Is Regional Labour Market Adjustment in Poland?" In S. Scarpetta and A. Woergoetter, eds., *The Regional Dimension of Unemployment in Transition Countries: A Challenge for Labour Market and Social Policies*. Paris: OECD.

Gottschalk, Peter, and Timothy M. Smeeding. 1997. "Cross-National Comparisons of Earnings and Income Inequality." *Journal of Economic Literature* 35 (2): 633–87.

Halpern, Lazlo, and Gabor Körösi. 1997. "Labor Market Characteristics and Profitability: Econometrics Analysis of Hungarian Firms, 1986–1995." William Davidson Institute Working Paper 41, University of Michigan.

Ham, John, Jan Svejnar, and Katherine Terrell. 1998. "Unemployment and the Social Safety Net during the Transition to a Market Economy: Evidence from Czech and Slovak Men." *American Economic Review* 88 (5): 1117–42.

———. 1999. "Factors Affecting Women's Unemployment Duration during the Transition in the Czech and Slovak Republics." *Economics of Transition* 7 (1): 47–78.

Jones, Derek C., and Takao Kato. 1997. "The Nature and the Determinants of Labor Market Transitions in Former Communist Economies: Evidence from Bulgaria." *Industrial Relations* 36 (2): 229–54.

King, Arthur E., and Vera A. Adamchik. 1999. "The Impact of Private Sector Development on Unemployment, Labor Force Reallocation, and Labor Market Flows in Poland." Paper prepared for the annual meetings of the Association for Comparative Economic Studies.

Krueger, Alan B., and J. S. Pischke. 1995. "A Comparative Analysis of East and West German Labor Markets: Before and after Unification." In R. B. Freeman and F. Katz, eds., *Differences and Changes in Wage Structures.* University of Chicago Press.

Milanovic, Branko. 1998. *Income, Inequality, and Poverty during the Transition: From Planned to Market Economy.* Washington: World Bank.

Mincer, Jacob. 1974. *Schooling, Experience and Earnings.* New York: National Buréau of Economic Research.

Munich, Daniel, Jan Svejnar, and Katherine Terrell. 1998. "Returns to Human Capital during Communism and in the Transition to Capitalism: Retrospective Evidence from the Czech Republic." University of Michigan.

Orazem, Peter F., and Milan Vodopivec. 1997. "Unemployment in Eastern Europe, Value of Human Capital in Transition to Market: Evidence from Slovenia." In Papers and Proceedings of the Eleventh Annual Congress of the European Economic Association, *European Economic Review* 41 (3–5): 893–903.

Psacharopoulos, George. 1994. "Returns to Education: A Global Update." *World Development* 22 (9): 1325–43.

Puhani, Patrick. 1999. "Unemployed Benefit Entitlement and Training Effects in Poland during Transition." William Davidson Institute Working Paper 226, University of Michigan.

Rutkowski, Jan. 1996. "High Skills Payoff: The Changing Wage Structure during Economic Transition in Poland." *Economics of Transition* 4 (1): 89–112.

Sorm, Vit, and Katherine Terrell. 1999. "Employment, Unemployment and Transition in the Czech Republic: Where Have All the Workers Gone?" William Davidson Institute Working Paper 140, University of Michigan.

Stefanova, Jana, and Katherine Terrell. 1998. "Gender Differences in Flows across Labor Market States in the Czech Republic." University of Michigan.

Svejnar, Jan. 1999. "Labor Markets in the Transitional Central and Easter European Economies." In O. Ashenfelter and D. Card, eds., *Handbook for Labor Economics*, vol. 3-4, North Holland: Elsevier.

Terrell, Katherine, and Vit Sorm. 1999. "Labor Market Policies and Unemployment in the Czech Republic." *Journal of Comparative Economics* 27: 33–60.

UN Development Programme. 1998. *Poverty in Transition?* Regional Bureau for Europe and the CIS.

Vecernik, Jiri. 1995. "Changing Earnings Distribution in the Czech Republic: Survey Evidence from 1988–1994." *Economics of Transition* 3 (3): 335–71.

Wolff, J. 1997. "Unemployment Benefits and Incentives in Hungary: New Evidence." William Davidson Institute Working Paper 111, University of Michigan.

World Bank. 1996. *World Development Report, 1996: From Plan to Market.* Washington.

DAVID E. HOJMAN

8 Inequality, Growth, and Political Stability: Can Income Mobility Provide the Answers?

Income mobility and distributional mobility are complex processes. Fast growth under conditions of great inequality provokes both favorable and unfavorable outcomes in economic efficiency, social welfare, social unease, and political stability. Only some of the initial mobility and the resulting mobility will be welcome. This chapter explores the basic issues, examines the data for Chile, and proposes a theoretical model that allows the reader to balance positive and negative aspects of mobility and identify survey questions for empirical research.

The chapter next explores possible reasons for the academic interest in income mobility and asks whether mobility should be pursued for its own sake. Next it discusses whether high mobility can compensate for great inequality. Five types of mobility, obeying distinct causes and provoking diverse consequences, are then explicitly identified. I argue that only one of these types, a market-driven, economically efficient medium-term mobility, unequivocally fulfils all the positive aims that have been attributed to mobility in general in previous studies. The problem of relative mobility, as outlined by Anthony Shorrocks, versus absolute mobility, as introduced by

The author would like to thank Markos Mamalakis for asking the relevant questions and offering concrete opportunities to try to answer them, and Anders Danielson and Carol Graham for their helpful comments. They are of course not responsible for any errors.

Gary Fields and Efe Ok, is addressed next.[1] I then examine aspects of distribution and mobility in Chile. A theoretical model that takes positive and negative outcomes into account is presented. The chapter concludes with some policy recommendations and research questions that remain unanswered and that should be considered in the design of future surveys.

When is more mobility preferable to less? A society without mobility is often associated with inherited privilege or inherited positions of underdogs. Mobility is perceived as one of the features that contribute to define modernity. However, more mobility is not preferable to less if it is a random event, and most members of society are risk averse. But mobility may not be random. A more dynamic society will result if, for example, a greater probability of upward mobility is positively associated with the amount of work effort, and a greater probability of downward mobility is positively associated with the absence of this effort. Yet more mobility has historically been associated with better opportunities for rent seeking, whether in late medieval and Counter Reformation (Golden Age) Spain, or during most of Spanish America's history, both in colonial times and during the import substitution period.[2]

What happens in the real world today? Some mobility is possibly random, but not all. In most societies a part of total mobility may be related to effort and another part to rent seeking. A further complication is that, also in most societies, some people are more exposed to mobility, random or not, than others. The length of time during which mobility is expected to have occurred or not occurred is also important. For instance, intergenerational mobility is associated with the transmission or absence of transmission of advantages and disadvantages from parents to their children. Thus much of intergenerational mobility would be good in that individuals' earnings would depend on their own achievements rather than on inherited privilege or inherited disadvantage. But short-term mobility tends to be associated with macroeconomic cycles and therefore would be bad.

Assume a society in which short-term mobility affects only people in the bottom quintiles 1 and 2. During the expansion phase of the macroeconomic cycle, the incomes of blue-collar workers in the manufacturing sector (who overwhelmingly constitute quintile 2) are higher than the incomes of white-collar social welfare officials (quintile 1). This is because during the expansionary phase all blue-collar workers have jobs, but many

1. Shorrocks (1978); and Fields and Ok (1996).
2. Roberts and Araujo (1997).

welfare officials are unemployed. This situation is reversed during the contraction phase of the cycle. Blue-collar workers in manufacturing lose their jobs, their incomes fall, and they are pulled down into quintile 1. At the same time, previously unemployed welfare officials get new jobs, their incomes rise, and they are pushed into quintile 2. The Lorenz curve remains constant over the cycle, unaffected by the economy's ups and downs. In dynamic terms, possibly this society would be better off without short-term mobility. Both social welfare and the rate of long-term growth are likely to be stronger without the uncertainty and instability associated with short-term fluctuations.

Some not repeated mobility may be caused by structural change. This type of mobility is different from that provoked by macroeconomic cycles because it is not reversible. It is also different from normal intergenerational mobility. One-off mobility caused by structural change may have been particularly relevant in Latin America since the beginning of the debt crisis in the early 1980s.

Why Are We Concerned with Mobility at All?

Concerns with income mobility have to do with concerns about economic efficiency, social unease, and political stability. These are the same concerns that drive interest in income distribution. There is considerable evidence that economic growth is faster where there is less income inequality.[3] Very convincing arguments have been put forward that, other things being equal, more even income distribution will reduce social unease and increase political stability. It is possible to think that conditions of great income inequality may somehow be moderated or compensated for or that the harsh effects may be mitigated by greater mobility. Maybe less inequality and more mobility go hand in hand. Nancy Birdsall and Carol Graham suggest that in Latin America "one plausible explanation for continued voter support for reform despite persistent inequality, for example, is enhanced mobility."[4] Anders Bjorklund and Markus Jantti show that, compared with the United States, "Sweden has both less income inequality and greater intergenerational mobility," and they cite studies by other authors that conclude, "economic equality in a country tends to be associated with

3. Birdsall and Londoño (1997).
4. Birdsall and Graham (1999).

higher social mobility."[5] But further analysis is required before accepting that these propositions apply more fundamentally than in just a trivial or definitional manner.

A more immediate reason for academic interest in income mobility is that for all their merits in other areas (including, at least in some countries, the alleviation of absolute poverty) recent programs of structural adjustment or the introduction of free market, open economy policies in the 1980s and 1990s have failed to improve income distribution. This is a particularly serious problem in Latin America, which has traditionally suffered one of the most lopsided income distributions in the world. Experience suggests that concerns with equality have led to theoretical and policy impasses. In policy terms they have led to economic populism, with possibly harmful effects on income distribution.[6] But if nothing can be done about equality, maybe at least something can be done about mobility? In some very poor countries, particularly in Africa, anecdotal evidence suggests that ordinary people are keener to accept inequality if they perceive that there is a possibility of some mobility. But maybe this happens only in very poor countries. We do not know whether tolerance of inequality (among its victims, as opposed to among academics) increases or diminishes with the level of absolute income.

There are, of course, ideological and political differences between the concern with equality and the concern with mobility. The latter is more individualistic. In England, for example, fast upward mobility for some is associated with the Thatcher era, which is also associated with worsening inequalities. But there are other associations that are much more positive. Mobility is at the root of the American Dream. It is the force that makes it possible for migrants to new lands to reinvent themselves and start new lives. Arguably, these new migrants do not displace others, since they arrive at empty lands, and they do not take natives' jobs or the natives' positions in the income distribution pyramid. What new migrants contribute is more than they take for themselves. The progress of a new migrant does not make anyone else worse off. On the contrary. And under favorable conditions even highly stratified and rigid societies may grant upward mobility to the best among their members, as was the case with the extraordinary amounts of mobility provoked in England by World War II.

5. Bjorklund and Jantti (1997, p. 1017).
6. Dornbusch and Edwards (1991).

New mobility follows after social, economic, technological, or institutional revolutions. If Latin America is adopting free-market, open-economy reforms along the lines of the U.S. development model, why should mobility along lines of the American Dream be denied to the Latin American peoples? Economists do not know whether there is more mobility in Latin America today than in the 1960s and 1970s (unless it is assumed that more mobility is an inevitable consequence of freer markets). Maybe one of the reasons they were not interested in mobility in Latin America during the period of industrialization through import substitution was not that there was no mobility, but that mobility tended to benefit rent seekers.

Mobility for Mobility's Sake?

Perhaps a society with at least some income or distributional mobility is better than an absolutely rigid society. However, income mobility is not always and automatically a good thing. Assume a society formed by three households, headed by Alice, Betty, and Carol, respectively. Their respective incomes are 1, 2, and 3, which is represented by the vector $(1, 2, 3)$. Assume that there is a one-off income mobility such that Alice's income increases from 1 to 3 and Carol's income falls from 3 to 1. The new distribution vector is $(3, 2, 1)$. Has social welfare increased, diminished, or remained constant? Social welfare may have increased if, for example, the new income distribution pattern is more conducive to faster economic growth. Or it may have increased if the new pattern is sanctioning ability and willingness on the one hand and on the other hand failure to follow market signals, and the relative prices are adequately reflecting social scarcities. Or social welfare may have increased if leisure, as compared to income, is more important as an argument in Carol's than in Alice's household utility function. But none of these conditions may apply, which means that this one-off mobility has led to a loss of welfare. Moreover, there may be a contradiction in that some of these conditions may be suggesting that social welfare will be improved by pattern $(1, 2, 3)$, which favors Carol, and other conditions by pattern $(3, 2, 1)$, which favors Alice. In Latin America, if not anymore at least until very recently, upward mobility has been associated with taking advantage of old and new opportunities for rent seeking.[7] In the 1980s and 1990s, structural adjustment and structural change

---

7. Roberts and Araujo (1997).

Table 8-1. *Short-Term and Long-Term Inequality Patterns*
Income per year in constant value units

Pattern	Year 1	Year 2	Year 3	. . .[a]	Long term
Pattern 1 (no mobility)					
Alice	2	2	2	2	2
Betty	2	2	2	2	2
Carol	2	2	2	2	2
Pattern 2 (high mobility with low short-term inequality)					
Alice	1	3	1	3	2
Betty	2	2	2	2	2
Carol	3	1	3	1	2
Pattern 3 (high mobility with high short-term inequality)					
Alice	0.5	3.5	0.5	3.5	2
Betty	2	2	2	2	2
Carol	3.5	0.5	3.5	0.5	2
Pattern 4 (Fields and Ok absolute mobility)					
Alice	1	3	5	6	n.a.
Betty	2	2	3	2	n.a.
Carol	3	1	1	1	n.a.

n.a. Not available.
a. For Pattern IV, this column corresponds to year 4.

may have provoked many instances of one-off mobility, both upward and downward.

Similar difficulties and ambiguities apply to repeated (as opposed to one-off) short-term mobility provoked by temporary income changes. Considering patterns 1 and 2 in table 8-1, possibly both Alice and Carol prefer pattern 1 (no mobility), which guarantees them the same income every year, to pattern 2 (high mobility), which imposes year-to-year income fluctuations, even if in the long term the results of both patterns are the same.

Freer markets will inevitably provoke more repeated mobility (and therefore it will be possible to say that this mobility is good because it is synonymous with freer markets) only if the product cycles are short, are frequent and independent from each other, there are no entry barriers, and the technologies are such that the economies of scale and scope are not important. But even in this case, which requires strong assumptions, the effects of product cyclicality will be much more benign for entrepreneurs than for wage earners. Mobility can be either upward or downward, and the declines are much more damaging for those who do not have any form of sheltering, protection, or insurance against them.

Can High Mobility Compensate for Great Inequality?

The short answer to the question of whether high mobility compensates for the lack of pervasive equality is probably not. Only some particular classes of mobility can compensate for strong inequality (I examine several types of mobility later). Indeed great inequality may be a necessary condition for high mobility, or high mobility may be a necessary condition for great inequality. Or mobility and inequality may be related to each other in a purely definitional way, which implicitly or explicitly excludes the possibility of causal links between them. As a matter of definition, "all countries have less inequality when a longer accounting period is used, and taking mobility into account reduces the amount of inequality when a multiple-year perspective is used."[8] This is because "those occupying the highest and lowest positions in the income hierarchy rarely remain there forever."[9] For example, in his deservedly popular definition, Shorrocks defines relative mobility as being higher, the greater short-term inequality is in relation to a constant level of long-term inequality.[10] He defines mobility, M, as one minus rigidity, R: $M = 1 - R$.

Rigidity itself is defined as the ratio between a long-term inequality index, IL, and the average of the relevant short-term (or year-to-year) inequality indices, IS: $R = IL / Average IS$.

R will always be positive because both IL and IS are positive. In general, R will be smaller than one except in the extreme case of a completely rigid society, where there is absolutely no mobility at all. Then R will be equal to one, and M equal to zero.[11]

---

8. Gottschalk (1997, p. 38).

9. Shorrocks (1978, p. 377).

10. This is logically the same as saying that mobility is higher, the lower long-term inequality is in relation to a constant pattern of year-to-year inequality. The two definitions are logically identical, but in fact the first is much more realistic than the second. Year-to-year inequality is always temporary and therefore flexible, whereas long-term inequality is conceptually permanent and therefore constant.

11. Several of the Shorrocks results apply only if the inequality indices IS and IL fulfill certain particular conditions; see Shorrocks (1978) for a complete discussion. For empirical applications of this index, also see Shorrocks (1978), which uses U.S. data, and Jarvis and Jenkins (1998), who apply

Incidentally, one may use the Shorrocks index once more to show that more mobility is not necessarily better. Consider again the society formed by three households headed by Alice, Betty, and Carol. Let Betty's annual income be constant and equal to 2, and let Alice's and Carol's income fluctuate from year to year according to the patterns 2 and 3 of table 8-1. Let the inequality index (*IS* and *IL*) be the ratio between the income of the richest household to the income of the poorest household. Under pattern 2 the short-term inequality index, *IS*, is equal to 3 (3 divided by 1) year after year. In pattern 3, *IS* is equal to 7 (3.5 divided by 0.5), again year after year. Because the long-tem inequality indices, *IL*, are the same in both patterns (and equal to 1), rigidity will be weaker and mobility greater in pattern 3. Thus, according to the Shorrocks index, there is more mobility under pattern 3. However, it would be extremely difficult to argue that social welfare is greater under pattern 3. This can only be true under many strong and crucially unrealistic assumptions. Paradoxically, pattern 1 presents both the highest level of equality (total equality, both in the long term and the short term) and the least Shorrocks-type mobility, zero. In the Shorrocks approach complete equality is by definition identical to zero mobility.

Mobility and inequality may be related to each other, with the "wrong" sign, in a more fundamental or structural rather than a purely definitional way. For instance, in the model developed by Oded Galor and Daniel Tsiddon (1997) mobility and inequality move together, following the different phases of a cycle of technological progress.[12] During periods of major technological invention, both inequality and mobility increase in favor of the highest-ability, best-qualified individuals, who generate the technological breakthroughs and benefit from them. During periods of technological diffusion, the new inventions become generally accessible and both mobility and inequality decrease. This or similar theoretical models seem to have been at least partly confirmed by recent empirical evidence.[13]

Five Types of Income Mobility

No serious analysis of income mobility or distributional mobility can be undertaken in developing countries unless a clear distinction is drawn

---

it to British data. In this chapter I use the term "relative mobility" to refer to the dimension represented by the Shorrocks (1978) index to distinguish it from the concept of "absolute mobility" presented by Fields and Ok (1996).

12. Galor and Tsiddon (1997).

13. Gottschalk and Smeeding (1997).

among five types of mobility: intergenerational, short term (or year-to-year, or dependent on the macroeconomic cycle), life-cycle, one-off (or provoked by structural change), and medium term (or economically efficient and market directed). These types are always present simultaneously, and it may be difficult in practice to distinguish them from one another. However, they are not only conceptually different but also different in their causes and consequences.

Intergenerational Mobility

A high rate of intergenerational mobility is largely the result of an open, fair, high-quality educational system. Restricted intergenerational mobility is typically associated with inherited privilege and inherited disadvantage ("Why do doctors' children become doctors? Why do manual workers' children become manual workers?"). In terms of compensating for social unease and increased political instability, intergenerational mobility is possibly useless and certainly not a substitute for other, shorter-term forms of mobility. It is unlikely that a high level of intergenerational mobility will ease social tensions in an extremely inequitable society, not even under the most favorable assumptions about discount rates and altruistic attitudes. It is also unlikely that a high level of intergenerational mobility will be present in such a society. Almost as a matter of definition, inequitable societies do not have open, fair, and high-quality educational systems, and therefore they cannot have high rates of intergenerational mobility. In this sense intergenerational mobility is a consequence rather than a cause of the processes that I am interested in here. In terms of diagnostics, there is no need to bother with intergenerational mobility because looking directly at the educational system will provide all the answers. In terms of policy, any direct attempts at changing other aspects of society rather than increasing intergenerational mobility will be easier and more rewarding.

Short-Term Macroeconomic-Cycle Mobility

Short-term, year-to-year income mobility is typically a consequence of the macroeconomic cycle. Possibly the most characteristic form of this type of mobility is represented by transitions in and out of unemployment. These temporary income fluctuations are not popular or desirable, and year-to-year mobility increases neither the well-being of its victims nor social welfare. A particularly undesirable expression of this problem appears when

Table 8-2. *Effects of Periodical Unemployment among the Lowest Earners*
Income per year in constant value units

Household	Year 1	Year 2	Year 3	Year 4	Long term
Alice	1	0	1	0	0.5
Betty	0	1	0	1	0.5
Carol	3	3	3	3	3
Sharon	5	5	5	5	5
Tracy	6	6	6	6	6

low permanent incomes are associated with sharp temporary fluctuations. Those workers with the fewest skills may be precisely the ones with the shortest periods of employment. In the absence of unemployment benefits (with income equal to zero during the period of unemployment), the evolution of the income distribution pattern would be as shown in table 8-2. This type of short-term mobility is thoroughly undesirable, but it is very difficult to avoid. However, some of its worst effects can be minimized in, for example, societies with high levels of life-cycle mobility.

Life-Cycle Mobility

High rates of life-cycle mobility (most of the poor are young and most of the young are poor; most of the rich are old and most of the old are rich) are typical of high-income, full-employment societies in advanced stages of their transitions to low rates of fertility and mortality. These societies also tend to be ethnically homogeneous. In some that are ethnically heterogeneous, high rates of life-cycle mobility may be observed among some ethnic groups (usually the most privileged ones) but not in the others. In the presence of high life-cycle mobility, every waiter seems to be also a university student who is waiting tables as a part-time job.[14] In societies with weak life-cycle mobility, such as the traditional Latin American societies, waiters may be old because they will be, or will have been, employed as such for their entire working lives. University students tend to be rich and do not need to wait tables.[15]

14. Reflecting patterns of either self-selection or sex discrimination that economic progress has been unable to overcome, these workers tend to be female, waitresses rather than waiters.
15. Lam and Schoeni (1993).

A high rate of life-cycle mobility is probably beneficial in easing social tensions provoked by income inequalities and in generating political stability. Additionally, societies with high life-cycle mobility may be more egalitarian because income differences between households usually depend at least partly on the age composition of the household. But nothing of this is very useful for the policies of developing countries, which are unlikely to fulfill the required labor market (full employment), demographic, ethnic, and educational conditions usually associated with high life-cycle mobility.

One-Off Mobility

One-off structural change provokes one-off distributional mobility. One-off mobility will be generated (it has been in Latin America during the 1990s) by the creation of new markets, the liberalization of old markets, and privatization. In general, one-off mobility is good for social welfare because it rewards those who attend to the new market signals and punishes those who ignore them. But there are questions that remain unanswered. Are relative prices conveying adequate market signals? Are markets competitive and well behaved? Are instances of market failure dealt with swiftly and adequately by using, for example, Pigovian taxes and subsidies to distort choices toward optimal outcomes? Are emerging instances of rent seeking being kept under control? Even if satisfactory answers are given to these questions, the one-off nature of this type of mobility makes it an unlikely tool for policy purposes.

Market-Directed, Economically Efficient Medium-Term Mobility

The final type of income mobility is a repeated, medium-term mobility that is both market directed and economically efficient. This is the only form of mobility that unequivocally facilitates economic growth, eases social tensions, increases political stability, and compensates for great inequality. Under the appropriate conditions it will also be compatible with or functional or possible under a range of policy instruments. Because this type of mobility is repeated, a household may benefit from it again and again, moving gradually up the income distribution pyramid. Different from year-to-year macroeconomic-cycle mobility, market-driven medium-term mobility is not an accident that fate inflicts upon helpless victims. It is permanent rather than temporary, provided that the household continues fulfilling the conditions that made mobility possible in the first place. It is also medium-term as opposed to long-term, or intergenerational, because incentives that require people to wait too long for the rewards are not good ones. This mobility is market directed in that it is entirely a reward for following the market signals conveyed by the price system when relative prices correctly reflect social scarcities. Finally, this mobility is not only optimal in static terms but also in dynamic terms: it is economically efficient in that it creates the most favorable conditions for fast growth in aggregate production. Medium-term mobility, just like intergenerational and life-cycle mobility, requires a good educational system. People need to be qualified if they are going to be prepared to take advantage of new market opportunities. The presence of medium-term mobility is the result of policies. Different policies generate new incentives that change attitudes.

Absolute or Relative Mobility?

I have already identified relative mobility in terms of the Shorrocks index. It may be useful to compare his concept with that of absolute mobility as defined by Fields and Ok. For them, absolute mobility is formed by the sum of two aspects: the transfer of income between households and the change in general well-being that results from aggregate economic growth (or contraction). Their definition of absolute mobility is illustrated by pattern 4 in table 8-1. Between year 1 and year 2, absolute mobility has only one component: the transfer of income between Carol and Alice. Absolute mobility amounts to four units: two that were taken from Carol and two that were given to Alice. Between year 2 and year 3 absolute mobility again has only one component, except that this time the component is aggregate growth. There has been no transfer between households, but the economy has expanded from a total income of six units to a total income of nine. Therefore, absolute mobility between years 2 and 3 is equal to three units (nine minus six). Finally, between years 1 and 3, absolute mobility is equal to seven. This total is formed by the sum of a transfer equal to four (two units taken from Carol plus two units received—one does not need to know by whom), plus aggregate output growth equal to three.

Fields and Ok's definition of absolute mobility makes it possible to distinguish between income mobility and distributional mobility. Between years 2 and 3 there has been (absolute) income mobility but no distributional mobility because the ranking has not changed. The problem with

Fields and Ok's approach is that any identification of aggregate growth with absolute mobility ignores distributional issues. For example, the same amount of absolute mobility (three units) and the same type of absolute mobility (caused by aggregate output growth only, but not by transfers) apply between years 2 and 3 and years 2 and 4. However, there are possibly several important consequences for the economy and society that will be different under the distribution vector (5, 3, 1) from what would obtain under vector (6, 2, 1). As mentioned before, these differences are likely to include growth rates, savings rates, human capital investment, health outcomes, demographic patterns, effectiveness of the tax system, social cohesiveness, political stability, the quality of policymaking, and even group identities.[16]

More generally, Fields and Ok's approach suffers from the same limitations as other attempts to apply the idea of Pareto improvement to this discussion. Pareto improvement occurs when someone has been made better off without anyone else having been made worse off (as mentioned before, a good textbook example is the typical immigrant in pursuit of the American Dream). But the concept of Pareto improvement cannot be assimilated to Fields and Ok's concept of absolute income mobility caused by aggregate output growth. For example, in pattern 4 of table 8-1, one cannot talk of Pareto improvement to describe the change from year 2, vector (3, 2, 1), to year 4, vector (6, 2, 1). In terms of absolute income, Alice is better off by three units, and the absolute incomes of Betty and Carol have not changed. However, for all the reasons mentioned in the previous paragraph, conceivably Betty and Carol may both be worse off in year 4 than in year 2.

The new situation may have been made even worse by the presence of rich-to-poor demonstration effects and imitation attitudes. In all unequal societies, from advanced industrialized or postindustrial ones to developing ones, the poor tend to imitate the consumption patterns and styles of the rich. In high-inequality (by European standards) England every woman aspires to get married in a wedding as similar as possible to the royal wedding between Charles and Diana. In low-inequality Norway, desirable weddings are inspired by the peasant traditions of the nineteenth-century national romantic style. Having a "proper" wedding is more expensive and more damaging to and difficult for the poor in England than in Norway. In Chile, other things being equal and after controlling for absolute in-

16. Birdsall and Graham (1999); Wilkinson (1996); and Hojman (1993, 1996a, 1999a).

come, great inequality makes child mortality among the poor worse, possibly because there is a negative relationship between the desirability of a consumer good due to rich-to-poor demonstration and imitation effects (the extent of visibility of a consumer good) and the effectiveness of the consumer good in improving child survival chances at the household level. Compare cars, holidays abroad, color television, or other household electronics goods with food, heating, over-the-counter medicines, or visits to the doctor.[17]

In contrast, the concept of relative mobility as expressed in the Shorrocks index imposes more stringent requirements as to whether or when mobility increases social welfare. If household A moves from quintile 2 to quintile 3, by definition this movement requires one or more compensatory movements, with a net effect such that another household B has to move from another quintile to quintile 2 (the number of households in each quintile must always be the same). For an unequivocal improvement in social welfare, not only the upward mobility benefiting A but also the possibly downward mobility affecting B must both be a good thing.

Chile: Income Distribution

The distribution of income by deciles in Chile between 1987 and 1996 is shown in table 8-3. This is household income (there is no information about individuals) and it includes all government subsidies. The picture that emerges is one of fast growth of absolute income combined with very great income inequality (and other inequalities).[18] The pattern of inequality is remarkably constant, although not completely rigid. Average real income grew by 55 percent between 1987 and 1996. In 1987 the top decile income was 24.2 times that of the bottom decile; in 1996 it was 24.3 times.[19] From 1987 to 1996 the real income of the bottom decile increased by 50 percent and that of the top decile, by 54 percent, suggesting that there has been some comparative improvement, albeit marginal, for the middle deciles at the expense (relatively speaking) of the top and the bottom of the pyramid. Deciles 3 and 4 improved by 61 percent, decile 6 by 60 percent, and

17. Hojman (1999a).
18. Hojman (1993).
19. This figure has been calculated using the raw CEPAL data in pesos at November 1996 prices. The 1996 value from table 8-3 is slightly higher because of rounding errors introduced by deflating using the consumer price index and by using thousands of pesos as the unit instead of the single peso.

Table 8-3. *Household Income in Chile, by Deciles, 1987–96*
Thousands of November 1987 pesos per month

Decile	1987	1990	1992	1994	1996
1	14	16	20	19	21
2	24	28	33	34	37
3	31	37	42	43	50
4	38	45	51	54	61
5	46	54	62	65	72
6	55	64	70	76	88
7	67	78	88	93	106
8	92	96	110	120	140
9	133	144	159	175	199
10	339	385	437	461	521
Total	84	95	107	114	130

Source: Calculated from Cómision Económica para América Latina y el Caribe (1997), which is based on the CASEN surveys, and Economist Intelligence Unit (various issues) data.

decile 7 by 58 percent. There has been substantial Fields and Ok absolute mobility caused by aggregate growth, but very little absolute mobility caused by transfers (only between 1992 and 1994 and affecting negatively decile 1 only). The Shorrocks index cannot be computed because there are no longitudinal data or individual case studies.

This remarkably stable income distribution has been generated by a number of factors, some of them equalizing and others the opposite.[20] Fast economic growth has been strongly labor intensive, gradually eliminating the large pockets of unemployment that were widespread in the mid-1980s. About 1.1 million new jobs were created between 1987 and 1994, a remarkable achievement in a total labor force of 4 million to 5 million.[21] Total participation in the labor force (men and women) increased from 51 percent of the economically active population in 1986 to 55 percent in 1994. The population has been getting older. Favorable external accounts have helped the currency appreciate. Real appreciation in relation to the

20. For a model addressing a situation in Taiwan that is in some respects similar, see Bourguignon, Fournier, and Gurgand (1998). On Chile, see Hojman (1993).
21. Hojman (1996a).

U.S. dollar was more than 30 percent during the period.[22] This has worked to the benefit of the lower rather than the upper deciles because the consumer basket of the former is comparatively biased in favor of tradables and against nontradables. By the end of the 1990s both the fast, labor-intensive economic growth and the currency appreciation were at least partially, and temporarily, under threat from the 1997–98 crisis in Asia. Technological progress and opening the economy have increased the demand for and the rewards to skilled personnel in relation to unskilled workers. Female participation in the labor force has increased, which helped the lower deciles in the 1970s and 1980s (women were taking jobs that men did not want, or those for which men were not wanted), but more recently female participation has been helping the upper deciles because only high-productivity female employees can afford expensive private child care arrangements. Since the 1970s or even before, there has also been a substantial increase in formal education. In particular, since 1990, subsidies to the poor (via cash or housing, health care, and education) have increased.

With the poverty line at about 40,000 November 1987 constant pesos, those below the line comprised 40 percent of the households in 1987 but only 20 percent in 1996 (table 8-3). Thus, households in decile 3, for example, were poor in 1987 (with an income of 31,000 pesos) but not in 1996 (an income of 50,000 pesos). These people can now afford to satisfy their basic needs. However, this does not seem to have been enough to make them happy. Even if their aspirations have remained the same, members of these households are now even further apart from the average Chilean. In 1987 decile 3 was 53,000 pesos away (84,000 minus 31,000) from the average income. By 1996 the gap had increased to 80,000 (130,000 minus 50,000) in pesos of constant value. The gap widened not only in relation to the average income but also in relation to the median. The median is important because it determines key political processes in a democracy. In 1987 the median income was 50,000 pesos and the gap with respect to decile 3 19,000 pesos. In 1996 the median income was 80,000 pesos and the gap in relation to decile 3 had increased to 30,000 pesos. So households in decile 3 were no longer poor, but the gap in relation to the average Chilean (either in terms of arithmetic mean or median) was worsening. Furthermore, aspirations may have been increasing. Large rich-to-poor demonstration and imitation effects may have been at work, inflating the

22. Hojman (1995).

number and the seriousness of those expectations that remain unsatisfied.[23] Thus it is not surprising that many low-income Chileans are being affected by feelings of increasing alienation in relation to the economy and the polity. In the December 1997 congressional elections, nearly 40 percent of the voters either failed to register (despite the fact that registering is compulsory) or spoiled their votes.[24]

Chile: Mobility

If income distribution is, if not dismal, at least not very good, mobility is not much better. In the absence of longitudinal data or individual case studies, there is some evidence of monthly earnings differentials and their evolution between 1986 and 1992 (table 8-4) and of hourly wage rate differentials according to occupational category and their evolution between 1993 and 1997 (table 8-5). Because the periods involved are not very long (especially 1993 to 1997), one may assume that there was little occupational mobility reflected in each table. Most people were in the same occupational category in 1986 and in 1992 and in the same category in 1993 and 1997 (comparison between the two tables is not possible because there is no information about hours worked for the first period). If this assumption is accepted, it follows that the two tables are the closest approximation to a longitudinal study that is available.

23. According to Oppenheimer (1998), "a funny thing is happening to this country: it has the most robust economy in Latin America, poverty has been cut in half this decade and virtually all business projections look great, yet a sizable part of its people look unhappy . . . when you talk with taxi drivers, newspaper vendors or people in the street, it's difficult to find many people who are happy now or upbeat about the future. Most of what you hear are complaints about . . . an uneven distribution of the country's rapidly growing wealth. . . . Many Chileans explain the country's malaise as a crisis of rising expectations: the poor are only a little less poor, while the rich are becoming substantially richer, generating widespread resentment among those left behind."

24. It would be misleading to suggest that the whole of voter attrition in Chile since the 1988 plebiscite and the 1989 election is the result of inequality and nothing else. Interest in voting was naturally higher during the early stages of the transition to democracy after almost seventeen years of military dictatorship. Since then, all the political parties have become gradually discredited. Still, traditionally Chileans have taken pride in their positive civic attitudes, and election day has traditionally been seen as a civic *fiesta*. Historically the participation rates at elections have been very high. The highest rates of nonregistration for voting purposes in the late 1990s are among the young, who are also affected by the highest rates of unemployment (in some regions and periods, up to three times the adult unemployment rate). Nonregistration has a high cost for whoever chooses to use it as a form of protest because registration is compulsory and proof of registration is often requested jointly with the identity card.

Table 8-4. *Index of Monthly Earnings in Chile, by Occupational Category, 1986 and 1992*

Each year average = 100

Occupational category	1986	1992
Average	100	100
Managers (*administradores y gerentes*)	419	515
Professionals and technicians (*profesionales y técnicos*)	178	168
Administrative employees (*trabajadores administrativos*)	91	88
Salesmen and women (*vendedores*)	115	114
Skilled white-collar (*trabajadores especializados: empleados*)	105	103
Skilled blue-collar (*trabajadores especializados: obreros*)	63	67
Unskilled workers (*trabajadores no especializados*)	51	53
Workers in personal services (*trabajadores en servicios personales*)	50	51

Source: Ramsden (1998).

The most notorious characteristic shown in table 8-4 is the large increase in the relative earnings of managerial personnel—from 419 percent of the average in 1986 to 515 percent in 1992. This was at the expense of practically everyone else, apart from some categories at the bottom of the pay scale. It is possible that this improvement at the top reflects not only rewards to human capital but rather a combination of rewards to human capital, rewards to property, rewards to entrepreneurial skills in short supply, and maybe even a gradual monopolization of the economy. Table 8-5 shows a similar process, except that the beneficiaries are now both managerial personnel and professionals (possibly highly qualified), mostly at the expense of categories of less skilled (but not unskilled) workers: technicians, skilled workers (possibly blue-collar), and machine operators. Both between 1986 and 1992 and 1993 and 1997 the data show a relative improvement of substantial size for those at the top of the pay scale.[25]

Intergenerational, life-cycle, and medium-term mobility are hampered because traditionally the Chilean educational system has acted more as a

25. There is no contradiction between table 8-3 (which shows roughly the same proportional improvement for all deciles) on the one hand and tables 8-4 and 8-5 (according to which the best paid are getting gradually better off at the expense of the rest) on the other hand. This is because table 8-3 includes all antipoverty subsidies. Data in all three tables are after income tax but before value-added tax.

Table 8-5. *Index of Hourly Wage Rates in Chile, by Occupational Category,*
1993 and 1997

Each year average = 100

Occupational category	1993	1997
Average	100	100
Managerial personnel (*personal directivo*)	428	445
Professionals (*profesionales*)	209	234
Technicians (*técnicos*)	160	156
Administrative employees (*personal administrativo*)	116	118
Personal services and security (*trabajadores en servicios personales y de protección*)	68	67
Salesmen and women in established commerce (*vendedores en locales*)	79	77
Skilled workers (*trabajadores calificados*)	101	92
Machine operators (*operarios de máquinas e instalaciones*)	97	90
Unskilled workers (*trabajadores no calificados*)	72	73

Source: Ramsden (1998).

tool for the reproduction of inequalities than as an instrument of mobility.[26] All studies consistently report large gaps in performance at school
examinations according to whether children come from state or private
schools. Performances in Spanish and mathematics among state school
children tend to be about 50 percent, whereas for private school children
they can be as high as 80 to 85 percent. As could be expected, there is a
strong association between parents' income and the type of school their
children attend.[27] Some recent reforms offer some hope for the future.[28]
Unfortunately, there have also been some steps backward, such as the recent move to deemphasize the teaching of economics in secondary schools.[29]
So-called educational experts in official agencies insist on providing less

26. See Arancibia (1994); Larrañaga (1994); Lehmann (1994); Sancho (1994); Aedo (1998); and
Sánchez (1998).
27. For reproduction of inequalities among the seriously disadvantaged see Buvinic and others
(1992).
28. Cox (1997); and Hojman (1999b).
29. "La semana económica" (1998).

vocational education than required, even against unequivocal market evidence of strong demand by employers and against the preferences explicitly expressed by parents and children.[30]

There is some evidence of the development of a new entrepreneurial middle class, which suggests the presence of at least some market-directed, medium-term mobility. However, characteristically those who tend to benefit are highly skilled people, professionals who already have university degrees.[31] This mobility favors only entrepreneurs or the self-employed; there is little evidence that it reaches employees. The privatization and market liberalization that took place in the 1970s and 1980s generated much one-off mobility. It is possible that, as the free market, open economy policies take hold, and they and their effects mature, there will be a constant gradual creation of new markets. This would have an effect analogous to that of technological progress in the model of Oded Galor and Daniel Tsiddon.[32] Following cyclical patterns, those directly involved in the creation of new markets would be rewarded with higher incomes and upward mobility. This would, however, increase overall inequality rather than diminish it. Still, although the general picture is that liberalization has diminished the opportunities for rent seeking, new rent-seeking possibilities have appeared, favoring, for example, some farmers, textile manufacturers, the national airlines, or even middle-class specialists engaged in the poverty-alleviating industries.[33] And, as mentioned before, unemployment has increased, at least temporarily, as a result of the crisis in Asia, and undesirable short-term mobility increased with it. Possibly one of the most interesting developments likely in the next few years is that gradually high earners and very high earners will receive their income more and more from the returns of financial investments rather than as salaries or profits. These people (in the top decile or deciles) earn so much already that they are saving a lot (at the same time that they also spend a lot). As their financial investments and the returns from them continue increasing, they will tend more and more to prefer leisure to labor. This will create new opportunities in the labor market and new opportunities for upward mobility for others (in middle or higher but not in the top deciles).

30. See Cáceres and Bobenrieth (1993); and Arancibia (1994).
31. Montero (1997).
32. Galor and Tsiddon (1997).
33. Hojman (1996a, 1996b).

A Model of Distribution, Growth, Mobility, and Political Attitudes

This section develops a theoretical model that may be used to assess both the positive and negative aspects of the evolution of growth and distribution in Chile since 1987 and balance these effects against each other. The most favorable aspect is the increase in aggregate production, and in Fields and Ok absolute income mobility.[34] The most unfortunate result is the persistence of inequality and the widening of the gap between average income and the incomes of low-income households, with many unfavorable consequences, such as a lower savings rate and rich-to-poor demonstration and imitation effects strongly and adversely affecting the consumption patterns of the poor.

The level of household utility, U, depends on access to leisure (or home production) time, consumption, savings, and some quality of life indicators, including, for example, the chances for child survival. The arguments in the respective utility function are leisure hours, L, the consumption of goods X and Z, and savings, S, so that $U = U(L, X, Z, S)$.

There is an important difference between consumer goods X and Z. X represents ordinary goods and services, including some that are demanded only because they contribute to improve child survival chances (some types of food, over-the-counter medicines, visits to the doctor, special heating requirements). Z represents high-visibility goods, which are demanded largely because of rich-to-poor demonstration and imitation effects (some types of cars, expensive holidays abroad, color television, other household electronic goods, luxury brand clothes).

To simplify the discussion, one may introduce composite good C, which is formed by fixed amounts (for ease of presentation, assume one unit each) of L, X, and S. By definition,

$$C = L + X + S.$$

In logarithms, the derived utility function is now $\log U = b0 + b1 \log C + b2 \log Z$. The respective parameters $b1$ and $b2$ are positive. The definition of a good as either C or Z is household specific. The same good may be defined as C by a rich household and as Z by a poor one.

34. Fields and Ok (1996).

Figure 8-1. *Household Utility Maximization and Income Inequality Constraints*[a]

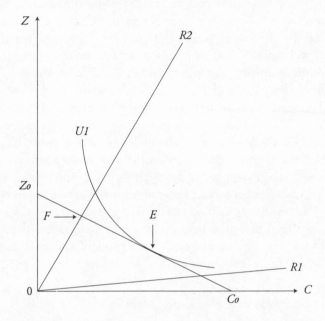

a. $U(F) < U(E)$. *R1:* low inequality; *R2:* high inequality; *F:* household (second-) best option under high inequality (*R2*).

Maximization with High Inequality

The household is faced by the usual optimization problem: to maximize U subject to the budget constraint $I = C\,pc + Z\,pz$, where I is household income (which may include access to consumer credit) and pc and pz are the prices of C and Z, respectively.

This is a conventional household optimization problem, but with a crucial difference. Households, including low-income ones, are under pressure to buy high-visibility goods. The actual demand for Z depends on the degree of inequality. The greater the positive-sign gap between average income, A, and the household income, I, the larger the proportion of household income that will be devoted to buying Z instead of C. If this proportion is represented by ratio R, by definition $R = Z/C$.

Parameters $r0$ and $r1$ are household specific. In general, $r1$ will be positive: $R = r0 + r1(A - I)$.

The household optimization problem is presented in figure 8-1. The consumptions of C and of Z are plotted along the horizontal and vertical axis, respectively. Given the budget line $ZoCo$, the conventional equilibrium is reached at point E, which is the point of tangency between the budget line and the respective indifference curve. However, whether the household will actually be able to go for E depends on the level of inequality. With little inequality, as represented, for example, by the line $R1$, the household is allowed to go for point E. With this low level of inequality, any combinations of consumption of Z and C to the northwest of line $R1$ are possible. However, under conditions of high inequality, such as those yielding line $R2$, the household will be under pressure to consume combinations of Z and C only if these combinations are to the northwest of line $R2$. Therefore, under high inequality the household cannot reach equilibrium E (because of either social or peer pressure: it has to keep up with the Joneses). The best the household can do is to go for point F, which represents a lower level of utility than E. By going for F rather than E, the household is worse off, despite having more goods Z, because it has fewer hours of leisure time, fewer goods X, and less savings.[35]

Growth without Market-Driven Mobility

What happens as the economy grows and there is a positive amount of Fields and Ok absolute income mobility but no market-driven mobility, as defined earlier? Assume that relative prices have not changed and that income shares by decile remain constant (these hypothetical conditions are as close as possible to the actual Chilean ones between 1987 and 1996). Also assume (this assumption will be relaxed in the next section) that there is no market-driven, economically efficient, medium-term mobility. This type of mobility is equal to zero. The optimization problem is shown in figure 8-2. The household income has increased, from I to I', and average income has increased from A to A'. The budget line has moved away from the origin to $Zo'Co'$. The new conventional or notional equilibrium is now at tangency point G. However, the income gap, $(A' - I')$, has also increased, and therefore the minimum proportion of Z to C that is now possible, or allowed, is greater than before. This means that line $R2$ has moved counterclockwise to become $R3$. The best that the household can now do is to go for point H.

---

35. Different (but possibly complementary) approaches to modeling similar situations have been presented by Leibenstein (1950); Kuran (1997); and Bowles (1998).

Figure 8-2. *Effects on Household Utility of High-Inequality Fast Growth*

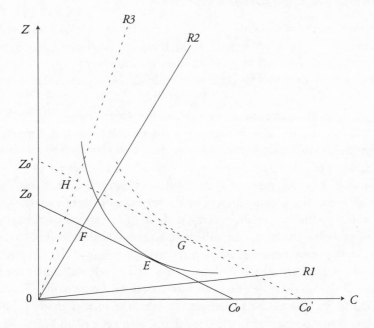

U(E) < U(G); U(H) < U(G). R3: very high inequality; *H:* household (second-) best option with very high inequality (*R3*).

Point *H* may or may not represent a higher level of utility than point *E* (*E* stands for equilibrium without growth or excessive inequality). This depends on only six parameters: the structural parameters of the household utility function, *b1* and *b2* (which determine the shape of the indifference map), the prices *pc* and *pz* (which determine the slope of the budget line), the household-specific parameter *r1* (which determines the amount of counterclockwise rotation in line *R*), and the rate of aggregate output growth. One may safely assume that the current political economy of fast growth with high inequality (which applied in Chile between 1987 and 1996) will be acceptable or not acceptable to a particular household, depending on whether it is or is not better off as the economy expands. If $U(H) > U(E)$, the outcome is likely to be political participation. If $U(H) < U(E)$, the outcome is likely to be political alienation.

It is worth pointing out that it is possible for the utility associated to point H to be even smaller than that associated to point F: $U(H) < U(F)$.

Growth with Market-Driven Mobility

How does the model change when the possibility of market-directed, economically efficient, medium-term mobility is introduced? By definition, in the presence of this type of mobility the economy grows at a faster rate. Postgrowth household income with mobility, Im, is greater than without it, I': $Im > I'$.

Faster growth of household income shifts the budget line $Zo'Co'$ further away from the origin to $ZmCm$ (figure 8-3). In relation to figure 8-2, average income has also increased, from A' to Am, and the gap between average and household income has increased as well: $Am > A'$ and $(Am - Im) > (A' - I')$.

Inequality is therefore worse than before. However, at least some of this high inequality is compensated by the presence of the market-driven, economically efficient, medium-term mobility. For example, under this type of mobility, incentives are different; households are now keener on higher savings, and they are more prepared to challenge any pressures pushing them toward buying high-visibility goods (and even low-income households will devote more resources to human capital investment). This is reflected in the size of the parameter rm, which is smaller than $r1$, and therefore it is also reflected in the slope of line Rm: $rm < r1$ and $Rm = r0 + rm(Am - Im)$.

Thus, depending on the values of the new, larger income gap $(Am - Im)$ and of the new smaller parameter rm, the Rm line may be either to the right or to the left of $R3$. In figure 8-3 it has been assumed that Rm is to the right of $R3$. This means that the market-driven mobility is important in compensating at least partially for high inequality. The notional equilibrium L is the tangency point between the budget line $ZmCm$ and the respective indifference curve. The best that the household can do is, however, point M. But the utility associated with M is clearly higher than that associated with H: $U(M) > U(H)$.

In other words, this type of mobility is a positive force. It increases the household utility of even low-income households in relation to the utility level reached under conditions of high-inequality fast growth without market-driven mobility. Still, it is not known whether $U(M)$ is greater than $U(E)$ or smaller in figure 8-3.

The aggregate data for Chile show that

—average real income per household expanded by 55 percent between 1987 and 1996;

—inequality remained constant and high, with a ratio between the top decile income and the bottom decile income slightly above 24;

Figure 8-3. *Maximization with High-Inequality Growth and Market-Driven, Economically Efficient, Medium-Term Mobility*

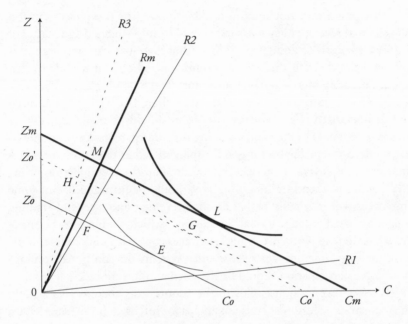

$U(G) < U(L); U(M) < U(L)$. *Rm:* very high inequality, partly compensated by market-driven mobility. *M:* household (second-) best option with market-driven mobility.

—information about mobility is far from complete, but the limited evidence available suggests that mobility was insufficient and inadequate to compensate for the negative effects of high inequality; and

—political alienation in the December 1997 elections increased to almost 40 percent.[36]

In terms of individual data or household surveys the only possible answers to a question about political participation are yes or no. However, a carefully designed survey or series of periodic surveys should be able to obtain much more information by concentrating on identifying the values of the household-specific parameters $b1$ and $b2$, and $r1$ or rm.

36. Again, it must be emphasized that possibly it would be wrong to attribute the whole of this massive political alienation to frustration caused by income and other inequalities. See note 24.

What Is "the Solution" for Chile? And How Much
More Do We Need to Know?

Although it may not amount to the solution, the previous discussion suggests that several policy measures should be implemented as a matter of urgency. In terms of doing something rather than just learning more, it is necessary to devote further efforts toward controlling rent seeking so that upward mobility increasingly rewards those who follow signals in competitive markets. The formal educational system should be further modernized and democratized. Good-quality education should be made available to everyone, not only to the children of high-income parents. Upward mobility should be possible also for good employees rather than only for entrepreneurial employers or the self-employed. Shop-floor, company-specific, evening and weekend training programs should be introduced. But some employees will inevitably be better off in evening and weekend training programs based in educational institutions, which should also be made available. To help workers earning low wages cope with undesirable short-term mobility, unemployment insurance systems that do not discourage labor force participation should be designed and introduced.

For low-income households in the countryside, there is also a rural, agroindustrial "solution" that is possibly labor intensive (in the late 1990s, but maybe not ten or twenty years later). It should also be technologically flexible so that it provides room for the gradual substitution of capital for labor as labor becomes relatively more expensive. However, it should not be technologically intermediate, since this could lock producers into rigid, backward production straitjackets. If possible, there should be few scale economies or none. Unconventional experiences such as that of Fundación Chile, which was instrumental in developing salmon farming and forestry in the 1980s and early 1990s, should be encouraged.

I hope the discussion has also highlighted the huge information gaps that afflict any effort at learning more about mobility. It is not enough to be able to say that some mobility has taken place. This is better than nothing, but it is not very good if we cannot identify precisely the characteristics of the mobility. What does it respond to? Who benefits? Why some and not others? Will it occur again if and when the same conditions apply? Both first principles and qualitative research methods should be directed to explore and understand (and eventually measure) the key concept of market-driven, economically efficient medium-term mobility. Resources should be invested in longitudinal studies and in individual case studies, both of ordinary people and of successes and failures. New appropriate questions should be added to the old surveys—What was your father's job? What do your grown-up children do? How much schooling, and how good, for the younger? What were you doing five, ten, twenty years ago? New purpose-designed surveys should be started. Much more effort and money should go toward monitoring school quality, rent seeking, subsidies, and special sectors of the population such as women. Efforts should be devoted toward linking income-expenditure surveys with surveys of political attitudes. There should be surveys of consumer attitudes, especially geared toward identifying rich-to-poor demonstration and imitation effects. More should be learned about the macroeconomic cycle and its effects on employment and periods of unemployment differentiated according to absolute income levels.

Statistics by themselves are not enough. Statistical data need theory if we are to be able to interpret and understand them. In line with the theoretical model presented earlier, longitudinal income and expenditure surveys should also explore ways of identifying the household-specific values of structural parameters of the utility function and of actual demand responses to inequality, with a view to eventually relating these numerical estimates to qualitative answers to questions on social and political attitudes.

References

Aedo, C. 1998. "Diferencias entre escuelas y rendimiento estudiantil en Chile." In W. D. Savedoff, ed., *La Organización Marca la Diferencia: Educación y Salud en América Latina*, pp. 45–84. Washington: Inter-American Development Bank.

Arancibia, V. 1994. "La educación en Chile: percepciones de la opinión publica y de expertos." *Estudios Públicos* 54 (Autumn):125–50.

Birdsall, Nancy, and Carol Graham. 1999. "Mobility and Markets: Conceptual Issues and Policy Questions." Brookings.

Birdsall, Nancy, and J. L. Londoño. 1997. "Asset Inequality Matters: An Assessment of the World Bank's Approach to Poverty Reduction." *American Economic Review* 87 (May):32–37.

Bjorklund, Anders, and Markus Jantti. 1997. "Intergenerational Income Mobility in Sweden Compared to the United States." *American Economic Review* 87 (December):1009–18.

Bourguignon, F., M. Fournier, and M. Gurgand. 1998. "Distribution, Development and Education: Taiwan, 1979–1994." Paper prepared for the Twelfth Annual Conference of the European Society of Population Economics. Amsterdam.

Bowles, S. 1998. "Endogenous Preferences: The Cultural Consequences of Markets and Other Economic Institutions." *Journal of Economic Literature* 36 (March): 75–111.

Buvinic, M., and others. 1992. "The Fortunes of Adolescent Mothers and Their Children:

The Transmission of Poverty in Santiago, Chile." *Population and Development Review* 18 (June): 269–97.

Cáceres, C., and E. Bobenrieth. 1993. "Determinantes del salario de los egresados de la enseñanza media técnico profesional en Chile." *Cuadernos de Economía* 30 (April):111–29.

Comisión Económica para América Latina y el Caribe (CEPAL). 1997. *Evolución Reciente de la Pobreza en Chile.* LC/R.1773, 97-12-1043. Santiago: División de Estadística y Proyecciones Económicas.

Cox, C. 1997. "La reforma de la educación chilena: contexto, contenidos, implementación." *Colección Estudios CIEPLAN* 45 (June): 5–32.

Dornbusch, Rudiger, and S. Edwards, eds. 1991. *The Macroeconomics of Populism in Latin America.* University of Chicago Press.

Economist Intelligence Unit (EIU). *Country Forecast: Chile.* Various issues.

Fields, Gary S., and Efe A. Ok. 1996. "The Meaning and Measurement of Income Mobility." *Journal of Economic Theory* 71 (November): 349–77.

Galor, Odid, and Daniel Tsiddon. 1997. "Technological Progress, Mobility, and Economic Growth." *American Economic Review* 87 (June): 363–82.

Gottschalk, P. 1997. "Inequality, Income Growth, and Mobility: The Basic Facts." *Journal of Economic Perspectives* 11 (Spring): 21–40.

Gottschalk, P., and T. M. Smeeding. 1997. "Cross-National Comparisons of Earnings and Income Inequality." *Journal of Economic Literature* 35 (June): 633–87.

Hojman, David E. 1993. *Chile: The Political Economy of Development and Democracy in the 1990s.* Pittsburgh University Press.

———. 1995. "Too Much of a Good Thing? Macro and Microeconomics of the Chilean Peso Appreciation." In David E. Hojman, ed. *Neoliberalism with a Human Face? The Politics and Economics of the Chilean Model,* pp. 225–48. Liverpool Institute of Latin American Studies.

———. 1996a. "Poverty and Inequality in Chile: Are Democratic Politics and Neoliberal Economics Good For You?" *Journal of Interamerican Studies and World Affairs* 38 (Summer-Fall): 73–96.

———. 1996b. "Rent Seeking and Corruption in a Successful Latin American Economy: Chile in the 1990s." In R. Espíndola, ed. *Problems of Democracy in Latin America,* pp. 35–51. Stockholm: Institute of Latin American Studies.

———. 1999a. "Poverty, Inequality, and Infant Mortality: A Simultaneous-Equation, Panel-Data Analysis of Health Outcomes under Social Exclusion and Fast Economic Growth." Economics Department, University of Liverpool.

———. 1999b. "Economic Policy and Latin American Culture: Is a Virtuous Circle Possible?" *Journal of Latin American Studies* 31 (February): 167–90.

Jarvis, S., and S. P. Jenkins. 1998. "How Much Income Mobility Is There in Britain?" *Economic Journal* 108 (447): 428–43.

Kuran, T. 1997. *Private Truths, Public Lies: The Social Consequences of Preference Falsification.* Harvard University Press.

Lam, D., and R. F. Schoeni. 1993. "Effects of Family Background on Earnings and Returns to Schooling: Evidence from Brazil." *Journal of Political Economy* 101 (4):710–40.

Larrañaga, O. 1994. "Reformas de la educación: una tarea urgente." In F. Larraín, ed., *Chile Hacia el 2000,* pp. 507–42. Santiago: Centro de Estudios Públicos.

Lehmann, C. 1994. "Hacia una educación de calidad." In F. Larraín, ed., *Chile Hacia el 2000*, pp. 543-62. Santiago: Centro de Estudios Públicos.

Leibenstein, H. 1950. "Bandwagon, Snob and Veblen Effects in the Theory of Consumers' Demand." *Quarterly Journal of Economics* 64 (May): 183–207.

Montero, C. 1997. *La Revolución Empresarial Chilena.* Santiago: Dolmen/CIEPLAN.

Oppenheimer, A. 1998. "Chileans Have More, Enjoy It Less." Heraldlink: The Oppenheimer Report. *Miami Herald.* April 27.

Ramsden, M. 1998. "From Excess Supply to Surplus Labour Exhaustion: Evolution of the Chilean Labour Market in the 1980s and 1990s." Ph.D. thesis. University of Liverpool.

Roberts, P. C., and K. L. Araujo. 1997. *The Capitalist Revolution in Latin America.* Oxford University Press.

Sánchez, X. 1998. "Reproducción de la desigualdad social en Chile: el caso de la educación." Paper prepared for the 1998 Congress of the Latin American Studies Association, Chicago.

Sancho, A. 1994. "Educación: las tareas de la nueva etapa." In C. Larroulet, ed., *Las Tareas de Hoy*, pp. 173-22. Santiago: Zig-Zag.

"La semana económica." 1998. *El Mercurio,* international edition (September 3–9): 3.

Shorrocks, Anthony. 1978. "Income Inequality and Income Mobility." *Journal of Economic Theory* 19 (December): 376–93.

Wilkinson, R. G. 1996. *Unhealthy Societies: The Afflictions of Inequality.* London: Routledge.

PART IV

Politics and Perceptions

CAROL GRAHAM

9 | The Political Economy of Mobility: Perceptions and Objective Trends in Latin America

After several decades in which authoritarian regimes dominated Latin America's polities, all countries in the region (with the exception of Cuba) are more or less functioning democracies that have held several rounds of elections. At the same time, the introduction of extensive macroeconomic reforms in the region has increased growth and reduced poverty. The effects of reforms on the region's deep inequality are less clear, however, with slight reductions in inequality in some countries and increases in others, with the rest remaining the same.[1] Not surprisingly, the region's experience in the 1980s with extensive eco-

I would like to thank Kristine McDevitt and Christina Aufhammer for excellent research assistance.

1. The Gini for wage inequality, for example, increased or remained high in all seven countries for which there are reliable data in two separate years. There were sharp increases in wage inequality in Mexico, Argentina, Bolivia, and Venezuela, and a mild worsening of wage inequality in Brazil. Wage distribution remained stable in Chile and Costa Rica. Although much of the current debate over inequality focuses on the effects of the crises and stabilization programs of the 1980s, Duryea and Székely (1998) argue that demographic trends and changes in schooling can explain a significant portion of the change in income inequality. First, the aging of the population increases aggregate inequality because inequality is greater among older age cohorts than younger ones. Second, the increased educational attainments of the new generations are leading to greater disparities in schooling, which increases inequality. Finally, the slow pace of educational progress has limited the supply of highly skilled people for the labor force at a time when demand for these workers is rising, driving a wider wedge between the wages of more skilled and less skilled workers.

nomic reform and political change has raised public expectations for progress both by individuals and countries.[2]

In this context there are significant concerns that without very high growth and better distribution of the growth, the region is vulnerable to a voter backlash against reform.[3] These concerns have been heightened by the effects on the region's growth prospects of the 1998 financial crisis in Brazil. They also stem from the region's history of populist policy swings. Most observers agree that the economic and political costs of major policy reversals would be very high. Yet there is far less agreement, and indeed understanding, of the factors underlying the political sustainability of the current policy framework.

One plausible explanation for continued voter support for reform despite persistent inequality is improved mobility.[4] Observers have noted that with the increased individual mobility (either upward or downward) and the weakening of labor unions and other collective organizations that accompany market reforms and globalization in many countries, traditional class or party-based voting has become less important. This has opened the door for mass-based support for neopopulist leaders, who use such classic populist political tactics as emphasizing the persona of the president to build support among unorganized lower-income voters.[5] There is a considerable number of studies and widespread debate on the political economy of macroeconomic reform. Although many of the studies have been concerned with distribution issues, none has dealt directly with mobility, much less in an empirical manner. This chapter seeks to shed new light on that debate by examining the effects of trends in mobility and public perceptions of those trends on public attitudes toward reforms. Because this is work in progress, it will raise more questions than it is able to answer.

2. This conclusion is drawn from the results of the 1996 and 1997 Latinobarometro surveys. There were variations among countries, however, and in some, particularly in South America, there was more optimism about the country's progress in 1996 than in 1997. The results are shown in table 9-1.

3. See "The Backlash in Latin America: Gestures against Reform," *Economist*, November 30, 1996.

4. Benabou and Ok (1998), for example, demonstrate theoretically how the hypothesis of the prospect of upward mobility explains how even when the majority of the people are poorer than the mean in current income, they expect to be richer than the mean in future income and therefore refrain from voting in favor of redistributive policies. They then substantiate their argument with empirical evidence from the United States.

5. See Roberts and Arce (1998, p. 220); Gibson (1996); and Dalton, Flanagan, and Beck (1984). Although in the 1940s and 1950s populist leaders such as Juan Peron and Haya de la Torre built political machines around their personas, in the 1990s the rise of the neopopulists has coincided with the decline in public faith in political parties.

This research is part of a study conducted by the author, in collaboration with Nancy Birdsall of the Carnegie Endowment for International Peace, that seeks to examine the effects of market reforms on mobility trends in Latin America.[6] An underlying assumption of the study is that the so-called second stage of economic and structural reforms can simultaneously improve equity and efficiency by eliminating distortions that have blocked the productive potential of low-income groups.[7] The study seeks to determine the extent to which reform has resulted in greater mobility, particularly for low-income groups, even though income distribution in the region, as captured by annual cross-sections, remains similar to what it was before the reforms.

This chapter is an initial attempt to assess the impact of mobility trends on public support for reforms, primarily as measured by opinion surveys. And because public perceptions are at least as important as actual trends in determining voter behavior, the study attempts to measure trends in public perceptions and expectations about mobility and, where possible, compare the perceptions with actual mobility trends.[8]

Work done by Petr Matějů in eastern Europe has found that perceived socioeconomic mobility, which is often very different from actual trends, has a much stronger effect on voting preferences than does objectively measured class and social mobility. In addition, objective mobility trends, either upward or downward, are usually very weak predictors of subjective mobility trends.[9] Mateju's conclusions are supported by the results of a recent pilot study of perceptions and mobility in Peru (discussed in detail later and in chapter 10): the respondents in the group with the most mobility in the sample were the most pessimistic of all respondents in self-assessments of their well-being. Although the explanation for these results is complex, it is likely that, as in eastern Europe, respondents' self-assessments will influence their opinion about the market process more than their actual mobility will.

---

6. For the purposes of this chapter, mobility is defined narrowly as movements up and down the income ladder. The research project, however, is concerned with a broader definition of mobility, which includes economic mobility (growth driven) and social mobility (movements across occupational and social status categories).

7. For detail on those reforms see Birdsall, Graham, and Sabot (1998).

8. Piketty (1995) develops a model demonstrating that individual experience of mobility, not only current income, matters for political attitudes, and that persistent differences in perceptions about social mobility can generate persistent differences in redistribution across countries.

9. The only clear predictor of upward subjective mobility was objective mobility into the realm of self-employment. See chapter 11.

An equally important and related subject, which this chapter does not go into in detail, is how perceptions influence mobility. Thomas Piketty, for example, shows how inequality increases with age for a given homogeneous cohort because of differences in individual effort that arise from experience with shocks. Even in a cohort where all agents start out equal, their efforts are affected by their experience with negative shocks—loss of a job, illness, and so forth. Those who face a number of these shocks may get discouraged and apply less effort to achieving well-being, while successful people continue to give more. The different attitudes that result from contrasting experiences can result in persistent inequality unless the discouraged people, who are more likely to vote for redistribution, are also politically effective enough to achieve it.[10] This suggests that individuals' perceptions of their mobility are not only important for their short-term effects on political economy, but that they can have long-term effects on incentives and allocation structures.

This chapter is based on eclectic sources. The first of these is the results from a regionwide public opinion survey, the Latinobarometro, which is conducted annually in seventeen countries by the Chilean-based Market Research International (MORI). At our request (and with financing from the Inter-American Development Bank) MORI included in the 1997 Latinobarometro survey several questions about respondents' perceptions of trends in their well-being (including access to important public services) and expectations for their children. The answers to each question were broken down by education and socioeconomic level.

The second component is an analysis of actual mobility trends in Peru, as captured by a unique set of panel data for 1985–97, and a complementary pilot study of perceptions of mobility trends. The pilot study, which was financed by the IDB and conducted by Richard Webb and his survey institute, Cuanto, S.A., covers a subset of the households in the panel and explores respondents' perceptions of their mobility as well as the influence of health shocks, community organizations, and a number of other variables on mobility. The results of the studies are then considered in the context of a detailed analysis of voting trends in Peru that I compiled for the same time period. Finally, the Latin American and Peru survey results are considered in light of some of the analysis that has been done on perceptions of distributive justice, mobility, and voting patterns in the former communist countries in eastern Europe.

10. This inequality results from what Piketty (1995) terms "endogenous beliefs dynamics."

Economic Reform, Mobility, and Voting Patterns

There are a fair number of studies on the politics of economic reform and the behavior of voters in the context of economic reform. We know, for example, that authoritarian regimes have no real advantage over democratic regimes in implementing economic reform and that elections can actually improve economic reform and performance.[11] Voters are more than capable of evaluating leaders according to their performance in achieving reform, and in some cases are quick to disapprove policies that seem likely to jeopardize the stability gained by reforms.[12]

Susan Stokes uses two classifications to distinguish voter behavior during reform from normal economic voting. In normal economic times voters hold their government responsible for the state of the economy and hold it accountable by reelecting it if the economy is healthy and voting it out if the economy is ailing. In the context of reform, however, voters may pay attention to what politicians say about the future instead of simply looking at economic performance under the incumbent's watch (intertemporal voting). And they view the past and future as inversely related: if the economy deteriorates, the public becomes optimistic about the future, and if it improves too quickly, they become pessimistic about the future. Voting during reform may also be antidotal: voters see reforms and their costs as necessary antidotes to the poor policies pursued by previous governments and thus are wary of policies that deliver benefits too quickly.[13] Voters also vary in the weight they attach to overall national conditions (sociotropic voting) versus that of their individual economic situations (pocketbook voting).[14] At times of national crisis or shortly thereafter, sociotropic attitudes tend to dominate, while pocketbook voting tends to surface as overall conditions stabilize.

Intertemporal and antidotal voting seem particularly prevalent in countries where reform was preceded by severe crisis or high levels of inflation or both, where voters often associate trends such as real wage increases with

---

11. See Haggard and Webb (1994); Geddes (1995); and Remmer (1993, pp. 393–407). For a discussion of elections and the fate of reformist politicians in eastern Europe and the former Soviet Union, see Aslund, Boone, and Johnson (1996, pp. 217–92).

12. See Nelson (1992); and Stokes (1996a, pp. 499–519).

13. Stokes (1996a).

14. Weyland (1998a) distinguishes between voting that pays attention to future prospects (what he calls prospective voting) and that which is primarily concerned with recent economic events or trends (retrospective voting). He notes that prospective attitudes generally favor economic reform.

the inflation of the past. Indeed, the collective experience with crisis usually results in a strong mandate for extensive reforms, often providing governments with the political opportunities to initiate structural reforms, such as independent central banks and new tax administrations, that lock in promarket macroeconomic policies.[15] Kurt Weyland takes this perspective one step further, and posits that, according to "prospect theory," voters become risk takers in times of crisis; they are willing to vote for the adoption of market reforms and then become risk averse as the economic situation improves. Thus as reforms bring stability and possibly prosperity, voters are unwilling to depart from market policies and will support their continuation and the locking in.[16]

Trends in Peru support many of these observations. Voters' approval during the Fujimori government's first term, for example, fell when real wages increased. There are two plausible explanations. The first is that real wage increases were associated with hyperinflation in the collective memory. The second is that the increases were concentrated in the formal sector, and most workers, who are in the informal sector, perceived that only a few were benefiting while they were not. This second interpretation is supported by the fact that pessimism about the future at times of real wage increases was much higher among the lowest-income groups than among the rest of society.[17]

In a similar study in Mexico, Robert Kaufmann found that views about general economic conditions are more important predictors of support for reform than are views about personal well-being. He also showed that expectations are consistent predictors of support for reform, but the effects of expectations may be stronger when crisis and adjustment are recent events than they are under more stable economic conditions.[18]

There is no equivalent body of studies to guide the analysis of mobility and voting behavior.[19] Yet several trends in Latin America and in some

15. Bruno and Easterly (1996). See also Cukierman, Webb, and Neyapti (1992).

16. Weyland (1998b).

17. This might also support the first explanation, as it was the lower income groups that were most hurt by hyperinflation, and therefore feared it the most. See Stokes (1996b). Respondents in the Apoyo opinion poll surveys, which provided the data upon which Stokes's article is based, were divided up into four socioeconomic groups, (a) to (d), with (a) the wealthiest and (d) the poorest. The negative correlation with real wages applied to all four groups but was insignificant among the wealthier two (Stokes, p. 558). An additional caveat is that voter support is determined by factors other than real wages.

18. Kaufmann and Zuckerman (1998).

19. There are, however, two excellent theoretical papers on mobility and redistributive voting, that do provide a starting point. See Benabou and Ok (1998) and Pikety (1995).

other regions provide a starting point for thinking about these matters. First, there is very clearly a regionwide trend in which public support for the established political parties and other traditional organizations has declined dramatically. This is not unique to the region and is at least in part explained by a worldwide trend toward market-oriented policy frameworks that has diminished the role of organizations such as unions in determining the mobility of individual workers.

> In a global era of increasing market individualism, increased social mobility, class heterogeneity, and weakened trade union organization, studies of European politics often assume that class voting is destined to subside in importance. . . . Distinctive class-based voting patterns in developing countries may also be diminished or transformed as a result of the marginalization of organized class actors and the erosion or dispersion of polarized social cleavages that yielded exclusive class projects in the political sphere.[20]

In Peru, for example, the broad support for President Fujimori and the decline of traditional parties illustrates these trends. Related to this is a more generalized weakening of interest in politics and an increased interest in private enterprise. As the editor of a prominent Peruvian newspaper has said, "Political news just doesn't sell newspapers anymore; everyone is interested in becoming a capitalist."[21] This trend has been supported by the rise of a small but visible number of successful entrepreneurs who began as poor migrants (*empresarios cholos*).[22] This stands in sharp contrast to a decade ago, when social mobility was much more closely linked to advancements within the public sector, unions, and political parties.

These trends are not unique to Peru. Gonzalo Sanchez de Lozada's unlikely alliance between the reformed wing of Bolivia's Movimiento Nacional Revolucionario (MNR) party, with its orthodox economic reform platform, and an indigenous movement, the Movimiento de Bolivia Libre (MBL), which was originally marxist, is another example of a political movement based on lower-class support that has at least to some extent bypassed unions, the party rank and file, and other traditional organizations. In Bolivia the Popular Participation reform, the bilingual component of the education reform, and the distribution of solidarity bonds (from

20. Roberts and Arce (1988, p. 220).
21. Jaime Althaus, editor of *Expreso,* cited in Graham (1998, p.113).
22. See Degregori, Adrianzen, and Cordova (1998).

the dividends of privatized national enterprises) to all Bolivians older than age 65 were measures that specifically aimed at building support for reform among the people and were for the most part opposed by the unions. In Venezuela, meanwhile, where two parties traditionally dominated national politics, a former military officer and coup leader with no party ties was elected president in December 1998. And in Mexico the long-dominant Partido Revolucionario Institucional (PRI) is gradually having to adapt to a more competitive party system, although the direction of that evolution and the depth of the opposition parties' public support is far from clear.

In addition, the ideological debate in the region has shifted with increasingly widespread acceptance of market economics and lower expectations of the state.

> With the demise of lower-class, antimarket collective actors, electoral competition has been largely purged of ideological content, and the public policy debate has narrowed to fit within the parameters of the neoliberal model. . . . The erosion of class-based collective actors and the emergence of more heterogeneous, atomized social structures in Latin America are conducive to the electoral mobilization of mass constituencies behind neoliberal projects.[23]

The long-term implications of these trends for democracy in the region are unclear. In the short term, however, they have been conducive to reform. Although some earlier political economy research suggests that reforms are less likely to be viable and sustainable in countries with weak or fragmented party systems, in recent years some of the most far-reaching reform programs have been started in countries where the party system is extremely weak, as in Peru, or fragmented, as in Bolivia.[24] In Peru the decline of parties coincided with increasing support for economic reform under the Fujimori government, in part no doubt because reform was associated in the collective mind with halting hyperinflation and ending the endemic violence related to the Shining Path movement.[25]

Another explanation for the erosion of support for political parties stems from the constraints imposed by the transitions from authoritarian

23. Roberts and Arce (1988, p. 241).

24. See Haggard and Webb (1994). One of their main conclusions is that reforms are less likely in countries with weak or fragmented party systems.

25. In addition, as I have argued elsewhere, the decline of parties in Peru has not been bad for democracy, at least in the short term, because it has given more weight to poor, rural voters, who previously were poorly represented in an urban-biased, party-list system. See Graham and Kane (1998).

regimes in the 1980s. In the 1960s and 1970s, political parties focused their attention and debates on social justice, and many, such as the American Popular Revolutionary Alliance (APRA) in Peru, the Peronists in Argentina, and Accion Democratica in Venezuela, were able to develop a mass-based following behind the cause of workers or of the lower classes. But in the 1980s elites of mass political parties were necessarily focused on establishing rules for the transition to democracy and on forming political pacts that promised adherence to those rules, thereby giving their authoritarian predecessors an implicit guarantee of political stability. Although such a focus was a necessity at the time, it had little appeal for the poor, who were facing the economic constraints imposed by the debt crisis and often experienced significant downward mobility. Thus political parties were increasingly seen as out of touch with the needs of the poor. This explains the appeal of authoritarian-style political independents such as Fujimori, who could simultaneously impose far-reaching economic policy changes and bypass existing political institutions.[26]

In the short term, political parameters in the region have shifted in a manner that seems conducive to economic reform. Yet given the weak organizational and institutional base of these new parameters and their basis in a collective memory of recent crisis, it is likely that other factors will begin to influence voting patterns and political parameters in the longer term. In the initial postreform period in most countries the public seems willing to sacrifice current consumption and wages for economic progress in the future, but parameters usually evolve to more normal economic voting. In the Brazil crisis, for example, the postreform optimism of the early and mid-1990s is likely to be tempered by the damper that the crisis has placed on the region's economic prospects.

Evidence from Peru indicates that approval ratings for the economic program began at a moderately high level (51 percent) and then fell during the government's first year. From that point until the 1994 growth boom and the reorientation of public expenditure, improved approval ratings of the program and the government were linked to political events such as the April 1992 closing of Congress rather than economic events.[27] As the pilot survey results on Peru's expectations suggest, respondents' economic evalu-

---

26. See Degregori, Adrianzen, and Cordova (1998). This kind of democracy has been termed "delegative democracy" by O'Donnell (1992). Another subject that is worthy of note is the high levels of abstention from voting in some countries, such as Colombia (as high as 70 percent in some elections) and Peru. I thank Alan Angell for raising this point.

27. Stokes (1996b, p. 553).

ations are clearly influenced by these political trends and events, or what can be termed the national mood. As more normal economic voting begins to dominate (moving from sociotropic to pocketbook voting), the economic opportunities available to people and their subjective evaluations of the opportunities are likely to be important factors influencing voter behavior.

Following is a review of the results of a regionwide survey of public attitudes about democracy and reform and of perceptions about living standards and expectations for progress. I then undertake a closer examination of the recent data on public expectations in Peru, one of the few countries where there is some evidence of mobility. (A more detailed regionwide examination of mobility trends and voting patterns will take place in the second stage of this research, when a second year of results is available for both the Latinobarometro expectations study and the Peru pilot.)

Expectations and Attitudes about Markets, Democracy, and Mobility

The Latinobarometro survey has been conducted by MORI since 1995 and attempts to gauge public attitudes about democracy, economic progress, and trade integration.[28] For all of the surveys, Mexico was included in the South America grouping because its size and GDP per capita are more comparable to the South American countries than to the Central American ones. One of the questions in the annual survey attempts to gauge people's confidence in others. As studies suggest, such trust is important to the efficient functioning of various institutions that affect economic performance and governance. Recent research has found a positive relationship between trust and economic performance and found that trust is greater in countries with greater equality and higher incomes.[29] At least at the ex-

28. For South America and Mexico, the sample size was 12,675 in 1996 and 11,716 in 1997. For Central America, sample size was 6,042 in 1996 and 6,051 in 1997. The sample was primarily urban, although as much as 30 percent of the sample was rural in some countries. Respected polling and survey firms were contracted in each country by MORI.

29. Much of the debate over the importance of trust, cooperative norms, and associations within groups was spurred by Putnam's (1993) research on the role of memberships in formal groups, which he used as a measure of social capital, in north and south Italy. Knack and Keefer (1997) have challenged the importance of associations but do find a positive relationship between trust and economic performance. For a broader discussion of these matters, see Crawford and Ostrom (1995). For some of the costs and consequences of lack of trust and institutional malfunction, see Graham and Naim (1998).

treme end of the spectrum, the relationship between trust (as measured in the Latinobarometro poll) and inequality in Latin America seems to support this: trust was weakest in Brazil and Paraguay, the two countries in the region with the highest Ginis (0.59 in each case).[30] In the rest of the sample, there was no clear relationship.

In 1996–97 the share of respondents professing interpersonal confidence rose from 19 to 20 percent in South America and Mexico and 22 to 29 percent in Central America. Support for democracy as the most preferable form of government increased from 61 to 63 percent in South America and 61 to 66 percent in Central America. Satisfaction with democracy is much lower than more general support for democracy as a form of government. Still, it increased from 27 to 36 percent in South America and Mexico and from 27 to 49 percent in Central America. While it is difficult to draw any definitive conclusions, this evidence suggests increasing support for democracy.

This increasing support is juxtaposed against a lack of faith in many of the traditional political and civil organizations, such as parties and unions, and by a trend toward reduced influence of class-based voting. In the Latinobarometro survey, political parties ranked below the government, large enterprises, and the military and above only banks when respondents were asked who held the most power. In Chile 28.5 percent of those surveyed in 1990 thought that the main union confederation, the Confederacion Unitaria de Trabajadores (CUT), looked only after its own interests. By 1995 the share had increased to 51 percent.[31] In a recent survey in Peru, just 3.6 percent of respondents said they trusted political parties, and only 13.4 percent trusted unions; 58.3 percent cited faith in the Catholic Church.[32] These attitudes in Peru and Chile are in keeping with a regionwide trend toward voting for independents and a decline of party influence, particularly at the local level.[33]

---

30. Countries ranked from most to least trust in others are Mexico (with a Gini of 0.55), Colombia (0.57), Uruguay (0.43); Argentina (0.48), Chile (0.57), Ecuador (0.57), Bolivia (0.53), Peru (0.46), Venezuela (0.47), Paraguay (0.59), and Brazil (0.59). The Ginis are from Barros, Duryea, and Székely (1998). The data for Argentina, Bolivia, and Uruguay are strictly urban, which surely pushes Bolivia's Gini downward. Information for Central America was more limited. Of the Central American countries for which there was information—Costa Rica, 0.46; El Salvador, 0.51; Honduras, 0.53 (wage income); and Panama, 0.56—the two countries with the highest Ginis had the lowest levels of trust.

31. CERC poll cited in Campero (1997, p. 41).

32. Agenda Peru poll, cited in Graham (1998, chap. 3).

33. For detail on this trend in Peru and references to other countries, see Graham and Kane (1998).

Underlying these trends, among other factors, seems to be a public attitude that evinces satisfaction with individual progress but expresses concern about the lack of an adequate safety net for the poor and vulnerable and about the efficacy of public institutions. Sixty-two percent of Chileans, for example, say that their situation is better than that of their parents, the highest percentage in the region. Meanwhile 50 percent of those interviewed said that poverty was the most important problem for the government, and 42 percent said the biggest problem was inadequate health care. In the 1997 Latinobarometro survey 58 percent of Peruvian respondents replied yes to the question "Is the country progressing?" Chile ranked second with 51 percent.[34] One could argue that these results are in keeping with the decline in class-based voting and an increased concern with individual mobility, but that it is a trend tempered by continued concern for overall national well-being. This is an example of the tension between sociotropic and pocketbook voting.

Optimism generally decreased slightly from 1996 to 1997 in the answer to the question "Is the country progressing?" In 1996 in South America and Mexico, 29 percent of respondents said their country was progressing; only 23 percent said so in 1997. In Central America optimism increased: 34 percent were positive in 1997 versus 20 percent in 1996. The net perception of progress (measured as the percentage of respondents who answered that their country was progressing minus those that answered it was getting worse) for South America and Mexico was only 2 percent, while for Central America it was 17 percent. Regardless of the decrease, the majority of respondents in the region still believed that their countries were progressing (figure 9-1). There were great variations among countries, however, with Chile, Panama, and Peru having 34, 29, and 25 percent net positive answers, while Ecuador and Paraguay had negative 23 percent and 27 percent, respectively. The most admired countries among South American and Mexican respondents were Brazil and Bolivia, with Bolivia moving from lowest in the rankings in 1996 to second place in 1997. Among Central American respondents, the most admired countries were Costa Rica and Mexico, with Argentina falling from the top of the ranking in 1996.

When people were asked about their individual (family) economic situations compared with one year before, 29 percent in South America and Mexico answered "better" in 1996 but only 20 percent did so in 1997. In

---

34. It is worth noting that in response to most questions young people were as optimistic as adults. Campero (1997).

Table 9-1. *Latin American Survey Respondent Satisfaction with Life, by Country, 1997*

Percent

Country	No reply	Very satisfied	Fairly satisfied	Satisfied	Not very satisfied	N
			Response			
South America and Mexico						
Argentina	0.4	10.0	23.2	36.6	29.7	1,196
Bolivia	1.8	8.0	15.7	39.6	34.9	796
Brazil	0.1	3.9	42.5	40.8	12.8	1,001
Colombia	0	19.6	29.0	38.5	12.8	1,200
Chile	0.4	10.6	33.2	35.1	20.7	1,200
Ecuador	0.3	11.7	13.5	43.8	30.8	1,200
Mexico	0.7	21.0	33.8	29.5	14.9	1,105
Paraguay	1.5	6.5	18.9	51.5	21.5	575
Peru	2.0	6.0	8.5	33.4	50.1	1,054
Uruguay	0.5	13.9	32.6	28.0	24.9	1,189
Venezuela	1.8	24.9	16.0	36.1	21.3	1,200
Total	0.8	13.0	24.7	36.8	24.8	11,716
Central America						
Costa Rica	1.5	34.9	23.1	28.3	12.2	1,007
El Salvador	1.5	15.1	31.6	37.7	14.1	1,010
Guatemala	1.7	18.7	21.6	38.4	19.6	1,000
Honduras	0.8	26.9	15.3	28.1	28.9	1,011
Nicaragua	0.6	31.8	23.3	24.3	20.1	1,002
Panama	1.3	16.0	28.6	31.0	23.1	1,021
Total	1.2	23.9	23.9	31.3	19.7	6,051
Latin America	0.9	16.7	24.4	34.9	23.0	17,767

Source: Latinobarometro (1997).

Central America there was a large increase, with 9 percent answering "better" in 1996 and 19 percent in 1997. Despite the drop in South America and Mexico, which may in part reflect a regionwide slowing of growth related to the Asian financial crisis, people's expectations for one year in the future were better in 1997 than in 1996. In 1997 36 percent of respondents in South America thought that their economic situation would be better in a year; in 1996 the figure was 30 percent. In Central America the increase was even greater, 29 percent in 1997 compared with 18 percent in

1996. When the responses for the 1998 survey become available, they may well reflect a general tempering of optimism related to the financial crisis in Brazil and its spillover effects.

Answers to questions about the general economic situation in a country often have a cyclical pattern and are influenced by factors other than economic trends, such as elections or the nation's fate in a world soccer tournament. Perceptions of individual or family situations often demonstrate similar cyclical patterns, but with much less variation.[35] This is hardly surprising because it is easier for people to gauge their own economic situations accurately than those of their country. Even then, however, individual evaluations are still subjective and can be influenced by variables such as expectations as well as by random events such as bad luck or poor health. The Peru pilot survey shows that the respondents who had done best in objective economic terms were more pessimistic in individual economic self-assessments than their counterparts who had fared more poorly. Another factor influencing general evaluations is that the countries in the Latinobarometro survey are at different stages in their economic reform, and the antidotal or intertemporal nature of their citizens' evaluations may vary depending on how recent the memory of crisis and reform is.

In general, public evaluations of democracy, economic progress, and trade integration were favorable in the region, which bodes well for continued support for reform.[36] This optimism provides the broader context in which to assess the answers to the specific questions in the 1997 survey pertaining to people's subjective evaluations and expectations of their own mobility and opportunity. Respondents were asked about their present living standards relative to those of their parents, as well as their expectations for their children. The survey also asked about access to major public services in the past and what was expected in the future. These are relevant because of the critical importance of access to such services, particularly

---

35. In Chile, for example, the public's marked increase in positive evaluations of the country's economic situation were very much influenced by the 1990 transition to democracy. The evaluations tended to moderate by 1996 despite continued high rates of growth. Campero (1997). For a good description of how public awareness varies in regard to politics, see Zaller (1992).

36. Public opinion about trade integration was very favorable and became more so between 1996 and 1997. In South America and Mexico 63 percent of those surveyed were in favor of hemispheric trade integration in 1996, and 78 percent were in 1997. The figures for Central America were 48 percent and 80 percent, respectively. Awareness of trade accords also increased slightly, with 55 percent knowing about NAFTA, 57 percent about Mercosur, and 49 percent about the Andean Pact in South America and Mexico, while the respective figures for Central America were 52 percent, 30 percent, and 24 percent.

education, if the poor and their children are to participate in new market opportunities. In addition, new forms of social spending accompanying market-oriented reforms have been crucial in generating political support for reforms among low-income groups.[37] There were also questions about level of family income, access to consumer goods, and job stability. Not surprisingly, answers varied widely among countries and according to the educational attainment and socioeconomic status of the respondent. Before I describe these variations, it is useful to explore the aggregated figures for the region as a whole (as in the previous section, South America includes Mexico; Central America does not).

In the answer to the question, "Did your parents live better than you?" 57.4 percent of respondents in South America answered that their parents had lived better, while 18.6 percent answered that they had lived worse. In Central America 57.9 percent answered "better" and 17.2 percent answered "worse." In response to respondents' expectations for their children, 48.8 percent in Latin America answered that their children would live better, while 19.1 percent said they would be worse off. In Central America 45.7 percent answered "better," while 19.1 percent responded "worse." In response to the question, "How many years will it take to achieve your desired standard of living?" 30.7 percent of South Americans and 32.5 percent of Central Americans chose the most common answer, three to five years. In South America 10.2 percent said "never," and in Central America 9.8 percent agreed. Two percent of South Americans and 1 percent of Central Americans answered that they had already achieved the desired level.

These results must be interpreted with care. One problem, which is highlighted by the Peru pilot study, is the difficulty that people have in providing accurate and objective assessments of their economic progress. The study found that their assessments of trends in their housing conditions and the quality of their public services, for example, which were often visible and tangible, were much more accurate than their assessments of their economic progress, which were much more subjective. Respondents' answers about their expectations for their children, meanwhile, inevitably reflect subjective qualities such as hope and determination as much if not more than economic conditions.

There were great variations among respondents in particular countries that did not necessarily correspond with their evaluations of their countries' progress. In response to questions about satisfaction with life, respon-

37. Graham (1994); Graham and Kane (1998); Roberts and Arce (1998, p. 240); and Lustig (1995).

Figure 9-1. *Percentage of Survey Respondents Stating Their Country Had Progressed, by Country, 1996–97*[a]

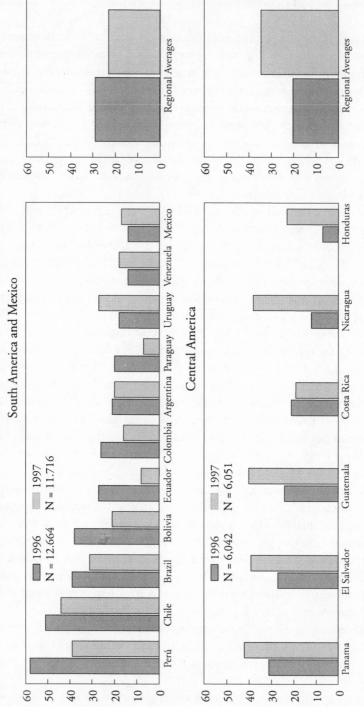

Source: Latinobarómetro (1996–97).
a. The question was "Do you believe your country has progressed, remained stagnant, or is in recession?"

dents were the most affirmative in Mexico, Colombia, Venezuela, and Uruguay, and least positive in Peru, Ecuador, Bolivia, and Argentina (figure 9-1). Yet Peruvians were the most optimistic respondents in the region when evaluating their country's progress. In Central America the most satisfied respondents were in Costa Rica and the least satisfied in Honduras.

In terms of time to achieve a desired living standard, the most optimistic of attaining their objective in three to five years were Peru, Bolivia, Colombia, and Brazil, while those countries with the highest numbers responding "never" were Uruguay, Ecuador, Chile, and Guatemala. These responses in particular must be approached with care because people's expectations of future earnings are influenced by complex factors and are endogenous to demographic and other noneconomic trends, such as luck.[38] In addition, the national mood may explain some of the differences, with optimistic answers tending to come from countries where the experiences of economic crisis and stabilization were more recent in the public mind.

The countries where the most respondents thought that their parents lived better than they did were Venezuela, Peru, Ecuador, Colombia, and Bolivia, and in Central America El Salvador, Honduras, and Nicaragua (figure 9-2). The countries with the most optimistic expectations for their children were Chile (by far the highest score), Brazil, Argentina, and Venezuela, and in Central America, Panama, Honduras, and Costa Rica. Those countries where a majority thought that their children would live worse than they, which seems the most pessimistic of expectations, were (from worst to better) Mexico, Ecuador, Colombia, El Salvador, Honduras, and Costa Rica.

For most countries, optimism or high expectations for respondents' children was related to higher socioeconomic levels (these were defined by where respondents ranked themselves on a socioeconomic scale ranging

38. There are a number of approaches to measuring people's income earning potential. One takes into account the permanent income hypothesis and savings as a function of the present value of life cycle earnings. Yet this is alone insufficient and does not account for the effects that expectations have on savings behavior. These expectations will reflect individuals' ages, education levels, other demographic characteristics, and past experiences. Another approach, taken by Carroll (1994) is to estimate permanent income with the assumption that people form their expectations about future earnings by comparing their income with those of individuals with a similar profile but who are much older. This is a fairly reliable approach as long as one accounts for "outliers," who form their expectations based on the experiences of those with very different earnings profiles. I am grateful to Miguel Székely for raising this point. The role of expectations in determining earnings potential, meanwhile, is explored by Piketty (1995) in his discussion of endogenous beliefs dynamics.

Figure 9-2. *Survey Respondents' Attitudes toward How Well Parents Lived and Expectations*

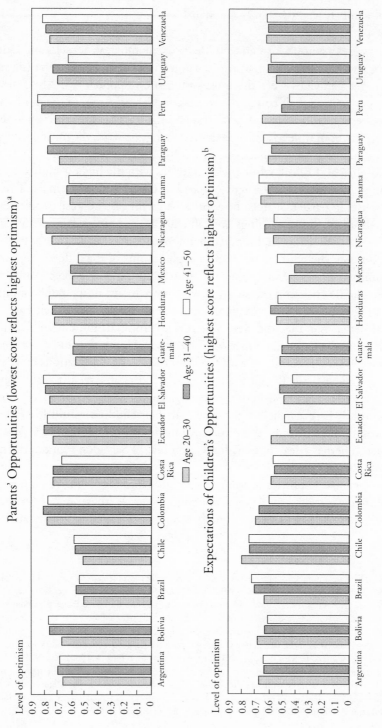

Source: Data from Latinobarometro (1997).
a. Higher scores mean that more respondents thought their parents lived better than they did.
b. Higher scores mean that more respondents thought their children would live better than they did.

from very bad to very good).[39] There was no clear relationship between socioeconomic levels and evaluations of their own versus their parents' living standards. One explanation for this may be found in a conclusion of the Peru pilot study: that more educated, wealthier, urban Peruvian respondents were much more likely to make bold statements and to assess their own situation negatively than were less educated, less wealthy ones, which reflected the wealthier respondents' higher expectations and greater experience with interviews. This may well be a more general tendency among the wealthier socioeconomic groups in the Latinobarometro survey.

There was no clear relationship between education levels and respondents' evaluations of their living standards and their expectations for their children. Although more highly educated people than other groups responded that they lived better than their parents, there was not that much variation among other education ranks. The relationship between education and expectations was positive from the lowest until the second-highest education level, incomplete university education. However, expectations were often slightly lower for the highest category, those who had completed university education.[40] A critical question in interpreting these results, which will be explored in the second stage of this research, is whether respondents' expectations in any way depend on the returns to education in particular countries. Recent research shows a great deal of variation in attitudes toward the returns to education among the various countries in the region.[41]

Another factor explaining variations in people's expectations is age, with younger generations tending to be more in favor of reform and more optimistic about the future than older ones. An analysis of the Latinobarometro results by age groups finds that in thirteen of the seventeen countries in the survey, respondents in the youngest generation (aged 20 to 30)

---

39. This obviously introduces a bias (most toward the center) into the answers because it is likely that not all persons in the highest socioeconomic category will place themselves there, while some of those in the lowest category may place themselves slightly higher when questioned by outsiders. In Peru, for example, in surveys conducted by Apoyo, a very well respected firm that conducted the Latinobarometro survey, only 7 percent of respondents in the highest socioeconomic category (A) placed themselves there when asked, while 81 percent of respondents in the A category placed themselves in the B category. Of respondents in the D category, 12 percent placed themselves in the B category, 44 percent placed themselves in the C category, and 42 percent in the D category. Data are from a survey conducted by Apoyo Opinion y Mercado S.A. in Lima and environs, July 1997.

40. Anecdotal evidence from several countries of university professors driving taxis to make ends meet suggests the kind of trend that can explain these results.

41. Duryea and Székely (1998).

demonstrate much more optimism in their evaluations of their individual economic situations vis-à-vis those of their parents. Their responses about their expectations for their children were also on average more optimistic than other groups, although much less markedly so than in their self-assessments. There were some clear outliers, however, such as Brazil and Uruguay, where the youngest groups were the least optimistic on both counts. The gaps between the expectations of younger and older groups (with younger groups far more optimistic than older ones both in their self-assessments and in their hopes for their children), meanwhile, were greatest in Peru and Ecuador.

The countries where variations in expectations were most closely linked with education and socioeconomic level were Chile, Brazil, and Peru, all countries with fairly high inequality. A greater percentage of Chileans (61.6 percent) than the regional average (40.7 percent) thought that they lived better or at least as well as their parents and that their children would do better than they (61.4 percent versus the regional average of 48.8 percent). There was a marked contrast, however, between the responses of illiterates and those in the lowest socioeconomic levels and the responses of most other groups. Only 28 percent of illiterates thought their children would do better, while an average of 68 percent of those in other education groups thought they would do better. Variations by socioeconomic level were not as great: 42 percent of those in the worst socioeconomic category thought their children would do better, while 61 percent of those in the top category did.

The very distinct responses of the poorest and least educated in Chile may reflect its still-high income inequality despite much progress in reducing poverty in the past decade. They may also reflect the changing nature of its poverty, which is increasingly like that of industrialized countries: a shrinking proportion of the population lives below the poverty line, and those people who are poor are increasingly concentrated in particular neighborhoods or racial or cultural groups, forming an underclass of sorts.[42]

A large percentage of Peruvians thought that their parents lived better than they did (69.6 percent versus a regional average of 57 percent), and responses were clearly correlated with education and socioeconomic

---

42. Chile's poverty rate has fallen from 45 percent in 1986 to 28 percent in 1994 and is projected to reach 17 percent by 2000 if growth remains at current levels. But while average incomes have increased across the board by 24 percent from 1990 to 1994, there has been much less progress in improving distribution. The ratio of the fifth quintile over the first has ranged from 17.9 to 19.5 percent between 1959 and 1994. Cowlan and de Gregorio (1996).

levels. And while only 25 percent of those with incomplete primary education thought that their children would do better, 53 percent of those who had completed a university education thought so. There was also a clear relation between responses and socioeconomic levels: 37 percent of those in the worst socioeconomic category thought their children would do better, and 61 percent of those in the highest category thought so. These variations are not reflected in the general response to the question on whether the country was progressing, on which Peru ranked first in the region.

Venezuela was the only other country in the region where a larger share of respondents (72.9 percent) than in Peru thought that their parents lived better than they, and there was little variation among socioeconomic or education levels. Both Venezuela and Brazil were outliers in that there was an inverse relation between respondents' socioeconomic and education levels and their expectations for their children. In Venezuela 73 percent of respondents in the worst socioeconomic category said that their children would live better, versus an average of 52 percent in the other income groups. In Brazil there was a similar relationship: 78 percent of illiterates thought that their children would live better than they, while only 45 percent of those who had completed a university education thought so. Again, these results must be interpreted with care because the responses reflect hope, determination, and other sentiments as much as they do realistic assessments of economic prospects.

Another important subject that was covered by the Latinobarometro survey was perceptions about the quality of health and education services, purchasing power and level of family income, and job stability. With health and education services, there was an across-the-board deterioration of evaluations of access to services at the time of the survey versus five years before (table 9-2). On a ranking of 1 to 10, with 1 being nothing and 10 being everything, 59.1 percent of respondents in South America were clustered from 5 to 8 on the scale ranking health services five years ago, while 54.3 percent were in those rankings for the present. Although the number in ranks 5 to 8 decreased even further for expectations of access to services in the future, this was counterbalanced by a much higher number in ranks 9 and 10. The percentages and trends were fairly similar for education (table 9-2). Overall, people thought that services had deteriorated but expected that they would get much better.

Public perceptions about job security, purchasing power, and level of family income show similar percentages and trends, with evaluations of the

Table 9-2. *South American and Mexican Survey Respondents' Attitudes toward Ease of Access to Health Care and Education Services, 1997*[a]

Percent

| | South America and Mexico | | | | | |
Scale	Access to health care five years ago	Access to health care today	Access to health care in five years' time	Access to education five years ago	Access to education today	Access to education in five years' time
No reply	2.3	1.8	14.2	2.8	2.9	14.3
Nothing	3.7	6.5	4.4	2.0	4.8	4.0
2	3.1	5.1	3.4	2.8	4.7	3.2
3	6.4	8.4	5.3	4.8	7.3	5.1
4	9.0	10.2	5.4	8.1	9.7	5.5
5	18.4	19.1	12.7	17.5	18.8	11.7
6	12.4	12.8	11.1	13.0	12.9	10.5
7	13.8	11.1	12.2	14.4	11.8	12.5
8	14.5	11.3	12.6	15.3	11.9	13.0
9	4.4	4.8	7.1	5.9	5.4	7.2
Everything	11.9	8.6	10.8	12.9	9.1	11.7
Other	0.3	0.3	1.0	0.6	0.7	1.3
N	11,716	11,716	11,716	11,716	11,716	11,716

Source: Latinobarometro (1997).

a. Scale of 1 to 10, with "Nothing" being the worst service and "Everything" being perfect service.

situation five years ago much more positive than attitudes toward the present. Yet unlike expectations about public services, which show an upward turn as a significant number of people expected services to improve markedly in the future, there is not a similar optimism in these other areas.[43] Job security in particular is a pressing concern: 63.3 percent and 64.9 percent of

43. In South America, for example, 2.5 percent of total respondents answered that they had no purchasing power five years ago; 6.0 percent answered that they had nothing now; and 4.7 percent answered that they would have nothing five years hence. Of those that placed themselves at the median, or 5 on a scale of 1 to 10, 18.7 percent felt they were at the median five years ago, 19.7 percent thought they were at the median at present, and 13.0 percent thought they would still be there five years hence, with most answers leaning toward less purchasing power in the future. In the responses to level of family income, 3.4 percent in South America answered "nothing" five years ago, 7.2 percent answered "nothing" at present, and 5.0 percent answered "nothing" in five years. Of those placing themselves at the median, 18.3 percent did so for five years ago, 20.8 percent did so at present, and only 13.5 percent thought they would be there in five years, with a slight shift toward higher (more optimistic) ranks (6–8).

Table 9-3. *Latin American Survey Respondents' Attitudes toward Job Stability, 1997*[a]

Percent

	South America and Mexico			Central America		
Scale	How much job security five years ago	How much job stability today	How much job stability in five years' time	How much job security five years ago	How much job stability today	How much job stability in five years' time
No reply	3.7	3.7	15.6	3.6	3.0	13.7
Nothing	3.5	9.2	5.7	3.4	8.1	5.3
2	3.3	7.1	4.1	3.6	6.3	4.1
3	5.8	10.2	6.5	6.1	9.0	6.1
4	8.8	11.8	6.4	8.4	10.6	6.1
5	17.0	18.5	13.1	16.9	17.9	12.6
6	12.8	11.7	10.5	13.6	13.6	11.2
7	14.1	9.4	11.5	13.7	11.1	11.7
8	14.7	8.6	10.8	14.1	9.5	11.5
9	5.9	3.6	5.9	6.1	4.0	6.7
Everything	9.7	5.2	8.3	9.7	5.8	9.3
Other	0.7	0.9	1.4	0.9	1.0	1.8
N	11,716	11,716	11,716	17,767	17,767	17,767

Source: Latinobarometro (1997).

a. Scale of 1 to 10, with "Nothing" being no job security or stability and "Everything" being total job security and stability.

respondents in South and Central America, respectively, are very concerned about losing their employment (table 9-3).[44] These uncertainties and concerns echo the opposing attitudes in which satisfaction with individual progress exists side by side with significant fears about the absence of a social safety net and may over time temper public support for economic reform.

It is difficult to draw many definitive conclusions from these responses until results are available for a number of years. Yet the responses do sug-

---

44. Comparative studies show that anxiety about unemployment often outstrips the unemployment rate because exposure to job insecurity and unemployment is not limited to the unemployed themselves, but affects their friends, family, and coworkers as well. Thus government approval is particularly sensitive to the unemployment rate, at least in the United States. Douglas Hibbs, cited in Buendia (1996, pp. 566–591).

gest that the same factors—education, initial position on the income ladder, level of inequality, access to the most important public services—that determine mobility rates also affect trends and patterns in the public's perceptions and attitudes about mobility. An examination of initial evidence of actual mobility trends in Peru as well as the results of the pilot survey of expectations will provide a benchmark for comparing attitudes and expectations with actual trends.

Case Study: Mobility and Expectations in Peru

Empirical studies of mobility for most countries in Latin America do not exist, in large part due to the absence of panel data. Yet there is some evidence on mobility trends for a few countries, and it is useful to consider information about expectations in light of actual trends. Peru is one of the few countries for which there are panel data. The data were compiled by the Instituto Cuanto from 1985 to 1997 for Lima and 1991 to 1997 nationwide. The panel is nationally representative and contains 676 households; there have been three observations: 1991, 1994, and 1996. The households selected for the subsequent pilot study were part of the original and smaller panel, which goes back to 1985. Initial analysis of these panels yields some insights into mobility trends. In addition, a pilot survey of 152 households in the panel, which sought to compare respondents' self assessments with objective mobility trends, provides some important insights into the matter of perceptions and mobility.

Peru stands out as a country where expectations are high, considering its large inequalities. Yet expectations are markedly different among various income and education groups, with much less optimism among low-income and less educated people. At the same time, the consistently large proreform vote has been strongest in poor and rural areas. In part this reflects the high costs that the extensive economic and political crisis imposed on the poorest. Despite the fact that the rewards from the economic recovery have been shared very unequally, most people see that the country is progressing, even if the expectations of poor people are much lower than those of other income groups. One possible explanation for this outcome is the mobility trends in the postreform years, which demonstrate substantial movement out of poverty, particularly for the extremely poor. Public expenditures, which have been reoriented to poor and rural areas in an unprecedented manner since 1993, are part of the explanation for the mobility of the poorest people.[45]

Transitions are defined here as movement either into or out of poverty or from or to extreme poverty from poverty. For the period studied, 39.8 percent of the total population had some mobility, and mobility was higher in rural than in urban areas: 34.9 percent of urban households made a transition, while 44.8 percent of rural ones did (see appendix table 9-A1). Upward mobility was higher in 1991–94 than in 1996, no doubt reflecting the stabilization of inflation and high growth rates of the first period and then the minor economic downturn of 1996. The percentage of the sample that moved up in 1991–94 was 26.8, while in 1994–96 it was 15.7 (appendix table 9-A2). The percentage that moved down in the first period was 10.8 and in the second period was 14.6. Thus in 1994–96 the percentage that moved up was only 1.1 points greater than that which moved down. Of the total poor the same percentage moved up as down in 1994–96: 11.4 percent. In Lima 13.4 percent moved down while 11.9 percent moved up. In rural areas 19.6 percent moved up while 16.0 percent moved down. The largest movements—across two poverty lines, either up or down—were in the rural areas.

Part of this story reflects the benefits of stabilization and the elimination of major distortions in the policy framework for both rural and urban groups. The downward trends for Lima in 1994–96 suggest that the 1995 economic adjustment had more direct impact on urban groups, which is not surprising. Yet another part of this story lies in dramatic changes in public expenditure patterns. After an October 1993 constitutional referendum, which President Fujimori won by a narrow margin but which he lost in most rural areas, discretionary public expenditures were dramatically redirected to rural areas, particularly to small, poor rural municipalities where Fujimori had fared the worst. Before 1993 Lima received 54 percent of total municipal fund expenditures; after 1993 it received 17.4 percent. The expenditures of the social fund, Foncodes, meanwhile, were directed to departments that voted no in 1993. Although this was clearly a politi-

45. This analysis of public expenditure patterns is based on Graham and Kane (1998). The evidence on mobility patterns comes from data compiled by Cuanto, S. A. as part of its annual living standards measurement surveys and was analyzed by Martin Cumpa of the Inter-American Development Bank. The author is grateful to both Richard Webb of Cuanto and Martin Cumpa for providing her with the data. For another analysis of the political effects of these spending trends, see Roberts and Arce (1998).

cally driven allocation of funds and resulted in the resignation of the head of the social fund, it also redirected funds to the departments with the worst social indicators in the country.[46]

Not surprisingly, the political returns on public expenditure investments in rural areas were much higher than they would have been in urban areas, where public services are of reasonable quality and where there are alternative providers of both basic services and food and income assistance. An interesting finding is that people's expectations of the state were higher in rural than in urban areas. Although most Peruvians believe that the primary responsibility of the state is to provide education, more rural than urban respondents believe so. In addition, rural respondents had much higher expectations of the state's role in promoting development in the country; urban respondents were much more likely to express faith in the private sector.[47] This may reflect the fact that most of the postreform market-led growth has been in urban areas. Although much of the rationale for the expenditure reallocation to rural areas was purely political, its beneficial effects on relieving poverty are clear.[48]

Results of the 1997 living standards survey, meanwhile, corroborate these general patterns. Although overall poverty remained fairly stagnant from 1996 to 1997, extreme poverty, which is primarily concentrated in rural areas, was significantly reduced. Preliminary analysis of the survey results suggests that transfers such as food aid explained much of the trend.[49] Food aid, a fairly insignificant share of total income for most quintiles, is a

---

46. Graham and Kane (1998, p. 89). While disbursements in 1991–93 correlated negatively with GDP per capita, suggesting some progressiveness, this did not guarantee targeting of the poorest. Funds were concentrated in more populated areas and in better-educated departments, and allocations were not affected by deficits in public services. As of 1994 this changed, and more funds were allocated to departments where Peruvians voted no. These were also the departments with the worst social indicators.

47. Agenda Peru poll cited in Graham (1998, chap. 3).

48. In addition, as Graham and Kane (1998) argue, this allocation occurred at the same time that political parties, which were very biased toward urban areas, lost a great deal of influence, and independents gained influence. Thus the weight of rural votes increased. Before 1993 people voted for party lists rather than for specific candidates and then indicated a preferential vote for a particular candidate. This meant that candidates had no local links, responsibilities, or representation. The 1993 Constitution eliminated assured congressional responsibility by department and established a single voting district. For the pros and cons of single district systems, see the discussion in Graham and Kane (1998, p. 70).

49. These are preliminary results from the 1997 ENNIV survey conducted by Cuanto. The author is grateful to Richard Webb for providing the data.

large proportion of the total for the poorest groups. Before 1993 most food aid was concentrated in Lima and was not progressively allocated to the poorest groups.[50]

These trends are clearly reflected in voting patterns from 1993 to 1996. Anti-Fujimori sentiment was very strong in the poorest rural areas in 1993 because people believed that they were not benefiting from reform. Support for Fujimori in the April 1995 elections increased the most in poor rural areas and declined the most in Lima. Although in general the proreform vote in Peru was driven by broad macroeconomic trends and the defeat of the Shining Path terrorist movement, the vote may also reflect more subtle trends in the mobility of the poorest income groups, trends that were in part driven by the government's public expenditure decisions. In 1995 rural voters rewarded Fujimori for expenditure increases that contributed to their upward mobility.

How these trends have affected expectations is less clear. Only a small percentage of the Latinobarometro sample was rural. Expectations were lower among less educated groups in the sample, yet the sample did not adequately represent the poorest rural groups, which experienced the most mobility. The inclusion of a more representative sample of rural areas that experienced significant and very visible increases in public expenditures might have shown raised expectations among the poorest respondents.

The survey covered 152 households, 40 rural and 112 urban.[51] The answers were affected by respondents' location, socioeconomic level, and expectations. The perceptions questionnaire addressed the following topics: perceptions of and satisfaction with changes in the household's economic welfare over the previous ten to fifteen years; perceptions and changes in the availability and quality of public services used by the household (health care, schools, security, water, sanitation, municipal government); perceptions of future economic prospects; presence and participation in community organizations; and family health history, especially the occurrence and effects of major problems. Five questions about economic trends in the previous five years were used to construct an index of perceived mobility (IPM). These were

50. In 1993 the proportion of families that used food aid was high only in Lima: 47 percent of low-income families used food aid, while 9 percent of those in the highest strata in the sample did (the wealthiest 20 percent of the distribution were excluded from the sample), a percentage that exceeded that of even the lowest socioeconomic levels in other cities. See Graham (1994, chap. 3).

51. A fuller, detailed description of the pilot study is found in chapter 10.

—Compared to ten to fifteen years ago, is the economic situation of your household much worse, worse, same, better, much better?

—Is your family's job situation much worse, worse, same, better, much better?

—Compared with yourself, did your parents live much worse, worse, same, better, much better?

—Compared with ten to fifteen years ago is the purchasing power of your household less, same, better?

—With respect to your current standard of living, is your degree of satisfaction very poor, poor, acceptable, good, very good?

All questions were given equal weight in the index except for the first two, which were assigned double weight because they most directly express economic mobility.

In objective mobility trends, 61 percent of households had income increases of 30 percent or more from 1985 to1990, which is better than the average for all Peruvian households during this period. Twenty-five percent were relatively unchanged, and 14 percent had income decreases of 30 percent or more. Self-assessments were startlingly at odds with the objective trends. Fifty-eight percent of households had very negative or negative views on their own economic experiences, while 28 percent were indifferent and 12 percent were positive. Most households, however (65 percent), were confident that their children would do better than they, while only 13 percent thought their children would do worse. The pessimistic economic assessments contrast with fairly optimistic self-assessments on housing improvements: 47 percent said that housing quality was better; only 5 percent said it was worse. This may reflect the contrast between the ease in identifying housing improvements and the difficulty in making accurate economic self-assessments about the past, particularly for the self-employed who do not earn regular wages. Earnings are also affected by external circumstances—luck, overall economic conditions, and shifts of jobs from one sector to another—as opposed to housing changes, which are more clearly determined by individual effort and savings. The respondents' generally optimistic assessments for their children, meanwhile, reflect hope, determination, and other noneconomic variables that are not necessarily conditioned by socioeconomic level or education.

Gaps between actual and perceived mobility were larger when answers were subjective and entailed a long recall period than when they were easily verifiable, as in the case of housing. And not surprisingly, responses about expectations for children were clearly the most subjective. In addition, the survey was conducted during a period of considerable economic instability, and also one during which several elections were held, leading to significant swings in public transfers and expenditures affecting the poor. These no doubt had some influence on the so-called national mood.

The correlates for the index of perceived mobility were gender, education, area of residence, and income status. There was a striking absence of correlation between IPM values and actual mobility. Of the respondents with per capita improvements in income of 100 percent or more from 1985 to 1997, 65 percent said they were worse off and only 11 percent said better off. Of the worst performers (with income declines of 30 percent more), 65 percent stated, accurately, that they were worse off, yet 29 percent said that their situation had not changed and 7 percent saw themselves as better off.

Women were more likely than men to take a negative view of past economic progress (63 percent of female-headed households versus 57 percent of male ones). Rural respondents were slightly less negative (53 percent) than urban ones (60 percent), and they were much less likely to use stronger "much worse" statements: 28 percent of urban households responded "much worse" while only 3 percent of rural ones did. Superior postsecondary education seemed to produce a similar effect: 35 percent of respondents with some higher education made the strong negative statement, as did 36 percent and 33 percent of the top two income quintiles. By contrast, none of those in the bottom quintile said "much worse," although 47 percent said that they were worse off. These variations are likely the result of cultural and class differences. In addition, urban respondents had higher expectations and more experience answering surveys—with an agenda in mind. This introduces a methodological problem that should be considered when interpreting the more general and regionwide Latinobarometro study: location-specific differences in answers to the same survey questions may create inaccurate or noncomparable survey results.

Some of these differences also reflect changes in perceptions of the overall national economic situation or the national mood. From May 1995 to May 1998, for example, households reporting an improvement in their economic situation dropped from 31 to 10 percent, while the proportion reporting a deterioration doubled from 22 to 47 percent. This shift in perceptions far exceeded changes in real incomes over those years, and likely reflects changes in optimism about the national state of affairs, reflecting political as well as economic trends, including declining support for President Fujimori.

Another interesting result was participation in community organizations. Sixty percent of the households in the poorest quintile were involved in five or more community organizations, while only 10 percent of the richest quintile were. The highest-achieving households (100 percent income increase or more) were less likely to belong to organizations and less likely to belong to five or more than were the lowest achievers. Meanwhile, perceived mobility becomes greater as organizational involvement increases, but the relationship is not strong and may reflect the same differences in culture and expectations that explain differences in perceptions among income and education groups.

These results seem to contradict Robert Putnam's influential work on the beneficial effects of social capital on economic development, a contradiction that may stem from the nature of the proxy measures used.[52] Yet they accurately reflect the extent to which community organizations in Peru are joint survival strategies for the poorest groups and are crucial to providing social safety nets in the absence of adequate public programs. Although such organizations are clearly useful, they can also become poverty traps: the perceived costs or risks of leaving joint efforts such as communal kitchens may discourage the poor from accepting or seeking other income-earning opportunities.[53]

More than anything else, the results of the Peru pilot project demonstrated the complex nature of perceptions and how far public perceptions about who is getting ahead and why can be from actual trends. Yet because people vote according to perceptions, and these perceptions may also have significant effects on individual effort and incentives, better understanding of them may be a key to achieving sustainable economic reform. Much more work remains to be done.

Latin American Trends in Comparative Perspective

The increased mobility (either upward or downward) and the weakening of collective organizations such as trade unions that seem to accompany market-oriented reforms have clear implications for voting patterns. In Latin America, market-oriented reform has signified a break with the severe economic crises of the past and thus has given voting patterns a clear

52. See Putnam (1993).
53. For detail on these kinds of effects, see Hoff (1996); and Akerlof (1997, pp. 1005–27).

intertemporal or antidotal character. In the same way, in many countries political parties are associated with the clientelistic political systems of the past. By the late 1980s and early 1990s the parties in the region were increasingly seen as representing the elite and concerned with political maneuvering rather than with the plight of the poor majority.[54] This perception was strengthened in some countries by a system in which internal party hierarchy dominated regional representation as the criterion for selecting candidates, as it did in Peru. This may explain the appeal for low-income groups of "can do" charismatic independents without links to the party systems. Yet the rejection of parties has not provided adequate representative mechanisms for the poor. Guillermo Campero's analysis of political attitudes in Chile, for example, finds a dissociation between favorable evaluations of progress at the individual level and concerns with poverty, inequality, and lack of solidarity in society. At the same time, distrust of traditional, class-based organizations such as trade unions has increased.[55]

A brief comparison with eastern Europe, another region that has experienced dramatic economic and political change since 1990, is illustrative. The policy reversals in both seem to have had an important effect on people's evaluation of social justice, their tolerance for inequality, and their subjective interpretations of how they have fared in the new market system.

Petr Matějů, in his analysis of previous research on social justice, finds that "subjective evaluation of economic inequalities is at least as important for the social climate and political attitudes as is the objective extent and origins of these inequalities." This also affects how the public defines and perceives mobility. "Mobility does not necessarily mean only individual mobility. Periods of major changes in stratification systems bring marked 'collective' mobility which people perceive as a change in the life chances typical for the social group or class they belong to."[56] This helps explain the divergent results in Peru, where individual expectations were lower than average for the region, but collective expectations for the country as a whole were much higher than average for the region.

Matějů notes that in established systems, high mobility reflects well-established and functioning allocation principles and thus is usually accepted as fair by most groups, even those that are not moving up. Many observers have attributed social and political stability in the face of very

54. See Degregori, Adrianzen, and Cordova (1998).
55. Campero (1997).
56. Matějů, (1997, p. 5); see also chapter 11 in this volume.

high levels of inequality in the United States to this phenomenon.[57] But in transition economies such as those in eastern Europe, high mobility is the result of changes in allocation patterns and principles, and thus individuals' evaluations of the fairness of mobility and of the new allocation patterns will depend on whether they are able to benefit from them. Matějů identifies a contradiction in the transition economies that is not unlike that identified by Campero for Chile: on the one hand evaluations are driven by egalitarian ideas and on the other by nonegalitarian and meritocratic concepts. In western democracies a person's inclinations to one of the main ideologies of distributive justice tend to predict his or her position on the left or right of the political spectrum; in most former communist countries these positions are just developing.

In the Czech Republic the patterns are more developed than in many other countries in the region, and by 1995 egalitarian ideology was clearly linked to left-wing political leanings. The links between meritocratic distributive ideology and right-wing political leanings were weaker. The tendency toward egalitarian ideology was linked to social status, while the tendency toward meritocratic ideology was more universal. Those with high status that was linked to education (the consistent group) were noticeably inclined to meritocratic ideology; those whose status was not linked to education (the inconsistent group) tended to reject meritocratic ideology. Matějů found that education is the most important determinant of respondents' evaluations of the market transition as beneficial.[58]

At the other end of the scale there are indications that the mobility of the poor is constrained by many of the same factors that limit the mobility of the poor in established market economies: inferior education, inadequate information, and income limitations. And thus far, at least in eastern Europe, these groups have demonstrated a fairly distinct tendency to vote against reform.

57. For an excellent description of mobility trends in the United States and the debates surrounding them, see McMurrer and Sawhill (1998).

58. See chapter 11. Mobility patterns at the upper end of the distribution in eastern Europe reflect two coexisting trends in many countries: elite reproduction and elite circulation. Elite reproduction is the capacity of former communist elites to adapt and to maintain their status at the top of the social order. Elite circulation suggests that the factors that promoted mobility into the elite during the years of the socialist state no longer exist and that new processes have resulted in a new elite with a new set of attributes. The degree of elite reproduction in the postcommunist period is directly related to the extent of circulation that took place before 1989. More pre-1989 circulation improved the technical competency of the elites, increasing their chances of surviving the transition to democracy and markets. See also Matějů and Vlachova (1997).

These trends are not surprising; in most countries education in particular has important effects on people's ability to participate in new market economies and to exploit opportunities. One such example is the voucher privatization program in the Czech Republic. Surveys of participants in the Czech voucher program found that the strongest predictor of a favorable evaluation of the privatization program was education, followed by wealth and relative youth. And education was also instrumental in determining who benefited most from the program. For example, although 62.7 percent of those with only an elementary education immediately sold off their shares in newly privatized enterprises rather than investing them, only 39.3 percent of those with university educations sold theirs. The university group fared much better financially because the returns on invested shares were much higher.[59] Continued participation in the voucher program (investing rather than selling shares) and positive evaluations of privatization were directly linked with voting in favor of reform, while those that perceived themselves as losers in the program were far more likely to vote for the socialist or communist parties.

In Latin America, education also affects peoples' abilities to benefit from or embrace opportunities in the market economies. Since the reforms went into effect, there have been widening wage differentials. This is explained by widening differences in the educational attainment of workers, with younger workers receiving more education than older workers did, and at the same time by the increasing returns to skilled labor. Because education increases have not kept up with the demand for skilled labor, the wages of skilled labor have risen much higher than those of unskilled labor. Preliminary evidence from Colombia shows that the younger (and most likely more educated workers) are the ones who experience the most income mobility.[60] In addition, in many countries expectations for future mobility were greater among younger and more educated groups, although there clearly were outlier countries where this was not the case.

Education and factors such as social networks influence mobility in most market societies, as the results from the Latinobarometro data analysis show. In Chile, for example, education and income levels of parents were determining factors in whether children used government-subsidized

59. Secondary variables important to the evaluations of subjective gains from the voucher program were social capital (defined as access to social networks) and business instincts. For details see Graham (1998, chap. 5).

60. Morley, Robinson, and Harris (1998).

vouchers to attend new private schools. In Peru it was the younger and more skilled workers who chose to join a new private pension plan. These same factors influenced perceptions of mobility, with younger, more educated groups tending to be more optimistic about their prospects in newly reformed economies. Yet the existence of outliers highlights the array of noneconomic factors that can determine and explain changes in expectations regardless of economic circumstances. What is striking is how dominant similar factors were in influencing mobility in societies as different in terms of distribution as the Czech Republic and Chile: the Gini coefficient in the Czech Republic is .27, while in Chile it is .57. Poverty in the Czech Republic affects less than 1 percent of the population, while in Chile in 1994 it was 28 percent. Yet in both countries similar forces seem to affect the ability to benefit from new opportunities introduced by market change, which is no doubt related to mobility trends in new market economies.

Political trends in Latin America are somewhat different from those in eastern Europe. Although voters are beginning to crystallize along ideological lines for the first time in eastern Europe, in Latin America traditional ideological lines are increasingly being blurred. Yet both patterns seem affected by changing mobility trends and seem consistent with a general pattern of proreform voting, at least in the short term.[61] In the longer term, with a return to more normal economic voting in both regions, it is plausible to assume that differences in individuals' mobility patterns, objective and subjective, may have even more influence in the way they vote. In addition, subjective patterns are clearly affected by hope, luck, changes in the national mood, and other noneconomic factors.

Concluding Thoughts and Matters for Further Exploration

An important matter that has not been explored in this chapter is the effect of the traditionally severe inequality in Latin America on mobility trends and the subjective evaluation of them. Also not explored is the effect of mobility trends and their evaluation on public expectations and voting behavior. Despite renewed growth since the reforms and possibly increased mobility, the region maintains the most unequal distribution of income in the world. Reforms have had important benefits for the poor and have the

61. For Latin America see Remmer (1993). For the postcommunist countries see Aslund, Boone, and Johnson (1996), pp. 217–313.

potential to increase efficiency and equity at the same time.[62] Still, the benefits of reforms have not been evenly shared in all countries, and in some, large income gaps have widened further. In Chile, for example, where there has been little occupational mobility during the reform period, the gap between the wages of skilled and unskilled workers has widened markedly. The relative earnings of managerial personnel rose from 419 percent of the average to 515 percent from 1986 to 1992. The earnings of unskilled workers rose from 51 percent to 53 percent of the average.[63]

Great inequality may affect people's perceptions of the fairness of reform. In the Latinobarometro study, for example, in some countries such as Peru, there were wide gaps among socioeconomic groups' evaluations of their economic situation vis-à-vis that of their parents and their expectations for their children. In Peru, only 37 percent of those in the poorest socioeconomic category believed that their children would do better than they had, while 61 percent of those in the highest category thought so. In Venezuela and Brazil, however, there was little variation among income groups, and there was an inverse relationship: those in the worst socioeconomic category were the most optimistic about the prospects for their children.

Clearly, expectations are affected by where people sit on the income ladder and how steep that ladder is, but the direction of those effects is neither clear nor uniform. In the Peru pilot project those respondents in the panel who had done the best were the most pessimistic in their self-assessments of their economic situations. A possible explanation is that the panel did not cover households in the highest income deciles, households that have for the most part fared very well in the reform. Respondents in the panel, who were slightly better off than the lowest-income groups and lived in urban areas, were more aware of the gaps between their own situation and those of the highest groups than were poor rural respondents. It is interesting to note in this light that the vote for President Fujimori and for the continuation of reform increased in poor rural areas from 1990 to 1995 but decreased in Lima. The existence of any generalized effect of inequality on voting, meanwhile, is far from clear. Some political economy research posits that high levels of inequality will cause voters to choose populist policies because the median voter will choose more redistribution and higher

62. This is discussed in detail in Birdsall, Graham, and Sabot (1998).

63. See chapter 8. For a more detailed review of distribution trends in the region see Inter-American Development Bank (1998).

taxes.[64] Yet research by Roland Benabou suggests that there are often steady states of inequality because political rights are often unequally distributed. Therefore theories of the median voter do not apply, and a powerful minority controls the political agenda and options available to median voters.[65] Thomas Piketty, meanwhile, describes how steady states of inequality result from people's expectations, which are determined by their mobility experience, and affect their effort levels.[66] There is some empirical evidence to support each of these arguments, and little agreement on the effects of inequality on voter behavior. A subject clearly worthy of further research, and one that will be critical to the political fate of economic reforms in Latin America, is the complex relationship between inequality, mobility, and public expectations.

Many questions presented here need to be further explored. One is whether increased mobility and higher expectations for one's children translate into proreform votes. Another is whether younger, more educated workers who are more upwardly mobile consistently vote for reform. A third is whether the rejection of traditional political parties and support for reform-oriented independents is related to mobility (upward or downward). A fourth and critical matter is the effects of severe inequality on mobility and the perceptions of it and on voting behavior. Other issues are pointed out elsewhere in the chapter. I have raised more questions than I have answered, but I hope this will serve to better formulate research questions about mobility, public perceptions, and political support for market reforms.

64. Alesina and Perotti (1994).
65. Benabou (1996, 1997).
66. Pikety (1995).

Table 9-A1. *Poverty and Mobility of Households in Peru, 1991–96*

Category	N	Percent
Total	676	100.0
Always poor	134	19.8
Moving up	166	24.6
Moving down	103	15.2
Never poor	273	40.4
Metropolitan Lima	344	100.0
Always poor	59	17.2
Moving up	71	20.6
Moving down	49	14.2
Never poor	165	48.0
Rest of country[a]	332	100.0
Always poor	75	22.6
Moving up	95	28.6
Moving down	54	16.3
Never poor	108	32.5

Source: Cuanto, S. A., data compiled by Martin Cumpa of the Inter-American Development Bank. The panel had 676 households.

a. Does not include rural coast and jungle.

Table 9-A2. *Poverty and Mobility of Households in Peru, 1991–94, 1994–96*

Percent

	1991–94			1994–96		
Category	Total	Moving up	Moving down	Total	Moving up	Moving down
Total[a]	37.6	26.8	10.8	30.3	15.7	14.6
MPE[b]	10.1	7.0	3.1	7.5	4.3	3.3
MPC[c]	27.5	19.8	7.7	22.8	11.4	11.4
Metropolitan Lima	30.5	21.5	9.0	25.3	11.9	13.4
MPE	7.0	4.9	2.0	4.7	2.3	2.3
MPC	23.5	16.6	7.0	20.6	9.6	11.0
Rest of country	44.9	32.2	12.7	35.5	19.6	16.0
MPE	13.3	9.0	4.2	10.5	6.3	4.2
MPC	31.6	23.2	8.4	25.0	13.3	11.7

Source: See table 9-A1.

a. The percentage of the total sample that had some mobility either up or down across poverty line.

b. Mobility within poverty from extreme to nonextreme.

c. Mobility across poverty line.

Table 9-A3. *Survey Respondents' Attitudes toward Parents' Past and Children's Potential Living Standards, by Country, 1997*

Percent

Country	Reply	"Did your parents live ____ than (as) you?"	"Will your children live ____ than (as) you?"
Argentina	No reply	4.0	9.7
	Better	58.6	53.3
	Same	16.8	16.7
	Worse	20.6	20.2
Bolivia	No reply	2.0	13.1
	Better	63.6	51.9
	Same	19.7	19.1
	Worse	14.7	16.0
Brazil	No reply	1.6	25.8
	Better	44.0	55.0
	Same	10.7	9.3
	Worse	43.8	9.9
Colombia	No reply	0.1	2.7
	Better	63.7	54.4
	Same	18.6	20.3
	Worse	17.7	22.6
Chile	No reply	1.0	4.6
	Better	37.4	61.4
	Same	36.9	28.1
	Worse	24.7	5.9
Ecuador	No reply	2.1	12.8
	Better	66.6	40.8
	Same	21.1	20.6
	Worse	10.3	25.8
Mexico	No reply	1.4	7.3
	Better	34.8	27.5
	Same	48.3	32.7
	Worse	15.6	32.5
Paraguay	No reply	4.2	16.5
	Better	65.2	46.5
	Same	17.9	24.6
	Worse	12.7	12.4
Peru	No reply	0.9	14.6
	Better	69.6	43.5
	Same	20.4	20.7
	Worse	9.0	21.2

Country	Reply	"Did your parents live ____ than (as) you?"	"Will your children live ____ than (as) you?"
Uruguay	No reply	3.7	14.4
	Better	58.3	47.7
	Same	15.9	19.1
	Worse	22.1	18.8
Venezuela	No reply	1.8	10.6
	Better	72.9	53.4
	Same	13.6	16.2
	Worse	11.8	19.8
Costa Rica	No reply	5.3	10.0
	Better	60.4	42.5
	Same	18.4	26.5
	Worse	16.0	21.0
Salvador	No reply	6.3	7.1
	Better	65.6	26.2
	Same	23.4	40.0
	Worse	4.7	26.6
Guatemala	No reply	7.2	24.3
	Better	46.2	33.8
	Same	25.3	25.8
	Worse	21.3	16.1
Honduras	No reply	1.2	9.5
	Better	65.8	43.0
	Same	17.2	25.2
	Worse	15.8	22.3
Nicaragua	No reply	1.0	5.4
	Better	65.8	41.7
	Same	26.0	36.4
	Worse	7.2	16.5
Panama	No reply	2.4	10.3
	Better	50.1	50.2
	Same	24.9	27.4
	Worse	22.5	12.0

Source: See table 9-A1.

References

Akerlof, George. 1997. "Social Distance and Social Decisions." *Econometrica* 65 (September): 1005–27.

Alesina, Alberto, and Roberto Perotti. 1994. "The Political Economy of Growth: A Critical Review of the Literature." *World Bank Economic Review* 8 (3): 351–71.

Aslund, Anders, Peter Boone, and Simon Johnson. 1996. "How to Stabilize: Lessons from Post-Communist Countries." *Brookings Papers on Economic Activity* 1: 217–92.

Barros, Ramon, Suzanne Duryea, and Miguel Székely. 1998. "What's Behind Latin America's Inequality?" Washington: Inter-American Development Bank.

Benabou, Roland. 1997. "Heterogeneity, Stratification, and Growth: Macroeconomic Implications of Community Structure and School Finance." *American Economic Review* 86 (3): 584–609.

———. 1996. "Inequality and Growth." *NBER Macroeconomics Annual.* Cambridge, Mass.: National Bureau of Economic Research.

Benabou, Roland, and Efe A. Ok. 1998. "Social Mobility and the Demand for Redistribution: the POUM Hypothesis." Economic Research Reports RR 98-23. C. V. Starr Center for Applied Economics, New York University.

Birdsall, Nancy, Carol Graham, and Richard Sabot, eds. 1998. *Beyond Tradeoffs: Market Reforms and Equitable Growth in Latin America.* Washington: Brookings and Inter-American Development Bank.

Bruno, Michael, and William Easterly. 1996. "Inflation's Children: Tales of Crises That Beget Reform." Paper prepared for the annual meeting of the American Economics Association.

Buendia, Jorge. 1996. "Economic Reform, Public Opinion, and Presidential Approval in Mexico, 1988–93." *Comparative Political Studies* 29 (5):566–91.

Campero, Guillermo. 1997. "Mas Alla del Individualismo: La Buena Sociedad y La Participacion." Santiago: CERC.

Carroll, Chris. 1994. "How Does Future Income Affect Current Consumption?" *Quarterly Journal of Economics* 59 (February): 111–48.

Cowlan, Kevin, and Jose de Gregorio,. 1996. "Distribucion y Pobreza en Chile: Estamos Mal? Ha Habido Progreso? Hemos Retrocido?" Paper presented to Ministry of Finance/ Inter-American Development Bank Workshop on Inequality and Growth. Santiago.

Crawford, Sue E. S., and Elinor Ostrom. 1995. "A Grammar of Institutions." *American Political Science Review* 89 (3): 582–600.

Cukierman, Alex, Steven Webb, and Bilin Neyapti. 1992. "Measuring the Independence of Central Banks and Its Effects on Policy Outcomes." *World Bank Economic Review* 6 (3): 353–98.

Dalton, R., S. C. Flanagan, and P. A. Beck, eds. 1984. *Electoral Change in Advanced Industrial Democracies: Realignment or Dealignment?* Princeton University Press.

Degregori, Carlos Ivan, Alberto Adrianzen, and Manuel Cordova. 1998. "Democracia e Inequidad en America Latina: El Caso Peruano." Paper prepared for the Inter-American Dialogue Meeting on Poverty and Inequality. Washington.

Duryea, Suzanne, and Miguel Székely. 1998. "Labor Markets in Latin America: A Supply-Side Story." Paper prepared for the annual meeting of the Inter-American Development Bank, Cartagena.

Geddes, Barbara. 1995. "The Politics of Liberalization." *Latin American Research Review* 30 (2): 195–214.

Gibson, Edward. 1996. *Class and Conservative Parties: Argentina in Comparative Perspective.* Johns Hopkins University Press.

Graham, Carol. 1994. *Safety Nets, Politics, and the Poor: Transitions to Market Economies.* Brookings.

———. 1998. *Private Markets for Public Goods: Raising the Stakes in Economic Reform.* Brookings.

Graham, Carol, and Cheik Kane. 1998. "Opportunistic Government or Sustaining Reform: Electoral Trends and Public Expenditure Patterns in Peru, 1990–95." *Latin American Research Review* 33 (1): 67–104.

Graham, Carol, and Moises Naim. 1998. "The Political Economy of Institutional Reform." In Birdsall, Graham, and Sabot, eds. *Beyond Tradeoffs.*

Haggard, Stephan, and Steven B. Webb. 1994. *Voting for Reform: Democracy, Political Liberalization, and Economic Adjustment.* Oxford University Press and the World Bank.

Hoff, Karla. 1996. "Market Failures and the Distribution of Wealth: A Perspective from the Economics of Information." *Politics and Society* 24 (4): 411–32.

Inter-American Development Bank. 1998. *Facing Up to Inequality in Latin America.* Washington.

Kaufmann, Robert, and Leo Zuckerman. 1998. "Attitudes toward Economic Reform in Mexico: The Role of Political Orientations." *American Political Science Review* 92 (2): 359–75.

Knack, Stephen, and Philip Keefer. 1997. "Does Social Capital Have an Economic Payoff? A Cross-Country Investigation." *Quarterly Journal of Economics* 112 (4): 1251–88.

Lustig, Nora, ed. 1995. *Coping with Austerity: Poverty and Inequality in Latin America.* Brookings.

Matějů, Petr. 1997. "Beliefs about Distributive Justice and Social Change: Czech Republic, 1991–1995." Social Trends Working Papers. Prague: Institute of Sociology, Academy of Sciences of the Czech Republic.

Matějů, Petr, and Klara Vlachova. 1997. "The Role of Politically Relevant Attitudes and Value Orientations in Electoral Decisions: The Czech Republic in 1996." Social Trends Working Papers. Prague: Institute of Sociology, Academy of Sciences of the Czech Republic.

McMurrer, Daniel, and Isabel V. Sawhill. 1998. *Getting Ahead: Economic and Social Mobility in the United States.* Washington: Urban Institute Press.

Morley, Samuel, Sherman Robinson, and Rebecca Harris. 1998. "Estimating Income Mobility in Colombia Using Maximum Entropy Economics." Paper Prepared for the Center on Social and Economic Dynamics Workshop on Social Mobility, Brookings Institution.

Nelson, Joan. 1992. "Poverty, Equity, and the Politics of Adjustment." In Stephan Haggard and Robert Kaufmann, eds. *The Politics of Adjustment.* Princeton University Press.

O'Donnell, Guillermo. 1992. "Democracia Delegativa?" *Cuadernos del CLAEH* 61: 5–20.

Piketty, Thomas. 1995. "Social Mobility and Redistributive Politics." *Quarterly Journal of Economics* 110 (3): 551–84.

Putnam, Robert. 1993. *Making Democracy Work.* Princeton University Press.

Remmer, Karen. 1993. "The Political Economy of Elections in Latin America." *American Political Science Review* 87 (2): 393–407.

Roberts, Kenneth, and Moises Arce. 1998. "Neoliberalism and Voting Behavior in Peru." *Comparative Political Studies* 31 (2): 217–46.

Stokes, Susan C. 1996a. "Public Opinion and Market Reforms: The Limits of Economic Voting." *Comparative Political Studies* 29 (5): 499–519.

———. 1996b. "Economic Reform and Public Opinion in Peru." *Comparative Political Studies* 29 (5): 544–65.

Székely, Miguel. 1996. *El Ahorro de los Hogares en Mexico, Banco Inter-Americano de Desarrollo.* Series de Estudios Economicos y Sectoriales, RE2-96-001. Washington: Inter-American Development Bank.

Weyland, Kurt. 1998a. "Peasants or Bankers in Venezuela? Presidential Popularity and Economic Reform Approval, 1989–1993." *Political Research Quarterly* 51 (2): 341–62.

———. 1998b. "The Political Fate of Market Reform in Latin America, Africa, and Eastern Europe." *International Studies Quarterly* 42: 645–74.

Zaller, John R. 1992. *The Nature and Origins of Mass Public Opinion.* Cambridge University Press.

RICHARD WEBB

10

Pilot Survey on Household Perceptions of Mobility: Peru 1998

W hen people look back on their earnings and welfare experience, do their perceptions match objective measures of that experience? What determines personal perceptions of one's own mobility? These questions bear on voter behavior and political attitudes, but they should be of interest also to welfare and development economists. How far can one go in assuming that measurable increases in the consumption of private and public goods create "satisfaction" or "development?"

This chapter is a report on a pilot study carried out in Peru to examine these questions. The study compares what households say about their own past mobility in terms of income and welfare change with objective evidence of that change—that is, it compares perceived and actual mobility. "Objective" information on household mobility was obtained by drawing on panel data from four World Bank Living Standards Measurement Surveys (LSMS) carried out between 1985 and 1997. Subjective data were obtained through a May 1998 Perceptions Survey especially designed for this study that asked a subset of households belonging to the LSMS data set to make retrospective assessments of their economic and welfare history since 1985.

This study should be described as an exploratory effort in that it was constrained by a small sample size and by a dearth of research precedents. The sample was limited by the size of the panel: the May 1998 survey covered 152 households from the LSMS panel. Moreover, studies on mobility had few pointers for the questionnaire design or for defining research hypotheses regarding the factors that determine the perception of economic welfare. The purpose of the pilot study, therefore, was to provide a first approximation to the relationship between subjective and objective data on mobility and to look for possible determinants of the relationship.

In that exploratory mode the survey included questions on two topics that have been at the center of much recent research on the causes of economic development. One focused on the significance of community organizations: does a person's participation in various of these organizations improve chances of upward mobility? Do they contribute to a person's more positive view of his or her circumstances? The second topic was health. Does a history of health problems correlate with less mobility? Or with a more pessimistic view of one's situation?

The study used an existing panel data set for Peru collected through a set of LSMS surveys. The surveys had tracked the income and welfare experience of a sample of Peruvian households from 1985 to 1997, applying the World Bank LSMS questionnaire design. Though the surveys were representative at the national level, the subset that comprised the panel was limited largely to households in Lima. Nonetheless, the panel provided a database containing detailed information on household expenditures, health, education, and housing conditions gathered at different times. Those data are here referred to as objective in that, although they were reported by household heads, they involved very short or no recollection because they referred to conditions at the time of the interview or to very recent events— mostly recent purchases and income receipts. Some of the responses, such as those on housing characteristics, could be verified by the interviewer and did not involve any subjective comparison with conditions or events at a different moment. By contrast, the information obtained through the follow-up survey in May 1998 deliberately sought a subjective assessment of the household's welfare experience. Room for subjectivity was created because the questions required the recollection of conditions and events at a considerable distance in time—the questions referred to "ten to fifteen years ago"—and because many of the questions were phrased as comparisons with current circumstances.

Method and Data

The panel information was obtained from surveys carried out in 1985, 1991, 1994, and 1997, each of which used the LSMS questionnaire and recommended procedures. All except the 1991 survey were representative at the national level and of about the same size: 3,800 to 4,000 households. The 1991 survey was of a similar size but did not include some major regions of the country because of the terrorist emergency. Those regions, both urban and rural areas of the jungle and rural areas of the coast, contain about 15 percent of the national population. The panel selected from those surveys was much smaller and also differed in size and composition for different comparison periods. For the longest period, 1985–97, the panel size was only 152 households, of which 106 were in Lima and 46 in the Departments of Cuzco and Puno.

The Perceptions Survey questionnaire was two pages and was applied to the panel of 152 households. Of that total, 112 were urban households, mostly in Lima, and 40 were rural. The interviews were carried out by Instituto Cuanto of Peru, a research and public information center that had been responsible for the 1991, 1994, and 1996 LSMS surveys. The survey used eight experienced interviewers, most of whom had worked on the previous LSMS surveys and who were trained especially for this survey to ensure maximum homogeneity in questionnaire application. The questionnaire and the interviewers were tested in the field before the survey began, and the survey itself was carried out May 22–28, 1998.

The survey questionnaire addressed the following topics:

—Perception of and satisfaction with changes in the household's economic welfare in the previous ten to fifteen years.

—Perception of changes in the availability and quality of public services used by the household: health, schools, security, water, sanitation, municipal government.

—Perception of future economic prospects.

—Presence of and participation in community organizations.

—Family health history, especially occurrence of and effects of major problems.

The results of the Perceptions Survey were compared household by household with the information on actual changes in living conditions contained in the panel data. However, responses to the Perceptions Survey were all ordinal rankings—"better," "same," "worse." Those perceptions were quantified by assigning values to each response and then summing across several questions to arrive at an Index of Perceived Mobility. The index, which can be considered a measure of the extent of positive or negative self-assessment of mobility, became the principal tool for comparing subjective assessments of mobility with actual mobility as measured by the panel survey.

The index was constructed from five questions, each of which could be considered an assessment of the respondent's economic success or upward mobility over ten to fifteen years. Those questions were the following.

—Compared with ten to fifteen years ago, is the *economic situation* of your household much worse, worse, same, better, much better?

—Compared with ten to fifteen years ago, is your family's *job situation* much worse, worse, same, better, much better?

—Compared with yourself, did your *parents* live much worse, worse, same, better, much better?

—Compared with ten to fifteen years ago, is the *purchasing power* of your household less, same, better?

—With respect to your current *standard of living*, is your degree of *satisfaction* very poor, poor, acceptable, good, very good?

The weights attached to each response were necessarily a matter of judgment. Our decision was to give equal weights to all except the first two questions, the responses to which seemed to express the idea of economic upward or downward mobility most directly and clearly and were therefore assigned a higher (double) weight.

A second index was calculated using a similar procedure to measure the perception of improvements or of deterioration in *public services*. Twelve questions were used, but some were almost directly repetitive; the index included nine different service items. These were health, education, water, sewage, electricity, security, municipal government, neighborhood night watchmen, and paving. The responses were also phrased comparatively, ranging from much worse to much better. Four items—health, education, security, and water-sewage—were given double weight.

The responses with regard to health history were classified into two groups: households that reported significant loss of income as a consequence of health problems and households that had not suffered major economic effects.

Finally, the information on community organizations determined the number of organizations to which the respondent belonged or from which he or she had received some benefit.

Results

The results of the study were surprising. Although the households in the sample showed significant upward mobility, the subjective assessments were significantly more pessimistic about having experienced that mobility. This negative slant was most evident among the upwardly mobile.

The Perception of Mobility

The panel data showed more families better off than worse off. This was true both when the comparison was between 1985 and 1997 and when the comparison was between 1991 and 1997 (table 10-1). The panel was therefore not representative of the less favorable experience of the average Peruvian household over those two periods: average household income either stagnated or fell slightly between 1985 and 1997. For the panel, significant improvement in per capita household income was far more common than major decline.

However, in considerable contradiction with those results, responses to questions regarding current economic status compared with that of ten to fifteen years before were sharply negative. When those responses are aggregated in the IPM, almost four times as many households (58 percent) had negative responses as had positive (15 percent), while 28 percent said "the same." Thus the starting point for this analysis was a negative emphasis in the array of self-assessments (table 10-2).

This strongly pessimistic outlook on their own experience, however, did not prevent households from making two very optimistic assertions. One was that a large majority (65 percent) were confident that their children would have a better standard of living than they themselves had: only 13 percent expected a lower standard of living for their children. A second positive response concerned housing quality. When asked whether their housing quality had improved or deteriorated, 47 percent said "better" while only 5 percent said "worse."

What explains these spots of optimism in the midst of a pessimistic general view? One explanation could be that housing quality (which was probably interpreted by respondents to mean wall, floor, and roofing materials, number of rooms, and general state of repair) is a far more observable, immediate, and objective matter than the necessarily vague comparison of living standards over a long time. The definitional vagueness and difficulty of measuring long-run changes in living standards (given changes in family sizes and needs, place of residence, and type of business) gives room for answers that are shaped as much by general attitudes and feelings, including the respondent's perception of his or her situation relative to that of others, as by objective assessment. This is less the case with the housing

Table 10-1. *Actual Income Experience of Households, 1985–97, 1991–97*

Household per capita income	1985–97	1991–97
Rose 30 percent or more	61	50
Were relatively unchanged (between +29 percent and –29 percent)	25	37
Fell 30 percent or more	14	13

Source: World Bank Living Standards Measurement Surveys (LSMS), 1985–97.

question. Yet the attitude that housing was better could also reflect a degree of pride in that almost all homes are self-built and and self-maintained. Their gradual improvement, therefore, is more directly a function of the homeowner's own accumulated efforts and resourcefulness than is the case with earnings, which can be imputed to a greater extent to external circumstances. Replies to the question on children's prospects, meanwhile, are more likely to be an expression of hope and determination than an objective observation, so that an optimistic view on prospects can be understood in part as a statement of priorities and perhaps in part as a normal emotional contradiction.

Correlates of Perceptions of Own Mobility

What are these positive and negative perceptions correlated with? Table 10-3 shows cross-tabulations between household perceptions as measured by the IPM and a variety of potential correlates that were included in the Perceptions Survey. The first two correlates—actual mobility over the longer period 1985–97 and the shorter period 1991–97—could be considered the "rational" determinants: if people are objective and informed in recognizing actual events, perceived and actual mobility would be highly correlated. Because this was not the case, other possible correlates—gender, education, area of residence, and income status—were examined for clues to explain the Index of Perceived Mobility.

There is a striking absence of correlation between IPM values and actual mobility. Of the highest performers in the sample of households (those with per capita income improvement of 100 percent or more between 1985 and 1997), 65 percent said that they were worse off and only 11 percent said better off. Of the worst performers (income deterioration of 30 percent or more), 65 percent stated accurately that they were worse off, yet 29 percent said that their situation had not changed, and 7 percent actually saw themselves as better off. The 1991–97 comparison produces a similar

Table 10-2. Index of Perceived Mobility

Index	Percent of households
Very negative	21
Negative	37
Indifferent	28
Positive	12
Very positive	3

Source: Perceptions Survey, 1998.

lack of correlation between perceived and actual mobility.

Examining other variables revealed, first, that women were more likely than men to take a pessimistic attitude (although it must be noted that the sample of 152 household heads included only 35 women): 63 percent of female heads but only 57 percent of men believed their income had declined. Comparing urban and rural households (again, the rural contingent was small—40 versus 112 urban) suggests what might be a cultural difference: rural respondents were a little less negative than urban (53 percent and 60 percent, respectively), but more clearly they seemed unwilling to make the stronger "much worse" statement than their urban counterparts: 28 percent of urban households used "much" but only 3 percent of rural households did. Superior (postsecondary) education and high income class seem to produce a similar, disinhibiting effect: 35 percent of respondents with superior education said their incomes were much worse, as did 36 percent and 33 percent, respectively, of the top two quintiles of the income distribution. None of the respondents in the bottom quintile said "much worse," although 47 percent said simply that they were worse off. These patterns of response suggest cultural, class, and psychological determinants of what is said in interviews by class-specific interviewers and, inevitably, using class-specific language that rural respondents might have more difficulty understanding or relating to. It remains an open question whether such determinants go beyond the adjectival character or manner of response to determine respondents' more fundamental stance between positive and negative views.

Perception of Public Services

The Perceptions Survey also asked respondents to rate changes in the availability and quality of different public services. For each household, the responses, which again took the form of rankings ranging from "much

Table 10-3. *Perceived Mobility and Potential Correlates, 1985–97, 1991–97*

Correlates	Very negative	Negative	Indifferent	Positive	Very positive
Mobility: percent income change 1985–97					
100 +	30	35	24	11	0
30 to 99	29	38	25	8	0
−30 to +30	19	31	23	23	4
−30 or more	36	29	29	0	7
Mobility: percent income change 1991–97					
100+	21	39	24	15	0
30 to 99	26	34	29	9	3
−30 to +30	25	27	29	16	2
−30 or more	11	44	33	6	6
Area					
Urban	28	32	25	13	3
Rural	3	50	35	10	3
Gender					
Women	29	34	29	6	3
Men	19	38	27	14	3
Education					
Primary	25	40	25	8	2
Secondary	12	41	32	12	3
Higher	35	15	25	25	0
Income quintile					
I (poor)	0	47	43	7	3
II	19	42	19	16	3
III	17	37	27	13	7
IV	36	26	23	16	0
V (rich)	33	33	27	7	0

Source: Perceptions Survey, 1998.

worse" to "much better," were aggregated into an Index of Perceived Public Services. The distribution of household views is shown in table 10-4.

In contrast to reponses regarding mobility, the reactions are now strongly favorable. Only 15 percent saw a deterioration of services. Moreover, none of the households used the term "much worse." For 62 percent of the sample, services had improved, and for 24 percent the improvement was described as "much better." These views fit what is known from aggregate statistics

Table 10-4. *Index of Perceived Public Services*

Perception	Percent of households
Total	100
Worse	15
Same	23
Better	38
Much better	24

Source: Perceptions Survey, 1998.

regarding the expansion in the delivery of most public services, especially during the past five years. The delivery of primary health care, water, electricity, and sanitation has expanded significantly. The status of security is harder to judge. The elimination of most terrorist activity perhaps remains uppermost in respondents' minds and is likely to continue to generate responses that security was better, even though criminal violence may be increasing. Still, the overall perception of better services largely fits the facts.

How does this strongly positive attitude toward the improved quality of public services relate to the opinions on the deterioration of family income? The most likely interpretation would seem to be that, as in the case of housing quality, the facts were very evident and immediate and left respondents with little room to express pessimism derived from their personal circumstances or as an effect of unexplained psychological determinants. Yet the answers suggest that there was little "transference" from the perception of services to that of their own income situation. Family income or purchasing power was clearly distinguished from the increased welfare provided by public services.

Health History and Community Organizations

The sample was divided into families that reported major effects on the family budget as a consequence of health problems and those that may have had illness or accidents but denied that the budget effects had been severe. Several questions were used, essentially asking the same question in different ways, to get at cases of major effects, and a positive response to any one of the questions was taken as sufficient evidence. Thus respondents were asked if sickness or accident to any family member had caused

Table 10-5. *Health Victims, Mobility, and Perceptions*
Percent

Response	Victims	Not victims
Perceived mobility	100	100
Very negative	23	38
Negative	46	21
Indifferent	21	17
Positive	11	21
Very positive	0	4
Actual mobility: income change, 1985–97		
(total households)	100	100
100+	40	30
30–99	21	15
−30 to +30	23	40
−30 or more	16	15

Source: Perceptions Survey, 1998.

"the paralysis or abandonment of a major family project, such as home improvements, studies, purchases, etc." or created an extant, unpaid debt or a continuing long-term expenditure or loss of employment or "a permanent reduction in the standard of living."

As a result of this rather liberal definition of major health effects, 70 percent of the sample households were classified in the category of victims, families that had suffered major economic costs from health problems. The correlation of health costs with other variables is shown in table 10-5.

The relationship between a costly health history and perceptions of mobility is clearly weak. Nonvictims did tend to be more positive—25 percent versus only 11 percent of the victims—but they also had a greater tendency to be very negative about their experience—38 percent versus 23 percent. Of course, the weak correlation between health problems and both actual and perceived mobility could be the result here of an overly broad definition of "victim." A next stage in this analysis should use a more demanding definition to test the effect on mobility of a more severe level of health problems.

The possible effect of community organization on actual and perceived mobility was also examined. Table 10-6 shows the distribution of respondents according to the number of organizations of which they were mem-

Table 10-6. *Relation of Mobility to Membership in Community Organizations*
Percent

Item	None	1 to 2	3 to 4	5 or more
Number of organizations	18	21	33	28
IPM				
Very negative	25	28	38	9
Negative	16	20	34	30
Indifferent	21	12	36	31
Positive	6	33	22	39
Very positive	25	25	0	50
IPM				
Very negative	29	28	24	7
Negative	32	34	38	40
Indifferent	32	16	30	31
Positive	4	19	8	17
Very positive	4	3	0	5
Income change 1985–97				
100+	24	24	35	16
30-99	29	25	25	21
–30 to +30	35	15	35	15
–30 or more	14	29	29	29
Income quintile				
I (poor)	0	13	27	60
II	19	16	42	23
III	13	17	40	30
IV	26	32	26	16
V (rich)	33	27	30	10

Source: Perceptions Survey, 1998.

bers or from which they had received some benefit. These organizations included some that were not located in the community but which provided benefits that reached the respondent. The complete list of reported organizations is shown in the survey at the end of the chapter. The most frequently cited organization (69 percent of households) was the local asociacion de padres de familia, the Peruvian equivalent of a PTA. Other important organizations were Christian (Protestant) community parishes, clubes de madres, and "communal organizations." Most of the latter were originally rural village or community self-government or mutual help associations, but membership was maintained by migrants who set up branches in towns and cities and continue to interact with their community of origin.

There is a greater correlation between the density of community involvement and income level than with perceived or actual mobility. Households in the poorest quintile were intensely involved in community organization: 60 percent had some form of association with five or more organizations, whereas only 10 percent of the richest quintile did. At the other extreme, all of the households in the poorest fifth belonged to at least one organization; 33 percent of the top quintile had no relationship to any organization.

Perceived mobility becomes regarded more positively as organizational density increases, but the relationship is not strong. Organizational density shows even less relationship with actual mobility. In fact, there is a suggestion of an inverse relationship: the strongest achievers (100 percent or more income increase from 1985 to 1997) were more likely to belong to no organizations and less likely to be among those who belonged to five or more organizations than the lowest achievers (30 percent or greater income decline).

Concluding Reflections: Some Clues and Suggestions

The strongest conclusion that emerges from this study is that for the particular sample studied, household perceptions of mobility were only weakly related to actual mobility. A second conclusion was that, on average, respondents took a more pessimistic view of their own experience than was warranted by the apparent facts.

But a more speculative conclusion can be drawn from the responses: the gap between perceived and actual experience was wide when the questions left a great deal of room for subjective interpretation but narrow when they referred to highly verifiable matters. The five questions used to derive the Index of Perceived Mobility were in the first category. They all asked for a long period of recall—ten to fifteen years. More important, the questions were vaguely defined, using terms such as "job situation," "economic situation," "comparison with parents' living standards," and "level of satisfaction with living standards." In addition, much room for interpretation was created by the fact that no explicit allowance was made for changing household needs. Over ten to fifteen years, considerable change could occur as a result of changes in family size and demographic composition, place of residence, and type of employment. Perceived needs could also change as a result of the greater availability and consumption of new goods and services. By contrast, questions on the availability of public services and on housing improvements may be judged to be more verifiable and objective, and to leave less room for interpretation, though some subjectivity was present in that these questions again referred to a ten- to fifteen-year period and some of the questions used to compute the Index of Public Services referred to quality rather than access.[1]

There was a marked contrast between the level of pessimism in the responses to these two categories of questions. When the room for interpretation was large, responses were at variance with objective information and displayed a negative bias. When the questions were more verifiable, responses were far more optimistic. In this study the "perceived versus actual" question was not tested in the cases of services and housing, but the positive slant of the responses to questions in both categories corresponds with macroeconomic information showing a substantial improvement in both availability and quality of public services.

A third category of question could be considered entirely subjective and therefore a measure of pure optimism or pessimism. These were the questions on future expectations of economic welfare for the household and, more specifically, for its children. Despite their negative bias regarding the past, respondents leaned to optimism regarding the future: 43 percent expected a better economic situation for the household while 23 percent saw a worsening. When asked how long it would take to reach a "satisfactory" level of living, 53 percent said ten years or less, 13 percent said ten or more, and 34 percent said never. The optimism, however, was most definite when it was a matter of the future of their children: 65 percent saw a better future and only 13 percent a worse one. Thus when the issue was the future, extreme subjectivity produced a highly positive or optimistic view.

As a basis for understanding these patterns of perception, three types of determinant should be examined: aggregate economic conditions, the prevalence of self-employment, and cultural or sociological factors.

---

1. In the total Index of Public Services, questions referring to availability represent 71 percent of the total weight while those referring to quality represent 29 percent.

Aggregate Economic Conditions

Self-assessments of upward or downward mobility are likely to be influenced by the national economic context, although neither the sign nor the strength of the causal effect is evident. As a starting point for interpretation, in any case, the reader should be aware of the main features of that background.

The 1998 survey on perceptions was carried out against a background of two decades of exceptionally high macroeconomic instability and falling incomes. Peru suffered major recessions accompanied by high inflation in 1975–80 and 1983–90. Recession continued, though with low inflation, in 1991–92. Short booms occurred in 1980–82 and 1986–87, but per capita GDP nonetheless fell 32 percent over the whole period. The period just before the Perceptions Survey, 1993–97, saw a sharp recovery with per capita GDP rising 31 percent. In addition, the almost complete elimination of price inflation after 1993 probably created the perception of an improvement in the standard of living over and above the actual increase in real earnings. These percentage variations do not, of course, cancel out because the earlier decline had been from a higher base: the net change in per capita GDP from 1975 to 1997 was a loss of 11 percent. For the average household, 1997 incomes were lower than those of 1975. For most of the population, income in 1998 would have been no higher, and probably lower, than that of their parents.

Structural and local changes added to the instability that households experienced. Substantial migration occurred: rural to urban, highlands to coca-growing jungle areas, towns to cities, and Peru to other countries. Between 1980 and 1992 a terrorist insurgency created enormous upheavals for much of the population in the highlands and jungle: a large part of the national territory was closed to normal productive relations and to public administration. In 1983 a major natural calamity occurred—a once-in-a-century El Niño. And throughout this period, technological change and investments brought major reductions in the cost of transport and communications.

One possible effect of such a difficult and changeable background on current perceptions is that economic hardship and insecurity produce a general sense of dissatisfaction and pessimism that colors recollections of personal experience. Another, reinforcing, possibility is that if people feel instability more keenly and recollect it more easily, their recollections will be biased in a negative direction. These two possibilities, the effects of the general context and of asymmetric recollection, seem to be borne out by the findings of this study. Yet alternative hypotheses cannot be ruled out on a priori grounds, even though they do not tally with the findings. Thus it would not be unreasonable to argue that instability causes households to be more tolerant and accepting of their own circumstances and to discount personal difficulties. Another reasonable possibility is that recollection is asymmetric in terms of time, with more recent events having a greater influence. If so, the particular sequence of events in 1985–97 could have been expected to bias recollections positively. Prolonged hardship in 1985–92 would have been discounted because it was followed by a short but significant economic recovery in 1993–97, whose subjective effects were, moreover, reinforced by the relief produced by successful price stabilization. These last two possibilities are contrary to the survey results but perhaps help explain the more positive expectations found with respect to the future.

The Prevalence of Self-Employment

Three out of four workers in Peru are either self-employed or unpaid workers in family-owned productive units. The largest categories of such employment are small farmers, shopkeepers, street vendors, and transport workers. The prevalence of self-employment spread during the past two decades, running counter to the long-term trend in Peru and in most developing economies. This reversal was probably driven by a combination of severe recession and growing government intervention in business operations. Small-scale production and informal organization increased the share of these operations in total employment, reinforcing the importance of self-employment and informal labor market arrangements vis-à-vis that of employees working in formal establishments. One measure of this trend to self-employment and informality is that the share of workers enrolled in the social security system contracted from almost one-third in 1980 to one-fifth in 1996.

The perception of changes in earnings over a specified period is likely to be different for the self-employed and employees. First, the variation in normal earnings is far greater for the self-employed than for wage earners. The net income of the self-employed is subject to the variability associated with profits. Wages normally move marginally and gradually, with little downward flexibility except under the unusual conditions of sudden and high inflation. Second, earnings from self-employment are more likely to be viewed as a measure of performance than is the case with wage income. Wages certainly provide a reward for productivity differences, but these are small in proportion to the effect of factors outside a worker's control—above all, the availability of jobs. For the wage earner, a decrease in earnings is commonly the result of reduced employment opportunities. The self-employed cannot so easily point to extraneous factors as an explanation of changes in their economic status. The third difference is that wage income is more easily determined than is net income from self-employment: in the typical household firm, household and business accounts are scarcely distinguishable. A fourth and related difference concerns the extent of openness regarding earnings: the self-employed, who face local and community tax collectors, thieves, and envy, have more reason to be reticent about their earnings and also have more capacity to conceal.

Changes in earnings are thus likely to have different meanings for the wage earner and the self-employed and to be reported in different ways. A work force that is mostly self-employed, such as the Peruvian, might report the same events differently from the way the more proletarian work forces of a Chile or an Argentina would. For one thing, significant income variability probably results in a greater tolerance for ups and downs and in a related tendency to discount particular changes. Also, the self-employed are both less able and less willing to disclose changes in their economic situation. As a result, their responses are more likely to be either intentionally misleading or to be perceptions that owe as much to general and subjective factors as to the facts of their personal situation. Finally, responses by the self-employed are likely to be colored by the fact that statements regarding their personal economic situation amount, to some extent, to self-evaluations as businessmen.

Culture and Psychology

Culture and psychology surely influence both perceptions of personal experience and the way respondents answer questions on that experience. One indication of such influence was provided in the survey results that suggest that the rich, the urban, the highly educated, and women are more likely to be outspoken and to make strong pessimistic statements regarding their economic situation. For each of those groups the sample results can only be considered as hints: the margin of error involved is very large and the results were not clear-cut. Nonetheless, the results are plausible and suggest that it would be worthwhile to explore response behavior in a larger sample.

Table 10-7. *Household Perception of Change in Family Economic Situation: Now versus One Year Before*

Percent

Date	Better	Worse	No change or no answer
May–July 1995	31	22	47
May–July 1996	18	36	46
May–July 1997	12	41	47
May–July 1998	10	47	43

Source: Apoyo Opinion y Mercado S.A.

The significance of national psychology in the responses is also suggested by a separate statistic, a monthly opinion survey carried out in Lima since May 1995 by the firm Apoyo y Mercado. One question in the survey asks respondents whether their family economic situation is better or worse than it was twelve months ago. The evolution of responses is summarized in table 10-7. The proportion of households reporting an improvement in their economic situation dropped by two-thirds between mid-1995 and mid-1997, while the proportion reporting a deterioration doubled. The shift in perceptions exceeds by far the changes in real incomes during those years and suggests instead what could be described as a changing national mood.

Survey of Perceived Economic Progress

Part One: Present Well-Being and Expectations

Good morning/afternoon, my name is . . . I am a representative of Cuanto S.A., a company which specializes in public opinion polls and inquiries, and we're taking the opportunity to carry out interviews to understand the public opinion about some aspects of the well-being of your family and the population in general.

I.   Evolution of Present Well-Being

1.1   The economic situation of your family, in relation to 10–15 years ago, is . . . (choose one)
      1 much worse   2 worse
      3 equal   4 better   5 much better

1.2   The work/employment situation of you and your family members, with respect to 10–15 years ago, is . . .
      1 much worse   2 worse
      3 equal   4 better   5 much better

1.3   In comparison to you, your parents lived . . .
      1 much worse   2 worse
      3 equal   4 better   5 much better

1.4   Would you say that the present access you and your family have to health services, in relation to 10–15 years ago, is . . .
      1 much worse   2 worse
      3 equal   4 better   5 much better

1.5   The access to educational services for you and your family, in relation to 10–15 years ago, is . . .
      1 much worse   2 worse
      3 equal   4 better   5 much better

1.6   Your present access to basic everyday services such as water, electricity, and sewer (plumbing), when compared to your access 10–15 years ago, is . . .
      1 poor   2 equal   3 better

1.7   The state of your life presently, with respect to your life 10–15
      years ago, is . . .
      1 much worse   2 worse
      3 equal   4 better   5 much better

1.8   The purchase-power of your family, in relation to 10–15 years
      ago, is . . .
      1 worse   2 equal   3 better

1.9   The level of security that currently exists in your region (violence,
      delinquency), in comparison to the level 10–15 years ago, is . .
      1 worse   2 equal   3 better

1.10 The management of your city government, in comparison to
      10–15 years ago, is . . .
      1 much worse   2 worse
      3 equal   4 better   5 much better

1.11 I will tell you some services that are offered to your community;
      please tell me how these services have changed in the last 10–15
      years.

	Worse	No Change	Better	N/A
Schools	1	2	3	4
Sewer	1	2	3	4
Water	1	2	3	4
Electricity	1	2	3	4
Community Police	1	2	3	4
Sanitation	1	2	3	4
Roads	1	2	3	4

II.   Prospects for the Future

2.1   The economic situation of your family in the future, in comparison
      with the present, will be . . .
      1 much worse   2 worse
      3 equal   4 better   5 much better

2.2   The standard of living for your children in the future, in relation to
      your present level, will be . . .
      1 much worse   2 worse
      3 equal   4 better   5 much better

2.3 How would you qualify your opportunity to have a higher standard of living in the future?
    1 very bad   2 bad
    3 equal   4 good   5 very good

2.4 How long do you think it will take you to reach a satisfactory standard of living?
    1 one to two years
    2 three to five years
    3 six to ten years
    4 more than ten years
    5 never

III.   Degree of Present Satisfaction and Prospects for Future Progress

3.1 With regard to your present standard of living, your degree of satisfaction is . . .
    1 very bad   2 bad
    3 the same   4 good   5 very good

3.2 Would you say that your present opportunity to improve your standard of living is . . .
    1 very bad   2 bad
    3 the same   4 good   5 very good

3.3 Would you say that the opportunity of your parents to access a better standard of living in comparison to your own opportunity was . . .
    1 worse   2 equal   3 better

3.4 Your opportunity to have a better standard of living than that of your parents has been . . .
    1 worse   2 equal   3 better

3.5 Would you say that the opportunity of your children to have a better standard of living than you will be . . .
    1 worse   2 equal   3 better

IV.   Organizations and Participation

4.1   Do the following organizations exist in your community?

4.2   Do you belong to, have some connection to, or have received some benefit from any of these organizations within your community?

4.3   . . . and outside the community?

	4.1		4.2		4.3	
Parents' Association (Asociación de padres de familia)	Yes	No	Yes	No	Yes	No
Christian/Parish Community (Communidad Cristiana/Parroquia)	Yes	No	Yes	No	Yes	No
Clubs and Associations (Clubes y Asociaciones)	Yes	No	Yes	No	Yes	No
Mothers Clubs (Club de Madres)	Yes	No	Yes	No	Yes	No
Community Organizations (Organizaciones Comunales)	Yes	No	Yes	No	Yes	No
Professional Associations (Asociaciones de Professionales)	Yes	No	Yes	No	Yes	No
Labor Unions (Sindicatos de trabajadores)	Yes	No	Yes	No	Yes	No
Political Parties (Partidos politicos/Frente Civico)	Yes	No	Yes	No	Yes	No
Town Councils (Municipios)	Yes	No	Yes	No	Yes	No
Soup Kitchens (Comedores Populares)	Yes	No	Yes	No	Yes	No
Milk Program (Programa del Vaso de Leche)	Yes	No	Yes	No	Yes	No
Nucleos Ejecutores	Yes	No	Yes	No	Yes	No
Development Committes (Comités de Desarrollo)	Yes	No	Yes	No	Yes	No

	4.1		4.2		4.3	
Brotherhood Fraternities (Hermandades Cofradias)	Yes	No	Yes	No	Yes	No
Community Police Watch (Serenazgo)	Yes	No	Yes	No	Yes	No
Organization of Self-Defense (Organización de autodefensa)	Yes	No	Yes	No	Yes	No
Community Enterprise (Empresas Comunales)	Yes	No	Yes	No	Yes	No
Farmers Cooperative (Campesina Comunidad)	Yes	No	Yes	No	Yes	No
Committee of Indigenous Peoples (Comunidad Indígena)	Yes	No	Yes	No	Yes	No
Immigrants Association (Asociaciones de Inmigrantes)	Yes	No	Yes	No	Yes	No

Part Two: Health Survey

1.   Has your family experienced any health problems?
      1 Yes   2 No

How has your family been affected?
2.   By the cost of the treatment?
      1 Yes   2 No

3.   Not being able to work?
      1 Yes   2 No

(If you responded "yes" in Question 2)
4.   Has the ill member received some type of medical or family insurance?
      1 Yes, public insurance
      2 Yes, a mix of private insurance and family insurance
      3 Yes, a public and private mix of insurance
      4 No

5.   Did the illness and treatment cause you to forgo your plans for the following: improvements/upgrading your home, purchasing goods and appliances, education, travel, etc.?
      1 Yes   2 No

6. Does the ill member have a steady job?
   1 Yes   2 No

7. Are there any pending debts in relation to the funds or external aid
   required for the treatment of the ill member, like: repayment of debts,
   interest, rescheduling debt, purchasing or repairing appliances/fix-
   tures, gifts, as well as compensating for the help of family and friends?
   1 Yes   2 No (*if "no" continue to question 10*)

8. Is the above-mentioned debt affecting the regular incomes of the household?
   1 Yes   2 No (*if "no" continue to question 10*)

9. What is the percentage of debt to total household income?
   _____%

10. Is there any permanent or long-term expense related to the treatment
    of the illness or accident that affects the family income, like: follow-
    up exams, special diets, rehabilitation, etc.?
    1 Yes   2 No

11. The experience made you drain your savings or other monetary re-
    sources that were targeted for education, appliances, cars, land, houses,
    home improvements, etc. . . .
    1 Yes   2 No

12. In the household budget, had you budgeted for preventative health
    care expenses for the members of your family?
    1 Yes   2 No (*if "no" continue to question 14*)

13. Have you increased the amount you budget for illness and treatment
    since that time?
    1 Yes (by what percent? ___%)   2 No

14. Has the illness and its ramifications caused any change in the struc-
    ture of the household, like: separation, divorce, departure or arrival
    of family members, etc. . .?
    1 Yes   2 No

15. In general, do you consider that the illness or accident of a member
    of your family adversely affected the permanent form of your family's
    standard of living?
    1 Yes   2 No

(If you responded "yes" in Question 3)
16. As a result of the accident or illness, has the ill member not been able
    to work on a full or part-time basis?
    1 Yes, part-time
    2 Yes, full-time
    3 No

17. How long has this person NOT been able to work?
    1 _____ Days
    2 _____ Months

18. Has the illness/accident of the ill member caused the permanent loss
    of the job: of the ill member OR another member of the household
    OR have they experienced permanent work problems like the reduc-
    tion of job status OR a cut in pay/wage?
    1 Yes, loss of job (ill member / family member)
    2 Yes, have had labor problems (ill member / family member)
    3 No

PETR MATĚJŮ

11

Mobility and Perceived Change in Life Chances in Postcommunist Countries

Since the 1993 parliamentary elections in Poland opened a string of election successes of left-wing political parties in formerly communist countries, students of social and political developments have been trying to explain changing voting preferences in eastern Europe by changes in socioeconomic inequality and people's perceptions by their social strata. Two main questions appear to dominate the research.

—To what extent can voting preferences for the left be explained by objective criteria of class and income mobility that people experienced after the collapse of state socialist regimes?

—What role in changing voting preferences can be attributed to subjective perceptions of life chances brought about by the change of the system, particularly by subjective perceptions of socioeconomic mobility and beliefs about changes in factors determining socioeconomic success?

Regarding the contribution of objective class and mobility in predicting voting preferences for the left, the results of analysis based on data from extensive mobility surveys carried out during the early stages of the postcommunist transformation have shown clearly that the effect of class on voting behavior was very weak and in fact weaker than in some western democracies.[1] A similar conclusion holds for a type of mobility during the transformation: it had a modest effect as well.

Regarding subjective dimensions of social stratification—perceived mobility and beliefs about factors determining success in life—analyses provide convincing evidence for two conclusions.

—Subjective downward mobility, which is a measure of relative socio-economic deprivation, predicted significant voting preferences for the left: other things being equal, the larger the number of people who believed themselves losers in a given country, the greater the chance of left-wing parties to win elections.

—Voting preferences for the left have been significantly related to subjective evaluations of changes in the role of ascriptive and meritocratic factors of life success. The belief that there is more ascription since the system change than before the collapse of the communist regime increases the probability of voting for the left. It shows that the feeling of unequal opportunity produces egalitarian norms.

The finding that perceived social status and socioeconomic mobility predicted voting preferences better than objective class and intragenerational class mobility prompts an important question about the relationships between the objective and subjective mobility people experience during turbulent political, economic, and social transformations.

The principal aim of this chapter is to shed more light on the relationship between objective and subjective mobility in the course of the first stage of postcommunist transformation in east central Europe. The core question is why does *objective* mobility between 1989 and 1993 show weak relation to *perceived* mobility? Almost 60 percent of economically active respondents in both years experienced a change in their position on a scale of subjectively defined socioeconomic status, while only 25 percent have changed their objective class or socioeconomic status. In other words, the feelings of change in relative socioeconomic status occurred among 60 percent of those who have been objectively immobile.

Because there are no similar analyses of the relationship between objective and subjective mobility in industrial nations, it cannot be decided whether the weakness of association between the two is a general phenomenon or one typical only of the postcommunist restoration of a modern stratified system. There are, however, strong reasons to believe that the latter is the case, primarily because postcommunist transformation has ini-

1. Matějů (1996).

tiated changes in social stratification and inequality that are taking place without causing class or status mobility: the figures presented earlier, as well as the results of other analyses, have been more modest than originally expected.[2]

Two concepts, *perceived change in life chances* and *collective mobility*, may clarify why the effects of objective class and mobility on voting behavior are weaker than the effects of perceived status and subjective socioeconomic mobility. It is certainly true that the transition to the market allowed an expansion of life chances for a large segment of the population, while for others it meant a loss of privileges or relative advantages, growing feelings of insecurity, and serious difficulties in coping with a new economic environment. Thus for sociologists to speak about winners and losers of the transformation is in fact to speak not only about opening a road toward open society, which is an activity that can hardly have any losers, but also if not primarily about life chances.[3] In other words, what political scientists tend to label an *expansion of freedom* in east central Europe, sociologists should approach as a *change in life chances*.

According to Rolf Dahrendorf, if there is any progress in historical development, it is primarily in the expansion of human life chances. Life chances have to be understood as a function of two elements, *options* and *ligatures*. Dahrendorf contends that options and ligatures "can vary independently of each other, and it is their specific combination at a given time that constitutes the chances by which the lives of people in society are determined. Options are structural opportunities for choice, to which individual choices or decisions correspond. Ligatures are allegiances; one might call them bonds or linkages as well. By virtue of his social position and roles, the individual is placed into bonds or ligatures."[4]

From this point of view, the collapse of communist regimes in east central Europe simultaneously introduced improved opportunities and increased inequality between social classes and strata, which in fact can be interpreted as an emergence of new links between options and positions in the social structure. Therefore, exploring effects of changes in social structure on political behavior during social transformation requires looking not only at mobility as a movement of individuals between social positions, but also at the change in opportunities attributed to various posi-

2. Domanski (1997).
3. See Popper (1952).
4. See Dahrendorf (1979, p. 30).

tions in the social structure, that is, on collective mobility perceived as a change in life chances even among those who have not experienced any objective class or status mobility.

Be assured, I am far from arguing that collective mobility can be identified with the feelings of change in a person's life chances. I only suggest that feelings of change constitute an easy-to-measure approximation of collective mobility and that analyzing perceived mobility while controlling for objective class or status mobility may bring a better understanding of the effects of social change on life chances of various population groups. I would also contend that understanding subjective mobility brings a better understanding of political behavior. It was Paul Lazarsfeld who claimed that people think politically how they feel socially.[5]

In regard to what I have said earlier, the following questions are of particular importance for this study:

—*What type of mobility has been stronger after the fall of communism: objective or subjective?* One assumes that during the first stage of the transformation of the eastern European nations, people experienced more subjective than objective mobility. Objective intragenerational mobility has been determined by, among other things, structural changes that have so far been modest. But the subjective dimension of mobility was affected primarily by the consequences of market transition on the life conditions of entire social classes and strata. The dismantling of socialist redistribution has put large parts of the populations of formerly communist countries on a downward economic track. These are typically those who profited from egalitarian policies, redistribution, and economic corruption of the lower social strata (the less educated, working class, lower social strata in general). But the market transition has been opening new opportunities for those who were disadvantaged by redistributive practices, people with higher education, most professionals, large segments of the middle class, people with entrepreneurial spirit.

—*Does the stability of one's location in the class structure really mean stability in life chances?* One would expect that not only those who have been objectively mobile but also those who have not changed their class, status, or occupation may have experienced a significant change in their life chances.

—*Do all patterns of intragenerational upward class mobility after the collapse of the communist regimes generate similarly strong feelings of social ad-*

5. See Lazarsfeld, Berelson, and Gaudet (1974).

vancement? And conversely, do all the downwardly mobile feel they are sliding down along relevant social hierarchies (status, income)? This question addresses a particularly important issue, which is the subjective meaning of various patterns of objective individual mobility during times of deep social transformation. Postcommunist transformation certainly has created specific circumstances for intragenerational mobility. For many people whose upward mobility was blocked during communism for lack of their explicit support of the communist regime, collapse has opened the road to higher positions. At the same time, one may assume that upward mobility within the bureaucratic sector has a different effect on life chances than mobility across the boundaries between the contracting state sector and expanding private sector. Similarly, patterns that are routinely labeled downward mobility (descent along the class or status hierarchies) may not necessarily cause feelings of narrowing life chances.

—What were the most important determinants of subjective mobility after taking objective class and status mobility into account? Is it education (human capital) that makes people feel as if market transition is to their benefit? One of the central assumptions about the changing role of cultural and human capital during market transition would be that education is one of the most important factors causing an increase in life chances, thus producing feelings of upward mobility even if a person has not experienced any significant change in occupation.[6] However, one expects some very significant differences between countries. A legitimate assumption is that the less importance education had as a determinant of life chances under communism, the stronger the feeling of upward mobility it causes after the fall. One should also look at the contribution of social and political capital. The relevant question is whether former party members believe their life chances have been narrowing and whether this depends on their objective mobility. The same question applies particularly to the cadres of the previous regime. Do they feel a significant change in their life chances after the fall of communism? And if so, in what direction and how does it depend on their objective mobility after 1989?

This chapter begins with an elementary examination of relationships between objective and subjective mobility from 1989 to 1993 using a cross-national, comparative perspective. Then it proceeds with the analysis of the most important factors generating different patterns of subjective status and income mobility. It pays particular attention to factors represent-

6. Treiman and Szelenyi (1993); Mateju and Lim (1995); and Szelenyi and Kostello (1996).

ing the most important assets influencing life chances during market transition: education (cultural and human capital), party membership and cadre position (political capital, social capital), entrepreneurial social origin (economic assets).

Data, Measures, and Variables

The data analyzed here come from a research project on social stratification in eastern Europe after 1989 conducted in 1993 in Bulgaria, the Czech Republic, Hungary, Poland, Russia, and Slovakia.[7] General population surveys were conducted on samples of about 5,000 respondents, representative for the population aged between 20 and 69 years.[8] Stratified random sampling was adopted by all participating countries. After weighting that brought the distributions of the most important variables (community size, age, sex, education) closer to the census data and after elimination of respondents with out-of-range ages, national data files presented the following number of cases: Bulgaria 4,907, Czech Republic 5,620, Hungary 4,286, Poland 3,520, Russia 4,734, and Slovakia 4,876. In this chapter I focus only on east central Europe: the Czech Republic, Hungary, Poland, and Slovakia.[9]

All measures of objective class position and class mobility are based on the EGP class schema.[10] Though there is no class schema that would not arouse doubts about its adequacy, the advantage of the EGP schema is that it was developed particularly for cross-national comparative analyses and has been widely used among students of social stratification both in the

7. The project was coordinated by Donald Treiman and Ivan Szelenyi. In each country a general population survey (about 5,000 randomly selected respondents) and an elite study (a survey of members of the former and current political elites) were conducted in 1993. The international research project was supported by the National Science Foundation (United States), the Dutch Social and Environmental Research Foundation (SRO/NWO), and the Dutch Social and Cultural Sciences Foundation (SSCW/NWO). In addition to international funds, all national surveys were also supported by national foundations. The Czech research team was supported by the Grant Agency of the Academy of Sciences of the Czech Republic, the Grant Agency of the Czech Republic, and the Ministry of Labor and Social Affairs.

8. The study of political, economic, and cultural elites was conducted in each participating country.

9. Bulgaria and Russia were excluded from the analysis for both technical and substantive reasons. The data from the two still show some consistency problems I was unable to solve, and I did not feel competent enough to interpret the results for them in a proper historical and social context.

10. See Erikson and Goldthorpe (1992).

west and east.[11] Because of sufficiently large sample sizes in individual nations, the extended coding schema rather than its collapsed version can be used (see the appendix for an explanation of EGP codes). A potential problem of using EGP class schema for my analysis, in which I used concepts of upward and downward mobility, was that Robert Erikson and John Goldthorpe explicitly rejected the idea that the schema could be treated as a hierarchy, unlike, for example, the index of socioeconomic status. Therefore, before constructing the categories of downward and upward mobility based on EGP class schema, I checked whether EGP classes could at least be ordered according to an average socioeconomic status of the occupations they comprise. The results shown in appendix table 11-A1 confirm the assumption of ordinality.

Two measures were created for objective class mobility: *EGPMOB1* and *EGPMOB2*. *EGPMOB1* measures a change in class position between 1988 and 1993 using five categories: downward mobility across two or more class boundaries, downward mobility across one class boundary, stability, upward mobility across one class boundary, and upward mobility across two or more class boundaries. Because in postcommunist countries an entry into the class of self-employed has been a specific type of mobility with particularly important consequences for life chances, I created *EGPMOB2*, a modified version of the mobility variable introducing an additional category comprising all respondents who became self-employed (regardless of other occupational characteristics). Thus the remaining categories of *EGPMOB2* contain only those persons who remained employed.

Status mobility was defined as a difference between the respondent's international index of socioeconomic status in 1988 and 1993 (*ISEI88, ISEI93*). A simple difference between two values of socioeconomic index was used only to check the assumption that there is an underlying hierarchical order beyond the created categories of class mobility.[12] To achieve

---

11. See, for example, Domanski (1997) for discussion of the appropriateness of the EGP schema for mobility analyses in postcommunist countries.

12. Average values of the change in the value of socioeconomic status in individual categories of class mobility variable are strong downward mobility −12.8, downward mobility −6.0, stability 0, upward mobility 5.5, and strongly upward mobility 12.0. Comparing with the averages of the variable ISEMOB in categories of objective class mobility EGPMOB2 (strong downward mobility −16.1, downward −5.9, stability 0, upward mobility 5.8, and strongly upward mobility 15.5, self-employed 1.7), I found that the only category that shows an exemption from ordinality is the category that contains respondents who entered the entrepreneurial class (became self-employed). The creation of this specific category improves the ordinality of other categories. From this point of view, the decision to create a specific category for those who became self-employed has proved appropriate.

metric comparability with the measure of subjective mobility, which, as will be shown later, was based on subjectively defined locations in decile structures, the variable *ISEMOB* was created after the two measures of socioeconomic index were transformed into decile structures. Therefore, the variable *ISEMOB* measures a change in a person's decile location between 1989 and 1993. For specific purposes this variable was collapsed into five categories (*ISEMOBC*): a decrease of three and more deciles, a decrease of one to two deciles, no change, an increase of one to two deciles, and an increase of three and more deciles.[13]

As far as subjective mobility is concerned, four variables capture the respondents' feelings about change in their position in important social hierarchies. Two items in the survey assessed subjective social status, one for 1988 (retrospectively) and the other for 1993.[14] These two (*SUBSOC88*, *SUBSOC93*) were used to define subjective status mobility as a difference between respondent subjective social status in 1988 and 1993. For specific comparative purposes a categorized variable *SUBSOC5* was defined by recoding the original continuous variable *SUBSOC* into five categories: a decrease of three and more points (deciles), a decrease of one to two points (deciles), no change, an increase of one to two points (deciles), and an increase of three and more points (deciles).

Two questions assessing subjective location in an income hierarchy (the respondents' perception of their family's income, *SUBINC88* and *SUBINC93*) were used to define subjective income (*SUBINC*).[15]

---

13. The collapsed version was used only for comparisons with class mobility, EGPMOB (EGPMOB2), defined as an ordinal variable.

14. The question for 1988 was: "In our society there are groups which tend to be toward the top and those that are toward the bottom. Here we have a scale that runs from top to bottom [the interviewer shows the card with a scale running from 10 (top) to 1 (bottom)]. Where would you have placed yourself on this scale in 1988?" Question for 1993: "Where would you place yourself now?"

15. The question for 1988 was: "Compared with [country] families in general, would you say that your family income in 1988 was far below average, below average, about average, above average, or far above average? [the interviewer shows the card with a scale running from 1 (far below average) to 5 (far above average)]." The question for 1993 was: "What about now?" An alternative to respondent's self-placement on a scale of family income would be to use a variable representing subjective evaluation of change in respondent's financial situation between 1988 and 1993 (question: "Since 1988, has your financial situation gotten better, stayed the same, or gotten worse?"). I chose the former strategy primarily because it reduces subjectivity in the direct evaluation of change. Because the correlation between the created variable (*SUBINC*) and the direct measure of change in individual financial situations (*CHANGE*) is very high (gamma = 0.8), the two strategies provide almost identical results.

Objective and Subjective Mobility in a
Comparative Perspective

Before turning to the changes in the economically active part of the population, where it makes sense to speak about class and socioeconomic mobility, I must emphasize that one of the most remarkable changes in social structures in postcommunist countries has been the decline in the proportion of gainfully employed. Official statistical sources report that between 1988 and 1993 the number of jobs that disappeared in the countries of east central Europe ranged between 15 and 38 percent.[16] Though most of the lost jobs were retirements (some of them early retirements), the people who were pushed out of the labor force certainly experienced a specific type of downward subjective mobility, particularly if they were members of the professional class or the economic, political, or cultural elite before the collapse of the communist regime.[17] Thus an interesting story can be drawn from analyses regarding the relationships between objective and subjective mobility. Because these analyses focus only on the gainfully employed, one should keep in mind that the story is not complete.

As far as the first question I raised for the analysis—What type of mobility has been stronger after the fall of communism: objective or subjective mobility?—figure 11-1 provides the background for a simple answer. Comparison of the results of the distributions of two mobility variables based on the same number of deciles supports the initial assumption that during the first stage of transformation the nations of eastern Europe have experienced more subjective than objective mobility. The figure also shows that, in general, feelings of downward mobility relative to others prevailed over feelings of social ascent. Figure 11-2 provides evidence referring to the second question: Does stability in terms of one's location in class structure really mean stability in life chances? The two almost identical lines, one for those who have been objectively mobile in social status, the other one for those who have been stable, support the hypothesis that not only those

16. According to the Organization for Economic Cooperation and Development (1994) *Short-Term Economic Indicators,* the number of jobs declined by 15 percent in the Czech Republic, about 17 percent in Slovakia, 21 percent in Poland, and 38 percent in Hungary.

17. Hanley and Szelenyi (1996), for example, show that the proportion of employed men older than age 60 dropped by about 50 percent in the four countries between 1988 and 1993 (Czech Republic, 48 percent; Hungary, 61 percent; Poland, 43 percent; and Slovakia, 33 percent). A similar drop was identified among women (Czech Republic, 49 percent; Hungary, 37 percent; Poland, 38 percent; and Slovakia, 30 percent).

Figure 11-1. *Objective (SESMOB) and Subjective (SUBMOB) Status Mobility in Four Postcommunist Nations, 1989 and 1993*

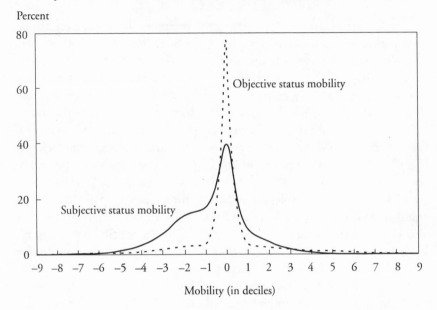

Percent

Source: Author's calculations based on survey data. See text.

who have been objectively mobile but also those who have not been mobile have experienced a significant change in their life chances. Figure 11-2, in fact, also confirms the very weak relationship between objective and subjective mobility.

As far as class mobility is concerned, tables 11-1 and 11-2 show that feelings of change in social status between 1988 and 1993 were far more frequent than actual changes.[18] What is striking is that about 80 percent of the people in east central Europe did not change their objective class position between 1988 and 1993 and that there were virtually no differences in this regard among the four countries included in this study (class stability ranged between 75 percent and 80 percent). I also found the flow into the

18. Objective mobility measured by changes in socioeconomic status does not show any significant deviations from class mobility displayed in table 11-1, so I have not shown the results here in a separate table.

Figure 11-2. *Subjective Mobility of Objectively Immobile and Mobile Persons in Four Postcommunist Nations, 1989 and 1993*

Percent

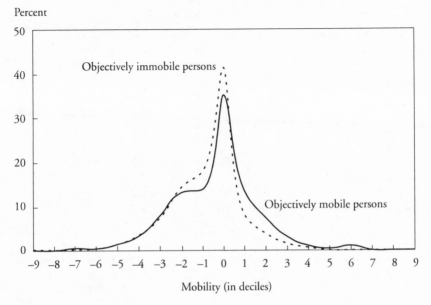

Source: Author's calculations based on survey data. See text.

category of self-employed to be the most important pattern of intra-generational mobility in all central European countries.

Only about 40 percent of the respondents declared no change in their perceived social status. This means that not only objectively mobile persons but also those who have not changed their class, status, or occupation felt a significant change in their social status. As figure 11-2 shows, the feeling of a downward shift significantly prevailed over the feeling of an upward shift (73 percent to 27 percent). Unlike objective class mobility, which showed remarkable similarity across nations, subjective mobility substantially varied. The Czech Republic reveals the most sure feelings in regard to social status mobility: the proportion of stable or upwardly mobile is the highest among the four nations. Hungary, however, has the most pessimism about status mobility: the proportion of respondents who felt downwardly mobile was by far the highest among the four nations (57 percent compared to 34 percent in the Czech Republic, 44 percent in Poland, and 46 percent in Slovakia).

Table 11-1. *Objective Class Mobility between 1988 and 1993 (Type II)*[a]

Category of objective class mobility (EGPMOB2)	Country				
	Czech Republic	Hungary	Poland	Slovakia	Total
Strongly downward	3.5	3.5	2.5	2.4	3.0
	2.0	1.3	−1.3	−2.1	
Downward	4.1	4.4	4.7	4.2	4.3
	−0.7	0.2	1.0	−0.3	
Stable	75.6	76.3	75.5	80.0	76.9
	−2.2	−0.8	−1.6	4.5	
Upward	3.7	4.5	4.5	3.2	3.9
	−0.8	1.6	1.6	−2.0	
Strongly upward	3.7	4.2	3.8	3.4	3.7
	−0.1	1.2	0.2	−1.1	
Became self-employed	9.5	7.2	8.9	6.7	8.1
	3.4	−1.7	1.3	−3.2	

Sources: See text.

a. Percentages and adjusted standardized residuals. Economically active respondents in both years.

Differences between nations in respondents' assessments of income mobility have two principal sources. First, although the subjective mobility was designed to be a measure of the perceived change in a person's position on the social status hierarchy relative to other people, apparently it is affected by a general feeling of change in standards of living, which dropped significantly during the first stage of transformation, most markedly in Hungary and Poland.[19] Second, in Hungary and Poland, where economic inequality was greater than in the Czech Republic and Slovakia at the initiation of the transformation, inequality has grown faster, particularly at the top of the social hierarchy.[20] This may explain stronger feelings of the relative deterioration of social status among people occupying the middle and lower layers of the Hungarian and Polish social hierarchy than in the same layers of the Czech Republic and Slovakia.

19. See the wording of the question assessing subjective social status.

20. It was partly because of a smaller circulation of economic elites in Hungary and Poland than in the former Czechoslovakia (see Matějů and Hanley [1997] for further details regarding differences in circulation of economic elites in the Czech Republic, Hungary, Poland, and Slovakia).

Table 11-2. *Subjective Status Mobility between 1988 and 1993*[a]

Category of subjective status mobility (SUBSOC5)	Country				
	Czech Republic	Hungary	Poland	Slovakia	Total
Strongly downward	10.5	13.1	15.4	15.1	13.3
	–5.6	–0.2	3.0	3.4	
Downward	23.5	43.6	29.0	31.0	30.8
	–10.7	13.9	–1.9	0.2	
Stable	46.3	32.2	36.7	39.8	39.7
	9.1	–7.8	–2.9	0.1	
Upward	16.6	9.6	14.7	11.9	13.5
	6.3	–5.7	1.7	–2.8	
Strongly upward	3.1	1.5	4.2	2.1	2.7
	1.6	–3.6	4.3	–2.2	

Sources: See text.

a. Percentages and adjusted standardized residuals. Economically active respondents in both years.

The results of a simple log-linear analysis of associations among three variables: objective class mobility (*OBJ*), subjective status mobility (*SUB*), and nation (*NAT*) displayed in table 11-3 verify the findings from the descriptive analyses. Two panels of the table show the results for two definitions of objective mobility: *EGPMOB1*, without a specific category for mobility toward self-employment, and *EGPMOB2*, separating mobility from self-employment.

Both panels of the table support the findings discussed earlier in several respects. First, among the models that allow for only one association, one model shows a particularly poor fit. This is the one allowing only for cross-national variation in objective mobility (model B). This model accounts for no more than 5 percent of the variation unexplained by the baseline model (model A). Models C and D show much better fit. In particular, this holds for the model that allows cross-national variation only in subjective mobility (model C). In the top panel this model accounts for 54 percent of the variance of the baseline model; in the bottom panel it explains 44 percent of the variance. The model assuming only the association between subjective and objective mobility (model D) shows a poorer fit than the previous one. There is, however, an interesting difference between the two panels: not only the percentage reduction in unexplained variance, but also Bayesian information criterion (BIC) statistics, show that the asso-

Table 11-3. *Log-Linear Analysis of Associations between Subjective Status Mobility, Objective Class Mobility, and Nation*[a]

Model[b]	df	L^2	p	d[c]	BIC[d]
		Objective mobility (EGPMOB1)			
SUB, OBJ, NAT (baseline)	88	601.5	0.000	0.0	–204.6
OBJ × NAT	76	576.6	0.000	4.1	–120.2
SUB × NAT	76	274.5	0.000	54.4	–421.8
SUB × OBJ	72	464.7	0.000	22.7	–194.8
OBJ × NAT, SUB × NAT	64	249.6	0.000	58.5	–336.6
SUB × NAT, OBJ × SUB	60	137.8	0.000	77.1	–411.8
OBJ × NAT, SUB × NAT,					
OBJ × SUB	48	115.9	0.000	80.7	–323.8
OBJ × SUBJ × NAT	0	0	1.000	100.0	. . .
		Objective mobility (EGPMOB2: mobility to the category of self-employed distinguished)			
SUB, OBJ, NAT (baseline)	107	742.3	0.000	0.0	–238.1
OBJ × NAT	92	704.7	0.000	5.1	–138.0
SUB × NAT	95	416.9	0.000	43.8	–454.1
SUB × OBJ	87	459.5	0.000	38.1	–337.8
OBJ × NAT, SUB × NAT	80	379.3	0.000	48.9	–353.5
SUB × NAT, OBJ × SUB	75	134.1	0.000	81.9	–552.9
OBJ × NAT, SUB × NAT,					
OBJ × SUB	60	105.0	0.000	85.8	–444.6
OBJ × SUBJ × NAT	0	0	1.000	100.0	. . .

a. Economically active respondents in both years (N = 9,500).

b. *SUB* = subjective status mobility; *OBJ* = objective class mobility; *NAT* = nation.

c. The percentage reduction in the L^2 for the baseline model that is achieved by a more complex model.

d. Bayesian information criterion statistic.

ciation between objective and subjective mobility is much stronger if the flow to self-employment is treated as a specific category.[21] Although in the top panel the association between objective and subjective mobility (model D) explains about 23 percent of the variance of the baseline model, which

21. BIC (see Raftery, 1986) is the statistic of a model fit that is independent for sample size and is especially recommended for selection between models if the number of cases in the analysis is very large, that is, when large N makes it almost impossible to get satisfactory fit according to standard criteria (statistical significance of $L2$). The rule for BIC is that the best model (particularly if one seeks for the most parsimonious one) is the model with the smallest BIC.

is less than half of the variance explained by cross-national variation in subjective mobility (model C), in the bottom panel it explains 38 percent, which is a number very close to the proportion of variance explained by cross-national variation in subjective mobility.

Combining two criteria, the percentage reduction in L^2 (explained variance) and the BIC statistic (parsimony), one reaches interesting conclusions regarding the relationship between objective and subjective mobility in a cross-national comparative perspective:

—Both the descriptive analysis and the results of log-linear analysis support the hypothesis that subjective mobility, defined as a feeling of change in one's position in the social hierarchy, was much stronger than objective intragenerational class mobility between 1988 and 1993.

—There is much more cross-national variation in subjective than in objective mobility.

—If the flow into self-employment (regardless of other characteristics of change in a person's occupation) is not treated as a specific pattern of objective mobility, then to understand the change in relationships between subjective and objective mobility between 1988 and 1993 it would be sufficient to analyze cross-national variation in subjective mobility represented by model C. If, on the contrary, the flow to the category of self-employed is treated as a specific pattern of objective mobility, then analyzing only cross-national variation in subjective mobility is not an adequate strategy and one has to consider two other important phenomena: a cross-national variation in subjective mobility as well as an effect of objective mobility on subjective mobility (model F).

Concluding this section, one may say that to understand intragenerational mobility in former communist countries in east central Europe, there should be a clear distinction between mobility that has brought people into self-employment and other types of mobility. Second, to understand the dynamic of life chances in general, one cannot analyze only objective class or status mobility but should also focus on subjective mobility and its cross-national variation. Third, to understand the structuralization of life chances in postcommunist countries, one has to analyze the relationship between objective and subjective mobility.

Relationships between Objective and Subjective Mobility

Subjective mobility is not a simple reflection of objective class or status mobility. Objective class or status mobility does not account for feelings of change in one's position in relevant social hierarchies (social status, income), leaving much of its variance unexplained. Although subjective mobility has been operating far beyond the limits set by objective class and status mobility, their interrelationship deserves closer inspection. Leaving cross-national differences aside, I have found that subjective status mobility not only operated independently of objective class mobility, but in fact the two types of mobility very often go against each other. As shown in table 11-4, the most evident discrepancy appears among those who have experienced upward class mobility and subjective downward mobility. As many as 43 percent of those who have experienced upward class mobility have felt a downward move along the scale of social status.[22] Meanwhile, downward class mobility often prompted feelings of an upward move along the social status hierarchy: almost 15 percent of the downwardly mobile have experienced relative improvement of their social status. As could have been expected, class stability caused deterioration rather than improvement of perceived social status: 45 percent of the objectively immobile have felt they moved downward in the social status hierarchy while only 14 percent reported a relative improvement in their position. These results confirm the existence of a strong feeling of relative deprivation in countries experiencing postcommunist transformation, as well as the fact that this feeling has been largely independent of the objective mobility people experienced after the collapse of the communist regime.

There was, however, one particular type of objective mobility that caused more consistent and distinct patterns of subjective mobility: mobility into self-employment. Becoming self-employed seems to be the strongest determinant connected with feeling that one's position in the social hierarchy has improved (36 percent) or at least has not changed (35 percent). Thus, compared with other types of class mobility, entering the new class of entrepreneurs apparently has been the most efficient mobility strategy in terms of avoiding feelings of relative deterioration in one's social status.

Factors Determining Subjective Mobility

The results I have discussed confirm the hypothesis that immobility in terms of one's location in the class structure has not necessarily meant sta-

---

22. In calculating these figures I did not distinguish between strongly upward mobility and upward mobility. The same holds for strongly downward mobility and downward mobility.

Table 11-4. *Subjective Status Mobility in Categories*
of Objective Class Mobility between 1988 and 1993 [a]

Category of subjective status mobility (SUBSOC5)	Category of objective class mobility					
	Strongly downward	Down- ward	Stable	Upward	Strongly upward	To self- employed
Strongly downward	17.5	14.2	13.2	15.7	13.3	10.9
	2.2	0.6	−0.5	1.4	0.0	−2.0
Downward	35.8	33.1	32.0	30.4	26.3	18.1
	1.9	1.0	4.8	−0.2	−1.8	−7.9
Stable	37.2	34.3	41.2	33.6	35.4	35.1
	−0.9	−2.3	5.2	−2.5	−1.7	−2.8
Upward	8.1	14.5	11.5	16.0	21.9	29.4
	−2.7	0.5	−10.5	1.4	4.6	13.4
Strongly upward	1.4	3.9	2.1	4.3	3.1	6.5
	−1.3	1.6	−5.9	2.0	0.5	6.9
Total	100.0	100.0	100.0	100.0	100.0	100.0

Sources: See text.

a. Column percentages and adjusted standardized residuals. Economically active respondents in both years. Pooled data (N = 9,500). Gamma = 0.172, p = 0.000.

bility in the perceived social status. The empirical evidence presented so far has corroborated the assumption that not only those who have changed their class or status but also a significant number of those who remained stable have felt a change in their life chances. With this evidence of the importance of collective mobility, I take a further step and ask the last question: "What social groups experienced collective mobility and what assets or characteristics could have been important determinants of collective mobility during the postcommunist transformation?" Therefore, the analysis will focus on determinants of subjective socioeconomic mobility for those who have not experienced objective class mobility.

For these analyses a new dependent variable measuring subjective socioeconomic mobility (*SSEMOB*) was created as a composite of two pairs of variables: subjective social status in 1988 and 1993 and subjective income in 1988 and 1993. Principal component analysis using the method of alternating least squares (*PRINCALS*) was applied. In both years two dimensions were extracted from pooled data for all countries. The first one expressed the feeling of upward mobility both in terms of social status and income (in both years this first dimension explained 66 percent of variance with loadings of about 0.800). The second dimension was rather inconsistent, a feeling of upward movement in the income hierarchy but downward movement in the social status hierarchy (in both years this second dimension explained about 34 percent of variance with loadings about 0.600 and !0.600). After standardization, the first dimensions were then used to compute the difference between subjective socioeconomic status in 1988 and 1993. Constructing the measure in this manner has the advantage of allowing the assessment of changing life chances in terms of both social and economic aspects of subjective mobility. [23]

One of the central theoretical assumptions in the study of collective mobility during the escape from socialism is that one of the principal characteristics of socialism was extensive redistribution, functioning not only as a major principle integrating the economy but also as an important instrument of fulfilling the ideological goal of homogenization of society as well as a mechanism of collective corruption of the lower social strata and those explicitly loyal to the communist regime.[24] Consequently, a gradual dismantling of the redistribution practices during transition to the market economy makes those who actually profited (no matter if absolutely or relatively) from the socialist redistribution feel they were losers as a result of transformation, whereas those who were not much favored by the communist redistributive system and who tend to believe that the new system is opening opportunities for their advancement and life chances may feel more like winners.

Thus, with some simplification, one may hypothesize that the winners under socialist redistribution tend to be the losers in the transformation and the losers very likely feel themselves winners after its demise and the penetration of market mechanisms.

As far as occupational classes are concerned, the results presented in figure 11-3 clearly support the hypothesis.[25] In all countries the upper classes (particularly professionals and controllers) felt significantly stronger up-

23. See the appendix for details about how the variable *SSEMOB* was defined.

24. See Polanyi (1944); and Szelenyi and Manchin (1987).

25. Because of the method of standardization (see the appendix), one can compare positions of individual groups within countries. Comparison between countries can be made only in regard to relative positions of groups in relation to a national mean (zero). In other words, no statements can be made from a direct comparison of values for one group across countries. The solid horizontal line crossing each bar is an average value of the dependent variable (the feeling of socioeconomic mobility) in a given group. The vertical bar represents a 95 percent confidence interval for these values (the range around the sample mean that will include the true, unknown population mean for a given group 95 percent of the time).

Figure 11-3. *Subjective Socioeconomic Mobility* (SSEMOB) *between 1988 and 1993, by Occupational Class*[a]

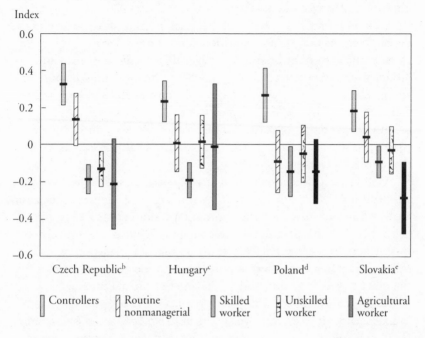

Index

Source: Author's calculations. See appendix.

a. Only individuals who have not changed their class. Means and their 95 percent confidence intervals. The class of self-employed is not shown because of the small number of those who were self-employed both in 1988 and 1993.

b. F-ratio = 13.5; p = .000.

c. F-ratio = 4.8; p = .002.

d. F-ratio = 6.3; p = .000.

e. F-ratio = 4.6; p = .003.

ward socioeconomic mobility than other classes. Members of the working class have felt that their life chances, measured by subjective assessments of socioeconomic mobility, have deteriorated. Though this pattern is common and is clearly the strongest one, there are also differences among countries. In particular, in the Czech Republic, where the egalitarian ideology and redistributive practice were the strongest among the four countries, the demise of redistributive practices and penetration of market principles have caused the most visible centrifugal tendencies for individual classes concerning subjective feelings of change in their life chances (the value of the *F*-ratio showing significant differences between classes in subjective socioeconomic mobility is by far the highest in the Czech Republic). A growing gap between nonmanual and manual occupations in the Czech Republic in terms of subjective mobility is in fact a mirror image of the development of their relative positions on various relevant social hierarchies (particularly of income and prestige) after the so-called socialist revolution, when wage differentials significantly shrank mainly because of a strong relative drop of average wages among professionals and other highly educated people in nonmanual occupations.[26]

Another interesting pattern is that skilled workers, an elite class according to socialist ideology, felt stronger downward collective mobility than unskilled workers.

Collective socioeconomic mobility of social classes shown in figure 11-4 confirms the assumption that, by and large, the winners of socialism are becoming the losers of postcommunist transformation, and groups not favored by socialist redistribution feel an improvement in their life chances.[27] In all countries the lower class is clearly on the losers' side, while both the middle and upper classes feel improvements in socioeconomic status. For the middle there is a clear distinction between the old middle class that, unlike the traditional definition of the term, has its background in a socialist intelligentsia (mostly employed nonmanual workers) and the new middle class, a postsocialist petty bourgeoisie. The difference between the two is obvious: although both feel improvements in their life chances, the postsocialist middle class is clearly ahead of the old one. Except for Hungary, the self-employed part of the middle class has experienced as much upward subjective mobility as the upper class, and in Slovakia the members of the new middle class have experienced even more upward subjective mobility than the upper class.

One of the most common assumptions regarding factors determining life chances during postcommunist transformation derives from the hy-

26. See Vecernik (1996) for details regarding the "history of equalization" in former Czechoslovakia as well as the analysis of major changes in wage differentiations after 1989.

27. Lower class was defined by EGP codes 8, 9, and 10 (manual workers, farm workers); upper class consists of higher professionals and controllers (class 1). To show the difference between the old and new segments of the middle class in east central Europe, in figure 11-5 there are two categories representing the middle class: "middle" and "middle, new." Although the former consists of individuals pertaining to EGP classes 2, 3, 4, 5, and 7 (lower nonmanual occupations and petty bourgeoisie) who have not changed their class position between 1988 and 1993 (to this effect there are only a few self-employed in this category), the latter represents those who became petty bourgeoisie during this period.

Figure 11-4. *Subjective Socioeconomic Mobility between 1988 and 1993,*
by Social Class[a]

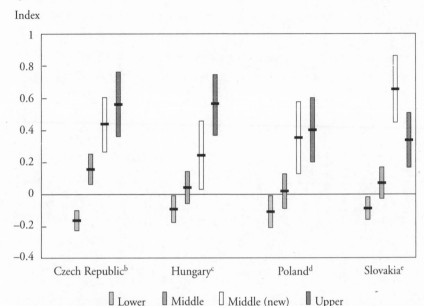

Index

Lower   Middle   Middle (new)   Upper

Source: Author's calculations. See appendix.
a. Only individuals who have not changed their class (except for category "middle new"). Means
and their 95 percent confidence intervals.
b. F-ratio = 38.9; p = .000.
c. F-ratio = 16.7; p = .000.
d. F-ratio = 8.6; p = .002.
e. F-ratio = 11.3; p = .000.

pothesis about a changing role of cultural and human capital in economic
success.[28] In short, the hypothesis says that human capital (education and
skills) as well as cultural capital (in Bourdieu's terms one's capacity to participate in symbolic culture) are highly generalizable assets that make people
more flexible and thus more adaptable to new opportunities created by the
market. This is why people with higher education or great cultural capital
or both are most likely to succeed during market transition. In accordance
with this hypothesis, I argue that education, as a proxy for both human

28. See Nee (1989, 1991); Treiman and Szelenyi (1993); Rona-Tas (1994); Matějů and Lim (1995);
and Szelenyi and Kostello (1996).

Figure 11-5. *Subjective Socioeconomic Mobility* (SSEMOB) *between 1988 and 1993, by Educational Group*[a]

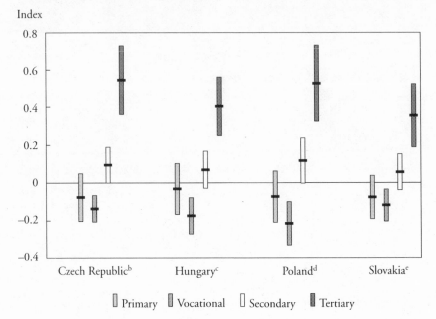

Index

Source: Author's calculations. See appendix.
a. Includes only individuals who have not changed their class. Means and their 95 percent confidence intervals.
b. F-ratio = 19.9; p = .000.
c. F-ratio = 11.7; p = .000.
d. F-ratio = 13.5; p = .000.
e. F-ratio = 9.3; p = .000.

and cultural capital, has been one of the most important factors determining life chances during transition to a market democracy. If this assumption holds true, even when compensating for the effect of individual class or occupational mobility, one should be able to find stronger feelings of upward socioeconomic mobility among well-educated as opposed to less well educated people.

The results shown in figure 11-5 provide strong support for this hypothesis. There is no doubt that, in general, people with college educations feel a strong upward shift in their socioeconomic status and that, in this respect, they differ significantly from other educational groups. Secondary education makes people feel that they are on an upward track as well, but not as steep a track as that provided by college or university education. Another result that deserves attention concerns the two lowest educational levels. Figure 11-5 suggests that the typical losers in the transition are not those with the least education (primary) but those who acquired only vocational training, the typical training of skilled workers in formerly socialist countries.

Much of the debate about social consequences of the transformation has focused on the importance of political capital from the old regime and particularly on the mobility of former cadres. Thus a relevant question for an analysis of subjective mobility is whether former party members believe that their life chances have changed, and if so, in what direction. The same question applies to cadres of the previous regime: Have former cadres of the communist regime felt a significant change in their life chances since the fall of communism? And if so, how does the feeling depend on their objective mobility experienced since 1989?

Figure 11-6 makes it clear that the difference between party members' and nonmembers' feelings of change in socioeconomic status is not statistically significant in any of the four countries. This result is in line with previous findings showing that party membership in and of itself does not provide the type of political capital that is directly convertible into marketable assets or advantages.[29] This is not the case, however, with cadre positions. Those who were in 1988 in the position of cadres perceived their life chances as better than did noncadres (figure 11-7).[30]

The results of more detailed analyses (figure 11-8) also show that it holds true not only for cadres that remained at their positions but also for those who experienced mobility after the collapse of the communist regime. Particularly interesting is that, in general, upward class mobility has not produced such a strong feeling of opening life chances as moving to

29. See Matějů and Rehakova (1993); and Matějů and Lim (1995).

30. I use the term "cadres" (or "nomenklatura cadres") in a broader sense than "nomenklatura" in strictly political terms (incumbents of the positions that require an approval of the central or local committee of the Communist party) . The cadres were defined in two steps using two variables: a code of occupation according to the International Standard Classification of Occupations (1988) and a position in the hierarchy of management (number of subordinates). All those whose occupations in 1988 were classified in major group 1 (legislators and senior officials, corporate managers, general managers) were coded as cadres. Titles classified from major group 2 (professionals) except primary and secondary school teachers were coded as cadres only if they had ten or more subordinates. Such a definition of cadres makes an implicit assumption that legislators, managers as well as professionals, with high supervisory power were people whose political commitment and loyalty to the regime was either explicitly (as in the case of genuine nomenklatura) or implicitly tested.

Figure 11-6. *Subjective Socioeconomic Mobility (SSEMOB) between 1988 and 1993, among Communist Party Members*[a]

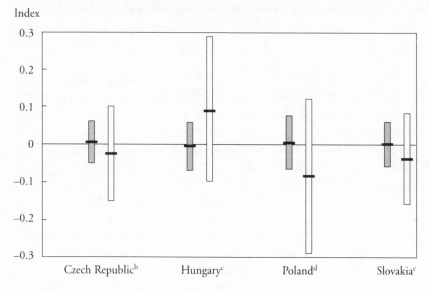

Index

Member of the Communist party in 1988: ▨ No ▯ Yes

Source: Author's calculations. See appendix.
a. Includes only individuals who have not changed their class. Means and their 95 percent confidence intervals.
b. F-ratio = 0.148; p = .700.
c. F-ratio = 0.829; p = .362.
d. F-ratio = 0.384; p = .536.
e. F-ratio = 0.249; p = .617.

self-employment. In addition, mobility from a cadre position into self-employment created significantly stronger feelings of increasing life chances than moving into self-employment from a noncadre position. This figure also shows that those who were pushed out of the labor force (through retirement and early retirement) apparently experienced the most acute subjective downward mobility no matter whether they were cadres or not before 1989.

There are, of course, strong correlations between various characteristics whose effects on subjective assessments of socioeconomic mobility were analyzed. Thus, to assess the net effects of these characteristics, by controlling for these correlations, a multivariate technique has to be applied. Table

Figure 11-7. *Subjective Socioeconomic Mobility (SSEMOB) between 1988 and 1993, among Cadres in 1988*[a]

Index

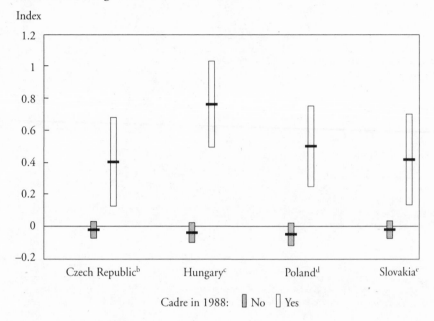

Cadre in 1988:   ▮ No   ▯ Yes

Source: Author's calculations. See appendix.

a. Includes only individuals who have not changed their class. Means and their 95 percent confidence intervals.

b. F-ratio = 10.9; p = .000.

c. F-ratio = 30.5; p = .000.

d. F-ratio = 19.5; p = .000.

e. F-ratio = 9.6; p = .002.

11-5 shows the results of the OLS regression of subjective socioeconomic mobility on the most important characteristics discussed earlier. The results support every relevant conclusion from descriptive analyses. Higher education, particularly a college or university diploma, is the strongest factor predicting one's feeling of upward socioeconomic mobility. As far as the effects of various patterns of objective mobility are concerned, the only one that significantly predicts feelings of upward socioeconomic mobility is movement into self-employment. Interestingly enough, neither upward mobility nor downward mobility caused a significant change in perceived life chances.

Figure 11-8. *Subjective Socioeconomic Mobility (SSEMOB) between 1988 and 1993 in Groups Defined by Type of Objective Mobility (Down, Stable, Upward, into Self-Employed, Retired) by Cadre Status in 1988*[a]

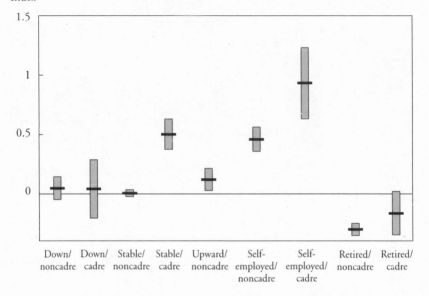

Type of objective mobility and cadre status, 1988

Source: Author's calculations. See appendix.
a. Means and their 95 percent confidence intervals.

Although Communist party membership does not have much effect on subjective mobility, the effect of cadre status remained strong even after controlling for education and type of objective mobility. There are, however, considerable differences among countries. The net effect of cadre status on subjective socioeconomic mobility was found to be strong in Hungary and Poland, weaker in Slovakia, and not statistically significant in the Czech Republic. These results support previous findings that in Hungary and Poland cadres (particularly enterprise managers) were more likely to succeed in retaining their positions than in the Czech Republic and Slovakia, where, because of greater elite circulation, to succeed in retaining their advantages, cadres had to rely more on entrepreneurial strategy.[31]

31. See Hanley and Matěju (1999); and Szelenyi and Kostello (1996).

Table 11-5. *Regression Analysis (OLS) of Subjective Socioeconomic Mobility (SSEMOB)*[a]

Item	Czech Republic	Hungary	Poland	Slovakia	All
Age	0.001	–0.002	–0.004	–0.002	–0.002
Education[b]					
Vocational	0.113[**]	0.017	–0.068	0.036	0.036
Secondary	0.273[***]	0.197[***]	0.154[*]	0.198[***]	0.211[***]
Tertiary	0.557[***]	0.533[***]	0.547[***]	0.447[***]	0.521[***]
Objective mobility[b]					
Downward	–0.043	–0.031	–0.085	0.083	–0.020
Upward	0.079	0.136	–0.009	0.047	0.069[*]
To self-employed	0.291[***]	0.208[**]	0.278[**]	0.545[***]	0.329[***]
Communist party in 1988	–0.095[*]	–0.103	–0.175	–0.034	–0.094[**]
Cadre status in 1988	0.119	0.447[***]	0.263[**]	0.204[*]	0.248[***]
Constant	–0.457[***]	–0.229[**]	–0.077	–0.276[***]	–0.276[***]
Multiple *R*	0.234	0.259	0.222	0.268	0.237

Sources: See text.

a. Nonstandardized regression coefficients. Economically active respondents in both years. Level of statistical significance: * < 0.05, ** < 0.01, *** < 0.001.

b. Primary education and category "stable" served as reference categories.

Conclusions

In the introduction to this chapter, I argued that the winners and losers of postcommunist transformation differ in regard to the life chances that opened after the collapse of the communist regime. I also argued that subjective mobility can be used to capture a change in one's life chances. Last, I assumed that the analysis of subjective mobility of those who have not experienced objective mobility can aid in understanding collective mobility during postcommunist transformation.

What are the main conclusions of the analysis?

Bearing in mind that the analysis focused only on the economically active population, leaving aside people who were pushed out of the labor force (mostly into retirement), one can conclude that subjective mobility has been a markedly stronger force than objective mobility. The analysis also confirmed the assumption that stability of a person's position in the class structure has not meant stability in life chances: the results show that not only those who have been objectively mobile but also those who have not changed their class position, status, or occupation have experienced a significant change in their life chances. Particularly interesting is that upward mobility within the bureaucratic sector has had a different effect on life chances than mobility across the boundaries between the contracting state sector and expanding private sector. Similarly, the results confirmed that mobility patterns that are routinely labeled downward mobility (descent in the class or status hierarchies) do not necessarily cause feelings of deteriorating life chances. Thus the findings from the analysis of relationships between objective and subjective mobility support the thesis that in postcommunist countries subjective mobility has been largely independent of objective mobility.

If one accepts the assumption that the subjective mobility felt by those who have not experienced any objective class or status mobility may be understood as a reflection of collective mobility, the results of the analysis strongly support the hypothesis that during postcommunist transformation collective mobility has been a more important factor determining life chances than individual mobility. This finding is consistent with the conclusions from previous analyses of factors determining voting behavior in early stages of the postcommunist transformation, especially the conclusion that perceived socioeconomic mobility had a much stronger effect on voting preferences than objective class and status mobility.[32]

The analysis also provided a strong support for the hypothesis that the dismantling of socialist redistribution has put large segments of the populations, typically those who were the winners during the socialist period—the less educated, the working class, and agricultural workers—on a downward track. Market transition has, however, opened up new opportunities, particularly for those who were not favored by socialist redistribution practices: people with higher education, professionals, the middle class, and new entrepreneurs. Education proved to be the most important determinant connected with the feeling that market transition was beneficial. Alhough this conclusion holds for all countries, there were cross-national differences supporting the hypothesis that the feeling of expanding life chances (collective mobility) among those with higher education was stronger in the countries where the importance of education in income differen-

32. See Matějů (1996).

tiation was particularly weak under communism. Consistent with this assumption, the results have shown that the link between higher education and the feeling of upward socioeconomic mobility was particularly strong in the Czech Republic.

As far as the importance of political capital is concerned, the analysis confirmed that Communist party membership has not been a significant factor affecting life chances after the fall of communism. One of the most important counterintuitive findings is that party membership during the communist era has not affected the perception of mobility after the collapse. This finding challenges the common wisdom that former communists benefited from the transformation: such a general conclusion does not seem to be true. However, the conclusion gets significant support from analysis of the mobility of former nomenklatura cadres. Cadres that did not retire felt a significant improvement in their life chances during the postcommunist transformation, independently of the type of objective mobility they experienced. Both cadres who have not experienced any mobility and those who converted their political capital into economic capital and became self-employed believed they were moving up in the socioeconomic hierarchy. Particularly interesting in this respect is the result showing that movement to the group of self-employed from a cadre position created significantly stronger feelings of improved life chances than becoming self-employed from a noncadre position.

Appendix

Definition of categories of subjective status mobility (SUBSOC5)

Question for 1988: "In our society there are groups which tend to be towards the top and those that are toward the bottom. Here we have a scale that runs from top to bottom [the interviewer shows the card with a scale running from 10 (top) to 1 (bottom)]. Where would you have placed yourself on this scale in 1988?"

Question for 1993: Where would you place yourself now?

The variable *SUBSOC* was created by the following transformation:
COMPUTE *SUBSOC* = *SUBSOC93* – *SUBSOC88*.

RECODE *SUBSOC* (lowest through –3 = 1)(–2, –1 = 2)(0 = 3)(1, 2 = 4)(3 through highest = 5) into *SUBSOC5*.

Table 11-A1. *EGP Class Scheme Used for the Definition of Objective Class Mobility*

Code	Original code	Description	Average value of ISEI in 1993[a]
1	I	Higher-grade professionals, administrators, and officials; managers in large industrial establishments; large proprietors.	65
2	II	Lower-grade professionals, administrators, and officials; higher-grade technicians; managers in small industrial establishments; supervisors of nonmanual employees	54
3	IIIa + IIIb	Routine nonmanual employees (both higher grade and lower grade)	45
4	IVa	Small proprietors, artisans, and so forth with employees	44
5	IVb	Small proprietors, artisans, and so forth without employees	40
7	V	Lower-grade technicians, supervisors of manual workers	39
8	VI	Skilled manual workers	35
9	VIIa	Semi- and unskilled manual workers (not in agriculture)	27
10	VIIb	Agricultural and other workers in primary production	22
11	IVc	Farmers and smallholders; other self-employed workers in primary production	25

Source: Erikson and Goldthorpe (1992).

a. The value of ISEI, international index of socioeconomic status (Ganzeboom, De Graaf, and Treiman, 1992) for all economically active individuals in 1993 (pooled data for the Czech Republic, Hungary, Poland, and Slovakia).

Definition of categories of subjective income mobility (SUBINC5)

Question for 1988: "Compared with [country] families in general, would you say that your family income in 1988 was far below average, below average, about average, above average, or far above average?" [The interviewer shows the card with a scale running from 1 (far below average) to 5 (far above average)].

Question for 1993: "What about now?"

Table 11-A2. *Principal Factor Solution for Dimension of Subjective Socioeconomic Mobility*[a]

Variable/statistic	Dimension 1	Dimension 2
1988		
SUBSOC88 (loadings)	.795	−.632
SUBINC88 (loadings)	.815	.617
Eigenvalue	.647	.389
1993		
SUBSOC93 (loadings)	.814	−.601
SUBINC93 (loadings)	.815	.600
Eigenvalue	.663	.361

Source: See appendix text.

a. To retain the frame of reference respondents used in the evaluations of their positions (comparison with "other people in the country"—see the wording of the two questions), the extracted dimensions were standardized within countries. The standardization was made by computing z-scores for each country separately. The first dimensions in each year representing subjective socioeconomic status were then used to assess subjective socioeconomic mobility *(SSEMOB)* as the difference between subjective socioeconomic status in 1988 and 1993.

The variable *SUBINC* was created by the following transformation:
COMPUTE *SUBINC* = *SUBINC93 − SUBINC88*.
RECODE *SUBINC* (lowest through −2 = 1)(−1 = 2)(0 = 3)(1= 4) (2 through highest = 5) into *SUBINC5*.

Definition of variable SSEMOB

Two pairs of variables were used to define subjective socioeconomic status in 1988 and 1993: subjective social status and subjective income in 1988 (*SUBSOC88, SUBINC88*) and subjective social status and subjective income in 1993 (*SUBSOC93, SUBINC93*).

Principal component analysis based on the method of alternating least squares (*PRINCALS*) was applied on the two pairs of variables to extract dimensions representing subjective socioeconomic status. To achieve comparability of measurement protocols (identical factor structures), the two dimensions for each year were extracted from pooled data.

To retain the frame of reference respondents used in the evaluations of their positions (comparison with "other people in the country"—see the wording of the two questions), the extracted dimensions were standardized within countries. The standardization was made by computing Z-scores for each country separately. The first dimensions in each year representing subjective socioeconomic status were then used to assess subjective socioeconomic mobility (SSEMOB) as the difference between subjective socioeconomic status in 1988 and 1993.

References

Dahrendorf, Rolf. 1979. *Life Chances*. University of Chicago Press.

Domanski, Henryk. 1997. "Constant Fluidity with Rise in Total Rates: Social Mobility in Six East European Nations." *Polish Sociological Review* 3: 267–83.

Erikson, Robert, and John H. Goldthorpe. 1992. *The Constant Flux: A Study of Class Mobility in Industrial Societies*. Oxford University Press.

Hanley, Eric, and Ivan Szelenyi. 1996. "Changing Social Structure during Market Transition: The Case of Central Europe." Paper presented at the Workshop on Economic Transformation and the reform of the State. Washington: National Academy of Sciences.

Hanley, Eric, and others. 1996. "The Making of Post-Communist Elites in Eastern Europe: A Comparison of Political and Economic Elites in the Czech Republic, Hungary and Poland." Working Paper 96:3. Institute of Sociology, Prague.

Lazarsfeld, Paul F., Bernard Berelson, and Hazel Gaudet. 1974. *The People's Choice. How the Voter Makes Up His Mind in Presidential Campaign*. Columbia University Press.

Matějů, Petr. 1996. "In Search of Explanations for Recent Left Turns in Post-Communist Countries." *International Review of Comparative Public Policy* 7 (May), pp. 43-82.

Matějů, Petr, and Eric Hanley. 1997. "The Making of Economic and Political Elites in Eastern Europe." In A. M. Hatschikjan and F. L. Altman, eds., *Elites in Transition in Eastern Europe*. Studies in Politics. Schöningh (forthcoming).

———. 1999. "Die Herausbildung ökonomischer und politischer Eliten in Ostmitteleuropa." In M. A. Hatschikjan and F. L. Altmann, eds., *Eliten im Wandel: Politische Führung, wirtschaftliche Macht und Meinungsbildung im neuen Osteuropa*, pp. 145–72. Paderborn: Verlag Ferdinand Schöningh.

Matějů, Petr, and Nelson Lim. 1995. "Who Has Gotten Ahead after the Fall of Communism? The Case of the Czech Republic." *Czech Sociological Review* 3: 117–36.

Matějů, Petr, and Blanka Rehakova. 1993. "Revolution for Whom? Analysis of Selected Patterns of Intragenerational Mobility, 1989–1992." *Czech Sociological Review* 1: 73–90.

———. 1996. "Education as a Strategy for Life Success in the Post-Communist Transformation. The Case of the Czech Republic." *Comparative Education Review* 40: 158–76.

Nee, Victor. 1989. "A Theory of Market Transition: From Redistribution to Market in State Socialism." *American Sociological Review* 54: 663–81.

———. 1991. "Social Inequalities in Reforming State Socialism: Between Redistribution and Market in China." *American Sociological Review* 56: 267–82.

Rehakova, Blanka, and Klara Vlachova. 1995. "Subjective Mobility after 1989. Do People Feel a Social and Economic Improvement or Relative Deprivation?" *Czech Sociological Review* 2: 137–56.

Offe, Claus. 1991. "Capitalism by Democratic Design? Democratic Theory Facing the Triple Transition in East Central Europe." *Social Research* 58: 865–92.

Organization for Economic Cooperation and Development. 1994. *Short-Term Economic Indicators*. Paris.

Parkin, Frank. 1971. *Class, Inequality and Political Order*. Praeger.

Polanyi, Karl. 1944. *The Great Transformation. The Political and Economic Origins of Our Time*. Boston: Beacon.

Popper, Karl R. 1952. *Open Society and Its Enemies*. London.

Raftery, Adrian E. 1986. "Choosing Models for Cross-Classifications." *American Sociological Review* 51: 145–46.

Rona-Tas, Akas. 1994. "The First Shall Be Last? Entrepreneurship and Communist Cadres in the Transition from Socialism." *American Journal of Sociology* 100: 40–69.

Stark, David. 1992a. "Path Dependency and Privatization Strategies in East Central Europe." *East European Politics and Societies* 6: 17–54.

———. 1992b. "From System Identity to Organizational Diversity: Analyzing Social Change in Eastern Europe." *Contemporary Sociology* 21 (3).

Szelenyi, Ivan. 1988. *Socialist Entrepreneurs. Embourgeoisement in Rural Hungary*. Wisconsin University Press.

Szelenyi, Ivan, and Robert Manchin. 1987. "Social Policy under Socialism: Market, Redistribution, and Social Inequalities in East European Socialist Societies." In Esping Andersen, ed., *Stagnation and Routine in Social Policy*, pp. 103–39. Armonk, N.Y.: M. E. Sharpe.

Szelenyi, Ivan, and Eric Kostello. 1996. "The Market Transition Debate: Toward a Synthesis?" *American Journal of Sociology* 101:1082–96.

Sztompka, Piotr. 1992. "Dilemmas of the Great Transition." *Sisyphus* 8: 9–27.

Treiman, Donald J., and Ivan Szelenyi. 1993. "Social Stratification in Eastern Europe after 1989." *Proceedings of Workshop: Transformation Processes in Eastern Europe*. The Hague: NOW-SSCW.

Vecernik, Jiri. 1996. "Earnings Disparities in the Czech Republic: The History of Equalization." *Czech Sociological Review* 4: 211–22.

Contributors

Jere R. Behrman
University of Pennsylvania

Nancy Birdsall
*Carnegie Endowment for
International Peace*

Gary S. Fields
Cornell University

Carol Graham
Brookings Institution

David E. Hojman
University of Liverpool

Petr Matějů
Czech Academy of Sciences

Isabel V. Sawhill
Brookings Institution

Joseph E. Stiglitz
World Bank

Miguel Székely
Inter-American Development Bank

Katherine Terrell
University of Michigan

Richard Webb
Banco Latino, Lima

Index